AVOIDING THE BRITISH EMPIRE

WHAT IT WAS, AND HOW THE UNITED STATES CAN DO BETTER

"...a great empire and little minds go ill together..."

Edmund Burke [1]

---

[1] "Speech on Conciliation With America" 22 March 1775 Drawn from Thomas H. D. Mahoney's introduction to a 1955 edition of <u>Reflections on the Revolution In France</u>.

CONTENTS

Introduction

The Imperial City is unsettled.

A new kind of politician has come to power. Despite being a child of great privilege, he says he speaks for the common man. He proclaims that those who came before him have been doing everything wrong. The country is in great danger. For too long the fools in charge have given away the empire's wealth. "We're being taken advantage of!" he claims. "The old way of doing things is giving power to our enemies!" The Empire's old masters gnash their teeth as they rattle around their profoundly shaken halls of power. This new man seems to be tearing everything down! "We are the indispensable nation!" the old guard exclaims "…and what would we be anyway without Free Trade?"

Do you think I'm talking about Donald Trump?

I'm not.

I'm talking about Joseph Chamberlain, one of the most prominent British politicians of the late nineteenth and early twentieth centuries. The British political system is quite different from the US system. Chamberlain was never Prime Minister, but he was a leader in parliament and served as the powerful Secretary of State for the Colonies between 1895-1903. Though one man was a career politician and the other is not, the parallels between Chamberlain and Trump are striking.

Trump has upended the Republican party if he hasn't destroyed it. Over his much longer political career, Chamberlain managed to do that to two parties. The issue that Chamberlain ended his career with, and for which he might be best remembered, is also Trump's signature issue. From the repeal of the Corn Laws in 1846, and to a lesser degree for some decades before that, the British Empire ran a world system based on free trade. Chamberlain insisted that this wasn't working for the British people. He wanted to create a system of "imperial preferences" involving protective tariffs and an emphasis on "better deals" between the United Kingdom and its many colonies.

Trump is working towards the same end. He wants to get away from the system of open trade the United States has been building since the signing of the General Agreement on Tariffs and Trade (GATT) in 1947. Trump loathes the World Trade Organization (WTO) that the GATT became. He wants bilateral "better deals" between the US and its partners.

Chamberlain was not as much of a rebel as he claimed to be. He dissented from his country's old leaders on free trade, but he shared the worst instincts of the older leaders as well. Chamberlain, like Trump, was obsessed with national decline. And like Trump, he pursued more vigorous versions of the same bad solutions favored by the elite he claimed to be fighting. Chamberlain, from his position as Secretary of State for the Colonies at the turn of the century, may have done more than any other figure to bring about those apocalyptic world wars. His answer to perceived decline was to militarize and to insist on the British Empire's privileges ever more strongly and violently. He may have been more extreme in advocating for this than others, but he shared this instinct with most of Britain's leaders, and with much of the British public.

Donald Trump is not the rebel he claims to be either. Trump's answer to perceived American decline is a record-setting military budget. He has turned our foreign policy over to retired generals and military contractors. He hasn't started any new wars yet, but he has let the generals intensify most of the many wars we are already fighting. He has also shaken our 7-decade old system of alliances. Trump may be a jump forward, but he's traveling in the same direction the United States has been going since 2001, if not 1990. Trump isn't as much of a rebel as he claims to be. The US problem isn't as unique as we think, either.

The parallels between the US World System today and the nineteenth century British Empire go far beyond these two politicians. The implications of those parallels are also terrifying. Eleven years after Chamberlain took his stand against free trade in 1903, the century old British World System died in flames. The First World War murdered millions, and set the stage for an even more apocalyptic conflict just two decades later. This book will argue that the fleeting dominance and catastrophic downfall of the British Empire teaches lessons that the United States desperately needs to learn.

American Decline

Most apostles of American Decline are getting it wrong. From Fareed Zakaria[2] to the folks commenting on my YouTube videos, many think that the United States has already been surpassed, and that our ability to influence the world is waning, or already gone. They are right about the trajectory, but their sense of timing is off. The United States will remain the "Indispensable Nation" for some time to come. Barring fiscal or some other sort of disaster (not impossible, but not as likely as some claim) the twenty-first century will be an American one as well. But it will probably be the last one.

By the end of this century, our relative economic and military weight will be dramatically diminished. China, India, and even Europe, if it ever gets its act together, are all likely to outweigh the United States economically and militarily. We will no longer be able to dictate world policy. We will not be as free of the world and its problems as we are today. What we do between now and then, however, remains an open question. Will we go the route of other declining empires? Will we choose to lash out, and insist on our privileges in increasingly violent

---

[2] Fareed Zakaria published the book, The Post-American World back in 2008

ways, as those privileges steadily wash away? That's certainly the current path.[3] Will we arrive at 2100 a universally loathed former hegemon, looking back at a century of violence and decline, clinging to more and more embarrassing stories about the good old days?

There's a model for that.

Avoiding the British Empire

The United States is not the first country to run the world. The British Empire first leveraged the Industrial Revolution, financial sophistication and maritime power into a comprehensive world system after 1815.[4] For just under a century, until 1914, the British Empire ruled the waves and the world. A small island off the northwest coast of Europe dictated to massive territorial powers like China and Russia. It was the first world empire. It had serious rivals in a few regions, but no real global competitors.

A century later, the United Kingdom has once again become just a large-ish island off the coast of Europe (with a few post-imperial bits and bobs). Britain's world system has largely disappeared or been absorbed by the United States. The British were lucky in that the new hegemon was friendly to them, but the costs to the world of the end of empire were immense. Two World Wars cost tens of millions of lives. Decolonization of British-held territories cost millions more. Most of the world's flashpoints today, from Cyprus to Saudi Arabia to Israel

---

[3] FATCA, the Foreign Account Tax Compliance Act, an absurd world-wide power grab by the US Internal Revenue Service, is a good example of an old-school imperialist play, if you are looking for further reading. I'd suggest my essay on this topic, FATCA and the New Birth of American Empire available on the Amazon Kindle.

[4] It's tempting to date this from the battle of Trafalgar fought in October of 1805. The British destroyed Napoleon's navy and established naval supremacy. But the distraction of opposing Napoleon on land, and blockading Europe kept the British from establishing a true world system. For example, the United States managed to do pretty well against the British in the War of 1812. 1815, and Napoleon's final defeat at Waterloo, is a good date for the beginning of British primacy.

and Palestine to India and Pakistan, are legacies of the fall of the British Empire.

The US World System is much more complex, all-encompassing, and fragile than the British System that ended 105 years ago. If the "Pax Americana" falls in a similar fashion, the consequences will be apocalyptic. A third world war won't need nuclear weapons to destroy life as we know it. In 1914, the majority of the world's 1.7 Billion people lived on the farms that fed them. Even back then, the disruption of war starved millions in non-combatant countries.[5] Today, the majority of the world's 7.5 billion people live in cities that rely on dense border-crossing networks for food and other supplies. The first minutes of a future "great power"[6] war will see the destruction of the web of communications we all rely on for daily life. Most communication satellites will be destroyed. The GPS system will go down. World-wide supply chains will be instantly disrupted. Mass starvation would be nearly immediate and world-wide.

There is another option. Abraham Lincoln saw the United States as the "Last best hope of earth"[7]. We can work towards fulfilling that hope with the time on top that is left to us. Every imperial system has attempted to justify itself with platitudes and the idea that it has some "civilizing mission". The US system, while always serving our own interests first and foremost, has involved a real flowering of independence across the world, on every continent. There have been unspeakable horrors perpetrated on our watch as well. Some have been committed directly by the US in places like Vietnam, Iraq, Syria and Yemen. Some were committed by monsters we created in Saudi Arabia, Chile, Indonesia and many other places. Some were committed

---

[5] The Persian famine of 1917-1919 might have been the worst, but it was far from the only one.

[6] This term can be defined a lot of ways. But even by an expansive definition, say the top 40 economies in the world, there has been no large scale great power military conflict in over 70 years. That's amazing.

[7] http://ask.metafilter.com/60189/Whats-the-origin-of-the-phrase-last-best-hope-for

by monsters who rose to oppose us in places like the Soviet Union, Cambodia and China.

But great progress has occurred as well. There are more people on this planet, living freer and healthier lives, than there have ever been. We deserve some credit for this, as well as the blame for our many mishaps. The peace and freedom (Pax Americana) we have policed and promoted[8] has served at least some parts of the world well. Seven decades without a "great power" war is an unalloyed good.

We can use our remaining strength to continue providing these benefits, and convince more people that those benefits exist. We can turn the US World System into a more representative system that everybody can happily buy into. Growing multi-lateral action through institutions like the United Nations and the World Trade Organization is an essential part of this. But there's also a lot we in the United States can do to change the world right here at home, from government reform, to the reorganization and rationalization of our defense industries.

The central concept here is peace. Peace is good.

Being pro-peace should not be controversial, but there is little in the actions of Washington, DC's foreign policy establishment over the past three decades that indicates that they understand that. We need to resist the militarist instincts of our Trumps and modern-day Joseph Chamberlains. This book will demonstrate that peace isn't just an economic and moral good, but that it's also an essential pre-condition

---

[8] Almost exclusively non-militarily. American military dominance created the Pax Americana, but most effectively so when it hasn't been used. There are numberless fault lines across the planet. India and Pakistan, and Turkey and Greece are only the most obvious ones. There are also many smaller countries that could easily have been swallowed up by larger, more aggressive neighbors. The fact that very few of these issues have flared up, and that they have been small when they have flared up, has a lot to do with US enforcement of peace. The best example would probably be the US defense of Egypt in the Suez crisis of 1956, when France, Great Britain and Israel's attempt to carve up that country was stopped diplomatically by Eisenhower.

for maintaining a modern world system. It's also good for whoever tends to run that system.

There's nothing worse for the country on top than a war. The British failed to keep that principle in mind, and their empire fell, at great cost to themselves, and tremendous costs to the rest of the world. If we can learn the lessons of Britain's fall then perhaps 2100 will no longer be a year to be dreaded. The United States could occupy a respected position as a founder of a greater, happier, and more peaceful world. The Pax Americana will end, but we get to choose how. It can be yet another story of sad, silly decline, or it can be one of transcendence.

To transcend our planet's sordid history of violence and conquest, we need to learn the lessons of the last folks who tried to run the place. The British also saw themselves as building a better world. Their failures are clear in retrospect. They did try to end slavery, and their system of government was better at building wealth and freedom (for the British!) than most others at the time. But the British Empire is rightly remembered as horrifically oppressive. The British enjoyed one of the greatest standards of living in history to that point, while their Irish and Indian subjects starved in their millions. We in the United States need to learn from British failures if we are to succeed where they failed. When we are immersed in the day to day news of failure in the Middle East, a vision of a world that can transcend humanity's vicious past may seem naïve. My hope is that when you finish this book you'll see this transcendence as very possible. We're already halfway there. But we'll never reach a world without war if we continue on the path the US government is currently on. What comes from here is too important to leave to the "experts".

A Note for Those without a US Passport...

You may be getting a bit of a "rah-rah America" vibe at this point.

I am from the United States, and I think it's better to have that out in the open than to pretend it isn't the lens through which I come at this thing.

All the same, my objective here isn't the continuing success of the United States so much as the continuing success of the world at large. This planet will be better off if American power fades in an orderly fashion rather than in the cataclysms that followed the collapse of other, older empires. I can't eliminate my own bias, but I hope that this book can persuade those outside of the charmed circle of US citizenship that a long, peaceful fade for US power is as useful to them as it is to the average American.

What We're Up to Here

In **Chapter One: Empires… How Do Those Work?** We'll define some terms, and lay out why the British Empire is the only real precedent for the world system the United States is running today. We'll also point out why it's indisputably fair to say that the US has an empire.

In **Chapter Two: The Two World Systems in Human History**, we'll do a bit of scene setting. Now that we've established why the US and British Empires are different from anything that came before, we will do a quick run through human history to tease out the outsize impact these two world systems have had. Situating the two world systems in the full arc of humanity's grim history will illustrate how this impact is much larger than is usually recognized, for good and for ill. This chapter will help establish the similarity of the two empires even though they look so superficially different.

In **Chapter Three: Geography, Good Government**, **and Luck** we'll take the British and US Empires down a peg or two. Chapter two talked a lot about the epic accomplishments and crimes of these entities, this

Chapter will focus on how essentially anybody can replicate these successes (hopefully with fewer crimes!) as long as we can keep the world at peace.

In **Chapter Four: The Rise of Britain,** we will lay out the story of one small island's improbable rise to world leadership. The propagandists of British Empire tell us the empire was acquired inadvertently. There's something to that, but not much. More importantly it was about enemies, the French in particular.

In **Chapter Five: The British World System,** we will lay out what Britain's century on top looked like, and how its success sowed the seeds of its own decline. We'll make it clear how the modern world system that the British created differed from all empires before it, and illustrate how there was so much more to British dominance than the sections of the map that were shaded "English red".

In **Chapter Six: Losing the British World System,** we will unwrap the thorny problem of what it is to lose control of a world system, and when and what we are talking about when we talk about the British Empire's fall. We'll run through the many candidates for the year British dominance ended, and lay out why 1914 and the beginning of the WWI is the best candidate. We'll also show why the British Empire bears the lion's share of the guilt for the World Wars.

In **Chapter Seven: The Disturbingly Similar US World System,** we will lay out the many ways that the United States is a successor to Britain, and why the lack of large territorial possessions shouldn't fool us into thinking that the United States isn't an empire, facing very British problems, and travelling down a very troublingly British Empire-like path.

In **Chapter Eight: Transcendence** we will lay out a few of the many reasons why the United States can hope to avoid a fully British path to apocalyptic war, and we'll lay out why I believe it is possible for humanity to transcend our vulgar history of war and thuggery.

Chapter 1

Empires… How Do Those Work?

The American Empire is going to end.

This may be a confusing statement to some. Whether or not the United States is running an empire remains a controversial subject. US politics has always had a strongly anti-imperialist bent. Our War of Independence was fought against an empire. Throughout the nineteenth century, we saw ourselves as opposing European Empires, and the British Empire most of all. This attitude lasted up until the First World War, a conflict that raged for three years before the US joined in. President Woodrow Wilson was almost as annoyed by British restraints on trade during that war as he was by the German U-boats the US eventually ended up fighting.[9] As we became one of two superpowers, and eventually the only one, we consistently told ourselves that we were fighting against evil empires. Sometimes this was even true.

The confusion here has a lot to do with the intellectual furniture of Western Civilization that clutters up all of our heads. What we think of, more than anything else, when we talk about empire, is Rome. Consciously or not, this is the model we reach for. This is a mistake.

We Are Not Rome

I believe in Western Civilization. I'd even consider myself an advocate. But it's a confusing concept, one that's worth its own book, so any definition here will necessarily be short and to the point.

More than anything else, Western Civilization is a set of ideas, and an agreed upon story of how those ideas evolved. The story often starts with the Renaissance, a rediscovery of the ideas of the classical

---

[9] Toomes, Adam <u>The Deluge: The Great War, America and the Remaking of the Global Order, 1916-1931</u>

civilizations of Greece and Rome, proceeds through the religious apocalypse of the Reformation, emerges in a new flowering with the Enlightenment, and pops us out into a self-satisfied Modernity, whatever that means. Every part of the story is suspect, and always oversimplified. Defining the intellectual, geographical or temporal limits of "Western Civilization" is a good way to get into a shouting match.

What is indisputable is that the models of ancient or "classical" Greece and Rome remain important to the way we think about ourselves in Europe and the United States,[10] and that they have been for over 500 years. The designers of every system of government in Europe and the Americas, from the propagandists of early modern absolute monarchs like Louis XIV's Cardinal Richelieu, to the 'Renaissance men' who wrote the US Constitution, to Marx, Lenin and Mussolini, have been in intense dialogue with ancient writers and centuries worth of their commentators. If you want an indication of how present these ideas still are, all you have to do is take a stroll down the national mall in Washington, DC. Neo-classical architecture is everywhere, from the White House to the Capitol Building, to the Mussolini-style Roman pastiche of the WWII monument. The neo-classical style of architecture is exactly what it sounds like, it's an attempt to build buildings the way the ancient Greeks or Romans of "classical civilization" are imagined to have built. The name of the US Senate itself is taken from Rome. Many of our conversations about how best to organize our lives have their origins in Greek deliberations about political systems and the Roman model of a Republic. These ideas have

---

[10] One amusing recent example is near-celebrity Stanford historian Niall Ferguson's "No, This Isn't The Fall of Rome" published in the Boston Globe on August 12th, 2019. In the column he makes the valid point that the constant comparisons of Trump to mad emperors and imperial decline don't make much sense. Alert folks on twitter quickly pointed out that Ferguson himself reached for an idiotic comparison to the fall of Rome himself in another Boston Globe column "Paris and the Fall of Rome" on November 16, 2015 in the aftermath of terrorist attacks in that city. I point this out, not to mock Ferguson specifically, but as just one example of how much a part of our mental furniture these comparisons are. As just one more example, as I was doing the final edits on this book, James Fallows published "The End of The Roman Empire Wasn't That Bad" in the October 2019 edition of the Atlantic Monthly.

evolved through centuries of discussions from Plato, to the Italian Republics and the Massachusetts Bay Colony, to modern Washington, DC think tanks[11] and everywhere in between. Interestingly, much of our current reverence for the Romans comes from the nineteenth century British. Victorian[12] propaganda tried very hard to jam the world-spanning British Empire into a Roman model.

Contemporary and Victorian writers take these comparisons with Rome too far. A vast gulf of time separates the agrarian societies and slave-based economies of classical Greece and Rome from our own. We have chosen to take the ruminations of the few elite writers whose works have survived as a guide to life and politics. Plato, Marcus Aurelius and many others have interesting things to say. But ancient Greek and Roman society was unrecognizable from a modern perspective. Athens may have given us the concept of democracy, but as much as two thirds of its population was made up of slaves. The vast majority of the population in "Freedom Loving Sparta" were *helots*, a permanently subjugated laboring caste.[13] The Roman Republic and Empire were slave-based as well,[14] with an un-enslaved population that became progressively more immiserated as those on top attained higher levels of "glory".

The obsession with using Rome as a model is especially pernicious when we discuss the decline of modern empire. So many of the basic facts of 2,000 years ago, from slavery, to the barbarians at the border, to military technology, to the dominance of agrarian life simply do not apply. Drawing out the lessons of Rome is endlessly fascinating. The fact that we've spent 500 years trying to do it means that we have to

---

[11] The Cato institute, as just one example, is named after a Roman statesman. I'm guessing it's the anti-imperial Cato the Younger rather than the genocidal Cato the Elder.

[12] 19th century Britons, and sometimes people from the United States and elsewhere, are often referred to as "Victorians" after the British Queen Victoria, who reigned from 1837 to 1901. Styles in housing, thought, and art from this era are often also referred to as Victorian. I have tried to avoid annoying historical jargon in this book, but I fall into it occasionally.

[13] Scott, James C. Against the Grain: A Deep History of the Earliest States P.156

[14] Scott, James C. Against the Grain: A Deep History of the Earliest States P.157

reckon with these long dead civilizations and their interpreters to fully understand anything in US and European history. But what we've thought and written about ancient history over the past 500 years is much more important for understanding ourselves than what actually happened in the Athenian agora or the Roman forum. Trying to use the events and characters of the fall of Rome to draw direct lessons for the twenty-first century American Empire won't work any better now than when the British were drawing on Gibbon. We won't make that mistake here.

Let's start with our terms.

Empire as a World-Wide System of Control

"Empire" calls many different images to mind. The horsemen of the Mongol Empire rampaging across Asia and Europe. Roman centurions turning the Mediterranean into an Italian *mare nostrum*. The Persian Emperor Xerxes having a body of water whipped because it failed to cooperate. The ambitions of Mughals[15] and Aztecs, Charlemagne and the Habsburgs. China's Middle Kingdom at the center of a world of barbarians, and Queen Victoria's world-wide empire "upon which the sun never set".

Only one of these comparisons really applies to the United States. The British Empire was the first world-wide system of control. The American Empire is the second. The only thing the American Empire has in common with the Mongols and Romans is that our empire will end, just as surely as theirs did. The important question is how.

To attempt to answer this question, we need to look closely at the British Empire, which is the American Empire's precursor. Great

---

[15] Fun fact: The Mongol and Mughal Empires are two different things. The Mongols came screaming out of the Asian Steppes in 1206 and conquered the known world. At its greatest extent the Mongol Empire stretched from China to Poland, knitting together the world's trade routes and diseases. The Mughals took over Northern India in the 1500s, and limped along for another 300 years, sometimes expanding, but most often falling apart until they were snuffed out by the British in 1857.

Britain's empire superficially had a lot more in common with the empires of the past than the US Empire does. Like the Romans, the British physically controlled a lot of land inhabited by people of different cultures. But it was much more than that.

The British Empire was a system of world-wide control. It leveraged financial, commercial and military superiority to spread its influence over every corner of the globe, far beyond the bits of the map that were technically shaded red. It had a defined ideology and sense of the "way things should be done" that it successfully imposed on countries everywhere. This is exactly what American Empire is. The United States does not yet operate much "formal empire". Compared to the British, there are few territories that fly that star-spangled banner. But our "informal empire" encompasses most of the globe.

Empire, Formal and Informal

The distinction between "formal" and "informal" empire is an extremely important one.[16] The popular image of the British Empire is wrapped up in its far-flung colonies on which "the sun never set". Large territories on the world map from the 1700s to the 1900s were directly controlled by the British. This "formal empire" was the most obvious exercise of British power, but historians have long known that the "informal empire" that Britain exerted worldwide was just as important, if not more important. The British never formally controlled most of Latin America, or China, and their formal control of most of the Middle East and Africa was fleeting, but they ended up controlling the politics of these areas through military, commercial and financial force for over a century, and in some cases for centuries. [17] This was

---

[16] I am told second-hand that these concepts of informal and formal British Empire stem from the work of Ronald Robinson and John Gallagher "in the 1950s". As with much of my understanding of the world I got this data point from C.A. Bayly's extraordinary Birth of the Modern World: 1780-1914. Bayly discusses these concepts on pps. 136 and 137 of that book.

[17] This whole discussion is indebted to the straightforward (and a teeny bit racist to twenty-first century eyes) discussion of these issues on pps. 174-177 of Lawrence James's The Rise And Fall of The British Empire

often the case in territories that formally belonged to other European and Asian empires as well. The formal power of the British soldier was much less important than the informal power of London bankers, diplomats, merchants and lawyers.

These two kinds of empire would often work in tandem. If a given country found itself tempted to renege on the details of a loan, or harass a British merchant, or object to Britain's pushing opium on their populace, they would have to deal with British military power. But it was never just stick, there was always lot of carrot too. Many, if not most of the world's governments from the 1800s on relied on loans organized in London to continue operating. Without the need for centralized organization from Whitehall, British financiers funded, built, and often ending up owning large chunks of the most valuable infrastructure across the US, Latin America, and the rest of the developing world. This investment is seen now, and was seen at the time, as both advantageous to the target countries and exploitative. It was both of those things. Industries and infrastructure that would not have been built otherwise were created, and the UK profited immensely.

This kind of "informal empire" is what the United States operates today. The American Empire is less violent, but that's because the US is more powerful, and has more sophisticated sticks to use. As of this writing, The United States hasn't invaded Venezuela, and I pray that it never will, but we've done almost as much to destroy the place as Venezuelan President Maduro has through sanctions, ongoing cases in US courts, and the unwillingness of US banks to continue funding the country's oil industry.

The world has been moving along under a world system for over two centuries now. When I say world system, I mean a set of economic and political relationships that govern the community of nations, imposed by one of them. Under the US system each individual country is better able to resist formal empire but they have also internalized many of the elements of informal empire (financial, legal) that used to come out of the barrel of a British cannon. It was British brutality that established a single world system. The US is brutal in fewer places because the world has learned the drill to some extent. Local elites in every country have adapted to the legal and financial priorities of the world system. US Empire is much more subtle than British Empire. It's so much more subtle that many people in the US can pretend that we don't have an empire at all.

This subtle world system also presents an opportunity. Despite the more fevered claims of US politicians on the left and right, the international institutions of one world government are not coming to get us. This idea is currently more associated with the right than the left, but it was the great big government advocate and New York Democrat Daniel Patrick Moynihan that first brought it to modern prominence as a US ambassador to the United Nations in the 1980s.[18] This makes for great politics, but the truth is that the UN, the WTO, and a whole host of other acronym-named institutions had their charters written by US bureaucrats, to serve US ends, and continue to serve US interests primarily. But the fiction of a more just and democratic system can become fact. *The* great virtue of a rules-based world system is that it can evolve peacefully. Moynihan's attack on the UN was a response to the countries of the "free world" no longer monolithically voting with the US as automatically as they had in prior decades. Taking the United Nations and other institutions more seriously than the post-WWI League of Nations could keep us from descending into war as the US loses relative power. Boring, legalistic

---

[18] The 2018 documentary Moynihan, illustrates how very different US politics were just a few short decades ago, on this topic and many others.

institutions of world governance can be much more powerful than control of vast tracts of land.

It's telling that the periods of greatest dominance for both the British and US Empires began with losses of land empires, not gains. In 1783, Great Britain lost the territory that became the United States of America. In 1946 the United States gave up its furthest flung territory, and its half century old imperial experiment in the Philippines. Direct military occupations and interventions in the region of the world that the US has abused the most, the Americas south of the US border, have been much less frequent post WWII than they were before. Both countries experimented with "formal" imperial control and found that "informal empire" was more profitable.

Informal empire is also a lot cheaper. This was the lesson that Britain learned from the stinging loss of the bulk of its North American territory in the 1770s. To some extent, the rise and subsequent fall of the British Empire was directly related to how well they adhered to a basic principle—that inexpensive informal empire was always preferable to ruinous formal military control. That principle remains relevant to the US World System today. It's clear we're not following it. It's not just our pursuit of more formal empire in Iraq, Syria, Afghanistan and Yemen. Our network of military bases is constantly metastasizing, and US soldiers are present in so many places that even hawkish Republican senators like Lindsey Graham can't keep track of them.

Our weakness for Roman comparisons helps to hide the importance of "informal empire" from us. Seductive Roman ideas of military virtue and Iron Age expansion blind us to the opportunities for peace that the modern world provides. Throughout this book I will refer to this problem as the **"Historical Hangover"**. Human beings love strength.

In the study of history we gravitate to stories of battles and military triumph. The world today is infinitely more complex than the world of the Romans and Greeks. But when we tell the story of the nineteenth and twentieth centuries we try to jam what happened into ancient ideas of strength and military glory. This is a problem, because what has really happened over the past 200 years has had progressively less and less to do with these ancient ideas.

The story of the rise of the British Empire is told through heroes, like Vice-Admiral Horatio Nelson defeating Napoleon's Navy, rather than the bankers and bureaucrats that were in truth more central to Britain's eventual economic sprawl. Celebrations of European wars from the 1700s through 1945 get added to the Historical Hangover too. We focus on dramatic stories of war in the rise of the United States as well. We focus on WWII, and we see Alexander and Hannibal when we look at US General and Allied Commander in Europe Dwight D. Eisenhower and German General Erwin Rommel. The historical hangover blinds us to the incredible opportunities for peace and prosperity we are already taking advantage of. It also risks killing those opportunities. This focus on historical battle and destruction leads both to the creation of military fetishists like John Bolton and to their elevation to positions of power within the American policy establishment. Left unchecked, war-happy, bullet-obsessed ideologues like Bolton will destroy the US power they think they are acting to preserve. If the United States wants to learn worthwhile lessons for using and preserving power in the modern world, our thinkers shouldn't be looking back 2,000 years. To see beyond the Historical Hangover, we should look instead to the only other country that has managed to run a world-wide system of control, the British.

Hiding the Ball—Who Us? An Empire?

In the United States we hate the idea that we have an empire. We come up with all kinds of different names and theoretical concepts to disguise our informal empire. The most popular of these among US political scientists is the idea that the world has been governed by a "Liberal International Order" since 1945. Donald Trump's critics are convinced that he is threatening this order and they are right, though they over-emphasize the degree to which this order was ever based on an international consensus. Ideas of democracy and free trade are enshrined in international institutions like the United Nations, the World Bank, the International Monetary Fund and the World Trade Organization (which grew out of the post-war General Agreement on Tariffs and Trade). While the ideals espoused by those institutions grow out of the Western Enlightenment generally, they were designed by and for the United States.

Consensus-based ideas of international cooperation are found throughout the charters of all these organizations. But lawyers and bureaucrats from the United States wrote most of those charters, and established the devilish details that most often work in the US's favor. And when individual countries transgress against the dictates of these organizations, it's always US power that enforces the consequences. This enforcement sometimes comes in the form of military power, but it most often arrives in the form of financial carrots and sticks. I prefer to call the world system the American World Order, or the Pax Americana. These terms are better but they are also ways to hide the ball. Pax Americana is taken from the Pax Romana, and it implies that it's just the US legions that are doing the job through military force. Both the US system, and the British system before it are about vastly more than military power. It's the bankers and the lawyers that really run the show. We think British empire was primarily about the navy, when it was just as much about the Latin American (Or US, Or Indian, or…) plantation and railroad investments that helped to fund that navy. We think US empire is about Iraq or Vietnam, when it's much more about the enormous flows of capital through New York that numerous international institutions enable.

The United States is currently operating a **world-wide system of control**. The British operated one before it. I'll try to use the term "world-wide system of control" or "world system" instead of "empire" going forward, but when I use the short-hands "British Empire" and "US Empire", it is world systems that I am referring to. When I refer to "Dominance" or "Primacy" in the following pages, I am referring to the ability to sit at the middle of a world system and reap the benefits. This involves both worldwide formal and informal empire, and the assumption that if there's a problem anywhere in the world, the dominant power has the right to be, and should be involved in solving it.

The British Ball Is Hidden Still

The British Empire also managed to "hide the ball". It seems ridiculous to (most of) us today, but the British believed that their Empire had a higher purpose that made it morally superior to all other empires, at the time and in the past. They believed they had a "civilizing mission" that was horrifyingly expressed in Rudyard Kipling's poem the "White Man's Burden", written in 1899 to celebrate the US occupation of the Philippines.[19] They professed to believe that what they had built was for the benefit of the world. This approach to British Empire has been preserved to some degree in the works of writers like Niall Ferguson[20], but it's not the majority position outside of England, to put it mildly. This British propaganda is widely mocked, and even Ferguson

---

[19] It's worth taking a look at a selection from the "The White Man's Burden: The United States & The Philippine Islands, 1899" to get a sense of the way these people saw the world. *Take up the White Man's burden— / Send forth the best ye breed— / Go send your sons to exile / To serve your captives' need / To wait in heavy harness / On fluttered folk and wild— / Your new-caught, sullen peoples, / Half devil and half child!...*
[20] In 2002 Ferguson wrote Empire: The Rise and Demise of the British World Order and the Lessons for Global Power

acknowledges the racist and brutal elements of the British World System.

There is another bit of British propaganda that we have internalized almost entirely, however, that makes the work of the defenders of British Empire much easier. The nineteenth century Age of Imperialism is still described to us as a competition between European powers. Up until 1815, this was true. From 1815-1914 it was not.

The British get to write their own history in the English-speaking world, so the extent of their power in the nineteenth century is constantly downplayed. The justifications of the imperialists have made it into the history books. Throughout the period of British dominance, the Brits always claimed to be threatened by somebody to justify their feverish expansion.

The closer you look at them, the sillier those notions of imperial competition are. The French had Indochina (Modern Vietnam), Algeria and a few other territories. The British held the entire coastline of Asia from Malacca and Singapore to the borders of Iran. Formally or informally the British controlled almost all of the "economically useful" territory between Indochina and Algeria. The Brits spent the 1800s pretending their wealthy coastal Asian empire was threatened by Russia's vast but nearly empty land acquisitions in Central Asia. We hear a lot about the "Great Game" played between British and Russian spies and soldiers. But Russia's first Trans-Siberian railway line wasn't completed until 1916. British India's railway network alone was more impressive, if not larger than that of the entire Russian empire circa 1914. The idea that Russia threatened British India was a fantasy that thousands of British and Indian soldiers died for in Afghanistan, first in the 1840s, and again in the 1870s.

Our focus on "European Imperialism" tends to obscure the central British role in the nineteenth century, the most damaging imperialistic era. Great individual horrors were committed by everybody from the

Belgians to the Germans and the Italians, but all these horrors were perpetrated in the context of a world system that Britain built. The British built the modern world with everything that entails, good and bad. That also means that they are responsible for what became of that first world system.

Many blame the British for the conflict between Israel and Palestine, and for the potentially nuclear conflict between India and Pakistan. I would go a good deal further than that, and blame the British for both World Wars. They created and ran the first world system, reaping the lion's share of the benefits, and they are as responsible for that system's calamitous end.

We can't emphasize enough just how different the British World System was from everything that came before it. The British Empire was born during one of humanity's great transitions. Prior to 1700 or so, it doesn't make much sense to talk about world history. 2,000 years ago, the Roman Empire was one of the most successful in history, but China was barely aware of it, and it had only indirect impacts on Sub-Saharan Africa and the Americas. 800 years ago the Mongols swept across the Eurasian "world-island" but their impact remained non-existent to tiny on five of the seven continents.[21] Thanks to industrialization, the British World System was unavoidable, no matter where you lived, just like the US World System today.

Portugal, Spain, the Dutch Republic, and the Myth of 'European Dominance'

To further illustrate the uniqueness of the British and US World Systems, we should now turn to the Spanish, Portuguese and Dutch Empires. These were world-spanning empires, based in Europe, and reaching multiple continents, but they weren't world-wide systems of control. Many, from European nationalists to the victims of European

---

[21] Mongol forces were turned away at the gateway to Africa by the Egyptian Mamluks at the Battle of Ain Jalut in 1260.

colonialism, like to imagine that European dominance lasted much longer than it did. You can hear commentators talking about "500 years of world dominance" or even "1000 years". This is largely bunk. The Spanish and the Portuguese attained great power in the Americas after 1492, but between the 1300s and 1683 as much as half of Europe itself was swallowed up by a Muslim power, the Ottoman Empire. The Ottomans held on to chunks of what they took well into the twentieth century.

The Portuguese, Spanish and Dutch empires were powerful, and thanks to new naval technology their geographic reach was unprecedented, but they were not "dominant" in the sense that I described earlier. They were not sitting at the center of a web of power that ran the world. They were wealthy coastal trading empires. They did not have the ability to determine the policies and politics of the great empires in Asia and the Middle East. When they tried to do so they failed.

Much is made of the Portuguese and Spanish empires, but it's important to remember that what we know as these empires were two very separate things, that did their work in two very separate political geographies.

The Portuguese and Spanish empires were able to subjugate the peoples of the Americas, long before the industrial era. This was more of a geographical and biological phenomenon than anything else. Jared Diamond's *Guns, Germs and Steel* famously (and super repetitively) offers a convincing explanation for why this happened. The geography of the "Old World" in Europe and Asia allowed for quick exchange of wealth and technology, and faster cumulative development of ships, firearms and urban centers. This put them ahead of the peoples they found across the Atlantic. Most importantly this mass of people allowed for the unknowing weaponization of disease that took care of the lion's share of indigenous genocide in the Americas. The quick transmission of disease across Asia and Europe led to immunity to a range of diseases. The more intensive use of livestock also contributed to this immunity. When the Conquistadores landed in the early 1500s, they carried a number of diseases that the Americans had no immunity to. The numbers are eternally controversial, but the indigenous population of the Americas is estimated by some to have fallen by between 90-95 percent between 1492 and 1700.

European influence was firmly established on the peripheries of these continents as early as 500 years ago. But it was influence, not dominance, and it was very coastal. The broad continental expanses of North and South America were barely touched by Europeans before the 1800s. The same cannot be said for Eurasian diseases unfortunately.

When it comes to Africa, Asia, and the rest of Europe, the Portuguese, Spanish and Dutch empires were important, but not dominant by any stretch of the imagination. Advanced naval technology allowed these empires to take over large parts of sea-going trade in Asia and Africa, but to the peoples of the interior they were barely an annoyance before the late 1700s. The Europeans had guns. The Ottoman, Chinese and Mughal empires had guns too. The Europeans were getting wealthier, but that wealth paled in comparison to the vast resources at the command of these Asian empires. In the 1680s, the English went to war with the Mughal empire that controlled India at that time. It didn't go well.[22]

The English East India Company was seeking trading privileges with the Mughal Empire in 1682. With prosperous trading posts on both coasts of India, Josiah Child, the company's governor, thought he was negotiating from a position of strength. Negotiations broke down, and the English sent out a fleet of warships in 1685. The English captured a few ships, and burned a few towns, but only succeeded in angering Aurangzeb, the last great, and probably most terrifying, Mughal

---

[22] p. 365 Scott, David Leviathan: The Rise of Britain As a World Power

emperor. He ordered that the English be wiped from the map of India. By 1690, England's prosperous network of trading posts, some of which had been around for over 70 years, were wiped out, and their last fortified posts at Bombay (modern-day Mumbai) and Madras (Chennai) were under siege. This wasn't even the Mughal Emperor's main focus during this period. In 1689 he won a more important victory against Hindu armies in the Western Deccan.[23] Aurangzeb had use for the English however, so they were allowed to pay a large indemnity and rebuild their trade, though not before English representatives had to prostrate themselves before the Emperor.

Strangely this episode hasn't made its way into popular memory the way Robert Clive and all those tales of English victory in the next century have. The Portuguese and Spanish empires established in the 1500s, and the Dutch empire that scooped up a lot of the most valuable parts of those empires in the 1600s, didn't come close to the sort of power that the British system attained in the 1800s, and is now exercised by the US World System.

Another good measure of this is probably the island nation of Japan. In 1635 Japan's rulers decided to drastically reduce European influence, and bar all access save for a single port for the Dutch. The Europeans, despite their hunger for Japanese goods, were unable to force the issue for another two centuries.

The Spanish, Portuguese and Dutch were forging much closer links in the world trading system. Their naval technology, and the Dutch use of finance in particular, were crucial elements of the first world system that the British eventually built. But these empires didn't really know what they were doing. The Spanish famously managed to throw the world financial system out of whack by mining a mountain of silver in Bolivia. The inflation that resulted had serious effects from Europe to China. But one of the largest victims of this dynamic was the Spanish

---

[23] P. 7 Bayly, C. A. Indian Society and the Making of British Empire

empire itself. Control of a certain commodity does not translate to dominance. Mansa Musa, a Malian emperor, had a similar effect on the gold markets of the Mediterranean when he embarked on a generous pilgrimage to Mecca in the 14th century. Saudi Arabian control of oil markets in the late twentieth century gave them power, but it did not make them dominant.

The Portuguese, Spanish and Dutch also controlled a wide network of forts in Africa, Asia and the Americas. But their systems of control rarely expanded much further than the water's edge. Control of a trading system provided great wealth, but it did not involve leveraging the human and mineral resources of these territories on anywhere near the same scale that the British did. The speed with which the valuable parts of these empires could be scooped up by other powers is an indication of how transient this power was. When the Dutch got into the game, about a century after the Spanish and Portuguese, they quickly took many of the most profitable bits of Asian empire away from their Iberian predecessors. And when the British got seriously into the game in the later 1600s they took a wide range of territories from the Dutch. Like New York, for example, where I'm writing this book today.

The dominance of a world spanning system, what we envision when we think about European colonialism and the subjugation of the world's other peoples, didn't really get started until the mid-1700s. And it was only in the aftermath of the Napoleonic wars in the early 1800s that European dominance could really get going. And that dominance was British.

The British Empire was the first to be dominant on a worldwide scale. The US Empire is the second.

American Empire

To fully understand the story of the American Empire, we have to tell the story of the British Empire as well. The value isn't just comparative. Many of the ideas embodied in the US World System were first articulated under British hegemony. Representative government has evolved mightily since 1815, but you can see elements of modern-day "Democracy promotion" in British projects like the liberation of Greece and their support for the liberation of Spain's American empire in the early 1800s.

More importantly the British were major promoters of the doctrine of free trade. British thinkers like Adam Smith (1723-1790) and David Ricardo (1772-1823) founded the modern discipline of economics. Prior to their work most saw trade as a zero-sum game, where military force created monopolies that could secure the benefits of trade exclusively for one country or another. Under the new version, now known as "classical economics" free trade was reckoned to lift all boats. Each country or region could focus on what they were best at, and everybody would get rich. On a macro level, I think it's fair to say that this has been proven to be true. Free trade under the British and American world systems has made the world fantastically wealthy from the perspective of the eighteenth century.

It's also fair to say that the largest share of the benefits accrued to the dominant countries sitting at the centers of these world systems of free trade. At the peak of the British Empire, in the middle decades of the nineteenth century, the British Navy opened and maintained markets violently, from China to South America. As their Empire faded in the early twentieth century, that commitment faded, with the introduction of a system of imperial preferences, that the rising American Empire then challenged. You can see this dynamic recurring with the Trump administration's turning away from the aptly named "Washington Consensus" on free trade and fiscal rectitude.

As I hope this chapter has made clear, the British managed to build something that was new: a world-wide system of control. The US is operating one today. As we face the inevitable decline of US power, and attempt to avert a collapse, we need to study the British Empire more honestly, and in more detail. The United States is an empire, but of a very new kind. Despite the neo-classical clutter of our national monuments, and the popular obsession with ancient Greek and Roman precedents, we don't need to look back twenty centuries to see our future. We just need to look back one or two.

We've talked enough about Rome. Let's turn our eyes toward London.

Chapter 2

The Two World Systems in Human History

For just over 200 years now, the British and US World Systems have driven world history. Intentionally and unintentionally they have changed the world out of all recognition. During this time period, other actors on the world stage were important, sometimes very much so, but they were reacting to a baseline geopolitical reality set by Britain and the United States. Innovations in technology, society and warfare were developed in other countries, but they were driven by an effort to compete with and within these world systems.

By forcing the planet into a single system for the first time, in a sense the British turned the whole world into immigrants in their own countries. Everywhere, the hierarchies and paths to power, or even survival, were upended. They continue to be upended. For over 200 years now, the wrecking ball of change has just kept on swinging, finding new barriers to flatten, and new realms of human experience to make uniform. A hundred and fifty years ago, this came in the form of heavily armed steamships forcing open new markets, and now it comes in the form billions of addictive electronic devices in what will soon be the pockets of every single human being. Globalization, Industrialization, Technology, Nationalism, all of these concepts are too often described as impersonal forces that just… kind of… happened. That's not how it went. The British and US World Systems jammed these developments down the world's throat quite forcefully.

Not many people are willing to emphasize British and US power as much as this book does. Despite the facts that those steamships were either British or trying to keep up with them, and that the internet was initially a US government project, the leaders and citizens of the countries who ran the world systems don't want to acknowledge how big their role was and is. British and US Patriotism aside, taking this sweeping a view of the past 200 years includes taking responsibility for the nightmares of the first half of the twentieth century as well. Blaming the Germans for both World Wars is a fervently held prejudice of US and British historiography that is only now slowly fading away. Nobody in the non-English speaking world wants to acknowledge the true importance of the British and US World Systems either, it's too much of an affront to national pride. From the French to the Indians, nobody wants to admit just how little agency they have had over the past two centuries.

Good Or Bad Or Is?

As friends have viewed drafts of this book it's become clear that many come at the history presented with some preconceptions. Some bristle at the suggestion that the British and US Empires ever did anything useful. Others are deeply offended by the idea that these two empires ever did anything destructive beyond being "occasionally misguided" or "no worse than anybody else back then." I think both postures miss the enormity of what has happened over the past 200 years, and how closely tied the British and US World Systems are to what happened. We're talking about nothing less than the complete transformation of human existence.

I've spent years trying to evaluate the morality of all this, and hope to spend decades more, but the question of "good" or "evil" initially functions mostly as a bar to understanding. Those who want to preserve the idea that these world systems were and are solely virtuous and helpful are obscuring the scale and grandeur of the accomplishment. Those that are carefully adding to their competing lists of atrocities are missing the true, Lovecraftian horror of what we're talking about here. The British and US World Systems aren't "good" or "bad" actors on the world stage. They are the stage.

The British Empire ran the world between 1815 and 1914. The US Empire has been dominant from 1989 to the present day, and depending on how you measure it, for a good deal of time before that. The story of the world during both eras was one of constant change and evolution. It was that constant ferment that made world-wide systems possible in the first place. And it's that constant change that ends empires as well. The British and US Empires look very different from each other, and the change the world has gone through explains that as well. To give a sense of what has changed so dramatically over the past few hundred years, we've got to tell just a bit of the story of human progress…

Progress!?!?!?

Yep, I believe in "Progress", with the full knowledge of how fraught and problematic that concept is. I find modern human civilization to be more of a wonder than a horror, and I remain optimistic about our ability to make it all work much better. My passion for history has a lot to do with my conviction that we really have been moving onwards and upwards as a species, and I enjoy the story.

The fact that we managed to get to this point, where I can write these words, and be confident that they will (hopefully) be read by people across the world within a couple months[24] is amazing. As writer and reader, we are relying on centuries of technological and social progress. The fact that we can sit in our climate-controlled rooms, read, and wonder whether or not we'd have been happier as hunter-gatherers is the result of such a multiplicity of factors, both in material terms and stretching back through time, that I can only see it as a kind of magic. The process that got us here, with its millions of small changes adding up to a general forward motion, is what I see as progress.

Progress has never been a straight line, though. Human history is one of horror, punctuated by brief periods of advancement. I believe it has

---

[24] Months or years… this project has taken a lot longer than I expected.

all been worth it. But perhaps that's my privilege talking. Let's look at where we've been…

Going All the Way Back…

For the first 35,000 years of the 45,000[25] or so since the emergence of modern humans, and throughout our development for hundreds of thousands of years before that, human beings and our ancestors lived by hunting and gathering. It's fashionable today to point out that the pre-agricultural people who survived childbirth lived a "better" life than we do today. There was more leisure time, supposedly, and people had more diverse diets, leading to healthier people than there were at any point after the agricultural revolution. Scholars like Jared Diamond have devoted hundreds of pages to the proposition that hunter-gatherers are more in tune with their environments, and that they make better use of human capacity. He claims that hunter-gatherers are just plain smarter than us.

As you might have guessed by now, I'm suspicious of this approach. I see a lot of conclusions being drawn from scant evidence that fit certain Western ideas and assumptions a bit too well. I'm not just talking about more current environmentalist ideas, but also the very tired Western trope of the "Noble Savage" who has so much to teach us fallen modern humans.

Elements of the current view of hunter-gatherers could very well be true. But I like things like reading and writing. Perhaps I'd be more in my element making cave paintings, but I wouldn't be me. And I like me. I also like humans. The fact that there are 7 billion of us rocketing around on planet Earth rather than a few tens of thousands strikes me as a great thing. And though our modern civilization is terribly fragile, with all its dependence on lengthy supply chains and technology we

---

[25] These numbers are always changing, based on whatever pops out of the ground, and our constantly shifting ideas of who "we" are. Every decade some new innovation in genetics or archaeology throws a different wrinkle into the story.

don't understand, I'm pretty sure it's less fragile than hunter-gatherer society was.

When Hurricane Harvey slammed into the Texas coast in August of 2017, 82 people are reckoned to have died. The greater Houston area is home to over 6 million people. Had it been home instead to 150 happy, fulfilled hunter-gatherers, I imagine the death toll would still have been somewhere around 80 people.

All that said, I have been convinced that the transition from hunter-gatherer modes of life to agricultural ones was a catastrophe for most people. James C. Scott's <u>Against the Grain: A Deep History of the Earliest States,</u> makes this case very well. Agriculture allowed for many more people, but settled agriculture and larger towns and cities also created deeper wells for disease. The transition from more diverse hunter-gatherer sources of nutrition to agricultural staples made most people shorter, dumber, and more sickly. It's only after industrialization, in the past couple hundred years, that this issue has begun to be dealt with. While I don't believe that agriculture invented man's inhumanity to man, it certainly gave it much broader scope. A chief of a band of Hunter-Gatherers band reserved her brutality for other bands, and she had to be concerned with the happiness of her scarce human resources. The king of an agricultural state could treat his thousands of subjects as interchangeable parts. He was more interested in volume than quality of life. While agriculture may not have invented slavery, it certainly gave it much broader scope. For thousands of years now, humanity has been led by vicious thugs who treat people as means to an end.

From the agricultural revolution,[26] thousands of years ago, down to around 1700 or so, compared to the eras we're discussing in this book,

---

[26] Dating the agricultural revolution is a tremendously difficult thing to do. The standard story is evolving as we speak. Somewhere between 9,000 and 5,000 years ago, the first agricultural states evolved. Farming allowed for surplus, and what we call civilization. But it was very uneven. These agrarian states were vulnerable to the pastoral "barbarians" at their borders. Settled states were constantly at risk of being consumed. That's how

the world didn't change much. But that's only compared to the centuries discussed in this book. Things changed. Things changed dramatically. All the processes of conflict, war and cultural clash that will be described in this book played out prior to 1700 as well, though on a smaller scale. Life was terribly unstable.

Empires rose and fell, new religions were founded, and most importantly, knowledge and technology slowly improved. Certain times and places, like ancient Greece, Song China, and Medieval Italy, combined new technologies and ideas to take great steps forward. The Roman Empire, and many others, managed to leverage agricultural wealth to create vast trade networks, with monetized economies. They created wonders that give us pause, even today. But all these places, and no doubt thousands of others that we know less well, or have forgotten entirely, were swept away.

The Pre-Modern era was not a nice place. The limits to progress in an agricultural economy were brutal. Disease, climate and weather all stood ready to destroy fledgling kingdoms. Early agricultural states were usually surrounded by seas of pastoral people who grew rich and numerous off of those states. The pastoral people would profit from trade, but they were also eager to swoop down on any sign of weakness, and take the fruits of whatever progress that had been made for themselves. The Germanic tribes that grew rich and numerous on the Roman periphery eventually swallowed the Western Roman Empire. Over millennia, from the Xiongnu to the Mongols and Manchus, pastoralists did the same thing to numerous Chinese dynasties. Ibn Khaldun, the great 14th century Arab philosopher was an early observer of this dynamic. It's recently become fashionable to see the 13th and 14th century Mongols as a great unifying force in Eurasia, but the pendulum is likely to swing back on that. The pastoralists' repeated

---

Rome fell for example. It's only around 1600 CE or so that the constant threat of barbarians from the steppes was eliminated.

eating of the goose that gave them golden eggs was enormously destructive. Tamerlane's 14th century capitol of Samarkand remains impressive, but that's because nothing that has happened in Samarkand since has been very impressive at all.

History was a one step forward, two steps back kind of thing for millennia. Great agricultural empires could fall entirely, and fall hard. James C. Scott calmly describes the result of one such collapse in the Middle East in the third millennium BCE.

> Of the magnitude of the depopulation there is little doubt: "According to one estimate, South Levantine population crashed to a tenth or twentieth of its previous level," wrote Broodbank. "Most large settlements emptied out to be replaced by a scatter of tiny, short-lived sites."[27]

The human stories left out of that matter of fact recounting must have been very, very bitter. There was great change and ferment throughout human history, but forward motion was hard to see. The tools and capabilities changed very, very slowly. One step forward, two steps back. For thousands of years.

Gross Domestic Product is a suspect measure in any time frame, and especially so if we're talking about historical eras. But the US Federal Reserve's estimates of historical economic growth help to illustrate how slowly things changed in the past. From 1960 to 2004, world GDP is estimated to have grown at 4 percent a year. From 1900 to 1960 it was 2.4 percent. From 1800 to 1900 it was 1 percent a year. And from 1700 to 1800 it's estimated to have been around .3 percent a year. Before that the world economy grew, but it was at a rate that was almost imperceptible by our standards.[28]

Thugs and Organization: A simple Equation

---

[27] Scott, James C Against the Grain: A Deep History of the Earliest States p.214 quoting Broodbank, The Making of the Middle Sea, 349

[28] https://minneapolisfed.org/publications/the-region/the-industrial-revolution-past-and-future

What slow growth meant, for most people, for most of the past 10,000 years, was a life of agricultural misery.[29] Good figures are hard to come by, of course, but it's fair to assume that 80 to 90 percent of all people living in settled states, everywhere, worked in agriculture. The more land a given empire controlled, the more wealth a small elite had to skim off the top. It was a pretty straightforward function. More land and people to oppress led to greater power. From the first Empires in Mesopotamia, down to 17th century "gunpowder empires" in Europe and Asia, the basics didn't change much. More land and people to oppress meant that the thugs on top could fund more conquest, and as a byproduct fund some pretty art and stuff. Human history's incredible diversity of culture masks this ugly fact. It was thugs on top, doing thuggish things, and misery for everybody else. For thousands of years. Everywhere.

I use the term "thug" intentionally. The word was initially derived from the experience of the British in India. It has its roots in the Thugee cult, which supposedly saw waylaying travelers as some sort of religious duty. The Thugees didn't get to write their own history. They were eradicated by the British in the 1830s. Since then the term "thug" has been applied indiscriminately to refer to criminals and gangsters, most often applied to minority populations. Re-appropriating the term to refer to the folks on top of society strikes me as a nice skewering of their pretensions. The aristocratic thugs on top in most countries for most of human history between the agricultural and industrial revolutions really were gangsters. They enriched themselves by providing a very debatable form of "protection" to their people in

---

[29] The degree of misery varied of course. At the first US Census in 1790, 90 percent of people worked in agriculture, but many owned their own farms, which allowed for a much higher standard of living than most of the world's farmers. The 18 percent of Americans that were slaves in 1790, of course, lived lives of unrelenting horror. Some Northwestern European farmers had standards of living approaching those of free farmers in the United States, but much of the world's agricultural labor force was made up of peasants, who did not own the land they worked, owed labor to their landlords, and often lacked the freedom to leave the land. The half of Russia's peasants (38 percent of the total population) that were tied to their land as serfs were not emancipated until 1861, as just one example.

return for taxes paid in food or money. Taxation without representation. Gangsterism, pure and simple.

(Land + People) * Organization = Power

There were exceptions[30], but for most of human history the outcomes of wars fit a fairly predictable pattern. The entity that did a better job of marshalling land and people tended to win. If one group of thugs had more people and more land, and controlled it effectively, they would win. The effective central control was the important thing. Great empires fell over and over, but that was usually because they failed to hold their lands and peoples together. The Western Romans fell to disparate groups of barbarians in the 400s, but that was after centuries of Roman civil wars. In an extraordinary few decades in the mid-600s the armies of the early Muslim Caliphs obliterated the Sassanid Persian Empire, and conquered the most lucrative parts of the Eastern Roman Empire. But this only happened after the Roman and Persian Empires had spent decades ripping each other to shreds. The Eastern Romans had allowed fights over Christian Orthodoxy to build up resentments and open rebellion in many of the provinces that the Arabs took. In the 1200s the Mongols ripped through the Abbasid Caliphate and the Song Chinese and everything in between because those empires were shadows of their former selves. If a group of thugs managed to keep a large selection of **Land** and **People** better **Organized** than the folks next door, then they could exert **Power** over their neighborhood.

Drawing more people and land into an empire required more organization. As a given entity got more powerful, be it a land empire

---

[30] The main exception that jumps to mind for me is the ancient conflict between Classical Greece and the Achaemenid Persian Empire in the 400s BC. This conflict was most recently celebrated in the movie 300 that came out in 2006. This may be a good counter-example to the phenomenon I'm laying out here, but then again it may not. Our accounts of this are almost all Greek. We know very little about what was really happening in the vast Persian lands. It's almost certain that the Persians did not ascribe the same significance to this conflict that the Greeks, and their millennia of admirers did. We just don't really know. That hasn't stopped Western historians like Victor Davis Hansen from fetishizing the Greek victory over the Persians and imputing to it some sort of intrinsic greatness of West over East.

like Rome, or a sea-based trading empire like the Venetians, there was a larger scope for people to benefit from serving the thugs on top. To a limited degree, these larger urban publics could exert pressure on their leaders. At its high point in the 100s CE, the city of Rome is estimated to have reached a population of around million people, a number which wasn't reached again in Europe before the 1800s. Some medieval Italian city states reached high standards of living within the city walls.

Urban publics could influence the politics of their cities and states through limited use of representative institutions, but also through the ever-present threat of mob violence. The people within these cities had to be placated to some degree, with bread and circuses for the mass, and with limited opportunities for social mobility for a hyper-talented and lucky few. But it's important to remember that this was possible only through the exploitation of vast agricultural hinterlands. These agricultural hinterlands, Rome's in particular, were often better organized than they were before, but this often meant outright slavery rather than a higher standard of living for farmers. Ancient Rome's massive population was possible because it managed to unite and organize the economy of the Mediterranean in a way that had never been done before, and hasn't been done since.

Brief moments of success were always tenuous. Rome fell due to a combination of the greed of the thugs it empowered (emperors and others) and invasions by the states and tribes on its borders, among many, many other factors. The medieval Italian city states that gave us the Renaissance were ruined by the early modern monarchs, from the Ottomans to the Habsburgs, that figured out how to take Italian trading networks for themselves. The urban publics that had managed to attain small slices of power from their thugs on top were either slaughtered by other thugs, or dispersed to the countryside to learn to farm or starve. The fall of Rome is the most famous example of this, but it happened over and over again, for millennia before and after that particular fall.

Something Changes...

Then something changed. It's fiendishly difficult to pinpoint exactly what it was, or even where it started to happen. We do know that the Europeans were the principal beneficiaries initially, and that the British Empire was the biggest winner of all.

It's tempting to pick out individual points that "changed everything," but that's usually misleading. In 1712, Thomas Newcomen, an English engineer, invented the first modern-ish steam engine, in an effort to pump water out of coal mines. You could say the industrial revolution started here. But did it really?

Newcomen's engine spread slowly, and it was a full sixty-nine years before Scotsman James Watt added a condenser and made applications like railroads and steam ships possible. There was no "big bang" for the industrial revolution; it was a cumulative process, that accelerated very slowly, and it extends back centuries. Economist Brad DeLong has pointed out that for most of the world's people, the industrial revolution's impact was virtually nil as recently as the late nineteenth century.[31] Whatever and whenever it was, the Industrial Revolution is generally recognized to have started in Britain, after centuries of scientific and economic development in Europe.

Europe had a number of characteristics that gave the sad 'thugs on top vs. everyone else' story some interesting variations. Its many navigable rivers and obstructive mountain ranges allowed power centers to build up in multiple places, and made it harder to conquer all of them and absorb them into one empire. History[32] led to an odd division between spiritual and physical power. Italian popes struggled with German

---

[31] http://www.bradford-delong.com/2018/05/1870-the-real-industrial-revolution-hoisted-from-the-archives-from-ten-years-ago.html

[32] Yes, that's very vague, but it's difficult to pinpoint what exactly it was that gave the Catholic church so much power. Was it the vestiges of Roman urban power that the City of Rome and its bishop managed to hold onto? Was it the way that the Eastern Roman Empire tended to format Christianity towards centralized religious and secular power, allowing the Pope to fill the void of centralized secular power in Western Europe? Was it the will of god? There's a lot to unpack here, and it's not the subject of this book.

"Holy Roman Emperors" for centuries, allowing all kinds of countries, and even individual cities, to set up their own little bases of power and land. It was the same story of thugs on top vs. everybody else, but it was much more fragmented.

Some interesting proto-democratic ideas developed here and there, with certain cities being run by sort of representative bodies. If you squint really hard you can see the beginnings of our ideas of representative government going back to the Middle Ages, in places like Florence and Venice. But you're probably fooling yourself if you do. Centuries worth of nationalist historians have worked hard to construct the idea of a special "western genius" for self-government in the "national souls" of Italian merchants, German tribal peoples and Greek hoplites. It's not that historians were inventing events and writings (most of the time[33]) it's that they were gravitating to the details that fit the nationalist stories they wanted to tell, and blowing them out of all proportion. The motivating ideologies are discredited to differing degrees, but the preoccupations of nationalist historians effect (infect?) everything we know about European origins. Early European oligarchies didn't create dramatically better places to live for most people. As we covered above, those living in the cities themselves had more interesting lives, but those in the agricultural hinterlands usually did not. At root it was the same story of thugs on top vs. everyone else. But there were more and more varied forms of thugs in Europe.

The wider range of thugs in Europe than elsewhere was important. In a relatively small geographical region there was a lot of competition. It's a story of almost continuous war and destruction. But it gave the Europeans a great gift. Innovations were adopted more quickly. There were more places for wealth and expertise to take hold and flourish. Each thug had to do everything in his power to beat out the thug next

---

[33] Scottish poet James MacPherson's fraudulent invention of the Ossian cycle of epic poetry in the 1760s is one extraordinary example of national minded intellectuals inventing an attractive history.

door, whether that thug was a noble, a merchant oligarchy, an emperor or a pope. That meant grasping on to any possible advantage. These innovations were most often military, but they spun off unpredictable opportunities. Competing naval technologies led to exploration and more markets to exploit. The need to get artillery trajectories right led to the dusting off and updating of ancient geometry and the perfection of trigonometry. This had implications for the development of science.

This process seems offensively slow from our perspective. But Europe's chaos led to steady upward progress in some places. Already by 1500 the percentage of the population of certain Northern European countries working in agriculture was lower than in the rest of the world. With so many little cities and kingdoms duking it out, a sort of natural selection made them stronger and meaner. It no longer made sense to have most everybody farming dirt. People needed to do more complicated things. The mercenary bands that were fighting most of Europe's wars by the high middle ages eventually got larger and more complex, and then they ended up as permanent standing armies in places like the Ottoman Empire and France.

The military technology got more complex and so did the supply chains. People needed to figure out how to fight for longer, further away from home. The supply chains led to administrative complexity, and the need for a more literate population. An English army of a few thousand that rides into Scotland can be collected by an illiterate agricultural aristocracy. An army that takes ships to invade France needs administrators that can read, more forethought and serious supply logistics. It's exponentially more complicated to get a British army to New York or India. Trade became more important, and more people got involved. The markets grew, as these more literate administrators and traders started wanting to live more like the thugs on top. This often violent process of innovation sparked and burned through Europe most intensely, but it had effects further afield, providing benefits to groups of merchants and princes from Northern Africa to South East Asia. Importantly, the process was most intense in Europe, but it created winners and losers over the world. The greatest beneficiaries ended up being in London, but its early effects were just as apparent in Istanbul and Nanjing.

The pace of change started to pick up. **England in 1440** didn't look too terribly different from England in 1340, 1240, or even, with some allowances, 940. The King of England in 1440 was a medieval monarch, as he had been for hundreds of years, running around trying to exert his will over the Scottish, Welsh, Irish and French, while also managing his uppity aristocratic underlings. The Hundred Years' War over English royalty's claims to France was just winding down. The Wars of the Roses for the English throne, between the Houses of Lancaster and York, were just about to get started. These two conflicts are largely what we think of when we envision the conflicts of "knights in shining armor". Our contemporary vision of medieval chivalry, the HBO TV series Game of Thrones, is based in part on the Wars of the Roses. A parliament existed in England in 1440, but it was a very different animal, and was more of an arena for battle between feudal lords than it was an institution that represented the people in any legitimate way.

By the 1540s, just 100 years later, Henry VIII was setting up an absolute monarchy, which is a much more modern animal than we commonly recognize. His assertion of independence from the Catholic Church, and appropriation of the Church's wealth set him up as probably the most (internally) [34] powerful king in English history, never matched before or since. Henry VIII and his six wives left a vast imprint in historical consciousness. He's easily the most famous British king. This has a lot to do with the length and scandal of his reign, but

---

[34] The power I'm speaking of here is Henry VII's power over his own countrymen and the governing apparatus. As far as geographic spread, or the ability to exert power over other nations, or even the Scottish or Irish, Henry VII was historically weak. Autocrats don't generally make for good competitors in geopolitics.

it also has a lot to do with that quickening pace of change. Henry VIII had a broader canvas to paint his lunacy on. The financial and political possibilities were wider than they had ever been.

Just 100 years after that, **in the 1640s**, the forces of the Long and Rump Parliaments fought against Charles I in the English Civil War. Different power centers in English and Scottish society had built up enough wealth to challenge the king when he tried to govern as absolutely as Henry VIII had. This conflict cost Charles his head in 1649, and ironically ended up costing Parliament its power as well, creating what is sometimes portrayed as the first modern dictatorship, that of Lord Protector Oliver Cromwell. This conflict, just two short centuries after the prime Game of Thrones era, can be seen as a forerunner to most modern civil wars from Russia in 1917 to Syria in 2011. All the relevant pieces were there, from competing propaganda to the inability to tell when a war has been "won" or "finished" in a revolutionary context. More groups and interests mattered than just a few aristocratic thugs on top. Things were changing quickly.

England's control over Scotland and Ireland had been much shakier just two centuries prior. In earlier times, an England in turmoil would have provided opportunities for those territories to go their own way. But because of growing wealth the potential for destruction was larger, and the connections between these territories were firmer. Scotland and Ireland were sucked into the English Civil War, and its aftermath tied them to England more tightly rather than less. Britain's precocious centralization here began to give it a lead on most of its continental European rivals.

Thuggery was evolving. Britain and, to a lesser extent those continental rivals, were getting richer. They were still desperately poor by our standards, but the classes of people who could benefit from conquest were getting larger. This allowed more sophisticated methods of control of the public and broader empires, but it also made for a broader mix of people who could demand things from the thugs on top. This was still a small class of people. We were nowhere near representative democracy, but it's fair to say that in the 1600s, if only in England and the Netherlands, the system of government was getting less thuggish for a broader slice of society.

Super Charged Thuggery

But this fading thuggishness relied on a profoundly sad development. Just as the growing privileges of a few urban areas in the Roman Empire relied on the deepening misery of a progressively larger agricultural hinterland, the less thuggish society of a few Western European states relied on growing misery elsewhere. A richer population, with slightly more widely distributed rewards, used their new freedoms to turn their thuggery towards the world. It was the wealth built by this process that allowed new freedoms to advance in Northern Europe. The brutality with which the English and the Dutch built American slave empires provided the resources necessary to challenge the thugs on top in their own societies.

This evolving thuggery in the 1600s led to more significant European impacts on the broader world. European empire in the Americas in the 1500s was about resource extraction more than anything else. The ships full of gold and silver were mined with slaves[35] taken from the diminishing native population. The larger American economies that began to be built around sugar, tobacco, indigo and cotton in the 1600s, however, required a higher volume of slave labor. Europe's exploitation of African labor began to kick into higher gear. Africa and the Americas provided the blood and toil that allowed Europe to begin to experiment with new ideas of freedom and government.

In the 1500s and 1600s, thanks to innovation in naval technology and financial organization, the world's resources as a whole began to grow

---

[35] Sometimes in name, but always in fact

more quickly. But the organization of world resources that brought this growth, perhaps inevitably, began to direct those same resources to the folks in Europe who were doing the organizing. It happened slowly. The expansive earlier centuries of China's Qing or Manchu dynasty, established in 1636, were fueled in part by American silver that came on European ships. Before being crushed by the British in the 1800s, China in the 1600s and 1700s grew to its greatest historical extent, fueled in party by wealth brought by the growing European organization of world trade. China's growing control over territories like Xinjiang (from 1759) and Tibet (from 1720) became possible because of the wealth that European networks of African slavery and American conquest provided.

This growing wealth also funded Europe's spectacularly brutal 1600s. It powered new and rapacious absolute monarchies, and began to form the modern idea of the nation-state. At the same time, it allowed the creation of unprecedentedly powerful representative institutions in England and the Dutch Republic. This bloody ferment produced thinkers like John Locke, one of the main thinkers behind the ideas in the US Constitution.

Bondage and slaughter across the world begat freedom in a few places. Our modern concepts of liberty and just government first flowered out of the sordid manure of world-wide networks of proto-industrial slavery and genocide. The very ability to conceive of slavery and genocide as bad things to be eradicated was born out of their perfection as engines of wealth. You see what I mean about Lovecraftian horror? And grandeur? Concepts like "good" and "bad" don't really begin to touch the deep, deep fucked-upedness of how our modern world was formed.

Nationalism: A Broader Kind of Thuggery

Long before it became known by the name, nationalism was driving this snowballing European organization of the world's resources.

Nationalism was central to the rise and fall of the British Empire, and it's an underappreciated factor in why the British and US Empires look so different. It's also a vital concept in the history of human progress, though many don't like that idea.

Nationalism, quite rightly, gets a bad rap today. We think of the evils of Hitler and other fascists. We think of the rise of a certain kind of nationalism in the United States today, that played such a troubling role in Donald Trump's victory in the 2016 election. But this story leaves a lot out. Prior to WWII, nationalism wasn't such a bad word. As an ideology it's not just about crushing the "other", it's also about identity, self-determination, and asserting the rights of any people to be free from outside interference. The idea of nationalism remains a useful weapon against the thugs on top of any given society, and against outside aggressors. Folks like to pretend that there is a firm division between nasty Nationalism and healthier ideas like "Patriotism" and the urge for "National Self-Determination", but they exist on a spectrum. In too many examples, like Myanmar today, the first thing a people does when it attains more self-determination is go out and persecute a minority. Nationalism is a dangerous tool, just like a steam engine or a computer, and its use and misuse is more important to how we got here than any individual technological development.

By the 1600s, and certainly the 1700s, something was happening in Britain, France, and to a lesser extent in other European countries. People were beginning to see themselves as **a people**. The modern legal concept of the nation-state had its origins in the religious conflict between Catholics and Protestants, but the idea ended up embracing a lot more than religious separatism. The long century of conflict between France and the British (roughly 1689-1815) involved a great deal of propaganda that defined **"who we are"** and **"who they are"**. The conflict itself provided a great deal of history and fodder for national myth making. The rising wealth of these countries provided broader literacy and allowed more people to become invested in new nationalist ideas. Loyalty to a city or region began to be rivalled by the concept of loyalty to the larger country. The struggles of what we can begin to call nation-states became something much more than the interests of whatever family happened to be occupying the throne. The idea of "Frenchness" or "Englishness" became a tremendously powerful tool, both for good and evil. It was a key part of the evolution from a straightforwardly thuggish mode of government, to one that provided benefits for a broader slice of the population.

I spent much of the past decade living in Turkey, a place where nationalism is more explicitly part of politics than it is elsewhere in Europe (or it used to be more explicit, the rest of Europe is catching up). Openly nationalist parties have been a significant factor in Turkish elections for decades. Nationalism is a central part of the ideology and cult of personality surrounding the modernizing founder of today's Republic of Turkey, Mustafa Kemal Ataturk (1881-1938). This can be alarming to the casual observer, and to some extent it should be. But in a lot of ways it's a throwback to nineteenth century European liberal politics.

In the nineteenth and twentieth centuries Nationalism was directly tied to the reforming and democratizing instincts of radicals throughout the world. "Liberal Nationalism" was not an oxymoron. The nationalist ideal of "the people", who deserved a larger say in government, and a larger share of the benefits of a country's success was a large part of bringing countries out of more thuggish modes of government.

The Possibility of a World System

In the 1600s, the ability to build a trans-Atlantic empire and profit from it was an extraordinary new development, and provided a boost to Europe's competitive advantages. The Spanish, Portuguese and Dutch empires discussed in Chapter One were demonstrating tantalizing new opportunities for wealth-building. But, again, it's important not to over-emphasize the significance of these empires in terms of world power. The trans-Atlantic economy of the 1600s made European world dominance possible, but it hadn't yet made it a reality. The Dutch, and to a lesser extent the British, scooped up the most valuable parts of the Asian trade networks the Spanish and Portuguese had hijacked a century earlier. They intensified some aspects of this trade, but were not yet that important to the Asian balance of power. The "Gunpowder Empires", of the Ottoman Turks, the Safavids of Persia, and the Mughals of India rubbed up against each other unhappily, and the Chinese empire prosperously growing China in the far East. Before the 1700s the Europeans had little to do with this. European empire was coastal.

A first look, **in 1700**, at what would eventually become the United States is helpful in illustrating the shallowness of European impact in the 1600s. The valuable bits of European empires were mostly in Caribbean islands, with their sugar and slave economies. There wasn't much European influence in North America yet. The three largest cities were New York with 4,937 people, Philadelphia with 4,400 people, and the big winner, Boston, with 6,700 people. The Massachusetts Bay Colony had to briefly abandon large swathes of territory during "King Phillip's War" with Native American tribes in the 1670s. The power of European empire was growing in the 1600s, but it wasn't anywhere near anything we'd call dominant.

By 1740 though, the growing empire of Great Britain was getting there. In 1707, England and Scotland adopted this name, and formalized their association with Acts of Union. Just 100 years after the turmoil of the English Civil war, and 300 years after the *Game of Thrones*-inspiring War of the Roses, London was sitting fat and happy at the center of a word-wide web of trade, political influence, and military power. The previously troublesome Scots had been incorporated, and the Irish had been more comprehensively suppressed. The slave economy in multiple Caribbean islands was operating at full steam, and was now expanding in the south of what would become the United States. There was slavery in the northern British colonies as well, but they were becoming more oriented towards trade, fishing and smaller-scale agriculture. The disarray of India's Mughal empire after Aurangzeb (r.1658-1707) had provided greater openings for European traders. Their profit-oriented appropriation of local armies and tax systems on the Indian sub-continent was building real Asian mainland empires for Europeans for the first time by the mid-1700s.

Nationalism was also a key part of the growth of the British Empire. Nationalist ideas were internalized by a public that was growing more powerful. By 1800, over fifty percent of Great Britain's population was working at something other than agriculture. And those that were still toiling in the fields were doing much more productive work. Literacy was becoming widespread, and many people gravitated to ideas of "Englishness" and "Scottishness" presented in the popular novels of the day. Industrialization and military technology was important to the British crushing of other peoples, but so was the fact that merchants, missionaries, and soldiers were all working toward the same goal of imperial power.

This embryo of British World System wasn't unchallenged however. The French had an Indian Empire and Asian networks of trade as well. They had fabulously lucrative slave islands in the Caribbean too. While they didn't have as many people in North America, they laid claim to a larger extent of land. And the Spanish were still competitive on a smaller scale. The stage was being set for the first world-wide wars. You can make a good argument that these wars were really just one big war that lasted for over a century (1689-1815).

After 1789, the French provided a master class in the weaponization of nationalism that the world is still recovering from (or benefiting from). The French Revolutionary government, and then Napoleon, used nationalist ideas to motivate the French to dominate Europe (1794-1815). The Napoleonic wars served as a wake-up call to the other peoples of Europe who engaged in a break-neck race to incorporate elements of nationalism into their own societies. History was ransacked to craft ideas of German and Italian national identity. This project resulted in successful unification of both Germany and Italy in 1871.[36] Less successfully, this project of national identity also had a lot to do with fascism, and the catastrophic defeat of both countries in WWII. Throughout the rest of Europe, a national language, national literature, and national history became obsessive topics of interest. Some of this had real basis in history, but a lot of it was invented as well.

Older tribal leaders, kings, and even emperors in Eastern Europe and across the world couldn't compete. They didn't have the human resources. The majority of the people outside Western Europe were peasants, who weren't necessarily all that invested in the complexion of the thugs who forced them to farm. The world was simply not prepared for the hyper-charged industrial thuggery of Britain and its rivals. Even continent-spanning empires like the Ottoman and the Chinese had this problem. Between 1850 and 1864, an estimated 20-30 million people died in the Taiping Rebellion. Chinese national identity had taken so many bruises from Europeans (primarily the British) by that point, that the country was vulnerable to this civil war with the Taipings, a profoundly idiosyncratic Christian sect made up primarily of Chinese people. By 1830, the Ottomans had already lost their first traditional territory, Greece, to these new concepts of nationalism, and this process would only accelerate in the coming decades. One can see why modern Turkey, the direct successor of the Ottoman Empire, takes nationalism so seriously.

---

[36] Using those dates is a tremendous oversimplification. The German and Italian unification processes were both the result of a long series of wars and diplomatic negotiations. They both reached completion with the defeat of France in the Franco-Prussian war. The Kingdom of Italy was established in 1861, but it was the loss to the Germans that got French troops out of Rome, allowing Italian nationalists to disown the Pope and complete the desired unification process.

The European head-start on the concept of nationalism dissipated rapidly in world-historical terms, but not rapidly enough to save the world from European empire. Most of the many heroic tales of resistance are sadly outside of the scope of this book, but it's important to remember that they happened. What followed European conquest, both formal and informal, was a period of adaptation. Panjak Mishra's fascinating book From the Ruins of Empire: The Intellectuals Who Remade Asia illustrates how thinkers from China to the Muslim world used elements of Western ideology, and their own rich histories to craft new national identities, and formulated ways to use the intellectual tools of the European oppressors against them.

By 1840 the British had won. In this rapidly changing world, the British industrialized first. The tale of the British Empire is fundamentally one of the first mover advantage. They had a commanding lead over their European rivals, were able to handily beat Europe's traditional French hegemon in 1815, and were effectively operating in a completely different century from most of the rest of the world by 1840. The military technology and motivated, literate, mercantile populace that the British had to bring to bear desperately outclassed anybody in Asia, Africa, Eastern Europe or the Americas in military and economic might. They had a smaller, but still very significant lead over the other West European powers as well.

The world they looked out on in the middle of the nineteenth century was a British playground. They could get away with a lot, and they did get away with a lot. The British formal empire, the lands actually flying the British flag, did not reach its widest extent until the 1920s, but the mid-19th century almost certainly represented the peak of British power. Settler colonies that eventually joined the United States as powerful independent countries had been established in Canada, Australia, and New Zealand. In 1840 the British formally controlled an ever-growing network of ports that allowed them to control world trade. The British attained strategic ports in Hong Kong (1842), Singapore (1819), Ceylon (modern Sri Lanka) (1815), Malacca (1824), Aden (in Yemen) (1839) and many others that allowed them to dominate trade in Asia. The British hadn't yet fallen victim to the passion for taking large territories that later caused them so many problems, but they had defeated the last serious rival to their dominance of India with the end of the third Maratha war in 1818.

The late nineteenth century Scramble for Africa, when European empires carved up the continent, had not yet started, but the British occupied strategic territories in South Africa and could dictate terms to the rest of the imperial and local powers on that continent. Their Caribbean territories were now much less important, but they were deeply involved both in encouraging the independence of Latin American countries, and the trade and finance of those countries. Again, the red bits on those British Empire maps only tell a small part of the story. Informal empire was just as important as formal empire. Naval, commercial and financial dominance meant that the British were able to re-write the trade laws of the Chinese and Ottoman Empires at the end of a gun. By the mid-nineteenth century, the British had successfully built a world-wide system of control.

By **1940** the British World System was finished. It didn't look this way on the surface. In the inter-war period, between 1918 and 1939, the British Empire reached its greatest extent, controlling almost a quarter of the world's land area, and an estimated 458 million people. India, large territories in Africa, and a growing selection of Asian and Middle Eastern countries had been agglutinated to this unwieldly mass. The final demise of the Ottoman Empire after WWI had added Iraq and Palestine, under the more nationalism-friendly title of League of Nations mandates. This gigantic British entity was running out of steam, and it was nationalism that helped it out the door.

By the time Europe shot itself in the face with two world wars the planet was irrevocably changed. The story of the twentieth century in every country in the world is one of rapid transformation. The processes that took centuries in North Western Europe, took generations in the rest of Europe and took decades elsewhere. Nationalism was perhaps the most vital part of this process. By 1945 every country at least had an intelligentsia that saw their people as independent by right. By 2018 most people in most countries could read the works of that intelligentsia, and insist on their right to self-determination. Nationalism is a profoundly tricky concept, but it's probably had as much to do with liberation as it had to do with horror.

The national aspirations of European peoples like the Serbians led to the cataclysm of WWI in 1914, and in 1940, nationalism's most demonic aspects brought about another cataclysm in WWII. In 1921, Britain's longest abused territory, Ireland, finally achieved de facto independence after decades of work by Irish nationalists. This was only the beginning. In the aftermath of WWII, Britain could no longer afford to crush the national aspirations of the peoples of its many territories. The British were broke. Worldwide nationalism was the largest ideological component in the end of the British Empire, and it is also what has made the US World System look vastly different from the British World System.

A bored US State Department official, stamping passports in some foreign consulate in 2019, looks like a very different animal from a swashbuckling British soldier pushing opium on China in 1849. Though roles like businessman, soldier and bureaucrat existed in both the British and US Empires, the details of what they did from day to day and country to country are different enough to make drawing comparisons look silly. This book argues that those comparisons are not silly. The seeming differences between the two world systems are more a product of the differences between the eras and the tools available than real differences between the goals and plans of the British and US World Systems.

Meet the New Boss...

The rise of the United States was meteoric. As we mentioned above, the British colonies in **1700** were tiny. Little more than 250,000 European and African settlers clung tenuously to the North American seaboard. **By 1800**, the newly independent United States had 20 times more people, with a population amounting to 5,308,403 in the census of that year. Despite independence, it could still be seen as part of Britain's informal empire. But it was expanding rapidly in geographic terms as well, sending settlers far over the Appalachian Mountains. **By 1900**, the census put the US population at 76,212,168, and the US economy was the largest in the world. The British still owned significant chunks of that economy, but the United States had spread all the way to the Pacific, and was getting seriously into the empire game itself in the aftermath of the Spanish-American war. The US had picked up formal colonies in the Philippines, Hawaii, Guam and Puerto Rico, and was beginning to exercise an aggressive type of informal empire over the rest of the Americas.

The rapid growth of the United States was truly unprecedented. It created a power that was more than capable of taking over after the British Empire collapsed. On a lot of metrics the United States is more powerful than the British ever were. More advanced communications networks mean that the attractiveness of the US model doesn't just speak to the elites of other countries, but also to their populations. Anybody with a laptop or a smart phone has a Hollywood-constructed idea of how life is lived in New York, Los Angeles or the US suburbs. Many find this idea attractive.

The British worked hard to make sure that their navy was always larger than that of the next two powers combined. The US spends more on its entire military than the other ten biggest military powers combined.

New military technologies, involving air power and communications satellites, provide capabilities that the British Imperialists could only dream about. As just one example, the US shares the ability to annihilate human civilization with only one or two other countries[37]. The British never had that. The British experimented with using concepts like free trade and the abolition of slavery to justify military aggression. The US has been able to institutionalize this approach in organizations like the United Nations and the World Trade Organization. The concept of Human Rights has been fully weaponized, turning countries like Syria who defy the US into pariahs, while allowing US allies like Saudi Arabia to do whatever they want. US economic interests are exerted in much more sophisticated ways. The British had gun boats, while the US has the IMF and the World Bank for carrots, and its control of the world-wide banking system and a complex system of sanctions than it can use as sticks. The US World System is much more powerful than the British system ever was. But US Empire looks very different from the British Empire. Why?

Why Does the US Empire Look So Different From the British Empire?

Part of the answer here is nationalism. The spread of military technology to the rest of the world has been important, but I would argue that the spread of literacy, and the internalizing of ideas of nationalism across the developing world is probably more important. As we mentioned above, these ideological tools were beginning to be used by developing country elites in the mid-twentieth century, and they have now been internalized by most populations as well.

The ability of the world hegemon to just run around shooting people who disagree with them, and take their territory, has mostly disappeared. It hasn't disappeared completely of course, but the US

---

[37] The number of countries with nuclear weapons is slowly expanding. But it's only the US and Russia that have thousands of these weapons. China's probably catching up.

needs ever more elaborate stories to justify the aggression it engages in. What happened in Vietnam in the third quarter of the twentieth century, and what is happening now in the Middle East is horrible. But it's worth remembering that the British were capable of doing that to everybody, not just a few "sacrifice" regions and countries. In the US, we like to congratulate ourselves for not taking territory like older empires. This is as much a question of inability than virtuous choice.

Necessity inspired the founders of the US system to make a choice. At its outset in 1945, the US Empire had to pitch itself as a liberating "friend" rather than an imperial power. The British told themselves and others that they were "helping" as well. But during the nineteenth century the rest of the world lacked the capacity to compete in this ideological realm, and lacked the ability to point out how pointless and brutal most British aggression was. Today, most countries have their own English-speaking lawyers and government spokespeople to bring to this legal and propaganda war. The developing world has forced the developed world to acknowledge them as people, and as peoples with the right to self-determination. The power of the world's peoples isn't just exerted in international talking shops like the UN. The Vietnamese and Iraqi people, and many others, have demonstrated that overwhelming military force is a lot less useful than it used to be. Literate people make nationalist ideologies their own, and exert costs on occupying forces long after the traditional battles are over.

As a citizen and supporter of the United States, witnessing my country's flailing in places like Iraq and Afghanistan has of course been frustrating. But it's also a sign of human progress. My country has hard limits set on what it can do with its hegemonic power, and that's a great thing for the world at large. The institutional architecture of US power is slowly transitioning into a system that can benefit all people. This is better for the world, obviously, but also better for the United States and its people as well, who experience fewer of the burdens of running the world, while also enjoying a slower fade of hegemony's privileges as well. This process is good for everyone who isn't in the business of selling weapons.

It's important to keep this story of change in mind as we compare the British and US World Systems. It's not just that the two eras, from 1815 to 1914, and 1945 to 2012 are different. The world changed completely over the course of each of those time periods as well. The wars got bigger and more horrifying. But the rewards of peace have increased exponentially as well. The stories this book tells all take place within this ever-growing wave of change.

The British and US Systems Set the Stage…

This book will tell an extraordinarily brutal story. But this brutal story also got us to a better place. The British and US systems built the world we know. For all of human history, being a part of a small country or people was tremendously difficult. If a large empire looked your way, you were in serious trouble. History is a tale of cities, peoples, and even whole empires, that were completely eradicated, sometimes by more powerful entities and sometimes by chaos. Imagine that. Whole cities full of daily routines, ways of life, cultures and human beings, wiped out completely. There are peoples whose names we barely know, and countless peoples we have never heard of. Today it's different. Homogenization and the loss of indigenous cultures still happens, but people aren't being wiped out wholesale anymore.[38] It's right to lament the loss of cultural diversity, and work to stave it off where it's convenient, but pretending this process is the same thing as the casual

---

[38] The attempted genocides of the modern era have all been failures. We rightly focus on the horrors perpetrated in Rwanda, Myanmar, and other places. But as bad as all those are, early eras were much worse. There may have been fewer deaths back then, because there were vastly fewer people, but there was much more comprehensive eradication of cultures.

eradications of peoples present throughout most of human history is ridiculous.

The consciousness of the world has changed. It has developed a conscience. The US World System, when it works well, treats the peoples of the world as people, not as obstacles. This has a lot to do with the US World System's effort to exploit all peoples economically, but it has had positive effects regardless. An argument can be made that the world's people are now forced to be consumers, which is dehumanizing in its own way. But that's better than the millennia of mass murder and enslavement we got before the world worked as a single system.

This book argues that we, as a planet, can truly transcend the dark history we've run through in this chapter. The fading of the US World System is more of an opportunity than a threat. If we can see through the "historical hangover" we can transcend this era of inter-state war and tragedy. If you open a newspaper today this argument looks transparently ridiculous. But if you consider how far we've come, the idea of transcendence won't look so silly. In fact, it's already happening.

Chapter 3
Geography, Good Government & Luck

The last chapter argued that the British and US systems made the modern world. From world culture to our ideas of nationalism and government, Britain and the United States have been vastly more influential than we like to recognize. But why? Was there some "Special Sauce" in the "Anglo-Saxon" model?

Nope.

Before we discuss how the systems developed by these countries ate the world, let's take them down a peg or two. These two systems really did develop a range of useful tools in government and society that are applicable everywhere. But they didn't do it because they were "special".

They did it because they got lucky.

Perfect Storms of Advantages

Empires are born from advantage. Every entity that has successfully become an empire has had some special quirk that led to outsize success. Both the British and US Empires had numerous characteristics that put them out in front. These characteristics placed them well to leverage the rapidly changing world that we discussed in Chapter Two. The leading position that the British held from 1815-1914, and, that the US has occupied from 1945 or so to today, also allowed these empires to take the leading role in shaping this evolving world of ours.

Many in both the United States and Great Britain maintain that it is our systems of government that put us out in front. "English Liberties" and "American Exceptionalism" in the forms of government are supposedly the "killer applications"[39] that created these eras of dominance. It's become common in the United States to look longingly at the social democratic forms of Western European government that have emerged under the US World System. Likewise, segments of the British chattering classes, even back during the empire, were always convinced that somebody somewhere else was doing it better (usually in France or Germany).

This isn't completely wrong. But the cores of British and American government, at least at the outset of their empires, really were better than anything else on offer at the time. They were out ahead in evolving from a more straightforwardly "thuggish" form of government, run exclusively for the benefit of a small class on top, to one that did a better job of incorporating the interests of a broader class of people. These governments also managed to harness the energies of those interests and point them in the same direction; the furtherance of a world-wide system of control. That almost every country in the world now has a parliament of some sort, and that everyone at least pretends to aspire to some form of representative government is an indication of this success. The United Kingdom and the United States were pioneering in their use of these ideas.

But I think this story of better government leaves something very important out. The advantage in government that these two countries have enjoyed didn't come from greater virtue, or some special characteristic of the Anglo-Saxon people and their history. It's geography, pure and simple.

Geography & Good Government

---

[39] Don't blame me, Blame Niall Ferguson

If this book has a central message it is the value of peace. And the geography of both Great Britain and the United States provided peace. One of the most persuasive cases for the success of England in government and industrialization is the fact that it has had longer, more stable periods of peace than anyone else. British success made them the winners in the colonization of North America, both giving the United States a powerful set of institutions to start with, and a continent to evolve in, largely free from outside interference.

Brits

The British were a major player in all of Europe's conflagrations. But those conflagrations rarely crossed the Channel. England's easily defensible position on an island allowed them to build pools of wealth and power that were not destroyed as frequently, and this eventually led to more centralized, better organized, more representative and more powerful forms of government. The wars that the British fought provided all the opportunities for profit and administrative sophistication that wars always bring, with little of the destruction. For centuries.

The last successful invasion of the British Isles took place in 1066. The religious conflicts stemming from the Reformation, which began shortly after Martin Luther rocketed to fame as a religious dissenter in 1517, were disruptive in England, but much less so than they were in Continental Europe. English government and society were only thrown into religious chaos for brief periods, such as the reign of Queen Mary from 1553-1558, the English Civil War between 1641-1651, and the Glorious Revolution of 1688-1689.[40]

The British had an island to themselves and these periods of religious chaos were therefore short and damage was limited. Distracted

---

[40] The Glorious Revolution could plausibly be seen as another invasion. A Dutchman came over with an army to replace a British king. But this "invasion" took place at the invitation of elements of the English aristocracy and left the populace and their wealth largely unscathed.

Catholic and Protestant outside powers couldn't easily intervene to prolong the agony. The periods of disruption forced innovation in British government. British statesmen could act to incorporate some religious minorities, tolerate others, and mercilessly crush others, like the long-suffering Catholics of Ireland. This mix in approaches allowed for a stronger central government, that did a better job of incorporating different views, first in religion, and later on in everything. Short periods of disruption tended to be followed by long steady periods of economic and political progress. With the exception of the decade of the English Civil War, the body counts of these periods of chaos rarely topped a thousand people.

On the European continent, the wars of religion after 1517 killed millions. The periods between chaos and war were times of instability rather than innovation and rebuilding. The repeated loss of significant portions of the population led to economic disaster. Religious conflicts in France and the Holy Roman Empire tended to rip apart old centers of power. France spent almost two centuries dealing with its Protestant minority, sometimes placating it, sometimes massacring it, and eventually driving it out completely, under Louis XIV (r.1643-1715). This process involved eight separate civil wars between 1562 and 1598, and was deeply mixed up with the struggles between the French nobility and the French king. The Catholic kings of France ended up crushing differing power centers rather than incorporating them. This produced a brittle system of royal absolutism that briefly awed the world under Louis XIV, before collapsing completely within 85 years of his death. The Holy Roman Empire was a barely workable medieval federation of territories that, as its name might indicate, did not handle religious differences well. The Reformation led to the three-century-long death throes of that system, keeping it from ever really unifying, and leading to cataclysms like the Thirty Years' War (1618-1648). The brief British conflicts over government and religion, on the other hand, tended to centralize government and give it new tools and powers.

Because it was on an island, England, and later Scotland as well, were able to develop peacefully (Ireland not so much). The thugs on top benefited the most, but everyone from great lords down to the peasants were able to take advantage of this peaceful accumulation of wealth. Continental Europe had roving bands of thugs that periodically dispossessed the population and razed large swathes of territory. England did not.[41] Wealth in England simply wasn't destroyed as often.

What resulted in Britain, in contrast to what took place on the Continent, was the slow, cumulative growth of wealth across the entire population. In a peaceful Britain, a mill built in 1300 could stay in service and become more productive through technological advancement until the Industrial Revolution. A mill built on the Continent, ravaged by the Hundred Years' War, the Thirty Years' War, the War of the Habsburg Succession, and dozens or even hundreds of other major and minor conflicts, had a much slimmer chance of long-term survival, let alone improvement. This destruction may have been at its most intense during the Reformation-fueled conflicts, but it was also present in the feudal wars before it, and the more modern conflicts between nations that followed.

This allowed the economy of England to prosper and specialize. Even those still working in agriculture by 1800 were more likely to be prosperous tenants or farmers owning their own plots than they were to be landless serfs. The secure home base provided by the island allowed for more naval expansion. Fewer forts and more warships led to a people that could more readily look outwards.

The logistical complexity of maintaining a naval force rather than a land one and maintaining longer supply lines than their continental adversaries provided another benefit. It just made the British better at stuff. Because they had to be. The skill sets and engineering culture

---

[41] England wasn't entirely free of this. The Wars of the Roses, and the wars between Scotland and England come to mind. But the intervals of violence were few and far between, and mercifully brief.

that made the first steamships and railroads in the 1800s was built over centuries of shipbuilding. British success owes almost everything to geography.

Geography led to a series of "virtuous cycles", or self-reinforcing positive processes, especially commercial ones. Domestic stability and peace led to more wealth, and therefore more domestic stability and peace. Britain was able to be the biggest winner in the Atlantic economy because it had a more secure island base to work from than the Dutch or the Spanish. The wealth and power that came from the Atlantic trade further contributed to the peace and security of that island base, leading to more wealth and power. You could be a self-made man in Britain to a degree that was not possible elsewhere. A prosperous merchant family's city was less likely to be sacked in England. This, shielded and accelerated by the way their island protected resources, gave the British a powerful mercantile interest in politics, and the entrepreneurial spirit that won them the world.

One of those virtuous cycles produced a form of government in Britain that did a much better job of providing power to a broader class of people and interests. This also meant that those interests were more likely to work for the interests of the government than against it. There are a lot of myths surrounding the much-imitated British system of Parliamentary representation. The standard story of "English Liberty" famously starts with the Magna Carta in 1215. The four surviving copies of the Magna Carta, or "Great Charter" are revered. They are kept on display in special climate-controlled rooms in London and Washington, DC. In 1215, the barons told the English king he couldn't tell them what to do if it was against the law, and that he needed their approval for taxation. The Magna Carta is an accomplishment worth celebrating, but it needs to be emphasized that the medieval parliament it helped create wasn't yet all that distinctive. Similar medieval assemblies of aristocrats were present across Europe, and in places like modern Poland and Hungary they were significantly more powerful. The long story of the evolution of Parliament through the centuries is interesting, but it wasn't dramatically different from the rest of the continent. Across Europe, these assemblies were an arena for competition between the thug on top, and the aristocratic and religious thugs just below him. The broader people neither had a real stake, nor saw much benefit from these assemblies.

It's only after the advent of early modern absolute monarchs, after 1500 or so, that the English system really began to diverge. Few of these older systems survived this period. France's Estates General didn't meet between 1614 and 1789, due to the French monarchy's establishment of royal absolutism. Francis Fukuyama's examination of Hungary in his fascinating Origins of Political Order, illustrated the way that strong medieval assemblies could actually hurt countries in European competition. Aristocrats often preserved their privileges over the survival of the larger political unit. The parts of Hungary that weren't conquered by the Ottomans in the 1400s and 1500s were subjugated by the Holy Roman Empire's Austrian princes in the 1500s and 1600s. The Polish Sejm, that country's fractious medieval assembly, survived all the way up until 1793, when Poland was swallowed up completely by Russia, Austria-Hungary and Prussia (the kingdom that later led German unification). What made Britain's experimentation different is the fact that it survived. None of these other institutions ever had an island. The barbarians never knocked down the gate. Britain's scribes and scholars never found themselves cast out to become subsistence farmers. And that's largely a geographical accident.

England was different. In the English Civil War (1642-1651), and the Glorious Revolution (1688-1689), British kings failed to set up their own system of absolute monarchy. The aristocrats in Parliament managed to preserve their old privileges, and add new ones. But unlike

Hungary or Poland, these new privileges came in the context of a system that provided new opportunities for financial and commercial privilege through centralization, not dispersal of power. The other great exception to this Europe-wide destruction of assemblies was the Dutch Republic. For a brief period from the late 1500s into the mid-1600s the Dutch managed to use a more representative system of government to build great trading and colonial wealth, and achieve a sort of early modern "superpower" status. But they didn't have an island. Dutch mercantile and military power was crushed by larger French and British rivals, and after a century long fade, the Dutch Republic devolved into a monarchy in 1813.

It took many centuries for what became the British Parliament to evolve into what we can now call representative democracy. It was a tremendously corrupt and inefficient system by modern standards. Some parliamentary constituencies had thousands of voters, some effectively just had one. Property qualifications for voting were not fully removed until 1918. And even after the succession of reform acts of the 1800s, the hereditary aristocracy maintained its control of both houses of the British parliament well into the twentieth century. But the results of the Civil War and Glorious Revolution in the 1600s were important nonetheless.

The aristocracy remained in control in government, but the peace and commercial power uniquely present in Britain made that aristocracy more porous. New families could insert themselves into this system. It could take a generation or two, but there was a whole system of schools and cultural institutions that allowed a limited sort of mobility. The most famous example of this would probably be the Rothschild family. Nathan Mayer Rothschild settled in Manchester in 1798, and leveraged his family connections in banking into great wealth and power. His grandson Nathan Rothschild joined the hereditary aristocracy, and his descendants remain influential in the UK down to the present day. You can find even earlier examples. Since 1732, the British Prime Minister has operated from 10 Downing street. Downing Street is named after George Downing, the son of a London lawyer who made his fortune in the Americas before rising to prominence in English government in the 1650s and 1660s.[42] The ability of commoners who made their fortunes in the broader empire to rise to the top of the system was much lamented by aristocrats, but it also helped to reinforce the aristocratic system.

The ability of the British system to evolve without outside interference, another gift of geography, is one reason why the aristocratic role in government has survived to the present day in institutions like the House of Lords. The power of this house of parliament was dramatically reduced over the course of the twentieth and twenty-first centuries, but hereditary nobility is still powerful in British society today. The survival of aristocratic power, however, did not keep the British from developing a modern form of representative government that has been imitated across the world. That, too, was a gift of geography.

The formal role of the aristocracy has been (more or less) completely wiped out in Continental Europe, which is certainly something this author prefers, but it's worth looking at what that means historically speaking. The rest of continental Europe arrived at modern representative government after 1945 in the West, and after 1989 in the East, but it did so through cycles of incredible destruction. The first French Republic dates back to the 1790s, but France spent the 1800s winning and losing great wars, experiencing repeated bouts of revolutionary ferment and foreign invasion, and oscillating between kings, a couple emperors, a commune, and another republic or two. The rest of Continental Europe experimented with assemblies at different times in the nineteenth century, but it was always a tremendously

---

[42] Scott, David Leviathan: The Rise of Britain As a World Power p. 194

contentious process. In the conflagrations of the First and Second World Wars, aristocratic power and wealth disappeared, but so did everybody else's. Media spectacles like modern British royal weddings make people like me grumble. But the fact that aristocratic power in Britain has survived to a degree means that everybody's power and wealth was also preserved to a degree in Britain that it was not elsewhere. Britain's development was simply less destructive than it was elsewhere. Because of geography.

Yanks

All the advantages described above meant that the British eventually won out in the battle for the North American continent against other European colonial powers. Theirs was a brief success, but it allowed for the transfer of many of Britain's advantages to a much larger stage. Geographic isolation, and the lack of serious competition on the continent of North America, allowed what became the United States to experience a super-charged version of the previous British success, both economic and governmental.

The Founders of the United States were descended from Scottish and English fortune seekers who were steeped in the ideas of English liberties. Somehow they managed to square this with slave-holding, and the genocide of America's indigenous population. Hypocritical as it was, self-government for whites was an important value for the United States from the get-go, and long before independence as well. It's staggering how many town governments on the North American coast date back to the 1600s and early 1700s. On the local level at least, the United States had constitutional government centuries before the rest of the world.

And the geographical stage these fledgling institutions had to play with had a size and openness unprecedented in human history. The genocide and dehumanization of North America's native populations gave the founders of the United States a sort of blank slate to work from. The native population was almost eradicated by disease before Europeans arrived in large numbers. While the struggle between "Cowboys and Indians" has made a large impact on US popular culture and mythology, the outcome was never in doubt.

The largest bar to the massacre and forced resettlement of Native Americans was the policies of elements of the British and then US governments. It was not an effective bar. The British attempt to limit the settlement of the interior of North America was one of the grievances that prompted the colonies to go their own way in 1776. When the US Supreme Court attempted to uphold the rights of Native American tribes in 1832, President Andrew Jackson simply ignored them. North America's vast, vilely acquired canvas was largely clear.

England's colonies in North America were also largely free of the unified social and religious structures that persevered in England itself. Many colonies were founded by religious dissenters, who fled from England's religious conflicts and often disagreed with each other as well. English Congregationalists, Scottish Presbyterians, the Quakers of Pennsylvania, and even the Catholics of Maryland, found a home for their divergent religious ideologies in North America. The United States was never going to have a single established church.

While rich planters in the Southern colonies had pretensions to landed aristocratic lifestyles, they were not successful in the long term. The Virginian wannabe aristocrats[43] who dominated the early United States tried mightily. Four of the first five US presidents were from Virginia. Slave interests were vital in the initial founding of the states of the American South but they saw their power first diminished by northern mercantile elites, and then wiped out almost completely by the US Civil War in the 1860s. There was simply too much space to allow these attempts at landed aristocracy to really take off. People (white

---

[43] Washington, Jefferson, Madison and Monroe, four of the first five Presidents were all wealthy Virginians

people) who were sick of deferring to their "betters" on the coasts could light out for the interior to try to build their own little empires.

This freedom from the old established societies of Europe can be over-sold. European pretensions, educations and goods were always attractive. But this freedom was real. Every attempt at reform had a clearer path in the United States. Property qualifications for white male voters were largely done away with in the United States in the 1830s, a full 80 years before their demise in the United Kingdom. Broad representative democracy for continental Europe had to wait until the 1950s (Western Europe), and the 1990s (Eastern Europe). This process was uneven, of course. Government funded public education made great progress in the United States in the nineteenth century, but its quality and reach depended on the state in which you lived (it still does). This diversity provided benefits as well, however. The multitude of distinct power centers kept any sort of centralized power from limiting economic development. In the nineteenth century, new states like Ohio (eight US presidents from Ohio between 1841 and 1923!) and Illinois could go from initial settlement to powerful economic engines in the space of decades. The settlement-and-growth process repeated in the twentieth century, when oil and new industries made California and Texas the most populous and powerful states.

Most importantly, the development of the United States was free from outside interference. As with all things Abraham Lincoln, said it best:

> Shall we expect some transatlantic military giant to step the ocean and crush us at a blow? Never! All the armies of Europe, Asia, and Africa combined, with all the treasure of the earth (our own excepted) in their military chest, with a Bonaparte for a commander, could not by force take a drink from the Ohio or make a track on the Blue Ridge in a trial of a thousand years. At what point then is the approach of danger to be expected? I answer. If it ever reach us it must spring up amongst us; it cannot come from abroad. If destruction be our lot we must ourselves be its author and finisher.

As a nation of free men we must live through all time or die by suicide.[44]

In the era of ICBMs and asymmetric warfare this US advantage has faded a bit, but it still remains a dominant fact of geopolitics. The British Empire benefitted from its home island. The United States has a home continent. Even at the height of British power, an invasion of the home islands remained possible. Napoleon and Hitler both put the resources in place to make it happen. During the late 1700s the French even launched an invasion of Ireland or two. No one, by contrast, has seriously contemplated an invasion of the United States since 1812. British leaders wanted to try in the 1850s, and their bankers told them no. Britain beat the Russian, Chinese and Indian empires on their own territories in the 1850s, but the United States was already seen as too tough a nut to crack. Japan's attack on Pearl Harbor in 1941 was an attempt to destroy the US Navy in the Pacific, not take Hawaii.

The US has always had the freedom to develop economically without interruption, and to find better ways to govern the fruits of that success. The fact that we've had a single Constitution since 1789 is deceptive. The system of government has changed in massive ways in multiple historic eras. The stability necessary to evolve so completely would have been absent if the country had any real local threats. To take the most obvious example, our Civil War would not have ended anywhere near as cleanly if we shared a border with a competitive power. To take another, the US managed to transition from a highly corrupt government in the late nineteenth century, similar to many developing countries today, to a more professional and less transparently biased

---

[44] Abraham Lincoln's Lyceum address, delivered on January 27, 1838 at the Young Men's Lyceum of Springfield Illinois. As much as I wish I could claim to have found this quote through exhaustive reading of Abraham Lincoln's works, I can't. I'm eternally grateful to New Jersey Punk band Titus Andronicus. Their fantastic 2010 album The Monitor (a civil war themed punk album) opened with this quote.

one in the early twentieth century.[45] This transition relied on the ability to focus on ourselves rather than preparation to face a nearby enemy.

Many of the ideas that were applied in the United States were European, and they weren't just British. All the ideologies around nationalism, liberalism, and the representation of the people were very present in Continental Europe in the 1800s. It could be argued that they were agitated for much more vigorously than they were in the United States. But the advocates for new ideas in each individual country had to deal with their neighbors. In 1848, new communication and transportation systems allowed Revolution to spread across the European continent. French, German, Italian and Eastern European territories erupted in a flourishing of insurrection, monarch deposition, constitution-writing and people's-assembly-assembling. The Russian Tsars weren't having that. With the cooperation of Europe's aristocratic thugs on top, including Britain's, the Russians sent its legions into Eastern Europe to restore order. This was influential in the places Russia intervened directly, but the show of force also undermined the revolutions in places that feared that intervention.

That was a tremendously over-simplified telling of 1848, about which hundreds of books have been written, but it illustrates the difficulty of enacting reforms in a crowded competitive environment. Europe's constant threats at the border acted to slow all attempts to move toward social justice and more representative government. This sort of thing still happens today, by the way. After 2011's Arab Spring, rich gulf monarchies worked to crush democratic aspirations across the Middle East, and paid Washington, DC think tanks to criminalize all talk of Middle Eastern democracy under the bogeyman label of the "Muslim Brotherhood".

---

[45] Pretty sure I got that from What Hath God Wrought, The Transformation of America 1815-1848 by Daniel Walker Howe

The US government has managed to be at the forefront of movements of social change and towards better government for its whole history. Even today, when Republican administrations have given us a reputation as reactionaries, this holds true. Everything from Environmentalism, to LGBTQ rights, to moves against smoking have a wider field of action in the US's vast, federal system. This freedom is a result of geography as well.

But Wait There's More!

I believe that much of the success of Great Britain and the United States can be explained by geography and the freedom in governmental development that flowed from it. But geographical security wasn't the only advantage given to these lucky countries. Both countries had extraordinary reserves of natural resources that facilitated industrialization and development. Factories grew up more quickly in Britain than on the Continent in large part because British coal mines were more easily exploitable and closer to navigable rivers and coastlines than those in mainland Europe.

Once again, the advantages of the United States were a couple of orders of magnitude larger. Gold and silver rushes created new economies out of essentially nothing in places like California and Colorado. Coal mines in Appalachia poured coke into northern factories, metal cropped up in every mountain range just as it was needed for foundries and construction, and just as US entrepreneurs and British military planners moved the world towards oil, we discovered huge supplies of it under California and Texas. This cycle hasn't ended yet—improvements to drilling and fracking technology have recently made the supply of oil and natural gas under the American continent seem limitless.[46]

---

[46] Any student of the history knows that the current confidence in unlimited supply is unlikely to persist indefinitely. Since the birth of the world-wide petroleum market in the mid-19th century, the market has oscillated between fears that we are running out, to convictions that oil will be cheaper than water for the

These natural resources, and the peace and rule of law necessary to exploit them, also drew the best human resources from all over the world. London and New York have been sucking up the world's best and brightest for centuries now. These people of course lead to more virtuous cycles, as the most talented craft lucrative new networks, industries and businesses headquartered in these cities or their hinterlands.

The culture of both countries is reckoned to be a large part of their success as well. There's some truth to this for sure. But these explanations bring up a sort of "what's first, the chicken or the egg?" question. Would these countries have the entrepreneurial spirit that they do if that spirit wasn't so constantly rewarded by a peaceful home base? Would the fabled benefits accruing to the "Protestant Worth Ethic" have materialized if these countries were as frequently invaded as others were? Germany and the Netherlands had a lot of industrious Protestants too, but they didn't end up running the world.

The governing systems, economies and cultures of the United States and the United Kingdom truly are marvels. They have inspired the world to follow these models in many ways. But we shouldn't let the brilliance of this accomplishment blind us to its underpinnings. At its root, the success of the "Anglosphere" has more to do with the fact that English language and culture developed on an island than anything else. If peace can be maintained, there's nothing standing in the way of the rest of the world developing just as impressively.

A Little Bit of Whig History

---

foreseeable future. Each cycle of conventional wisdom tends to last for 10 to 15 years. Daniel Yergin's book The Prize is excellent on this. It's certainly possible that Texas innovations, efficiency and the advent of the electric car will make things different this time around, but I wouldn't necessarily bet on it. It may take extraordinary regulatory interventions to bring about another cycle of scarcity, but the politics of climate change will probably provide those interventions.

Chapter four will describe the extraordinary emergence of the British World System by providing a brief survey of the conflicts, European political players, and British institutional changes that made it all possible. In the process of doing that, it will lean in to a very old-fashioned and discredited way of telling the story, known as "Whig History". Confusingly, this is only tangentially related to the Whig political parties that were important in the 17th-19th centuries in Britain and the United States.

With his 1931 book <u>The Whig Interpretation of History</u>, British historian Herbert Butterfield launched a long and completely justified tradition of trashing the old way of looking at British history. "Whig history" supposedly portrays British history as a tale of improvement and progress towards liberty and Enlightenment. The Glorious Revolution of 1688 in particular, had a worshipful cult set up around it. It was seen as one of the most important steps in the victory of the British Parliament, and all of humanity, over royal despots. If you had studied history in the 1800s or the early 1900s you wouldn't be able to avoid this approach, in Britain or the United States.

Since the 1930s, Butterfield and his successors have poured an extraordinary amount of scholarly energy into tearing this approach down. It's seen as simplistic, too focused on white men, ignorant of the sufferings of others, Eurocentric, and about a million other nasty things. These critiques are all valid. "Whig History" hides the true complexity of what happened in favor of telling a pretty story. It makes history into a fairy tale that serves British and US nationalist aims. It leads to complacency, and incorrectly assumes that history only moves in one positive direction. Whig History also plays into the distinctly American version of the "historical hangover". If the United States is the custodian and best example of some special narrative of human progress, then all manner of atrocious actions are justified to protect it.

This narrative has been systematically removed from curriculums all over Britain and the United States, and I'd be surprised if one in one thousand US citizens could tell you what England's Glorious Revolution of 1688 was about today.

How Important Was the Glorious Revolution?

Fast forward to 2012 and the publication of Why Nations Fail: The Origins of Power, Prosperity and Poverty. It's a great book that places the emphasis squarely on institutions and the importance of their character and functioning for the success and failure of countries. The book is by two Harvard professors, Daron Acemoglu and James Robinson. It is scrupulously politically correct, and it was rightly celebrated by all the elite outlets that have spent 50-70 years making fun of Whig History. One of the central claims of the book, as far as I can see… is that the Glorious Revolution of 1688 is one of the the most important things that ever happened.

The Harvard Professors see 1688 as a crucial turning point in world history. "The Glorious Revolution brought much more inclusive, pluralistic political institutions, which then led to a transition towards more inclusive economic institutions."[47] They'd no doubt be horrified to see it put this way, but these Harvard guys ended up writing a modified sort of Whig History.

Everything goes in circles.

This book will not shy away from "Whiggishly" pointing out the many ways that the Brits and the Yanks got things very right. But it will always try to emphasize the many lessons learned through almost 90 years of tearing down the traditional narrative. A slow evolution towards prosperity and good government is not some special thing that

[47] Acemoglu, Daron and James Robinson, "Why Nation's Fail FBBVA Lecture" May 21, 2012

only English-Speakers can do. All it requires is peace. The Brits and the Yanks got peace from owning an island and a continent. The past seventy years of relative world peace have demonstrated, over and over again, that people on every continent are more than capable of doing the same thing. If we can effectively manage US decline without catastrophe, then every country in the world can experience its own "Whig History" of boundless progress. But nothing is guaranteed. We've got to work for it.

"It is good to hate the French."

-Al Bundy

Chapter 4
The Rise of Britain
1485-1815

So Why Empire?

Citizens of Britain and the United States at the outset of their respective periods of dominance were some of the safest people in human history. So why bother conquering the world, or forcing the world into their particular world system? The answer is fear, fear of outside ideologies that were sometimes in fact, but almost always in imagination, coming to get the countries that formed the two world systems.

For each system, the enemy ideology was embodied in one opponent above all. For the British it was France. Over the course of one hundred and thirty years, Britain's French enemy transitioned from a force of Catholic reaction into one of revolutionary republicanism, and then "enlightened" empire. The conflict barely skipped a beat. Aggression towards and fear of that one opponent didn't diminish even after the ideological underpinnings of the initial conflict faded away. For the US, the eternal enemy was and remains Russia. Over forty years, the United States's Soviet enemy transitioned from an ideological and economic juggernaut, appearing to conquer whole continents, to a ramshackle kleptocratic petrostate. Thirty years on from the fall of the Soviet Union, Russia is a tin-pot kleptocracy with diminishing regional power, shorn of its original threatening ideology, but our fear remains. Amusingly, even after an unbroken century of alliance, the British and the French still don't seem to like each other that much either.

There's a lot of paranoia in these tales of imperial foundation, but it's important to emphasize that there was some justified fear as well. 16th-18th century militant Catholicism, and mid-twentieth century Communism did present real threats. Both were novel, promising a new kind of subjugation. A hostile foreign power alone, over the sea, wasn't necessarily all that threatening. The Catholics and the Communists, however, in their two very different time periods, threatened something special. The Catholics would pervert your very soul, forcing you to bow down to their unholy Pope. The Communists didn't just want to take your country, they wanted to turn your kids against you, take away your hard-earned money and give it to the lazy ethnic guy down the street. These are caricatures of course, but these were the threats that were deeply felt by the founding leaders and publics of the two world systems.

Competition & Nationalism

For most of the countries of Europe and the broader world, the nationalist project was a conscious effort that elites and peoples worked on. The development of national languages, histories and myths were intentional nationalist projects engaged in over the course of the nineteenth and twentieth centuries, spreading outwards from Europe. In most countries, this project was defensive in nature. It was necessary to counteract the physical and ideological onslaught of European Empires, chiefly the British. The French, British, and American experiences are different. The process was less conscious. So much less so, that it can even seem odd to talk about nationalism in these countries. But nationalist dynamics are very present in these countries too. They're just older. They developed more organically and are harder to see.

British and French nationalism developed first. Their use of nationalism forced the rest of the world to adapt to it. British and French national ideas were firmed up by competition between these two countries, and when this competition turned outward, it forced everybody else to scramble to keep up. Without ever using the term, the British and French were the first to really use nationalism as a weapon. It grew out of a diverse soup of influences. Earlier and deeper centralization than the rest of the countries in Europe played a role. Their glorious history of competition going back to Medieval stories of the Hundred Years' War played a role. Ruling elites steeped in classical influences, chiefly imperial Rome, played a role. But more than anything else, it was about Religion.

Nationalism & Religion

The nationalism of the United States is instructive in teasing out the role of religion in the British experience. The US has a unique ingredient in our national make up, the Constitution. It was born out of the Enlightenment musings of both French and British thinkers, like Locke and Montesquieu, who were very involved in proto-national projects in their own countries. At our best we in the United States take our identity from that Constitution. Throughout our history we have fought to prove that this Constitution can be for all people, and apply to an ever-expanding circle, including women, former slaves, and migrants from all over the world. But there are many other skeletons hidden in the closet that is US national identity, and most of them are taken from the British, and the English most of all. These skeletons jump out of the closet periodically, and get in the way of the great project of the ever-expanding circle. Some aspects of the English inheritance are positive, like the common law, and its age-old focus on rights. Some less so, religion most of all.

Hating on the Catholics…

It seems ludicrous today, and it's fading from living memory as we speak, but all the vitriol in US public life that is currently aimed at Muslims used to be aimed at Catholics. In the mid-nineteenth century there was a nation-wide party, the Know-Nothings, dedicated to anti-

Catholicism. It was legitimately surprising when John F. Kennedy, a Catholic, was able to win the presidency in 1960. In 1959 Dr. Fields of the Southern Baptist convention declared "…many Baptists feel that a Roman Catholic candidate would prove a real danger to many of those freedoms that we enjoy."[48] Many questioned whether he would be too loyal to the Pope. Kennedy had to defend himself against these accusations the same way Barack Obama had to defend himself against even more groundless accusations that he was a Muslim.

It's not something we emphasize much in the history classes, but anti-Catholic hysteria was a big part of the US independence struggle. The British took Canada from the French in the Seven Years' War (1756-1763). This left them governing a sizeable Catholic minority in Quebec. With 1774's Quebec Act, Parliament ordained that the Catholic religion would be tolerated, French Civil law could be used for some purposes, and the Catholic church was to be allowed certain rights. This was a humane law, indicating the progress that the British had made from earlier attitudes towards Catholicism that we'll get to in a moment.

That's not the way the inhabitants of the Thirteen Colonies saw it. The Northern colonies were deeply rooted in various flavors of the Protestant faith, and saw any toleration of Catholicism as a betrayal, and possibly a sign of things to come in their own territories.[49] Two years later, in part because of this controversy, the US founding fathers declared independence. With the central place that Catholics have taken in US culture since the nineteenth century, this bit of revolutionary history has been dropped down the memory hole. But anti-Catholicism was a serious stream in US culture well into the twentieth century. You can still find it flourishing in the darker reaches

---

[48] P.92 Brown, Deward C. Anti-Catholicism in Contemporary America 1920-1960 a January 1966 master's thesis that can be found at this link…
https://digital.library.unt.edu/ark:/67531/metadc130656/m2/1/high_res_d/n_03271.pdf
[49] P. 104 James, Lawrence The Rise And Fall of The British Empire

of the internet today. It's worth mentioning that Kennedy was our first and last Catholic president.

"Remember, Remember, The Fifth of November…"

As is the case with many diasporas, more virulent strains of anti-Catholicism lasted longer in the United States than it did in its English homeland. But it's still there if you know where to look for it. Many of the pop culture touchstones that make up British identity today are deeply entwined with the international clash between Protestantism and Rome. The Spanish Armada that failed to take England in 1588 was very much a Catholic one. It was held to be so in the propaganda of both countries at the time. Whenever I read about that Armada's defeat by weather and fire ship, I envision Clive Owen as Walter Raleigh, yelling from a mast, thanks to a not very good film from 2007. Guy Fawkes, of course, is the most relevant contemporary example. The 2005 film "V for Vendetta"[50] turned Guy Fawkes masks into an international symbol of protest in the mid-2010s, leading to its adoption by the hacker group Anonymous (remember them?). Guy Fawkes, the man memorialized every fifth of November, was a Catholic terrorist who tried to blow up the Houses of Parliament in 1605. The "Remember, Remember the fifth of November…" British folk poem was used to great effect in the 2005 film. The V for Vendetta film-makers wisely chose not to include the later verses of some versions of that poem, which include extended fantasizing about ways to assassinate the Pope.[51]

Anti-Catholicism in the twenty-first century doesn't make much sense. In 16th and 17th century England it made a lot of sense. The fact that it lingers on 500 years later, in YouTube comment sections at least, is an indication of how calamitous the conflict was. The epic of the

---

[50] V for Vendetta is a great film. The comic book it is based on, by Alan Moore and David Lloyd is even better.
[51] "…A rope, a rope, to hang the Pope, / A penn'orth of cheese to choke him, / A pint of beer to wash it down, / And a jolly good fire to burn him. http://www.potw.org/archive/potw405.html

emergence of the British Empire is inseparable from holy terror of "popish plots" and Catholic domination.

Eras of Conflict, Eras of Empire

The Protestant battle against Catholicism had two distinct phases, with two different "big bads". In the 1500s and first half of the 1600s the main enemy was Spain and its Habsburg kings, as well as, to a lesser degree, their Habsburg cousins in Austria, who were attempting to manage their unruly Holy Roman Empire. By the late 1600s and into the early 1800s, well beyond the era where religion was the main justification for war, the enemy was France.

At the outset of the first "Spanish" phase of this conflict, England was a marginal player, without much influence in Europe, and without much of an extra-European empire either. England's efforts to play a larger role in European competition entailed consolidation on the islands it shared with the Welsh, Scottish and Irish, and the beginnings of its overseas empire. These efforts were successful, and by the second "French" phase of European competition, Great Britain, later the United Kingdom, took center stage. The battle between France and Britain became the dominant factor in European competition and spread to almost every continent and ocean.

As you can already see, the consolidation of power in the "British Isles" created some confusion in naming. In 1707, due to Acts of Union in each country's parliament, England joined with Scotland to become **Great Britain**. In 1801, due to separate Acts of Union passed by the British and Irish parliaments, Ireland was forced into the **United Kingdom** of Great Britain and Ireland. The Scottish and Irish parliaments were folded into the British Parliament in London with these Acts. To add to the confusion, people in the nineteenth and twentieth centuries, and some today, use the terms "England" "Great Britain" and the "United Kingdom" somewhat interchangeably. I have made an effort to do a better job of sticking to the historically appropriate nomenclature in this book, but I'm sure I've screwed it up in places as well.

The rest of this chapter will tell the tale of British competition with European rivals, the expansion of its overseas empire, and the key role religion and nationalism played in all of this. For convenience I've divided it into four separate sections. As the complexity and scale of these conflicts and the emerging British World System grows, these sections will naturally get longer. In **Empire of Failure** (1485-1558) we'll discuss the historical reasons why the British pretty much missed out on the earlier phases of imperial competition outside of Europe, and the religious and political dynamics that kept England on the margins of geopolitics. In **Empire of Theft** (1559-1625) we will cover the opportunistic way that England began to muscle in on other European empires, and took advantage of religious strife on the European continent to become a bigger player. In **Empire of Wealth** (1625-1689) we'll cover Britain's great internal consolidation, improving institutions, and the accelerating opportunities of overseas empire that took England from a growing power, to one of the only two that mattered. In **Empire of Competition** (1689-1815) we will cover the century long battle with France that created the British World System.

Empire of Failure (1485-1558)

Henry VII, Henry VII, Edward VI, Mary I

Britain did not begin the European age of overseas empire-building on top. In fact, they pretty much missed out on the first century or so. Back in Chapter Two, I mentioned that the popular TV series Game of Thrones is loosely based on a real battle between English aristocrats lasting roughly from 1455 to 1485. Let's extend the metaphor. Prior to the romantically named "Wars of the Roses" England had sometimes been a big player in Medieval Europe. But England had fallen into disarray at exactly the wrong time. Winter was coming.

The Game of Thrones TV show worked out a little differently, but in Medieval England, it was the Queen Daenerys figure, the slim chance monarch from over the seas, who won out. Henry Tudor founded a dynasty and reigned as Henry VII from 1485 through 1509. Thanks to England's many advantages (see Chapter Three) he did a great job restoring the country's wealth, but wow was England unprepared for the White Walkers.

On the TV show, the "White Walkers" are magical zombie hordes, who take advantage of the kingdom's disarray. In real life it was a combination of three unprecedented geopolitical factors that kept England playing catch up throughout the 1500s: the Reformation, the Habsburg-driven revolution in European power politics, and the wealth of the Americas that started flowing into countries like Spain and Portugal while Henry VII was still picking up the pieces.

Henry VIII & the Reformation

The extraordinarily prudent and competent Henry VII was succeeded by Henry VIII, a notoriously larger than life figure (r.1509-1547). Not only was he legendarily fat towards the end, he was a guy whose personal life was so disastrous that it doesn't need dragons to make good TV. Whether you have watched TV shows like The Tudors and

Wolf Hall or not, you may be familiar with Henry VIII, Anne Boleyn and his other five wives. Henry VIII is probably the most famous English king.

England's separation from the Catholic Church was not high-minded. Henry VIII was determined, given his continuing lack of a surviving male heir, to divorce his very Catholic, very Spanish first wife, Catherine of Aragon. The Pope, closely tied to Catherine and her family's Iberian kingdom, wasn't going to give it to him. In the end Henry declared himself the head of the English Church with 1534's Act of Supremacy.

Henry VIII wasn't particularly interested in the new reformed approach to religion, but there were members of his court, like Thomas Cromwell and Henry's second wife Anne Boleyn, who were. Henry was very interested in the new source of income that breaking up monasteries and confiscating church land gave him, so these religious reformers were given a broader scope of action. The Protestant rebellion against the Pope, and many other aspects of the universal Medieval Church, was making great progress in Continental Europe. From 1517, through the end of the Thirty Years' War (1618-1648) the battle between Catholicism, and a dizzying array of Protestant interpretations was a, if not the, dominant factor in European politics. Unwillingly at first, what would become the British people found themselves drawn deeply into this conflict.

England's Strange, Semi-Reformed Christianity

Europe's sixteenth and seventeenth century wars weren't just about religion, of course. The justifications put forth for those conflicts all got churned around in a soup of proto-nationalism, and very British loathing of the French and foreigners in general, but by the end of the 1500s, unique forms of Protestant religion had taken firm hold in England and Scotland. England's Queen Mary (r.1553-1558, Henry VIII's daughter with his first, very Catholic, very Spanish wife) tried to bring Catholicism back, but her reign was too short, and her rather sad marriage to Phillip II of Spain forever tainted her religion with the stench of foreign influence. There would be "Catholic-curious" monarchs and even one full-on openly Catholic King of England[52] over the next 130 years, but public opinion came to see itself as Protestant over the course of the 1500s. That notion was pretty central to the formation of public opinion, in fact. It remains a big part of British identity today, consciously or not. Queen Elizabeth II (r.1952-present) is still the head of the United Kingdom's established Church. The UK's official form of Christianity is known as Anglicanism, to add another name to keep track of.

Anglicanism has a number of characteristics that made it different from the way Protestantism was practiced elsewhere in Europe in the 1500s. The success or failure of the "reformed church" everywhere was related to the wishes of the rulers of a given territory or city. But in Britain, at least initially, opting for Protestantism was more about dynastic politics than religious conviction. Henry VIII made himself the head of the English Church. In a lot of ways, he replaced the Pope, a figure that was done away with completely in a lot of the "read the bible and decide for yourself" versions of Protestantism present elsewhere. Non-Anglican Protestant interpretations, set down by clerics like Martin Luther, John Calvin and Huldrych Zwingli were also influential in England, but the English monarch was in charge of the national church in a way that was more or less unique. The Anglican Church preserved a more hierarchical form of church organization, with bishops and archbishops, that many Protestant interpretations did away with. This allowed for some pretty wide swings. A lot depended on the proclivities of the monarch in a given period. Henry VIII's direct successor Edward VI (r.1547-1553) was more influenced by the mainstream protestant clerics on the continent. Mary I (r.1553-1558)

---

[52] James II didn't last very long.

allied with Spain to try to swing the country back to Catholicism. Elizabeth I (r.1558-1603) brought the Reformation back, but as with many things, she refused to be pinned down on what exactly that meant. The monarch was in charge, and you could get in a lot of trouble for questioning that, but beyond that, things were a little vague. Each new monarch put a different swing on things.

The Rivals: Religion & Conflict in the 1500s

Almost uniquely in the 800 years of British history up until 1815, **France** was not England's main problem in this period. There were wars between France and England in the 1500s, and even an attempted invasion by France, but they were brief and inconclusive, and nothing like prior or later conflicts in their impact. These expensive wars were limited in their effect because of English weakness and French disarray. The diverse centers of agricultural wealth that had made French nobility such a Mediterranean-wide terror throughout medieval history became a serious problem during the Reformation. Some French power centers opted for Protestantism, and the French Monarchy most often stuck with Catholicism. After spending centuries engaging in crusades against Eastern Orthodox Christians, Muslims and domestic "heretics", France's nobility spent much of the 1500s crusading against itself.

France also had to deal with the **Habsburgs of Spain and Austria,** who emerged as a European and world-wide super-state in the early 1500s. The Habsburg empire was a weird entity, with one foot in the thuggish medieval past, and one in the modern world of trans-continental empire building. It was the first European state to start benefitting from world-wide networks of power. In its heyday, roughly the 1500s, followed by a spectacular burn-out in the first half of the 1600s, it formed a continent-wide system that every European power had to reckon with, much as the British did on a vastly larger scale in the 1800s. The wealth of other continents was a big part of this

European power, but the Habsburg system was a European one, not a world-wide one.

Maximilian I, the Holy Roman Emperor from 1508 to 1519, brilliantly capitalized on the already strong set of dynastic holdings his Habsburg family had built from its base in Austria. His son Charles V, was the first ruler to govern territories described as an empire "upon which the sun never set." Between 1519-1556, he ruled the **Holy Roman Empire**, the diverse collection of German and other territories in the center of the continent. He ruled the economic dynamo that was the "Low Countries", modern Belgium and the Netherlands, which had recently been controlled by members of the French royal family. He ruled the recently consolidated and fervently Catholic territory of **Spain**, and the rich empire of theft that it was building in the Americas. For decades, Charles V battled France, the peaking Ottoman Empire, and most frustratingly the many cities and states of the Holy Roman Empire that opted for Protestantism after 1517. He found this whole thing so exhausting that he abdicated in 1556, and divided his unwieldly domains between his son Philip II of Spain and his brother Ferdinand I of the Holy Roman Empire.

From 1556 on, the Habsburg domains were ruled by two separate dynastic lines of the family, but they often worked in concert. Their sometimes-conflicting interests were unified by their fervent pursuit of Catholic politics and their loathing of countries like England that had opted for Protestantism. But they also worked against their competitor in Catholic France. They had a ton on their plate.

In the 1500s, England was kind of an afterthought. The great Asian and American trading empires of Spain and Portugal started the process of reorienting European trade and politics away from the Mediterranean, but it didn't happen immediately. The old Italian city-states and their trade networks were still tremendously important in the 1500s, sometimes allying with the Habsburgs, sometimes allying with France to fight the Habsburgs. Under Suleyman the Magnificent (r.1520-1566) the Muslim Ottoman Empire reached its height. The Ottomans controlled the modern Middle East and growing sections of North Africa, and they also moved further into Eastern Europe in this period, besieging the Habsburg capital of Vienna in 1529. The Ottoman siege of Vienna failed, as did their attempt to seize control of the Mediterranean by besieging Malta in 1565, but these battles were close-run things that devoured immense resources on both sides. English, Scottish and Irish sailors and soldiers fought in the great set-piece battles of this era, but they certainly weren't leading them. Charles V and his Austrian Habsburg successors found the English deeply annoying, but they usually had better things to do than worry about Protestant kings and queens out on some islands in the North Atlantic margins.

Spain was a different story. Henry VIII's initial break with Rome had involved discarding his first wife Catherine of Aragon, a member of the Spanish royal family. Philip II, the son of Charles V that got the Spanish Empire, had briefly ruled as King of England and Ireland (1554-1558) through his marriage to Mary I. He deeply resented the fact that Mary's sister Elizabeth I took England back to Protestantism after Mary's death. Phillip too had a million other things to attend to. He had his growing American and Asian empires, in places like the Philippines (that name is not a coincidence). In 1581 he took over Portugal and its world-spanning trading empire as well. But England was always in the back of his mind. This was a terrifying thing for English leaders. England was a gnat that had angered an elephant. It had no international empire, and couldn't even consolidate power over Scotland and Ireland.

The Empire of Failure

The reign of Queen Elizabeth (r.1558-1603) is popularly seen as the beginning of the British Empire. Virginia was named after her choice to never take a husband, and the East India Company, which was to become one of history's most powerful corporations, was founded during her reign. These seeds did bear great fruit, but their produce in Elizabeth's reign, and the following decades, was not all that impressive. In fact, the Virginia Company was not founded until after her death in 1606, and the foundation of the East India Company only came at the very end of her reign in 1600.

Elizabeth I's reign is fondly remembered, for Shakespeare and for much else, but that emphasis gives us an exaggerated impression of her power. England was further behind in the Empire game than its island advantages would suggest. As we mentioned above, its ruling classes had been distracted in those crucial years in the second half of the 15th century. While visionary thugs like Henry the Navigator of Portugal (1394-1460) or Ferdinand and Isabella of Spain[53] (r.1474-1504) were sending expeditions out around Africa to Asia, or to discover the Americas, England's thugs had been spending their energies in the Wars of the Roses.

Henry VIII's dad Henry VII (r.1485-1509), the victorious Queen Daenerys analogue, tried to get in on the game after winning the last War of the Roses by sponsoring a few expeditions to North America. Giovanni Caboto (John Cabot), the Venetian he hired, failed to find the Northern passage to Asia in his initial voyage, and then in 1498 he failed to come back. Failure and disappearance became a theme throughout the first century of "British Empire".

Henry VIII's (r.1509-1547) decision to go and get himself excommunicated by the Catholic church in the 1530s didn't help with empire-building either. Resources that might have gone towards exploration were needed to defend England from wealthy sea-going

---

[53] Basically Spain. Ferdinand ruled Aragon, Isabella ruled Castile, and upon Ferdinand's death in 1516 both realms passed to Charles V, knitting together most of the kingdoms and territories that make up modern Spain.

Catholic powers like Spain. Henry VIII's dissolution of the monasteries did briefly give the English crown great wealth, but it was quickly dissipated in a more backward-looking attempt at empire building. Henry wasted extraordinary sums on a fruitless attempt to take territory in France.

Henry's multiply-wived final years, and the brief and religiously fraught reigns of his successors Edward and Mary didn't provide much opportunity for empire-building either. Henry VIII did manage to use some of the wealth generated by the dispossession of the Catholic Church's lands to build an impressive Navy. It managed to defend his realm, but disease and the difficulty of keeping ships at sea for long periods in the 1500s did more to defeat Spanish and French invaders than English naval power. At the end of Henry's reign, English sailors began to develop a taste for preying on Spanish merchant ships that would become more important later on.

The policy of the initial decades of Elizabeth's reign was defensive as well. As a woman and a non-Catholic, Europe was an unfriendly place, and Elizabeth very much wanted to avoid making the Spanish even angrier than they already were. It wasn't until war with Spain finally broke out in 1585 that the English started to try to build an American empire in earnest.

Empire of Theft (1558-1625)

Elizabeth I, James I

Elizabeth I (r.1558-1603) might not have been much of an empire builder, but she is rightly remembered as one of England's greatest monarchs. In recent decades she's been played by such famous actresses as Cate Blanchett, Margot Robbie and Dame Judi Dench. Her private life provides plenty of drama. Her many suitors, her dangerous path to the throne, and her lethal conflict with Mary Queen of Scots[54] all come to mind. But unlike her similarly dramatic father, Henry VIII, she also accomplished an extraordinary amount. She did not rule a great extra-European empire, but she did more than any king to forge the identity of the British people that eventually built that empire and constructed the British World System.

Elizabeth I's long reign is seen as the beginning of British religious toleration. It wasn't a toleration we would recognize. She executed both Catholics and Protestants for questioning her control of the established Anglican Church. But her reign did provide a broader scope for toleration than was present anywhere else in Europe. Her preservation of church hierarchy, combined with developments in later centuries, left the Anglican church of today looking a lot more like the Catholic church than most other Protestant denominations. By the dawn of the 1600s, Elizabeth and her servants had established that England was Protestant, but it was Protestant in a very idiosyncratically English sort of way.

The power that the English monarch retained made the church a more useful tool for forming national identity than it was elsewhere in Europe. For centuries the official bible in the English language was the King James Bible, pulled together by a large committee under Elizabeth's successor. To be sure, there were many English Protestants

---

[54] Important Note: Elizabeth's cousin Mary Queen of Scots is a very different person from Elizabeth's sister Mary I of England. I got that confused for years.

who dissented from the official established Anglican Church, conveniently known as "Dissenters" in the historical literature, but mainstream English Protestantism was a force for centralization rather than the discord it often represented on the European Continent. The Medieval Church performed many of the functions that we now associate with government today. The local religious establishment was often a center of life, government and law. The Reformation's extraordinary destructiveness in Europe came from the way that it upended all of those relationships, warping and rending the fabric of communal life. It was not as destructive in England. The English monarchy managed to replace the Pope at the top of the church, and do a better job of preserving the old church hierarchy than most. That too added to English power.

One of Elizabeth's greatest gifts to the project of British consolidation was dying childless. To keep England under her wise control she had refused to marry any of her foreign and domestic suitors. By the end of her reign she knew that her successor would be James VI of Scotland, the son of Mary Queen of Scots, the rival she had executed. James VI became James I of England in 1603 and he reigned until 1625. This was a good deal for England. James I lost interest in his poorer and uncooperative Scottish realm, only visiting once in his 23 years on the British throne.

This was not a unification of the separate kingdoms, it was a personal union, meaning that Scotland and England preserved their own laws and parliaments of nobles. The churches weren't unified either. Scotland had a more unified Calvinist Presbyterianism (a stricter form of Protestantism) approach to church reform, and they weren't interested in Bishops or elements of the English church that they saw as "Popery".

The Stuart dynasty James I initiated would have a tremendously complicated and unhappy time on the throne until its final fall in 1689.

Two of the three Stuart kings that succeeded James I left the throne involuntarily, one without his head. The process of unifying England and Scotland was difficult, and there was intermittent violence, especially in the English Civil War (1642-1651), but the geographic benefits of island living also brought long periods of peaceful, prosperous consolidation and overseas expansion. None of it would have been possible if Elizabeth I had tried to continue her own dynasty.

Unlike his son and grandsons, James I himself had a largely unremarkable reign, which was damn impressive in Europe's apocalyptic 1600s. He was mocked for his scholarly pursuits, and castigated for not championing the Protestant cause in Europe's many conflicts. From our perspective, that just looks wise. There was one great exception to this wise path of moderation. With the "Plantation of Ulster" in 1609 James sent Protestant Scottish and English settlers to colonize Northern Ireland. This certainly contributed to the consolidation of English control of Ireland, but it also sowed the seeds of centuries of discord and violence.

The Rivals: **Let's You and He Fight**

During the reigns of Elizabeth and James **(1558-1625)**, the main show in Europe was still the attempt by **Spanish and Austrian Habsburgs** to control Europe and the world. With the large exception of intermittent and undeclared Anglo-Spanish War (1585-1604) at the end of Elizabeth's reign, James and Elizabeth were largely content to let the European great powers fight, and steal stuff from them at the margins. The nineteen years of the Anglo-Spanish War may look long, but with the exception of a few large naval campaigns, most famously the failed invasion by the Spanish Armada, it was more simmering animosity and piracy than a sustained conflict. It definitely contributed to the anti-Catholic bent in English national feeling, however.

During Elizabeth's reign, **France** was caught up in what might have been the most intense period of the French monarchy's religiously-tinged effort to consolidate control. With Henry IV's attainment of the French Crown in 1589, religious strife began to dissipate. France began to get its great power groove back, but in this period they were far more interested in thwarting the Habsburgs than they were worried about England, or even Protestantism.

The **Ottomans** were still threatening South Eastern Europe and the Mediterranean, but that was getting less important as wealth from America and Asia continued to pour into Western Europe. In North Eastern Europe all manner of interesting things were happening, involving exotic powers like the **Polish Lithuanian Commonwealth**, **Russia**'s first stabs at European relevance, and **Sweden**, an aggressive Protestant superpower from the North (yes, Sweden). All of this is fascinating stuff, but it didn't have much to do with England. Trading links with these exotic realms existed, but thanks to ocean travel, North America and the coasts of India were in some ways closer. For Elizabeth and James, Spain and its battle to control what would become the **Dutch Republic** were their main interests.

The "Low Countries", today's Belgium and the Netherlands, more or less, had been a great commercial area since the late middle ages. Their position at the northern coastal end of the Rhine river, facing England, and right between the French and Baltic coastlines made them a center of trade and proto-manufacturing. An inconvenient death in the 1470s and a whole bunch of dynastic weirdness ended up with this dynamic economic region being attached to Habsburg Spain. The graft didn't take, and the "Low Countries" were split apart by an 80-year long war of independence from Madrid (1568-1648). This exhausting conflict ended up with a Protestant Dutch Republic, more or less on the land of the modern Netherlands, and Catholic lands that Spain retained for a bit, that eventually, more or less, became modern Belgium.

The Anglo-Spanish war broke out in 1585, and it featured England's most direct intervention on the continent between 1585 and 1587.

Robert Dudley, the Earl of Leicester, took a position in the government of the Dutch provinces rebelling against Spain. This direct intervention was a disaster, managing to enrage the Spanish, and greatly disappoint England's Dutch allies as well. After this point the English limited themselves to financial support for the Dutch in their Eighty Years' War of liberation from Spain.

In 1588, Philip II attempted to finally take his revenge on England, putting together a massive Spanish Armada for the purpose. The Armada failed due to poor planning, bad weather, and an impressive effort from the English Navy, in that order of importance. The English Navy was subsequently wasted in failed attempts to capitalize on this victory on the Spanish coast and in the Caribbean. James opened his reign by making peace with Spain in 1604, and he tried to keep out of the fight in Europe through the rest of his time on the throne. His placid attitude towards Spain and the rest of the Continent allowed England to focus on the beginnings of the British Empire in the Americas.

James's efforts to maintain neutrality became more difficult with the advent of the Thirty Years' War (1618-1648). This conflict involved the intensification of the Spanish Habsburg Eighty Years' War against the Dutch. It also involved the Austrian Habsburg attempt to crush Protestantism in a bewildering variety of territories across the Holy Roman Empire. It's estimated that the war killed somewhere between 25 to 30 percent of Germany's entire population. This conflict drew in powers across Europe, most significantly including Protestant Sweden and Catholic France. France was more interested in heading off Habsburg dominance of Europe than furthering the Catholic cause. By the end of the Thirty Years' War in 1648 Spanish power had been largely broken, and the Holy Roman Empire was forced to accept the existence of the few Protestant states that were left. Spain continued to play a role, but resurgent France was now the aspiring European hegemon. Despite the vigor with which they had defended Protestant enemies of the Habsburgs, now that that threat was mostly dealt with, French kings were happy to take up the mantle of Catholicism's champion. Religion always serves politics.

The Empire of Theft

England's first colony in North America, Roanoke, founded in today's North Carolina in 1587, managed to disappear. This isn't so surprising, as it was intended to serve as a base for privateers, basically English pirates given letters of marque from the Crown and official permission to prey on the Spanish. It's possible that the Roanoke colony was wiped out by the Spanish. The first builders of the British Empire had their eyes on trade to some degree, but it was mostly about theft. Walter Raleigh, Sir Francis Drake, John Hawkins and the other famous figures of this era were pirates first and foremost. The Portuguese and the Spanish had built large and rich empires on Asian and American coasts, and the English found it much easier to steal the fruits of those empires than to found their own. A single stolen Spanish or Portuguese treasure trip could make a significant difference to the English treasury and economy. Early efforts to build Caribbean colonies failed. The focus was theft until the foundation of the first island colonies of Barbados, Nevis and St. Kitts in the 1620s.

James I chartered two companies in 1606 with the purpose of settling North America. The initial efforts of the Plymouth and Virginia companies were disappointing. The Virginia company founded Jamestown in 1607, for the purpose of finding gold. Large scale starvation and ruinous wars with the natives greeted the early colonists. It wasn't until the 1620s and the firmer establishment of the tobacco economy that the colony became viable. The Plymouth Company's first colony at Popham in Maine didn't last a year. The colonists didn't like it and promptly sailed back to England. The pilgrims of 1620 were longer lasting. Despite the fact that the Massachusetts and Virginia colonies eventually succeeded, both the Plymouth and Virginia Companies failed as commercial ventures by the late 1620s.

The East India Company's first incarnation, the "Governor and Company of Merchants of London trading with the East Indies", chartered in 1600, found most of its early success in capturing Spanish and Portuguese ships. Small trading posts were established at Bantam on Java in 1603 and at Surat in India in 1612. After winning a battle with the Portuguese in 1612 and negotiating a concession with the Mughal Empire shortly thereafter, the India trade began to expand. But the early English Empire's successes were about war, piracy and theft far more than trade and colonization.

Empire of Wealth (1625-1688)

Charles I, the English Civil War, Oliver Cromwell, Charles II, James II, and the Glorious Revolution

In this period, England made up for its slow start in empire building. It put together a trading and land empire of great wealth despite considerable civil and religious strife. Vigorous anti-Catholic Protestantism was a crucial part of the British Empire's development beyond one based on theft. To be clear, there was as little agreement on what being "Protestant" meant in England as there was anywhere else. The **English Civil War (1642-1651)** was fought between a king, Charles I, who likely saw himself as an Anglican Protestant, and a bunch of rabid fundamentalists who thought the king was threatening their right to be their particular Dissenting versions of Protestant. Once they killed Charles, these fundamentalists proceeded to fall out among themselves over the best form of government and religion. It's all maddeningly confusing for someone like me, who grew up in a sedate suburban town in the United States where the Catholic, Episcopalian (Anglican), Congregationalist, Presbyterian, and Quaker churches would organize non-denominational picnics together. At some point in the 1600s, each of these groups was actively trying to kill or forcibly convert each of the other groups in England Scotland or Ireland. Except for the Quakers. They were just being killed. #Pacifists #TheOnlyRealChristians?

In the United States, and in Britain as well, we tend to gloss over the religious aspects of these 17th century British conflicts. They don't make much sense to us, so we ignore them. We choose to see the English Civil War and the later **Glorious Revolution (1688)** as primarily about revolutions in government, even though religion was usually foremost in the minds of the people involved in these conflicts.

Our emphasis on secular politics isn't all wrong though. The English Civil War was about religion, but it was also about the roles of King and Parliament, and England's age-old effort to establish dominance over Scotland and Ireland. England had usually been the aggressor in these conflicts, though Scotland would occasionally act as a junior partner in French wars against England. By the 1600s, Ireland hadn't acted as the aggressor in any of these conflicts since the Viking age over half a millennium prior.

English Civil War

Charles I, (r.1625-1649) had a relationship with Scotland that was considerably worse than his father James I's neglect. It ended up costing him his throne and his head. This conflict is still known as the English Civil War despite the large role Scotland played, and the ruinous effects it had on Ireland. Charles was interested in setting up the sort of absolute monarchy that was developing on the Continent in Spain and France. In both of those countries, monarchs with pretensions towards Absolutism were trying to aggregate all authority to themselves, filling their civil bureaucracies with middle-class professionals (instead of hereditary nobles) and undermining the powers and privileges of the aristocracy. This was a hard road for Charles, because England had a powerful parliament that resented his pretensions and was unwilling to vote him the money or power that he wanted. The Protestant-leaning parliament also resented his marriage to a Catholic, and his taste for a "High Church Anglican" form of worship, that looked too Catholic to more serious church reformers. After a lot of back and forth, Charles dissolved a Parliament in 1629 and refused to call a new one, attempting to rule by fiat like his Spanish and French brothers-in-monarchy. He came up with a number of stratagems to fund his government, and managed to avoid calling a new Parliament for over a decade.

It was religion that ended Charles's grab for absolute authority in England. Charles may have had some Catholic leanings, but he liked playing Pope, and enjoyed being the head of his Church. This led him to attempt to appoint bishops and impose the suspiciously-popish Anglican Church on the very Protestant Presbyterians of Scotland. The Scots rose in rebellion forcing Charles to convene a parliament to try to induce his nobility to approve new taxes. After eleven years without meeting, however, this parliament was not disposed to be helpful. Dissenting Protestant resentments in England, and the broader question of the rights of Parliament to constrain the king, kept anything from being accomplished. In 1642 Charles I gave up on negotiating with the Parliamentarians and left London to raise an army.

This account will spare you the ins-and-outs of that decade of campaigning, but Charles I lost the war, and lost his head on January 30th 1649. Ironically, the Parliament lost as well. Oliver Cromwell, the head of Parliament's "New Model Army" decided that the Parliament wasn't doing a good job, and installed himself as a forerunner of modern dictators, running the Commonwealth of England, Scotland and Ireland as Lord Protector (r.1653-1658 but Cromwell was in charge from 1649 more or less). Cromwell's Commonwealth was a monster, crushing all opposition and violently unifying all three realms under one government for the first time. I don't think it's unfair to characterize Cromwell and his New Model Army as waging something of a "Protestant Jihad". For Cromwell and his ilk, religious uniformity was part of their project of political unity. Iconoclasm, the destruction of "idolatrous" statues that ISIS is such a fan of today, was part of the New Model Army's toolbox. Cromwell's campaigns in Ireland enforced a new level of English control, and viciously crushed Catholic resistance in notorious battles like the Siege of Drogheda and the Sack of Wexford.

After establishing this control, in the 1650s Cromwell set his gaze on the wider world, causing great damage to the Spanish and Dutch in inconclusive wars. His forces took the Caribbean island of Jamaica, laying the foundations, along with some smaller earlier acquisitions, for the sugar and slave economy that would be so important to the British Empire's first flourishing of wealth. His armies also took Dunkirk in Flanders, which I believe to be the last occasion that a British Army took territory in Northern Europe.[55] European history might have looked much different if Cromwell had not died in 1658 at the age of fifty-nine.

Cromwell's son and successor as Lord Protector was not equal to the task. Richard Cromwell is known to history by the delightful nickname "Tumbledown Dick" for the speed of his fall. The English were sick of war, and most were not on board with the Protestant extremism of Cromwell and his New Model Army. In 1660, through the connivance of George Monck, one of Cromwell's best generals, Charles II, the son of the decapitated Charles I, was restored to the throne. "The Restoration" (1660) brought the English Civil War era to a close, but it left many questions of religion and government unresolved. This conflict is half-remembered but still has some fading cultural relevance. After those non-denominational church picnics in my suburban New England town in the 1990s, inter-faith groups of tipplers could grab a drink at a bar called "Tumbledown Dick's".

This complicated narrative of war, royal failure, and Protestant dictatorship may seem to contradict the image of a peacefully developing England presented in Chapter Three. A glance at the timeline of the 1600s, however, shows that it does not. James I reigned largely peacefully from 1603 to 1625. Though Charles I always had a strained relationship with the aristocratic and mercantile interests

---

[55] Great Britain also sort of held Hanover, a smallish German principality, for much of the 1700s, complicating its approach to the European continent. This was a result of Britain's importation of some German kings after the Stuarts died out. This was a personal union as well, meaning that all those King Georges ruled over Hanover and the Great Britain as two separate entities. This mostly served to make Britain's eighteenth and nineteenth century wars on the continent more complicated. I'm not going to go into this in any detail, because it's boring, and doesn't add much to the story. This complicated problem was solved in 1837, with the accession to the British throne of Queen Victoria. Hanover's rules of succession didn't allow for queens, so Hanover was given to Victoria's uncle Ernest Augustus. This was probably viewed with a sigh of relief from the folks running Great Britain's foreign policy.

represented by Parliament, he reigned for fifteen years years before war broke out in 1641. Cromwell's Protectorate in the 1650s was brutal to Ireland and crushed Scotland too, but in England it provided new feats of military and political organization and new vistas for overseas conquest. Charles II ruled peaceably and profitably from 1660-1685. His brother James II fell after less than four years in what has become known as the Glorious Revolution of 1688, renowned for its bloodlessness. In one of Europe's bloodiest centuries, England consolidated control over the British Isles, built an overseas empire of extraordinary wealth, evolved a world-beating new system of government, and did it all with only a decade of open civil war. The English got off easy. Before we can explain the Glorious Revolution, we'll have to dive in a little on the European rivals.

The Rivals: How You Like Me Now?

The 1600s saw great religious and civil strife in England, but it also saw rapid growth in the scale and power of England's efforts on the European and world stages. Despite all the confusion[56] between different sects there was a real sense of Protestant solidarity between English and Scottish Protestants and their Protestant brothers abroad in the Holy Roman Empire, France, and the Netherlands. Both of the kings who lost their thrones in the 1600s, Charles I (1649), and his Catholic son James II (1688), lost them in part because they failed to support the Protestant cause in the rest of Europe to the extent that the English public wanted them to. There was a lot of Protestant suffering to alleviate. One historian estimates that in 1600 half of Europe was Protestant. In 1700 it was down to a quarter.[57] And this transition

---

[56] If you want an amazing introduction to this whole pivotal era of history, and don't want to bother with the whole history book thing, you could do a lot worse than checking out Neal Stephenson's extraordinary Baroque Cycle. It's a rip-roaring adventure yarn, and it's the first thing that got me interested in this period of history. The second book in the three part cycle is entitled The Confusion.

[57] Scott, David Leviathan: The Rise of Britain As a World Power p.217

wasn't brought about nicely. The Thirty Years' War (1618-1648) wiped out as much as a third of the population of Germany.

The Thirty Years' War also largely broke the power of the **Spanish and Austrian Habsburgs**. They were still powerful, but they never recaptured the dominance of the 1500s. The direct family link was broken with the death of the last Spanish Habsburg king in 1700. The Spanish would continue to control a vast American and Asian Empire until the end of the 1800s. Catholicism remained important in both the Austrian Holy Roman Empire, and in Spain. The rulers of these entities continued to try to impose Catholicism in their domains, but in international politics they were more worried about the French, and often had to ally with Protestant powers like Britain from the late 1600s. England and Spain clashed many times up through the early 1800s. Religious propaganda was always part of the wars they fought, but the conflicts were more about European politics, or British muscling in on Spanish Empire, than any real religious conviction.

In the 1600s, the previously threatening **Ottoman Empire** was fading, managing one last failed siege of Vienna in 1683. They didn't start losing large chunks of their European empire until 150 years later, but that was more because their rivals were busier fighting each other than their historic Muslim enemy. That ancient republic **Venice** had one last gasp of relevance, taking much of modern Greece from the Ottomans for a few decades (1685-1714), but Austrian and Russian rivals kept them from capitalizing on those gains. The whole Mediterranean sphere of international competition became less and less important over the course of the 17th century. Fading powers were still squabbling over it, but the center of European politics moved north and west, towards powers that were operating on the scale of oceans, not seas. England's trading networks, however, were also reaching into the Mediterranean Sea in this era, just as they were everywhere else.

At the end of the 1600s, **Russia** began to play a larger role on the European stage under Peter the Great (r.1682-1725). The superpower that was **Sweden** rose and fell over the 1600s. **Poland** had some good moments, but it was largely a story of continued decline. **Prussia** survived the Thirty Years' War and began its slow climb to leading the formation of Germany in 1871. All of this was terribly interesting, and England's growing commercial power meant that it had some commercial links with all these powers and regions. But the British did not yet have a serious impact on these fascinating conflicts.

France's terrible century and a half after the Reformation ended with the extraordinary and extraordinarily long reign of Louis XIV (r.1643-1715). This most famous and most absolutist of French kings, whose childhood had been marred by yet another civil war, finished the French monarchy's project of crushing other French power centers. The consolidated French monarchy once again became the terror of Europe. There was a strong religious component to this as well. In 1685, Louis XIV (despite having a grandfather who had been Protestant for a time) revoked the Edict of Nantes that had protected his country's Protestant minority for 90 years. 400,000 people are estimated to have fled the country. Many died. Louis XIV also spent much of his more than seventy-year reign beating up on Protestant powers like the Dutch Republic. The European rivalry between the English and the French that would dominate the period between 1688 and 1815 began under Louis. But it did not start at once. Charles II, the English monarch who was restored in 1660, spent part of his exile in France. His brother and successor James II was a Catholic. So for the period between 1660 and 1688, England was more or less aligned with France. Louis XIV straightforwardly bought the loyalty of these two kings and their courts. England's Protestant-leaning nobles and public were not happy about this. Perceived sympathy towards Catholic powers was one of the reasons they had killed Charles I, after all.

The English Civil War was fought, in part (there were a lot of parts to these things), over the English Parliament's reluctance to give Charles I money to fight the wars he wanted to fight. They didn't trust him to serve their commercial and anti-Catholic interests. Once the English people had leadership that they trusted to fight the Catholic threat, under Cromwell, however, they were willing to devote sums to European wars that Charles couldn't have dreamed of.[58] Weirdly this too involved a lot of warring on a Protestant power, the Dutch Republic.

What? You may be asking, that doesn't make any sense at all! I'm making the case that the birth of the British Empire is all about fighting for Protestantism, but some of the largest expenditures made by this proto-empire were used to fight the Protestant Dutch?

Yep.

Money + Politics > Religion

The English fought three separate wars against the **Dutch Republic** from 1652-1654, 1665-1667, and 1672-1674. All of them were brief compared to the epic, century long struggles against the Catholic powers of Spain and France. But they conflicted with the Protestant ideology of the English public and parliament. This was especially jarring in the first Anglo-Dutch war, which was fought by Cromwell's hyper-Protestant Commonwealth Navy. Even Cromwell, the Protestant Jihadist, allied with Catholic France! Politics always beat religion, and the English wars against the Dutch illustrate about as basic a truth of politics as can be found: Money always trumps ideology.

The United States, for example, has been "encouraging democracy" in the Middle East for seventy years, where its main ally is a corrupt absolutist petro-monarchy. The sentiments we use to justify our military adventuring, and the stories we tell ourselves about what we

---

[58] Scott, David Leviathan: The Rise of Britain As a World Power p.217

do never match all our actions. This doesn't mean the publics of the British or US World Systems didn't or don't believe in the guiding principles (or guiding fears) of their foreign policies, but it does mean we're willing to violate them for gain. The past eighteen years of the "War on Terror" have mostly been about the absurd contortions our US leaders have put themselves through to avoid facing the true source of "Radical Islamic Terror": Saudi Arabia. We want to fight terror, but Saudi Arabia is also an immense gravy train for US defense contractors. The English wanted to work with the Dutch out of religious solidarity, but they were also the main obstacles to England's commercial growth.

English action against the Dutch had its roots in economic facts.

Most folks who find themselves in an eighty-year struggle for independence end up with a ruined economy at the end of it. Not the **Dutch Republic**. You've heard of Rembrandt and Vermeer, right? Those painters came out of what was known as the Dutch Golden Age. For most of the 1600s, this small country on the margin of Europe was a world superpower. The Dutch accomplished that feat with a winning combo of trading might, naval power, international colonies, financial sophistication, and crusading Protestant vigor. They held their own against Catholic Spain and ended up beating it. They ended up fighting off the much closer Catholic France of Louis XIV as well, though the conflict exhausted them and ended their golden age. In this 17th century process, they developed a world-wide empire that included New Amsterdam (New York), parts of modern South Africa and Indonesia, and much more. As Ben Wilson wrote in his *Empire of the Deep*:

> Many of the leading figures in the English government believed that the future of the English state was as a republican mercantile oligarchy, similar to their neighbours across the Narrow Seas. Flourishing overseas trade,

imperialism and enterprise would lay the basis for remodeling English society, making it more like the Netherlands.[59]

The English wanted what the Dutch Republic had. The Dutch proposed to include them in a system of free trade in the 1650s, but the English weren't having it.[60] England still saw trade in Mercantilist terms. In their eyes, a rising tide emphatically did not lift all boats. There was a fixed amount of trade out there, and you had to fight and kill to get it. So that's what the British and Dutch did in three short wars. In the end, the British were bigger, more secure, and didn't have long land borders with Catholic powers to deal with, so they won.

The period of British conflict with the Dutch was brief. After the Glorious Revolution of 1688 and the expulsion of the Catholic James II from the English and Scottish thrones, the two Protestant powers finally did unite for a time as a Protestant superpower. But the damage had already been done to the Dutch. The British and the French, in an odd combination, had managed to destroy Dutch power. The Netherlands remains one of the world's wealthiest countries today, but it never quite got back that golden age juice. The Dutch retained an overseas empire and great commercial weight in the 1700s, but they owed their survival to European powers that found them useful for balancing purposes rather than their own power.

This interaction with the Dutch also revealed something about the nature of the of the early British Empire. Yes, it was put together out of fear of Catholicism, but what was built initially wasn't panicked. The initial structure of the British Empire was put together with commercial realities first and foremost. They wanted to take lucrative sugar islands in the Caribbean and wealthy coastal ports in Asia, not endless unprofitable territories. The British Empire was built with hard-nosed ideas of economic gain in mind, not according to the vague

[59] P.193 Wilson, Ben Empire of the Deep: The Rise and Fall of the British Navy
[60] P.194 Wilson, Ben Empire of the Deep: The Rise and Fall of the British Navy

ideas of prestige and "credibility" that eventually killed it in the twentieth century.

With the Dutch effectively out of the way by the late 1600s, the British were free to move on to the conflict with France that would dominate the entirety of the next century. But let's not get ahead of ourselves. Before the Dutch fell into second rank status, they managed to briefly pick up the throne of England and defeat Louis XIV of France.

The Glorious Revolution of 1688

Throughout the 1600s England became a dramatically richer place. But it was also deeply schizophrenic on issues of religion and politics. It failed to unify to act consistently in its treatment of the "near abroad" in Scotland and Ireland and in the broader European and extra-European world. The English Civil War (1642-1651) had made it clear that Parliament was a force to be reckoned with, and under the Commonwealth (1649-1660) Cromwell's fervor had given an indication of what a united Britain might be capable of achieving, but these questions of religious freedom and political structure remained very unsettled. It's hard to see how a country that was as confused about these issues as it was, was going to end up running the world just a century or so later. The Glorious Revolution made the British World System possible by settling many of these issues, at least for a time.

The Glorious Revolution and the decades that followed created a new balance between Parliament and the King, in the Parliament's favor. This period also brought Scotland and Ireland more firmly under English Control. Religious issues got a new settlement as well, firmly exiling Catholics from the public sphere, and cementing the British government's Protestant orientation for centuries. The Glorious Revolution also brought about a political realignment in geopolitics.

From 1688 on the English were almost always focused on defeating France. There was a lot going on here.

What Actually Happened in The Glorious Revolution of 1688?

In 1660, England decided it was sick of all the strife, and that it wanted a king again. Parliament invited the Stuart Monarchs back, and Charles II (r.1660-1685) agreed to a number of conditions and took the throne. Charles II was an agreeable sort, and he ruled happily for 25 years. He was flagrantly corrupt, both in his governing and in his private life. He took bribes from France's Louis XIV, and his court was famously Dionysian. But he was agreeable, didn't take religion too seriously, and was capable of working with Parliament. He was popular enough that he was able to dissolve Parliament for the last four years of his reign without sparking another civil war. His successor was not so lucky. Charles II's brother James II (r.1685-1688) was not an agreeable sort. One of the conditions of the settlement that brought back the monarchy were laws[61] stating that public officials had to be members of the Church of England. This was aimed both at Catholics and at Scottish Presbyterians and other Dissenting Protestants who disagreed with the established Anglican Church's approach. James II, who took the throne in 1685, was an open Catholic. And he started taking steps to re-introduce the religion to England.

This did not sit well with England's Catholic hating public. James II's foreign policy was likewise objectionable. Charles II and James II both had sided with France's super-Catholic Louis XIV in continental struggles. Charles II seemed to do this largely because he liked French money, and as long as the wars against the Protestant Dutch were increasing British trade, the public wasn't going to complain too much. James II seemed to be helping the French out of love for Catholicism,

---

[61] Corporation Act 1661, 1st Test Act 1673

and was open to using French aid to turn England Catholic. His conspicuous heroism in wars against the Protestant Dutch might also have been seen as suspect. James II's daughters Mary and Anne were next up in the succession and they had both been raised in the Protestant Anglican Church, against James II's wishes. This kept the anti-Catholic tensions from boiling over. When James II's wife produced a male, Catholic heir in 1688 he was finished.

James II's daughter Mary was married to William, the Protestant Prince of Orange, the Dutch Stadtholder[62]. Some nobles invited William to come on over, and he invaded with a large army. The support for James II disintegrated quite quickly. There was no large scale fighting in England, and it was, in part, the bloodlessness of the revolution there that made it Glorious. The speed with which a war-hero king, who wasn't regarded as being too bad at his job, was thrown over, indicates how unhappy the English were with a Catholic monarch.

The Glorious Revolution settled the principle that the king wasn't going to be a Catholic, and in part because of this principle, 1688 also represents a giant step towards the British Monarchy's contemporary irrelevance. Kings and Queens weren't immediately powerless, but after 1688 they were clearly losing their battle with Parliament. The development of Parliament, from an assembly of thugs taking privileges from the thug on top, to the form of representative government we know today took centuries. And, despite its reputation, the Glorious Revolution of 1688 didn't permanently settle the question.

---

[62] I have read a couple thousand pages of history of the Dutch Republic, and I'm still not 100 percent on what the relation between the House of Orange and the Republic was. From the beginning of the Republic there was somebody leading the fight from the House of Orange, occupying the office of Stadtholder of one or more of the constituent parts of the United Provinces. The Stadtholder occupied a sort of executive position. The exact nature of the Stadtholder's role in the Dutch Republic depended on the personality of the particular Stadtholder, how successful the Republic's many invaders were, and the always tumultuous state of internal politics in any given year. The House of Orange ended up treating the role of Stadtholder as a hereditary office, but that was often quite tenuous. Eventually, with the end of the Dutch Republic in 1795, the House of Orange did end up as monarchs of the Netherlands.

In the fight against France, William III (r.1689-1702) often chafed against Parliamentary requirements, but he had to deal with them. If the politics were right, the disfavor of a king could lead to the fall of a government in the 1700s. As recently as the 1800s the death of a monarch required a new parliamentary election. The developments of the 1600s were big steps towards Parliamentary pre-eminence, however. The English Civil War established that Parliament was a permanent feature of English life. 1688 enforced that principle, and it also established a sort of stability that allowed the institutions of the modern British Parliament to start to develop.

The first modern-ish British political parties, the "Whigs" and "Tories" began to emerge in the late 1600s and early 1700s. Generally speaking, the Tories tended to be more favorable to Royalty, and the official, established, more lightly Protestant Anglican church that the monarch led. The Whigs were less deferential to royal power, and more sympathetic to harder, Dissenting forms of Protestantism.[63] These parties were still just separate factions of the aristocracy in the 1700s, though the Whigs began to incorporate more of the financial interests of large urban merchants. The voting public in this massively corrupt system was less than 5 percent of the British population, and many of the seats in the House of Commons were outright controlled by the mostly hereditary members of the House of Lords. Though the office of Prime Minister was not legally established until 1937, it began to emerge in the early 1700s, largely through the political genius of one man, Thomas Walpole. Parliament didn't really begin to transition into an institution that represented the wishes of all the people until the Reform acts of the 1800s, and the elected House of Commons didn't fully assert its dominance over the hereditary House of Lords until a controversy over taxes in 1910. But it was the Glorious Revolution that made all this evolution possible. The stabilizing of the rivalry

---

[63] P.42 Webb, R.K. Modern England 2nd Edition

between monarch and parliament in parliament's favor after 1689, and after Queen Anne's death in 1714, allowed the whole British government to focus more seriously on the business of building empire and building wealth.

The new stability in government brought about by the Glorious Revolution allowed the English to subjugate the Scots and Irish. This age-old English goal was largely accomplished in a few decades around 1700. James II attempted to use Catholic Ireland as a springboard to take England back from William III. He failed, and this failure prompted William III to complete the English conquest of Ireland. The "bloodless revolution" of 1688 was very bloody in Ireland. The Williamite-Jacobite War in Ireland (1688-1691) more strongly established a "Protestant Ascendancy" of landowners that controlled Ireland for over 200 years. Some Protestant Northern Irish today still rally under the color orange, in tribute to William III's House of Orange. Ireland had been the target of English and Scottish "Plantations" since medieval times. English monarchs would import their own subjects to Ireland as a strategy of subjugation. The Glorious revolution completed the process. The conquest of Ireland involved extreme cruelty and mass expropriation. After 1690, Catholics were legally precluded from buying land. They couldn't hold political office.[64] The fact that Ireland remained Catholic in spite of all this is deeply impressive. Ireland had a parliament of its own until 1801, and representation in the Parliament in London after that. But until the late 1800s, Ireland's Parliamentary representation was controlled by rich Protestant landlords, not by the Catholic majority.

The hard-earned and tenuous religious tolerance in England and Scotland allowed an aristocratic controlled parliament to govern without too much resentment. Crucially, this tolerance initially

---

[64] P.66 Webb, R.K. Modern England 2nd Edition

extended only to different forms of Protestantism, not to Catholics. This made Ireland's parliamentary representation just another instrument of occupation until the parliamentary reforms of the nineteenth century. In 1707 the Act of Union created Great Britain, unifying England and Scotland. Scotland was incorporated fairly bloodlessly, but only after the merciless crushing of the independent mercantile aspirations and international investments of Scottish elites. None of this consolidation would have been possible without the real economic juggernaut that the English were finally developing in this period.

The Empire of Wealth: The West

Kings and Queens had chartered joint stock companies for the purposes of trade since the 1550s, but they only began to have a real impact in the mid-1600s. After the Glorious Revolution of 1688, they slowly began to be tied together in a more consistent imperial project. It was also in the two decades around 1700 that "the phrase 'The City' came to mean, as it still does to the English, what 'Wall Street' means to an American. It was in London that the great overseas companies had their headquarters."[65] London became the hub of growing trading, financial, government lending, and insurance industries. The centralization of all these influences in one place, and the lessening of 17th century distractions over government and religion would make for a dominating eighteenth century. London grew in power and sophistication, but other ports and cities in England were also key to overseas expansion as well.

The British Empire first acquired large territories in the Americas. The conflicts of the mid-1600s gave some real impetus to the British Empire in North America. Small numbers of religious Dissenters had

---

[65] P. 19 Webb, R.K. Modern England 2nd Edition

founded North American colonies like the Plymouth Bay Colony (1620), Maryland (1634), Rhode Island (1636), and Connecticut (1639). The English Civil War provided a steady stream of refugees, many religious, and many simply seeking to get away from the fighting. The Virginia colony, after years of starvation and bruising conflict with natives, began to find stability and prosperity through tobacco.

I was surprised to find, when I started looking into this, that the territory of today's United States was not the focus initially. It turns out it's not always about us! Piracy, slave-trading, and sugar production in the Caribbean was the first focus of imperial wealth creation and violence. "In 1688, 213 ships are known to have docked at Port Royal [Jamaica], almost as many as the total number calling that year at all of New England's ports."[66] Virginia and the Plymouth colony may have gotten started around the same time, but their later economic dynamism followed the earlier success of the sugar islands. Islands like Nevis, Montserrat, Antigua, Barbados and more were acquired in the first half of the 1600s, without a high degree of enthusiasm from the kings of the time.[67] Jamaica was taken from Spain by Cromwell's Protestant Jihadists in 1655.

The 17th century passion for sugar in Europe made these islands incredibly lucrative by the 1650s. The money that they pumped into the British system helped to fund the great consolidation of England Scotland and Ireland, and the wars against the French.[68] All the capital and economic activity created then inspired the growth of other aspects of the British Empire. Calling something that was so reliant on the brutality of the Atlantic slave trade a "virtuous cycle" just doesn't work, but it was certainly a cycle of accelerating economic growth that

---

[66] P.4 Colley, Linda The Ordeal of Elizabeth Marsh: A Woman In World History
[67] P.338 Scott, David Leviathan: the Rise of Britain As a World Power
[68] P.339 Scott, David Leviathan: the Rise of Britain As a World Power

connected European sugar fiends, growing colonies, and the brutalization of Africa and the Americas.

The Empire of Wealth: The East

The English had been a player in the eastern spice trade, or had at least tried to be players for quite some time. This was a crucial arena for their competition with the Dutch and the Spanish. In the 1600s the Dutch generally did better. The Dutch initially blocked the English from large-scale trade with eastern spice sources like Malaya, Java and the Molucca Islands. So the English made do with supplanting the Portuguese in India. They developed a healthy textile trade on the periphery of an Indian subcontinent still dominated by a vigorous Mughal Empire.

The economic and emotional weight that India was to acquire for the British Empire by the 1800s and 1900s sometimes leads us to over-emphasize the role of the East India Company at this point. In the 1600s England's trade with India was important, but it was much less important than the emerging Atlantic wealth machine. In 1674-1675 the value of goods imported into Britain from India amounted to £860,000.[69] Annual exports from the Caribbean island of Barbados alone amounted to £3 million in the 1660s.[70] "Asia still remained marginal to European trade and world power; until 1820 the Caribbean and the Americas were vastly more important."[71] The India trade was growing, but it was nowhere near inhabiting the dominant role in British minds that it did later.

---

[69] P.26 James, Lawrence The Rise And Fall of The British Empire
[70] P.338 Scott, David Leviathan: the Rise of Britain As a World Power
[71] P. 4 C. A. Bayly Indian Society and the Making of British Empire

Empire of Competition (1688-1815)
Britain versus France
The Second Hundred Years' War, the French Revolution, and Napoleon

Throughout the different periods of conflict described in this chapter, the scale of Europe's influence beyond its borders was increasing. Already by the end of the 1600s, wars between European powers often included battles in the Americas and Asia. Over the course of the 1700s, those fights grew from small skirmishes of pirates and settler militias to large set-piece battles fought between professional European or European-led armies as far afield as Montreal in Canada and Pondicherry in India. As Europe's scale of conflict grew, England's role in those larger conflicts grew as well. By the end of the 1600s, England was no longer a marginal player ambushing treasure ships when it could, it played a leading role in wars on the European continent.

The complex tale of William III's battles to consolidate England's dominance of Ireland were key parts of the Europe-wide Nine Years' War (1688-1697). Queen Anne sent English generals to the continent and helped to fund the larger War of the Spanish Succession (1701-1714) against France, again allied with the Holy Roman Empire, and the elements of Spain that did not want to be ruled by France. These major conflicts between England and France were inconclusive, but England and Great Britain (est. 1707) largely succeeded in preserving the Dutch Republic and limiting France's growth. As the century wore on, the role of France and Great Britain became more central, and the other powers, no matter how they were aligned in a particular war, found themselves playing less important supporting roles. From the Seven Years' War in the middle of the century (1754-1763), the British prioritized winning battles overseas, gambling that victory there would lead to victory in Europe. They chose wisely. This global focus allowed the British to build the first world system.

The Importance of Royalty Fades

The Glorious Revolution of 1688 did not instantly make British royalty powerless, but it changed the trajectory of the relationship between monarch and parliament drastically. You may have noticed that the title of this section no longer lists all the kings and queens concerned. This is because over the course of the period 1689-1815, monarchs got a lot less important. 1688 had some direct legislative consequences, like the Bill of Rights of 1689 that limited the royal ability to act outside parliamentary authority.[72] The last Stuart monarchs, however, retained great power in the period from 1689 to 1714. William III and Mary II reigned together between 1689 and 1694. After Mary II's death in 1694, the Dutch William III was allowed to continue to reign until his death in 1702, when he was succeeded by James II's other Protestant Daughter Queen Anne (r. 1702-1714). William III ruled over a Protestant Super-State in a personal union of the Dutch Republic and the Kingdom of England Scotland and Ireland. But it was a new, tenuous form of ruling, that had to deal with contentious representative bodies run by nobles and newly powerful mercantile interests in both realms. This was frustrating for William III, but it also gave him the ability to punch far above the weight in land and population of his two contentious realms as he confronted his massive and now consolidated French enemy. The elites that William III had to persuade were more capable and more dedicated once persuaded than the French elites who were compelled towards war.

William III, was probably the last real "fighting king" in British history. Later monarchs would occasionally have a limited role in

---

[72] P. 41 Webb, R.K. Modern England 2nd Edition

picking governments, and play an important propaganda role, but after William, none took a serious part in directing the wars day to day. George II (r.1727-1760) was the last British king to take part in a battle, but he did not take the lead in determining policy. At the end of William's reign, England and the Dutch Republic went their separate ways. England to rope in Scotland to become Great Britain and build a world system, and the Dutch Republic to begin a long slide into irrelevance. William's successor Queen Anne recently got a rather unfriendly portrayal in the 2018 film The Favourite. While I haven't found any indication that her relationship with her favorite courtiers was as physical as the movie portrays, it does a surprisingly good job depicting the political history. The course of Great Britain's participation in the War of Spanish Succession really was determined by Olivia Colman's shifting relationships with Rachel Weisz and Emma Stone, sorry Queen Anne's shifting relationships with Sarah Churchill and Abigail Masham. Queen Anne was the final monarch from the Stuart family. She was also the last monarch to veto a bill passed by parliament.[73] After Anne royalty had power, but in much less straightforward ways.

Parliament found an unimpeachably Protestant royal family to succeed the Stuarts in the German Electors of Hanover. The impact of the unremarkable Georges was limited by their initial foreignness, and then by the lengthy incapacity of George III (r.1760-1820), the first Hanover king who grew up speaking English. In England's unwritten constitution, tradition counts for a lot. A century's worth of foreign and mad Georges gave up a lot of power to Parliament that later monarchs were incapable of taking back. Later Kings and Queens will crop up in this account, but after Queen Anne they ceased to be as important in the day to day running of the British Empire. Their opinions of a given politician could influence the forming of a government, but in ways

---

[73] P. 49 Webb, R.K. Modern England 2nd Edition

that are too subtle and complex to really dive into in a book of this length. Kings and Queens played a role in parliamentary politics, but they could no longer act in opposition to the very idea of parliamentary politics.

British Government Grows

The (temporary) settling of the eternal British religious, political and territorial conflicts after the Glorious Revolution took a lot of money. So did William III's war against a continental superpower at least three times the size of his combined realms. This prompted England to take a page out of the Dutch book, and get a lot more financially sophisticated than its French antagonist. The Bank of England was founded in 1694 to finance the reconstruction of William III's navy.[74] This institution eventually evolved into something like a central bank, financing a large national debt, which allowed the British to continue to punch above their weight in their century long struggle against their French rival. This regularly serviced and supported debt helped to make London a financial center, while also giving the UK government the money it needed to grow to meet its many challenges. And grow it did. "The number of full-time state employees would treble between 1689 and 1714, from 4,000 to 12,000—a proportionally greater increase than in any other period in British history."[75] The Bank of England was subject to panics and turmoil, but it never failed. This stability was a key part of Britain's eventual victory over France, a country that never seemed to be able to get its finances in order. French finance was subject to the whims and extravagance of kings and emperors between revolutionary upheavals. The British debt, as enormous as it got, paid a regular income to its holders.

---

[74] P.248 Scott, David Leviathan: the Rise of Britain As a World Power
[75] p. 249 Scott, David Leviathan: the Rise of Britain As a World Power

The Great Rivals

We apply the names WWI and WWII to two twentieth century conflicts. But many scholars have argued that the first true World War can be found in the eighteenth century. In the United States we remember this conflict as the French and Indian War, but it was much bigger than our little piece of it. This titanic struggle between France and Great Britain, waged on five continents, is more widely known as the Seven Years' War (1756-1763). It involved all the great powers of Europe and established British dominance of India and the seas.

Some go even further and refer to the period between 1688 and 1815 as the "Second Hundred Years' War". If you tail together the "Nine Years' War" (1688-97) and the "War of the Spanish Succession"(1701-1714) against Louis XIV, the "War of the Austrian Succession" (1740-1748), the "Seven Years' War" (1756-1763), the War of American Independence (1776-1783) and the French Revolutionary (1792-1802) and Napoleonic Wars (1803-1815), this designation makes a lot of sense. As the names indicate, there were multiple parties, and a lot going on in all of these conflicts, but in all of them France was on one side, and England on the other. Again, it was this conflict that gave us the eternal naming confusion that may have already irritated you in this book. To review, England roped in Scotland to become Great Britain in 1707, and roped in Ireland to become the United Kingdom of Great Britain and Ireland in 1801. The conflict with France allowed for the British consolidation of power both in the closer islands and in the world at large. It was this century-long rivalry that produced the British Empire, planet Earth's first system of world-wide control.

British and French Nationalism

The name, the "Second Hundred Years' War", is a call back to the medieval conflict between France and England that took place between 1337 and 1453. This first "Hundred Years' War" is a fantastic example of the "thugs beating up on other thugs" era of history I talked about in chapter 2. The English Monarchy, through more dynastic weirdness it doesn't make much sense to get into, had a claim to significant chunks of the territory of modern France. Henry II (r.1152-1189) controlled the western coast of France, and significant inland territories, from Normandy down to the border of modern Spain. The glory-seeking (Richard I (r.1189-1199)) and fecklessness (John "Lack-land" (r.1199-1216)) of two of his sons lost most of this territory. From the 1330s to the 1450s, the English kings attempted to take it back. There were great victories, but in the long term they failed. This conflict was crucial to the eventual formation of both English and French national identity. From Joan of Arc to Henry V, both countries got some of their greatest heroes out of the conflict.

Many argue that the first Hundred Years' War was the birth of mass national identity for England and France. I question the extent to which this identity went beyond the standard loathing of the other you can find in any of our ancestors from the primates on down. The medieval Hundred Years' War was a horrible conflict, carried out in the context of the Black Death, the outbreak of bubonic plague beginning in 1347. The plague continued to break out repeatedly over the ensuing decade and century carrying off somewhere between 30 percent and 60 percent of the European population. The French peasantry was regularly brutalized, and large sections of the English expeditionary forces never came back. Climate change also contributed to this nightmare. The four century long "Medieval Warm Period" came to an end, producing colder temperatures and years of failed harvests. The last thing these people needed was a thuggish war for land. I doubt the courtly tales of

English victory at Agincourt or French triumph under Jeanne D'Arc provided much consolation to the largely illiterate people forced to participate in this conflict. The descendants of these brutalized peasants made great use of these national myths and legends though. The glorious stories that came out of the first Hundred Years' War were certainly important to the growing nationalism of the French and British peoples in the 1700s and 1800s.

Unlike the First Hundred Years' War, there was a lot more at stake in the second than which group of hereditary monsters would control which sections of France. The difference in numbers alone is fascinating. It gives a good sense of the meteoric rise in the stakes we are dealing with in more recent centuries. The most famous battle[76] of the first Hundred Years' War is probably the one that took place at Agincourt in 1415[77]. The battle was immortalized in Shakespeare's Henry V, written around 1599. The play brought the English language immortal lines like "Once more unto the breach, dear friends…" and "Band of Brothers". The army that Henry V used to invade France in 1415 totaled 6,000-9,000 troops. Napoleon's invasion of Russia in 1812 included 685,000 troops on the French side.[78]

The stakes weren't just higher in aims and numbers. The fears motivating the belligerents came from all-encompassing nationalist ideologies. The degree to which individuals or certain groups within the French and English publics were captured by these ideologies can be argued for academic lifetimes, but the presence and power of these ideologies was indisputable. They fed into a feeling of nationalism that grew up more organically in these countries than it did elsewhere. The fact that the justifying ideologies shifted almost completely as a result of the French Revolution did not make the nationalism they helped

---

[76] Perhaps I'm revealing a bit too much Anglophilia here…
[77] https://en.wikipedia.org/wiki/Battle_of_Agincourt
[78] https://en.wikipedia.org/wiki/French_invasion_of_Russia

form any less powerful. Throughout the reign of Louis XIV, and even long after the courts of his successors had drifted off on clouds of fashionable Enlightenment ideas, France was seen by the British people as a Catholic aggressor. The French didn't just want British land, they wanted to fundamentally change English and Scottish life. They wanted, or were seen as wanting, to crush the tentative religious independence that was developing in Great Britain (not for Catholics).

World-Wide SCALE

The all-encompassing nature of ideological fears, the new weaponization of nationalism, and the scale of the new style of warfare forced changes in the government in England, Scotland and Ireland. On paper it was not an equal fight. The French population in 1700 stood around 21 million. The total population of England and Wales was only 5.1 million. To beat France in the Second Hundred Years' War, England needed to first subjugate Scotland and Ireland, and then build the British World System. In the climax of this conflict under Napoleon, France managed to construct, for brief periods, a "Continental System" that arrayed all of Europe from Spain to Russia against the British. In a very real sense, the climactic Napoleonic wars of this period arrayed Europe on the French side, and much of the rest of the world on the British side. The construction of a world system that could beat a united Europe required the British to be everywhere. So they were.

A Supporting Cast of Rivals

Outside of the consistent battle between France and Britain, The Second Hundred Years' War saw many great shifts in allegiance and rivalry. But France was always on one side, and Britain was always on the other. More importantly it saw a massive shift in the relative weights of the smaller powers involved. In the earlier conflicts of this period, roughly from 1689 to 1714, the lesser powers that mattered were still familiar from the 1500s. The later more intense period of conflict from 1740 or so to 1815 formed the great European power structure that would stay largely in place all the way down to 1914.

Spain's time as a superpowered empire was pretty much done. The world-beating Habsburg Spanish / Holy Roman Empire (Austrian) / American / Asian monster state of the 1500s and early 1600s had collapsed. Charles II (of Spain, not England!) (r.1665-1700) was the final Habsburg king of Spain. It was his death in 1700 that kicked off the War of the Spanish Succession. France attempted to absorb the Spanish Empire by installing Louis XIV's grandson Philip of Anjou on the throne. Though the Spanish empire was a financial ruin at this time, it still held large territories in modern Belgium, the Americas, and the Philippines. So everybody wanted a piece. The Austrians preferred a different candidate for the Spanish throne, and the British and the Dutch supported them. After fourteen years of war, the French candidate won, the Austrians got what became Belgium, and everyone else got a promise that the French and Spanish crowns would never be united.

Spain would participate seriously in the wars of the later 1700s. Its large territories in the Americas forced it to. Sometimes they fought the British, sometimes they fought the French. But each new conflict left it in a worse position than the last, culminating in occupation by Napoleon and the loss of Spain's mainland American empire in the early 1800s. Spain, much like the Dutch, its great antagonist from centuries past, was now a small player in Europe rather than a great power. Spain was sort of like Russia today. A once great power scrapping to hold on to what was left. Spain was still capable of packing a punch, but it was no longer one of the main protagonists of world history.

The **Dutch Republic** limped on through the 1700s. The conflict with Louis XIV, and the English usurpation of important parts of its trading empire had exhausted it. It remained a wealthy country, with an Asian empire in modern Indonesia that lasted until 1949. But its continued independence in the 1700s and 1800s owed more to rivalry between France and Britain than it did to its independent power. The French Revolutionary era finally brought an end to the Dutch Republic in 1795, first through repeated French intervention in the Dutch revolutionary process, then through outright annexation to the French Empire. When it regained its independence in 1815, it was as the Kingdom of the Netherlands rather than a Republic.

A range of other European powers that had been significant in earlier centuries were being shuffled off the stage in various ways. **Sweden**'s losses to Russia in the early 1700s had pretty much deprived them of possessions south of the Baltic sea. **Poland**, at one point the territorially largest country in Europe, was on its way to being completely devoured by its neighbors in 1795. The **Ottoman Empire** didn't start to get carved up until the 1800s, but it had long since stopped growing, and a process of decay was setting in. Like the Dutch Republic, the Ottoman survival as a European power in the 1700s owed more to the fact that the great powers didn't want strategic Ottoman land going to any other power than any great vigor coming from the Sultans in Istanbul.

The **Austrian Empire** was the only power other than France to remain a great power on the European stage all the way from the 1500s down to 1914. England, remember, wasn't a major player until the mid-1600s. The nature and territorial limits of Austrian Habsburg rule changed dramatically over that near half millennium. The Second

Hundred Years' War saw Napoleon put the Holy Roman Empire out of its misery in 1806. But the Austrians had spent much of the 1700s slowly morphing away from that medieval structure and its religion-based legitimacy. A series of "enlightened despots" modernized the Austrian Empire, attempting to rule its unwieldly mix of territories. To the south and east Austria justified its power over a range of Eastern European peoples through the fading conflict with the Ottomans, and a rising conflict with the Russians. Austria's attempts to exert power over their traditional German territories to the north and west were complicated by the continued emergence of the powerful German states of Bavaria, Saxony and most importantly **Prussia**.

The rising power of these three German states, and some smaller ones, had been a problem for the Austrians since the Thirty Years' War (1618-1648) and before. It was thrown into high relief with the War of Austrian Succession (1740-1748). France, Bavaria and Prussia disputed the right of Empress Marie Theresa, a woman, to succeed to the Austrian throne. With the help of Britain and Saxony, she kept her throne, but she did not succeed in keeping Prussia from taking Silesia. That acquisition was an important milestone in Prussia's rise to great power status under Frederick II "the Great" (r.1740-1786).

Frederick opposed the British in the war of Austrian succession, but he became the great British ally in the Seven Years' War (1756-1763). Prussia, the state that would eventually force the unification of Germany over one hundred years later, had a great military, but not a ton of land and resources, and its rise became very reliant on British subsidies. Frederick II's Lutheranism (a sect of Protestantism) helped to make him a hero to the British people. His prime enemies the Holy Roman Emperor and the King of France were Catholics. Though these religious conflicts were losing meaning among the "Enlightened" elites of the day, sticking it to the Catholics was still a great way to get the

British public on your side, and Frederick's Protestantism was a key part of his popularity with the British. It's fascinating that the state that would eventually produce the Kaiser and Hitler was given its first leg up by British subsidies to fight the French. There's some "blowback" for you. Interestingly, every late twentieth and twenty-first century adversary of the United States, from the Soviet Union, to China, to Vietnam and Iraq and Iran, benefitted from a similar dynamic. The US supported all of these powers, to differing degrees, against other enemies before they became "rivals".

Rounding out the set of five great powers that took us down to the First World War, we have **Russia** (the other four being Britain, France, Austria, and Prussia (later Germany)). Russian power and influence steadily marched west across the 1700s. For the first half of the century, Russia was more focused on the Ottomans to the south, and crushing more Eastern European powers like Sweden and Poland. Russia was largely successful in these conflicts, and by 1795 it had partnered with Prussia and Austria in swallowing up Poland completely. This inserted Russia into the mainstream of Central European politics, where it shared a border with Prussia (later Germany) and the Austrian Empire until 1918. Russia would remain a major player in European and world politics all the way down to 1989.

The Wealthy Pause (1714-1740)

Some readers will have noticed that there was is a rather large gap in the "Second Hundred Years' War" chronology provided above. Between the end of the War of Spanish Succession in 1714 and the War of the Austrian Succession in 1740, things eased off a bit. Europe's colossus, Louis XIV of France, the Sun King, scourge of the Protestants, finally died in 1714. His decades of constant war against the Dutch, the English, and various German states hadn't really yielded all that much for France, and it had been financially ruinous. Despite a series of brilliant advisors, the French monarchy had never figured out war finance to the extent that the British did, and they needed a breather.

That breather, between 1714 and 1740, was very good to the era's two main antagonists. Both France and Britain's empires grew significantly. But Britain was doing better. London was replacing Amsterdam as the center of European finance and trade. Beyond the Caribbean and Indian empires that were already growing, the Treaty of Utrecht that ended the War of Spanish Succession in 1714[79] also awarded Britain her first Mediterranean possessions. It was a satisfying turn-about, a little more than a hundred years after the Spanish Armada loomed off the English coast, for Britain to take a little chunk of Catholic Spain. Gibraltar, at the mouth of the Mediterranean Sea, is still held by the UK today.

Historians dispute the extent to which Industrialization was an important factor in this period. Every decade or so, a different interpretation comes to the fore, asserting that the last interpretation either under or oversells the role of new technologies and styles of economic organization in the 1700s. Nobody doubts that innovations were taking place, and certain industries were mechanizing and beginning to feel the effects of steam. The flying shuttle (1733) and the spinning jenny (1764) revolutionized the textile industry. The Marine Chronometer (1761) allowed for more precise navigation. Perhaps most importantly, the pressures of naval battle from the 1500s led to rapid development of naval technology and scale by historical standards. One of Henry VIII's most impressively new-fangled ships famously tipped over in a naval battle due to poorly designed gun ports.

---

[79] The Treaty of Utrecht was apparently not a single treaty, but a collection of them between a range European players.

Innovation had its costs. By the 1700s the progressively larger and more numerous ships of the French and British navies were finely tuned machines. The engineering and administrative skills necessary to establish these navies spun off innovations and skilled workers for other endeavors. The massive naval dockyards built valuable skills that were applied to commercial fleets. For our purposes it's enough to note that the steadily accelerating drum beat of industrial progress was a factor here. We talked about this a lot back in Chapter Two. It gave both the British and the French empires broader horizons, capabilities and opportunities than any empires that came before them.

With hindsight, it's clear that the British did a much better job of capitalizing on the opportunities of the "Wealthy Pause". British North America steadily gained in population and economic sophistication, while French North America remained sparsely populated with an economy focused on fur trapping. On the eve of the Seven Years' War (1756-1763) all of France's vast American territories held about 70,000 Europeans. British North America held almost 1.6 million Europeans, and it was growing quickly. The roots of the conflict in North America can be found in this mismatch of territory and population. The comparatively teeming shores of the British colonies were completely encircled on land by vast, largely European-free French and Spanish possessions. New France spread from Montreal and Quebec in modern Canada, across the great lakes and down the Mississippi to Louisiana. The French hold would prove to be fleeting, but their influence is preserved by city names like Montreal, Detroit, Cadillac, St. Louis and New Orleans. The Spanish held Florida. Britain's colonists were eager to get their hands on these territories. The native populations were, wisely it turned out, eager to preserve lower-impact French control.

In India, as well, the French were far behind the English and the Dutch. During this early 1700s pause in European fighting the French greatly expanded their network of trading posts, building up a flourishing center at Pondicherry on the South Eastern Indian Coast. But they were too far behind. Britain's decades of experience, flourishing relationships with petty Indian princes, and growing native armies outclassed the French position.

The roots of France's problem lay in the previous century. In the 1600s, while the British were struggling with the Dutch for overseas trading routes, Louis XIV had been focused on his dreams of domination on the European continent. It's similar to the way the United States has spent trillions in just Iraq and Afghanistan over the past two decades, while China has won much more influence in many more countries, with much smaller investments. Later French kings and their advisors saw the benefits of a large trading empire, but they had lost too much time. The French had the resources necessary to put together large and impressive navies, but they didn't have the experience necessary, institutionally or in their corps of sailors, to compete with Britain on the sea.

Historian Linda Colley's excellent book, <u>The Ordeal of Elizabeth Marsh</u>, illustrates the way that the expanding empire of this wealthy pause was providing some extraordinary opportunities for social mobility. The technological sophistication required to run a navy was breaking down the old rule of thugs in novel ways. "The skills involved in maintaining and sailing these vessels were so specialized, and in such high demand, that possessing them could sometimes trump a man's skin colour, just as it often trumped social class."[80] In her book, Colley tracks the success of a humble family of ship wrights, and one of their daughters in particular. In her short life, the titular Ms. Marsh managed to involve herself in commercial schemes and adventures across the world, from Jamaica, to Florida, to Morocco, to England and

---

[80] P. 14 Colley, Linda <u>The Ordeal of Elizabeth Marsh: A Woman In World History</u>

India. Her family's skills and diligence got them chances at great wealth and power. Marsh's ability to travel relied to a great extent on her Uncle George Marsh, who rose from a lowly clerkship to a position of wealth and power as Commissioner of the Navy.[81] As with everything, luck was important. Colley documents how one of Elizabeth Marsh's grandchildren was born a hereditary British aristocrat, while one of her great grandchildren started her life as an Indian orphan before the historical record loses track of her completely. The opportunities that the growing empire of competition provided were vast. This luck could be aided by warfare.

The wealthy pause, that had done so much for trade, was ended due to commercial interests. Under the government of Robert Walpole from the 1720s, a forerunner to modern prime ministers, British governments largely aimed for peaceful expansion, slashing military budgets and getting out of the way of commercial growth. This worked well for a while, but mercantile rage at Spain's continued insistence that only they could profit from trade with their colonies, led to the "War of Jenkins' Ear" starting in 1739. The extent of time between the Spanish Coast guard's severing of the ear of British trader/smuggler Captain Jenkins, in 1731, and the commencement of hostilities in 1739, indicates how unwilling the Walpole government was to go to war. They were finally forced to do so, initiating a conflict that would drag on for another nine years.

In 1742, war with Spain became part of the larger War of Austrian Succession fought between all of the European powers. The most important feature of this war from the British perspective was the French-supported invasion of Scotland by Charles Stuart or "Bonnie Prince Charlie", the grandson of the Catholic James II who had been dethroned in 1688. The invasion in July of 1745 met with some initial

---

[81] P.38 Colley, Linda The Ordeal of Elizabeth Marsh: A Woman In World History

success in Scotland, winning some battles and briefly invading England before being defeated at the Battle of Culloden in April 1746. Charles and his French supporters had overestimated the amount of support they could pick up for a Catholic in England. Disaffected Scots who thought they might be in a better position with one of their own back on the throne were one thing, but the wide support Charles had expected in England simply didn't exist. In the 1750s, he briefly converted to Protestantism to make his claim to the throne more legitimate, but the time when a British public might have hankered after a lost king had passed.

Seven Years' War

The Seven Years' War is the first of the great clashes between European powers that started outside Europe. Throughout the 1700s, even during the wealthy pause, there was low-level strife between the European imperial powers, especially at sea. These skirmishes were far away, deniable, and often quite lucrative, but in 1754 they exploded into something more. Clashes along the border between France and Britain's North American possessions escalated. These clashes took place in and around the territories of Montreal and Quebec in modern Canada, and territories to the southwest in what would become the US state of Ohio, and the western reaches of Virginia and Pennsylvania. George Washington first came to prominence during this conflict. The Seven Years' War started in North America, but it didn't stop there. As ever, the main theater of conflict, for the belligerents other than Britain, was the European continent. But the war wasn't sparked by anybody's succession, it was initially about the French and British rivalry for Empire. The other European powers threw their territorial disputes on top of the fire. In 1756, Austria thought it would be clever and team up with its historical enemy France to attack Prussia.

The Seven Years' War (1756-1763) involved every European Power. Great Britain, Prussia, Portugal, Hanover, and some other small German states were aligned against France, Russia, Spain, the Austrian-led Holy Roman Empire (which included Bavaria, Saxony and other German states), and Sweden. Borders changed very little in Europe, but the British won great victories against the French in North America, India, and West Africa, and on the high seas. For the British elites, protecting and growing empire became the rationale, but for the public religion remained a factor. Through the 1700s, and even into the 1800s, beating up on Catholics was an important part of the propaganda rationale for warring on France.

William Pitt The Elder

Under the government of "Prime Minister"[82] William Pitt the elder, in the Seven Years' War, Britain embarked on a strategy of balancing Europe and the world that would take it through the Napoleonic wars, and to some extent all the way through to end of the Empire in the twentieth century. Unlike earlier leaders of British war efforts, Pitt was explicitly focused on imperial expansion. He consciously strove to deprive the French of their empire and trading routes. Unlike in previous wars, the conflict in Europe was a side show for the British. The British subsidized allies fighting on the European continent to allow their Navy free rein for empire building across the planet.[83] Frederick II of Prussia was crucial here, battling France, Austria and Russia to retain the territories he had previously taken from the Austrians.

---

[82] The office of the Prime Minister is supposedly traced back into the 1700s, but nobody really used the name until the 1800s. The informality here is illustrated by the elder Pitt's career. He's best known for his stewardship of the Seven Years' War, but his semi-official time as Prime minister isn't reckoned to start before the late 1760s.
[83] P.400 Scott, David Leviathan: the Rise of Britain As a World Power

Pitt's strategy of paying continental allies to fight in Europe while the British scooped up foreign territories worked marvelously. 1759 was the "Miracle Year"[84]. The British took all of French Canada, swept up the sugar island of Guadeloupe in the Caribbean, (which had more revenue than all of French Canada), and most importantly smashed the French Navy at the battle of Quiberon Bay. Guadeloupe was given back in the treaty that concluded the Seven Years' War, but the British ownership of Canada and the seas was much more lasting. Over the course of the war, British Naval supremacy also allowed them to scoop up a range of French trading posts in Africa, from Senegal to the Gambia. The Seven Years' War also prompted the birth of British India, a more complicated story we will cover in the next section.

The British were doing very well out of this war, but naval victory was terribly expensive, and war certainly wasn't helping trade. Other European powers became more jealous of the British the more successful they became. William Pitt the Elder, the architect of the war's winning strategy felt compelled to resign in 1761. Interestingly, at this late date, the attitudes and preferences of the new king George III were still important, and figures the king liked better took over the conduct of the war and quickly sought peace.

The speed with which peace was agreed with the French left Britain's allies in the lurch. The 1763 Treaty of Paris gave some international territories back to the French, but left the British in a massively better position. Britain's Prussian ally didn't get much at all. Hundreds of thousands of European soldiers had died, and central Germany, the kingdom of Saxony in particular, had suffered greatly. The Prussians were forced to negotiate peace with their Austrian antagonists separately. Prussian prestige had advanced greatly, solely through

---

[84] Many historians will still use the Latin "annus mirabilis" for this, like anybody knows what that means in 2018.

surviving, but the European borders didn't move much, despite a great deal of sacrifice. It was clear to everyone in Europe, British ally and British enemy, that there had only been one winner of the Seven Years' War. Everybody other than Britain had lost.

France was able to build large navies again, and take one last brutal stab at Egypt under Napoleon, but after the Seven Years' War it never really competed with Britain's overseas empire. Britain scooped up most of North American New France, including Canada, and all the land East of the Mississippi river. Spain got the still largely European-free land west of the Mississippi river, including the nascent New Orleans, but in return the British got Florida. France retained some lucrative islands in the Caribbean, and lesser trading posts in Africa and Asia, but the 1763 treaty of Paris did not allow these trading posts to be fortified to the extent they previously were. France also acquired some significant "me too!" imperial territories later in the nineteenth century, but being knocked out of the North Atlantic and Asia put France permanently into the second rank of imperial powers outside Europe. Prior to the Seven Years' War there was real competition for extra-European land empires between France and Britain. After its conclusion in the 1760s, that rivalry was over. France's one large extra-European victory after this point was moving a large British territory to independence, rather than into the French empire. The British hadn't fully built their world system yet, but the way was now mostly clear.

The winnings from the Seven Years' War were truly extraordinary. But European resentment also set up a future loss. Britain's continental European allies thought they had suffered greatly for the British, with no reward. This made the great reverse of American Independence possible. But before we look at that, we'll need to turn to the other side of the globe, and the true beginning of British India.

British India Begins

The British campaigns that won them their first significant Indian possessions were part of the worldwide conflict, but crucial battles took place years after the end of European hostilities. The Seven Years' War provided the opportunity to crush French interests in the region, but more importantly it led to a transition in the nature of British Empire in India.

Political control of even the margins of India did not begin to appear before the mid-1700s. As I described in Chapter One, the British attempted to invade the Mughal empire in the 1680s, and were quickly defeated and embarrassed. But Augrangzeb, the emperor who made such short work of the English, was the last strong Mughal emperor, and he died in 1707. Aurangzeb's endless wars to subjugate southern India had drained the Mughal coffers, and he had embraced a more extreme form of Islamic orthodoxy than the other Mughal Emperors. This alienated many of his Hindu subjects. His successors were nowhere near as powerful or long-lasting, and the Empire began to disintegrate. The British were not the first outside power to take advantage of this decline, but the third. The Afghans and the Persians had already rampaged through northern India before the British started building their inland empire in the 1750s. Though the Mughal ruling family survived until the first war of Indian independence in 1857, their suzerainty became more and more nominal, with local princes asserting greater power. Throughout the 1700s, power in India became less and less centralized, allowing the French and the British to make in-roads from the coasts.

British historians used to characterize India in the 1700s as falling into chaos, and the East India Company's growing control as a benevolent way to deal with anarchy. More recent scholarship has contradicted that self-serving narrative.[85] Central control was falling away, but more compact regional powers were emerging and becoming wealthy. As ever, India's story in this period was one of bewildering diversity. The anarchy that the British Empire's propagandists described may have existed briefly in some jurisdictions, but the broader picture was one of a shifting but growing economy. It was the sophistication and predictability of Indian land revenues and financial systems that made it such an attractive target for British exploitation. "The British were sucked into the Indian economy by the dynamic of its political economy as much as by their own relentless drive for profit."[86] Local Indian capitalists, merchants and money lenders played a significant part in the expansion of British control.[87] They often preferred the stability that the British could offer.

Conquest was only a small part of the growth of British domains in India. The British East India Company slowly expanded over the decades, always as a money-making institution, sometimes conquering, but more often insinuating themselves into local governing systems chunk by administrative chunk. The company formed numerous "partnerships" with petty Indian monarchs. The English would "help" to administer systems of taxation, or provide protection from competitors. Client princes that tried to end these relationships, or fell too far into debt, lost their kingdoms to direct rule by the East India company. It was always a hybrid system, mixing both formal and informal empire. Many of these petty kingdoms fell, but some lasted all the way to Indian independence in 1947.

At the outset of the Seven Years' War, British traders and military entrepreneurs were firmly established around ports on the west coast of India around Bombay (Mumbai), on the southeastern coast around

---

[85] P. 3 C. A. Bayly Indian Society and the Making of British Empire
[86] P.46 C. A. Bayly Indian Society and the Making of British Empire
[87] P.47-48 C. A. Bayly Indian Society and the Making of British Empire

Madras (modern Chennai), and most importantly for this section of the story, in the northeast around Calcutta. Bombay in the west had yet to establish the importance it had later. It was on the east coast that "British India" was born.

The most important Seven Years' War battles between France and Britain occurred around modern Chennai. The French trading post of Pondicherry had been established less than 100 miles down the coast from the British colony of Madras. In 1760 the British won the battle of Wandiwash (Vandavasi)[88] which decisively ended French ambitions in India. In the closing years of the war, the British conquered Pondicherry, and other French settlements in India. There were still serious battles to fight against Indian powers, but after the Seven Years' War British influence in India was largely free of interference from Europe.

The importance of France's defeat, however, pales in comparison to what Robert Clive (1725-1774) was up to in Bengal. Clive is one of the great heroes of the British Empire, controversial at the time, who has now become internationally recognized as a personification of greed and conquest. Bengal, a territory which is now divided between Bangladesh and neighboring Indian states, was "probably… the wealthiest province of Mughal India"[89]. Some sources argue that it was richer than Great Britain itself at the time, and it was certainly more populous.

In the decades up to 1757, the East India Company had begun to adopt an innovative scheme to deal with an issue they were facing. It was difficult to pay for all the products that foreign consumers wanted out of India. It cost a great deal of silver.[90] So the company began to take

---

[88] P.404 Scott, David Leviathan: the Rise of Britain As a World Power
[89] P. 51 Bayly, C.P. Indian Society and the Making of British Empire
[90] P. 49 Bayly, C.P. Indian Society and the Making of British Empire

on more administrative tasks within the tumultuous Indian states they traded with. In some places they operated state monopolies, or acted as tax collectors. Most importantly they had begun to develop native armies. These could be used to defend the Company's interests, and they could also be used to favor one group or another in India's many wars, large and small. The Company had built up networks of relationships with rulers and mercantile and banking interests within Bengal and many other states in India.

In 1756, Bengal got a new ruler, Siraj-ud-Daula who attempted to consolidate power both by squeezing some of the native Indian bankers, and eventually by trying to kick out the East India Company. Conflicts with France down the Indian coast had led to a larger contingent of British troops in India than normal.[91] This gave Clive options. At the Battle of Plassey in 1757, Clive and his Indian allies defeated Bengal's army, and installed their own choice, Mir Jafar. Historian C.P Bayly points out that this sort of thing happened all the time in India, but that the British brought something different…

> All this had happened within the context of a system of world trade in which the British were rapidly becoming dominant. The Bengal revenues could therefore be used to counterbalance the Company's trading performance which had been deteriorating since about 1740 as a result of war and competition from the private trade of its own servants. The revenues could also be used to pay for the Company's ever-growing army. [92]

India's riches had created a situation where "informal empire" led to a rare profitable form of "formal empire". After the battle of Plassey, the East India Company no longer needed all that imported silver to finance its operations. They could use the revenues of Bengal itself to

---

[91] P. 50 Bayly, C.P. Indian Society and the Making of British Empire
[92] P. 51 Bayly, C.P. Indian Society and the Making of British Empire

build its armies, and to support its trade across the world. From this point onward British India became a sort of engine. In the century to come, British commercial interests swallowed up all of India's wealth, and then eventually forced many of China's markets into the British World System as well. This engine of wealth creation eventually drove the British World System off a cliff. The desire to protect Indian revenues led to the conquest of unsustainably large territories, that were nowhere near as remunerative as Bengal. That all happened later.

Bengal, however, went off the cliff very quickly. Mir Jafar, the ruler installed by Clive did not last a decade. The ever-increasing demands of the East India Company drove him to revolt. He roped in other Indian rulers, and the participation of his nominal lord, the Mughal Emperor Shah Alam II himself. All these forces were defeated at the Battle of Buxar in 1765 by a British army composed of 859 European and 6,215 Indian troops. The resources of India were used to defeat the Mughal empire that had humiliated English forces less than a century before. The British weren't yet interested in deposing the Mughals, however. The East India Company took Bengal for itself, and gifted some of the land they won back to the Mughal emperor. In return they got a series of Imperial Firmans that formally established the British role in India.

Clive, who was not at Buxar, and many other East India Company employees became fabulously wealthy. At least a quarter of Bengal's population died in a famine starting in just the fourth year of British rule, in 1769. It would not be the last famine.[93] Many of the British Empire's first formal subjects in India were reduced to eating each other.[94]

---

[93] P. 33 Bayly, C.P. Indian Society and the Making of British Empire
[94] P. 21 Read, Anthony & David Fisher The Proudest Day: India's Long Road to Independence

American Independence and Informal Empire

What eventually became the United States benefitted mightily from British neglect during the wealthy pause in wars between 1714 and 1740. The sugar islands of the Caribbean were where the real action and profit were in the 1600s and 1700s. London was largely content to leave the adventurers and religious whackos of what became the United States to their own devices. Though economic activity in North America intensified greatly throughout the 1700s, London was not too rigorous in insisting that it reap the majority of the benefit. Since the 1660s, as part of their conflicts with the Dutch, the English developed the wherewithal to enforce a series of "Navigation Acts". These laws required that all trade with English, and later British colonies be carried out on English, and later British ships. But from the 1720s through the 1760s, these laws were not particularly rigorously enforced. This allowed great wealth to begin to be built up in North America, primarily through trade with Britain's Caribbean colonies.

Many of the English colonies were also founded with rather serious chips on their shoulders. A lot of this was the traditional obsession with "English liberties" but some additional factors gave that inclination a harder edge. Towards the North, many colonies were founded to be fundamentalist religious utopias of one flavor or another. This necessarily required a high degree of self-government, to protect against the infidels. Distance from London also encouraged local government in both the Northern and Southern American colonies. It's easy to forget just how distant North America was from London in the age of sail. As wealth began to be built up and down the seaboard, folks became more and more invested in the systems of local government that they had set up. Prior to the Seven Years' War this wasn't a problem.

After 1763 it was a big problem. The British had spent a great deal of money to win their larger empire. Defending and expanding their North American colonies was a significant portion of this expense. London's financial sophistication had allowed the British to foot this cost much more successfully than the French, but a sizeable national debt had accumulated. It seemed only natural that the North American colonists be required to help in paying off this debt.

War fatigue was also a large factor in the end of the British Empire's relationship with what became the United States. The imperial center wanted to consolidate its gains after the Seven Years' War. Parliament wanted to pay down the debt and avoid sparking any new conflicts. This meant seeking peace with the Native American tribes of the North American interior, and seeking to incorporate the largely French Catholic inhabitants of its new territories peacefully and profitably. In the Proclamation of 1763 George III forbade any settlement west of the Appalachian Mountains. This enraged the colonists, who expected that victory in the Seven Years' War would have led to greater expansion. This anger was present up and down the economic distribution. Elites had titles to land beyond the Proclamation line. Those who aspired to higher status, or at least to their own plots of land in new territory, were similarly frustrated.

As discussed above, the Quebec Act of 1774, with its toleration for Catholics, and incorporation of some French law, inflamed the Protestant prejudices of many colonists as well. The attempt to start taking the Navigation Acts more seriously again was probably the largest problem of all. This attempt to funnel more of the colonies trade through the imperial center was a direct threat to the commercial elites of North America.

In brief, the imperial center in London went from asking very little of its North American colonies to asking quite a lot. The agenda of consolidation and profit transgressed against the financial interests and religious prejudices of large segments of colonists. In 1763, North America was home to a population that largely saw themselves as proud British subjects (the free and non-native parts of the population that is). By 1776, and the Declaration of Independence, this was clearly no longer the case. Many remained loyal to the Crown, but the British had lost enough of the elites that they eventually lost the war in 1781.

This was the result of a long process of give and take, that will be familiar, if only dimly, to most
US readers. As much fun as the Boston Tea Party, the Intolerable Acts, Thomas Paine's Common Sense and all that are, we won't be running through the litany again here. From 1763, and on into the war itself, The British Parliament would alternate coercion with attempts satisfy some of the colonist's concerns. This effort failed. But American Independence would have been much harder to win without the French Navy.

A Poorly Managed Europe Is Bad for Empire...

The loss of the US colonies in the 1780s taught the British a valuable lesson: the importance of not alienating all of their continental allies. The British had started to build world dominance, but they never had the safety at home that the United States does today. The balance of power in Europe remained paramount. If everybody there was united in opposition to Britain, the dominance of the seas wasn't everything.

The British had screwed up. They had left their allies feeling burned after the end of the Seven Years' War in 1763 and unwilling to help the British in their time of need. In 1778, the French came into the war on the side of the colonists, and none of Britain's traditional continental allies were interested in helping to balance that threat. The Spanish, unsurprisingly, and the Dutch, much more surprisingly, eventually joined in on the French side as well. Much of the rest of Europe joined a League of Armed Neutrality[95], committed to blocking British attempts to hamper trade with North America. Great Britain stood alone against all of Europe. With the exception of some brief periods during the Napoleonic wars, and between the fall of France and the invasion of Russia during WWII, this is the only time this has ever happened.

The British learned that its vast territories didn't mean all that much if all the world's powers were arrayed against it. The French, for one of the only times in its long "Second Hundred Years' War" against the British, were free to focus on building up their navy, rather than fending off British allies. In league with the Spanish, the French were able to use their refurbished navy to put together a smaller imitation of the world-wide strategy that the British had carried out against it in the Seven Years' War. A French and Spanish fleet briefly threatened the British Isles. The Spanish attempted to blockade Gibraltar. Large British merchant fleets were captured. The French initially managed to take some islands in the Caribbean. And, of course, the French supported George Washington's battle against British occupation. Washington's victory at the battle of Yorktown in 1781 would not have been possible without the support of French ships.

Britain was still overwhelmingly powerful. Even with all of Europe against it, or sitting the fight out, it wasn't going to lose everywhere. The French succeeded in securing the independence of the United States but that was about it. Europe's situation forced Britain to do a sort of triage. They prioritized their much more lucrative Caribbean

---

[95] P.451 Scott, David Leviathan: the Rise of Britain As a World Power

island possessions over pricklier and harder to access territory on the North American mainland. They were largely successful in fending off the French in the sugar islands. The French had a large new Navy, but the British had the experienced commanders and crews. The war allowed Britain to take France's now lightly defended trading posts in India. This focus on the more lucrative and easily handled points to another lesson taught by the War of American Independence, a preference for formal over informal empire.

Keeping it Informal…

Managing large settler territories was difficult. Britain learned earlier than most that imperial success was not measured in mass of territory. What mattered was control of trade and financial power. The loss of the territory that became the United States was painful, but with Britain's growing and more sensible focus on informal empire, it wasn't necessarily even a loss. The US economy grew faster as a free country than it would have as a British territory, and it did so at zero cost to the British in terms of soldiers and administration. Even better, much of the capital involved was still British. The British bought the cotton that made the South prosperous. Northern English textile mills were so reliant on that cotton that, despite the Empire's professed hatred of slavery, it seriously considered intervening on the Southern side in the US Civil War. British capital helped to build the railroads and other infrastructure that connected the growing US economy. And the British profited mightily. As just one example, the majority of the shares in the vast Illinois Central, in 1856 the longest railroad in the world, were owned by British investors. British investors owned large chunks of the US economy throughout the nineteenth century and all the way up until the First World War.

Informal empire was almost always cheaper and more profitable than formal empire. The proclamation of 1763 that the North American colonists found so irritating, limiting the expansion of colonial territory, was one British attempt to act in accordance with this principle. The War of American Independence reinforced this inclination. The shifting status of Florida is another example of this principle in action. The British had attained it from the Spanish in 1763's Treaty of Paris ending the Seven Years' War. Between 1763 and the confusingly redundantly named 1783 Treaty of Paris that ended the War of American Independence, Florida had begun to turn into a prosperous colony. Florida's colonists had remained scrupulously loyal. Regardless, the British were happy to let the southernmost colony return to Spanish control in the second Treaty of Paris. Vast, distant territories filled with settlers with interests that often diverged from the imperial center were a challenge, and one that the United Kingdom managed more successfully through most of the 1800s.

There were settler colonies after the USA went its own way, of course. Refugee British loyalists from the lower colonies became the first significant non-French population to reside in Canada in the 1780s. Australia was getting its first ships of convicts around the same time. The Dutch and British settlers of what became South Africa were an escalating problem throughout the 1800s. But the British managed these settler colonies much more cleverly than they had the prior ones. When 19th century British settlers began to develop their own identities, and their own desires for self-determination, London did not stand in their way. The success of this policy was demonstrated by Canada, Australia and New Zealand's significant participation in the twentieth century's two world wars, even though they were largely independent by that point.

The British were more willing to acquire large tracts of territory in India, but that was because running the subcontinent's petty kingdoms and principalities directly provided opportunities for profit for the East India Company. The Company's eagerness to expand often led to conflict with the officials running the British Empire from London. London's preference for administering the subcontinent through nominally independent principalities lasted all the way to the demise of British India in 1947. The drift away from the lesson of the American War of Independence, and the willingness to acquire large territories of dubious economic value in the latter half of the 1800s was one of the largest factors in the end of the British World System.

A Revolution in Nationalism

Anti-Catholic sentiment remained widespread among the British people into the 1780s, even as elite opinion moved on. As we saw earlier, the government's attempt to welcome French Catholics into full citizenship in British Canada had more to do than we like to remember with US independence. Another well-meaning piece of legislation sparked some of the worst civil unrest in London's history in 1780. The delightfully named "Papists Act" sought to lessen some of the official prejudice against Catholics. The streets of London went wild under the leadership of Lord George Gordon, the head of the Protestant Association, who demanded the repeal of the act. Hundreds were killed, and buildings ranging from prisons to Catholic Churches to foreign embassies and the Bank of England were damaged or burned down. More modern Enlightenment ideals had inspired a less religiously bigoted approach to geopolitics among British leaders. But that equanimity had not yet filtered down to the man on the street.[96]

---

[96] https://en.wikipedia.org/wiki/Gordon_Riots

One would think that the start of the French Revolution in 1789 would have knocked the base out from under British-French rivalry. The Revolution was made up of many strands of thought, but the fight against Catholic influence was a key element of the Revolutionary platform from the early 1790s. At one point, revolutionary leaders set up a new quasi-religion whose object of worship was Reason itself. France's emperor Napoleon famously made his peace with the Pope in 1801[97], but it was a very new settlement, and not one that was favorable to the ancient rights of the Catholic Church. The Code Napoleon, the new civil law code, which was forced on many of the conquered territories, and often survived French control, booted Catholic clerics out of many of their traditional roles in favor of a modernizing state. Catholic invasion of Britain as any kind of legitimate threat died with the French Monarchy.

But the British-French rivalry persisted. In some ways Great Britain and France had switched roles. France had been the world leader of Catholic reaction, but Britain now became the leader of anti-Revolutionary reaction. We can see an echo in the geopolitical and ideological shift that has taken place in my own lifetime. For over seventy years, the nominally revolutionary Soviet Union struggled against the "counter-revolutionary" West, led by the proudly capitalist United States. Modern Russia has morphed into an enthusiastically crony capitalist oligarchy, which often positions itself as the standard-bearer for older ideas of sovereignty, Christianity, patriarchy and "whiteness". In both the eighteenth century and twenty-first century examples, the conflict survived jarring jumps across the ideological spectrum. Once again, nationalism proves to be more important than we recognize.

---

[97] https://en.wikipedia.org/wiki/Concordat_of_1801

In the first years after 1789, there had been a great deal of British sympathy for the Revolutionary cause. The British had been complaining about French despotism for centuries, after all. The Ancien Regime's reorganization in favor of the people was something to be celebrated! In the earlier days, many in Britain were inspired by the French struggles. But the initial excitement faded. As the revolutionaries first disrespected their king, then killed him, British sympathy faded away. Perhaps more importantly, when the French revolutionaries annexed the territory of modern Belgium, they crossed a red line. Britain went to war in 1793.

Democratic War

The French Revolutionary State was something new and strange. David A. Bell's *The First Total War* describes the way that France's Revolutionaries brought about a change in the nature of war itself. The 1700s had seen a great expansion of the geographic scope of European war, but, in Western Europe at least, it had also gotten about as civilized as war could be. The hereditary nobility that controlled these wars was no longer gripped by the occasionally exterminatory religious passions of the 1500s and 1600s. Great soldiers of the 1700s like Frederick the Great of Prussia saw themselves as men of the Enlightenment. They hoped to make war scientific and civilized.

The surprising fate of Tadeusz Kościuszko, one of Poland's great heroes, at the tail end of this era, helps to illustrate the surprising civility of eighteenth-century war. After returning from heroic service on the side of the colonists in the American Revolutionary War, he attempted to secure the independence of Poland from Russia. In 1794, he led an uprising and was defeated and captured. The experience of captured independence-minded Poles in the following 150 years was usually brief and violently ended, but not in this era. Kościuszko was pardoned by the Russian Tsar and lived out his life in the United States and Switzerland, dying in 1817.

Wars were fought by men who saw themselves as gentlemen. This gentlemanliness of course didn't extend to indigenous populations anywhere, or the Muslims of the Ottoman Empire that the Russians were so enthusiastically expropriating in the 1700s. Enlisted men who were seen as failing in their duties were still subject to barbaric punishments. But on a broader level, war in Western Europe had become limited, formalized, and even polite.

The French Revolution demolished all pretenses to civilization. The initial years after 1789 saw all sorts of high-minded proposals in France, including banning war entirely.[98] But the pressures of democratic politics, and the mounting fears of international intervention soon made war look much more attractive. One faction of Revolutionary politicians, the Girondins, led by Jacques Pierre Brissot, began to advocate for war as the solution to all their problems. It would help them consolidate power. It would punish the Austrians and Prussians who were seen as interfering in France on the behalf of exiled French nobility and the embattled French monarchy.

This would be a new type of war. It wouldn't be some petty noble war for land, it would be a war for the independence of all peoples! It supposedly wasn't religious, but France's revolutionary government injected a new exterminatory vigor into warfare. "Out of a toxic mixture of ignorance, wishful thinking, and pure naked ambition, the Girondins were pushing France towards wars that would last for twenty-three years and cost millions of lives"[99]. The French declared war on Austria and Prussia in April 1792.

France's response to initial defeat was to inaugurate the famous *levée en masse* in August 1793. This was the first mass conscription of the entire male population in modern European history. War was no longer going to be between polite aristocrats and their professional armies.

---

[98] pps. 98-102 Bell, David A. The First Total War
[99] p. 114 Bell, David A. The First Total War

Henceforth, it was to be fought between whole peoples, by national armies. France's leveraging of their people's fears and resources is an important moment in the history of nationalism. Peoples throughout Europe and the world have been trying to bottle that magic ever since. This new fervor was to take the French people to victory over victory over the next two decades. The costs were immense. The warmongering Brissot and the Girondins didn't survive 1793. Neither did the French royal family. The French Republic didn't survive the decade. As the French Revolutionary Wars wore on, a general from Corsica distinguished himself. Napoleon Bonaparte first won great battles in Italy and ended up as the dictator of the French state.

With short breaks, the British Empire would be at war with France for the next twenty-three years. The prolonged hostilities required the utilization of extraordinary resources and drove administrative reforms to use those resources. The public largely supported these efforts. The fight against the Americans had been difficult from a public relations perspective. The colonists were widely seen as countrymen, who were (mostly) just protecting their homes. They eloquently expressed time-honored British ideas of liberty in the English language. Facing crazed French revolutionaries was much easier. The wars starting in 1793 crushed any reservations about conquest that the American War of Independence had created. Empire was now a vital tool for survival.

Napoleon and The Historical Hangover

Napoleon is a puzzle. How did the French go from fighting for Liberte!, Egalite!, and Fraternite! to dying en masse for one of history's greatest despots? Napoleon was careful to position himself as a great reformer, but he marshalled the tools of the Enlightenment and nationalism to pursue one of the oldest ideas in the human playbook: conquest.

Many books have been written about the strange demise of the French Revolution, but I'd like to introduce another possibility, a central concept for this book, The Historical Hangover.

The French Revolutionaries wanted to create a new world. They wanted to be people of peace. But they couldn't wipe away what they came from. Their lived experience and their intellectual underpinnings were all mired in the glories of war. The French people in 1789 already knew war very well. Depending on their age, the generations alive at the time had participated in multiple world-spanning conflicts before they got to the Revolution. The Roman Republican archetypes most of them favored were great warriors. Despite early leanings towards pacifism, it only seemed natural that their great revolutionary ideas should be spread by the sword. When a new Caesar rose up, France fell in line quite eagerly. Those who disagreed died or left. It's worth emphasizing just how old world a figure Napoleon was. In 1809 he threw over his wife Josephine to marry a Habsburg princess. He may have been a legal reformer, but he was very happy to set his family members up as royalty in many of the countries he conquered. There wasn't much push-back on these developments until he started losing. All of the great aspirations of the French Revolution were quickly thrown over in support of older historical hangover assumptions about power, and martial vigor.

The fact that the French Revolution somehow produced a Napoleon is an extreme example of a historical hangover but it is not the only one. No matter how noble the aspirations we aspire to, we are still human beings. If a threat arises, or seems to arise, we quickly gravitate towards violence. All of the world's countries today aspire to some degree of democracy, peace and fellow-feeling. Yet the main historic accomplishments most countries celebrate or mourn are wars. After seventy years of great power peace, the United States still spends outrageous sums of money on its military, and eagerly jumps on any excuse to use it. Is any of this necessary?

An Easier Enemy

The rise of Napoleon made the jobs of British propagandists much easier. His coup and appointment as first consul in 1799 and self-coronation as Emperor in 1804 set up a one-man despotism that was less attractive to the average Britisher than the Enlightenment values of the Declaration of the Rights of Man and the Citizen put together by the revolutionaries.

The wars with Napoleon both cemented the imperial system that Britain had set up and forced it into a higher degree of efficiency and aggression. With French help, Ireland rebelled in 1798. The British crushed the rebellion and took Ireland's parliament away with the establishment of the United Kingdom of Great Britain and Ireland in 1801. This more consolidated entity had its traditional disadvantages in terms of population, but also had to deal with the fact that Napoleon kept winning every battle he fought. He didn't just have the resources of France to draw on, but at some points those of all of Continental Europe as well.

The series of battles that culminated in Napoleon's final defeat at Waterloo in 1815 was known as the "War of the Seventh Coalition". The fact that defeating Napoleon took seven coalitions should give an indication of how demanding these conflicts were.

> More than a fifth of all the major battles fought in Europe between 1490 and 1815 took place in just the twenty-five years after 1790. Before 1790, only a handful of battles had involved more than 100,000 combatants; in 1809, the battle of Wagram, the largest yet seen in the gunpowder age, involved 300,000. Four years later, the

battle of Leipzig drew 500,000, with fully 150,000 of them killed or wounded. During the Napoleonic period, France alone counted close to a million war deaths, possibly including a higher portion of its young men than died in World War I.[100]

Over and over again, the British would put together a coalition of European powers and fund it with generous subsidies. Over and over again Napoleon would defeat that coalition in battle. It's a testament to both the superiority of British finance and the already significant money-raising potential of the empire at this point that the British were able to keep coming back until Napoleon's winning streak finally ended in Russia.

The era of the Napoleonic wars saw the introduction of a surprisingly modern income tax in Britain, and the practice of announcing an annual budget each year, which is still maintained today.[101] The modernity of these budgeting practices was especially surprising given that the French Revolutionary armies and Napoleon himself, despite their reforming reputation, brought back a very old school thuggish approach of funding conquest with plunder.[102] British debt, income taxes, and a (relatively) higher degree of transparency and efficiency won the day.

The treasure expended was enormous. "The National debt, some £900 million, had nearly quadrupled its prewar figure; the interest and charges on the debt were £32 million, about a third of total government expenditure in 1815, two thirds in 1818…"[103] British naval supremacy was an expensive thing to maintain, but was clearly worthwhile. With two battles, at the Nile (1798) and Trafalgar (1805), the British

---

[100] P.7 Bell, David A. The First Total War
[101] P.143 Webb, R.K. Modern England 2nd Edition
[102] How do you cite a podcast? I'd highly, highly recommend the third season of Mike Duncan's excellent Revolutions podcast, which covers the era of the French Revolution in delightful detail.
[103] P.161 Webb, R.K. Modern England 2nd Edition

managed to beat the French badly enough that Napoleon simply stopped bothering to attempt an invasion for the duration of the war. Britain's territory was largely unscathed throughout the course of the war. In addition to subsidies to allies, Britain funded its own armies in Spain in the Peninsular War between 1807 and 1814. These armies then participated in the final battle of Waterloo in 1815 under Arthur Wellesley, the Duke of Wellington.

All in all it was a colossal struggle. And it won Britain the World. Alone among the era's major combatants, Britain managed to use the conflict to expand and consolidate its empire, building a world-wide system of control that lacked any serious competitor. The serious competition had been destroyed. What the British World System looked like is the topic of Chapter Five.

What It All Might Mean… Towards Transcendence

The finish of this Second Hundred Years' War is puzzling. The French had more people and land under their direct control than the British did. That old equation **(Land + People) *Organization = Power** should have come into play.

In the First Hundred Years' War (1337-1453) between France and England, the English were competitive with the French because they were much more organized than the French, allied with many petty princes on French territory, and to various extents, in control of large territories along France's coast. The English used French land and people to wage war on the French. Once the French got more unified, the English ability to compete faded away. King Henry VIII of England (r. 1509-1547) wasted most of the capital he'd raised by expropriating Church property on French campaigns that went nowhere. For most of recorded history, if the country with more land and people was unified, it would win. If it was easily divided, or poorly administered, it might fall apart.

The French were not divided or poorly administered either at the beginning of their Second Hundred Years' War with the British, or at the end. Louis XIV was able to impose a higher degree of control over France than any king before him. But he and his successors were continuously frustrated by the British and their allies. French monarchy eventually collapsed under the financial strains of this fight, but it was replaced by the Empire of Napoleon. This empire, with its vast citizen armies, was able to sweep away most European armies. By 1812 Napoleon, didn't just have the resources of France to draw upon, but also the resources of most of Europe up to the Russian border. In both quantity of land and people and quality of morale and leadership, Napoleon was the most powerful thug the world had seen to that point. He lost to the British anyway.

The Napoleonic wars were horrific, but there was a kernel of hope to be found there. The British that defeated Louis XIV and Napoleon represented a new type of thuggery. Make no mistake, it was still thuggery, but it was a real shift, and represented something new. The British could bring to bear more than just people and land. British victory showed that technological and financial power could beat the old equation. For the first time the wealth of the land did not determine victory. Thinkers like Alfred T. Mahan argued that what mattered most here was sea power, the British control of the sea, and he's certainly not wrong. But he may have missed a more important point. The British demonstrated that developing technologies and use of resources meant you didn't necessarily need conquest to prosper. The British did use the Napoleonic Wars to consolidate power in places like India and South Africa, but they weren't yet calling up Indian soldiers to fight in Europe. A "nation of shopkeepers" had beaten one of history's greatest conquerors mostly by using their scarcer resources more cleverly than he did.

The British and US World Systems both used the new tools of industrial and financial prosperity to craft new weapons of war and devise new and planet-wide forms of thuggery. But was any of it really necessary? If that old equation of Land + People = Power was broken, then what was the point of war anyway? The intensity and destruction of the wars since Napoleon quite rightly grabs our attention. The intensity of conflicts like the World Wars, however, might indicate how difficult and pointless land grabs have become. The ballooning costs incurred by the US Empire over the past century, in places like Vietnam and Iraq, for smaller and smaller gains in territory and influence, might be a reason for hope. The militarism of the British and US systems are a historical hangover, brought on by older ideas of power and prestige that no longer fit the post-industrialized world we live in.

We really could transcend this whole mess of conflict and suffering that has taken place over the past two centuries, and in all the centuries before them. A closer examination of the British World System should shed some light on the possibility.

"We desire no extension of Our present territorial Possessions; and while We will permit no aggression upon Our Dominions or Our Rights, to be attempted with impunity, We shall sanction no encroachment on those of others. We shall respect the Rights, Dignity, and Honour of Native Princes as Our own…"

Queen Victoria, in the 1858 proclamation that formalized the British Empire's most dramatic extension of its territorial possessions.[104]

Chapter 5
The British World System
1815-1860

Being on top is a very nice thing. People just do stuff for you. Following the July Revolution of 1830, France, the United Kingdom's traditional rival, tried to turn itself into Great Britain. The July Monarchy of Louis Phillippe set itself up as a constitutional one. The folks who manned the Paris barricades in 1830 were fighting for many of the ideas that British thinkers and (some) leaders of the time cherished. The leading figure of the July Monarchy's final government from 1840 to 1848 was Francois Guizot, a historian of Britain, described as the "arch-apostle of English-style constitutional monarchy."[105]

When you're on top, leading the world can seem effortless. People race to get in line. Between 1815 and 1848 it wasn't just France. The world could see that the United Kingdom had gotten something right, and

---

[104] Proclamation by the Queen in Council to the Princes, Chiefs and people of India (published by the Governor-General at Allahabad, November 1st 1858)
[105] P. 185 Evans, Richard J. The Pursuit of Power Europe 1815-1915

those that were aware of the model tried hard to emulate it. At certain moments, in certain places, you had revolutionaries fighting old establishments, even though both groups were trying to make their country more like Britain in different ways.[106] For a few decades in the first half of the nineteenth century, the Brits were the envy of the world! It should go without saying that this enthusiasm for the British model provided great opportunity for British merchants and financiers.

The US is having a similar moment on a much larger scale. The world's countries in the period of US dominance have more capacity than they did in the nineteenth century, and more independence to use in their pursuit of the US standard of living. The unquestioned notion that that standard of living is worth aiming for is beamed into everybody's heads and pockets through a propaganda machine that would amaze any ninteenth century imperialist. Though the "Washington Consensus" is looking a lot shakier after the 2008 financial crisis, we haven't left the moment of peak US dominance quite yet. Or at least I don't think we have. Have we? It's hard to say.

The Difficulty of Measuring Dominance

Talking about world systems is a tricky business. Which metrics are important? It's tempting to deal with the simple figures of people and square miles under a given empire's control. On this measure, the British Empire reached its peak in population and territory between the two World Wars in the third and fourth decades of the twentieth century. Nobody would argue that the British Empire was at any kind of peak of power and prestige at that point, however. Britain's informal empire was evaporating. In financial terms, World War I had turned the account books upside down. Britain had shifted from the world's largest creditor nation to one of its largest debtors. "In 1914 British public debt had stood at only £694.8 million. Five years later the figure

---

[106] I'm thinking of Spain during nineteenth century civil wars here specifically, but If you stretch the idea a bit I think it's true of multiple places in Europe and even the broader world, though perhaps later on that one.

had mounted to a dizzying £6.142 billion, of which £1 billion was owed to America, and not in sterling but in dollars."[107]   A lack of resources led to the evaporation of old privileges. Insurgent powers like Germany, Italy, and Japan were running roughshod over continents where Britain's informal empire had once held almost effortless sway. Most importantly, the United States had taken over the British role in Latin America and the Caribbean, and the Americans had the capacity to do so everywhere else, if only they could be convinced to do so. So no, the power of the British World System did not peak with its size in the 1920s and 1930s.

The economics of a world system are just as important as the political questions of people and territory. The economic and political factors fuel the even more difficult to measure factors of reputation and perception. These amorphous factors then feed back into the system to fuel more political and economic opportunities. Space is yet another important variable. In a world full of different countries and territories, with their own political, economic, cultural and ideological idiosyncrasies, the prestige or attractiveness of a given model can be at its height in one place, but already falling elsewhere. Long after the fall of Communism as a world-wide project, countries as diverse and North Korea and Algeria still hold onto elements of its ideology and culture. Right now, despite endless agonizing over how "embattled" democracy is in the developed world, we're seeing a bit of a democratic renaissance in less developed (and publicized) regions. We're seeing strong men like Robert Mugabe (Zimbabwe) and Najib Razak (Malaysia) drop like flies, and we're watching people power bring about real change on the streets of Algeria, Armenia, Bulgaria, and Ukraine, for better or worse.

Britain's Peak: The 1850s

---

[107] Loc 4965 Tooze, Adam The Deluge: The Great War, America and the Remaking of The Global Order 1916-1931

British dominance started in 1815 with victory over Napoleon. As we'll lay out in the next chapter, it ended with World War I between 1914 and 1918. Throughout this period, the power of the British Empire wasn't just "indispensable," it was unavoidable. The date range for dominance is easy to argue for historically. The question of a British peak is much more controversial.

The standard story is that the empire ended due to competition from other powers like Russia, France, Germany, Japan and the United States. This book argues that it was an internal change in the focus of the people leading the British World System that was much more important. This shift in focus had its roots in much earlier periods, and aspects of it could be seen in earlier conflicts and imperial strategies. But it was in the 1850s that the focus and character of British policy began to change in significant ways. This shift was sold as a response to the rise of other powers, but that wasn't what was really going on. British power was a good deal more secure than we are told in most history books, and the British government had a broader range of policy options than it claimed. The shift in British focus did more than anything else to bring about the British World System's demise. This is the central lesson that US leadership needs to learn.

The state of the British World System in the mid-nineteenth century is important because it was strikingly reminiscent of where we are now in the United States. Since 2001, the United States has been going through a shift in policy, a great mistake that I see as quite similar to the British shift in focus after the 1850s. Just because US Empire is passing its peak, or has passed through it already, doesn't mean we're through making an impact, or even that we are done growing in power and prestige. The choices the United States makes now are vastly more important to the survival of our world system than the growing power of any other country.

Formal and Informal Empire, Again

The British shift in focus or general mood, Britain's great mistake, was a shift in emphasis from "informal" to "formal" empire. Through the 1850s or so, the policies of the British Empire were more geared towards commercial profit and building "informal" networks of influence and financial power. After the 1850s, the British became more oriented towards "formal empire," the acquisition of vast new territories, almost completely free of any commercial logic or economic utility. They undertook this shift in focus in service of misguided notions of imperial prestige and an over-estimate of the threat posed by their imperial competitors.

I don't want to mislead with the specificity of the years I chose there. World systems are vastly complicated things, and in the 1800s the folks on the ground had a lot more power over imperial policy than they do today. Local British generals and administrators, and the shifting leadership in London, pursued policies that worked against the general mood of each period. In this chapter and the next, we'll talk about chunks of formal empire that were unwisely acquired before 1857. We will also talk about individuals, and even British Prime Ministers after 1857 who strenuously argued against the shift towards formal empire. It's not like the British public and leadership woke up one day and decided as a whole to do empire differently. The transition took decades, and there were always people who loudly proclaimed that the shift was unwise. But that shift in focus was real. The choice of 1857 as the turning point is somewhat arbitrary, but there were two general moods that prevailed over the course of the British World System. The initial focus on informal empire led to great success, and the latter focus on formal empire led to disaster.

Sound Familiar?

I fear that a similar shift in focus is in the process of destroying the US World System today. The focus of US foreign policy is beginning to move from informal to formal empire as well. The early periods of the

British and US World Systems involved great injustice. In the first phases of these systems, the British took territory, and the United States felled governments it didn't approve of, but these actions were usually taken with an eye towards hard-nosed economic realities. British expansion in India in the 1700s and early 1800s was about money-making first and foremost. When the CIA toppled governments in the second half of the twentieth century, it was almost always with the interests of some US or friendly multi-national in mind. The actions were taken with one eye always on the bottom line. If a policy, like the British repression of the Maori, or US support for dictators like Suharto in Indonesia or Marcos in the Philippines wasn't working out, these younger, savvier imperialists cut the cord and moved on.

It's the transition to dumber ideas of "Imperial Glory" or "Globo-cop credibility" that kill world systems. With the British, the shift in mentality meant the taking of large swathes of territory with little economic value out of paranoia, and a new focus on martial virtue that generated an accelerating series of mistakes. In the US it involves the ceaseless expansion of military bases, and a previously quite un-American worship of soldiers that has already resulted, in 2019, in a foreign policy run by generals. We are now seeing the semi-permanent occupation of places like Afghanistan. As just one example, the US military industrial complex's exploitation of Iraq (1991-2018) has already lasted almost twice as long as British control of that country (1917-1932). As this chapter tells the story of the British World System's initial, more successful phase, it will occasionally highlight the parallels with the US World System. Dominance sows the seeds of its own destruction, but those seeds don't have to be harvested.

Dominance Defined

Before we can get to the physical components of the British World System at the outset of the nineteenth century, we need to deal with two factors that made that system new and different. In Chapter One, I defined "dominance" as the ability to sit at the center of a world-wide system and reap the lion's share of the benefits. This had never happened before the nineteenth century, because the necessary tools did not exist. In 1815, the British had achieved a form of political hegemony that was not unique in history. The Mongols in the 1200s, the Romans for a few centuries, the Chinese at any one of a number of times in their history, and many others, had reached similar victories over their neighbors. But the British ability to forge a world-wide system with its political and martial success was new.

Two forces built this success, working in concert, accelerated by the calamity that was the Napoleonic Wars. **Industrialization,** after centuries of slow development, surged forward in the nineteenth century. Most are aware of this. What's less widely understood is that much of what we know as modern **Finance** was also invented in the early nineteenth century. Not all of it was invented in London, but British investors took the lead in exploiting everything that worked. These two forces, creating and funding new technologies, built a true world-wide system of control for the first time. These two forces created and funded the telegraph lines and steam ships that made physical control across the planet more practicable. More importantly, they provided the less tangible web of ownership of new structures like national debts and railroad corporations that made a complete world system of informal empire possible.

Industrialization

As we mentioned back in Chapter Two, the process of industrialization is a difficult thing to nail down. It's got something to do with those steam engines that started to become more prevalent in Britain in the early 1700s. Throughout the eighteenth century, mechanization and industrial wealth slowly accumulated. It was imperceptible at points, but it was in the first half of the 1800s that it became unavoidable. Dramatically improved steam engines got thrown on trains and ships.

New inventions spread mechanization to more and more industries. Later, the telegraph linked the world in a web of near instantaneous communication. The British lead in the process of industrialization was immense.

But it wasn't just about factories and steam engines. All of Britain's advantages, in government, literacy, and finance combined to put it in a leading position. And wow did it lead.

> During the French Revolutionary and Napoleonic wars, Britain had forged ahead economically, leaving the European Continent far behind. Per Capita industrial production in Britain in 1830 was almost twice that of Switzerland or Belgium, more than twice that of France, and three times that of the Habsburg Empire, Spain, Italy, Norway, Sweden, Denmark or the Netherlands.[108]

This industrial leadership was accompanied by leadership in other dimensions. Of the 3,128 newspapers that are estimated to have been published in 1828, almost half of them were published in English-speaking countries.[109] None of this would have been possible without the sophisticated pools of British capital that were available to be invested in the country and world-wide.

The British also benefitted from a smaller version of the dynamic that launched US dominance in the mid-twentieth century. In the 1790s and 1810s there wasn't much industrial capacity in Europe to destroy, but those decades of war acted to destroy a lot of industry's underpinnings on the Continent. Napoleon's Continental System did allow for some limited growth in textile manufacturing in Europe by shielding it from British competition. Those beginnings did eventually lead to industries that could compete seriously with Britain, but it took decades. The most important result of the Napoleonic wars was destruction. Agricultural land, capital, and lives were wasted on an extraordinary scale.

---

[108] P. 143 Evans, Richard J. The Pursuit of Power Europe 1815-1915
[109] P. 20 Bayly, C.A. The Birth of the Modern World 1780-1914

Amsterdam, which still held great importance as a financial center in the late 1700s, was invaded and occupied by the French, and eventually annexed by Napoleon[110], making London a much more secure destination for investment and credit by comparison. The British, as ever, were insulated from the destruction of the Napoleonic wars to a large degree. With the exception of some early skirmishes in Ireland, the United Kingdom's physical plant wasn't impacted in the slightest.

It's worth teasing out the consequences of just one of these new industrial technologies, the railroad. William Cronon's superb book Nature's Metropolis: Chicago and the Great West documents the many ways that railroads completely transformed a range of industries in one section of Britain's informal empire. Railroads could carry new bulk at new speeds. That was nice, but rivers could do that. Rivers weren't everywhere, however. The Rails could be. And rails didn't freeze. They didn't dry up or get blocked (usually). Commercial activity was freed from the tyranny of the seasons. The rails encouraged the conquest of the interiors of the Americas and later Africa that had largely been untouched by Europeans before the 1800s.

Railroads allowed for a new reliability and consolidation in trade. Frontier merchants didn't have to buy a year's worth of goods all at once, on long trips to commercial cities on major bodies of water. They could send orders up the rail lines on a monthly or even weekly basis. Everything got faster, and volumes went up exponentially. Commodities like grain weren't traded piecemeal in bags on the sides of rivers anymore. They could be stored in large grain elevators in places like Chicago, and flow through the economy like water. The increase in pace and volume was extraordinary.[111] The nineteenth

---

[110] Loc. 2124 Ferguson, Niall The House of Rothschild: Money's Prophets 1798-1848
[111] This whole section on railroads is drawn from William Cronon's extraordinary Nature's Metropolis: Chicago and the Great West. I only came across it in research for this book, but it's already easily in my top five historical books of all time, if not top two.

century introduced the possibility of reliably mounting economic growth from year to year.

This allowed for commodities to be financialized in futures markets that provided whole new arenas for wealth-getting. Chicago became rich, but many of its profits, and the bulk of its most prize investment opportunities streamed back to New York. New York became richer still, but many of its profits, and its most prize investments streamed back to London. And the nineteenth century was full of chains like the one that originated in America's hinterland, all of which terminated in British cities. Which leads us back to finance.

Finance

The story of Finance is less often told than that of industrialization, which is surprising given that its origins are in some ways more straightforward. The Napoleonic Wars were ruinously expensive. The volumes of money sent out by the British government to continental allies required complex financial systems. It's not like there were a bunch of boxes of silver lying around that London could ship directly to Austrian, Russian and Prussian soldiers. Napoleon's "Continental System" attempted to block all British trade with the European continent, throwing up considerable physical and administrative obstacles. Bankers found ways to surmount these obstacles and became rich in the process.

The British national debt itself was one of the main movers in building modern financial markets. After the war, unlike another country that runs a world system that I could mention, the British decided to pay down much of that debt, in full, with interest. The repayment of the debt left a large pool of money that wanted new opportunities. That mountain of cash allowed London bankers, led by the House of Rothschild, to create a new system for the originating and transfer of government debt, largely the one that we have today.

> The system they developed enabled British investors (and other rich "capitalists" in Western Europe) to invest in the debts of those states by purchasing internationally tradeable, fixed interest bearer (that is transferable) bonds. The significance of this system for nineteenth century history cannot be over-emphasized.[112]

If any country in the world wanted to borrow money, they now usually looked to London. And over the course of the century, almost all countries did. The payment of these debts was sometimes enforced by the Royal Navy.

A country's need to borrow money for war and other projects was not new to the nineteenth century. Jakob Fugger (1459-1525), a German Catholic banker and mining magnate, is a leading candidate for the title of richest man who ever lived. His family's fortunes were greatly enhanced by his position as banker to the Spanish and Austrian Habsburg ruling houses. But the Fugger family's fortunes were very dependent on those Habsburg kings and emperors. The Spanish crown's serial bankruptcies, followed by the generalized disaster for the Catholic cause that was the Thirty Years' War (1618-1648) pretty much wiped out the Fuggers. Like the Medici before them, their descendants survived as landed nobility, but their continent-moving financial power was gone. So was much of the financial system that had underpinned Europe's development.

For better and worse, London's innovations in the early nineteenth century liberated capital from the failings of individual monarchs, countries and religious causes. In a larger bond market the risk was distributed. We hear a lot about a few famous and fabulously wealthy nineteenth century banking families like the Morgans, the Barings and the Rothschilds, but the financial world was much larger and more diverse than that. By 1825 there were already many "other banks—some sixty in London and almost eight hundred outside..."[113] in

---

[112] Loc. 222 Ferguson, Niall The House of Rothschild: Money's Prophets 1798-1848
[113] P. 175 Webb, R.K. Modern England 2nd Edition

Britain. The owners of these banks still represented a small class of capitalists, but it was a far broader selection of plutocrats than the landed magnates of former centuries.

A country that became an unreliable risk found money much harder to come by. The power dynamic between money and nation-states shifted towards money, and it's still shifting in that direction today. London's bankers have not been wiped out by the many sovereign bankruptcies of the past two centuries. Individual banks fail, but the system founded in the early nineteenth century as a whole is much more durable than the Fuggers or the Medici were. The ability of international capital to preserve itself has had many negative consequences, the travails of Greece since 2009 being one prominent example, but there have been many positive effects as well. Wealth is preserved, not just for the Morgans and the shareholders of Citibank, but for others as well.

The railroads led to another revolutionary financial innovation—the modern stock market was invented in the nineteenth century as well. There are a number of romantic origin stories for stock markets before the 1800s. The New York Stock Exchange was famously formed under a buttonwood tree in 1792, and the Amsterdam Bourse dates back to 1602. But the shares traded by the Dutch in the early 1600s were mostly in a few trading companies. Two-hundred years later, the securities on offer on what would become the New York Stock Exchange weren't much more diverse. A few banks and insurance companies mostly. Prior to the nineteenth century, forming a corporation in Britain required an act of Parliament.

Railroads changed all that. The enterprises that built and maintained rail infrastructure needed large pools of capital for construction and maintenance, long before they made a dime, and for years to come. These new corporations couldn't be formed on the ad hoc basis that had governed much of capitalism to that date. Into the early twentieth century, most of the stocks available on public markets were railroad stocks. But the public stock markets and more easily set up corporate forms put together for railroads allowed all manner of enterprises to be built.

The British head start in trade, industry and finance gave London a lead in banking and legal services that hasn't completely disappeared even today. Industries like insurance, sovereign lending, and the "invisible" trade in services that made the world run kept Britain on top all the way up to 1914, even after they had ceded their edge in industry to places like Germany and the United States in the later 1800s. The unparalleled pool of capital a century of world dominance had given them meant that they could continue to profit off the success of competitors, even as their lead in more concrete industries slipped away. This was endlessly frustrating to aspiring competitors in New York and Berlin. German and American success in any economic endeavor just made Britain richer, because London financiers inevitably had a stake in the companies, railroads, and factories that built world-wide prosperity.

Industrial Heaven, Industrial Horror—A Brief Note On Atrocity

The modern rail era began in 1830 with the opening of the Liverpool and Manchester Railway. The opening celebrations were marred by one of the first railway accidents. William Huskisson, one of the leading figures in British government at the time, was killed when he wandered on to the tracks.[114] It was a fitting beginning.

The tales of rapid industrial progress and domination above may have given the impression that it was all sweetness and light. In the aggregate I believe the effect of industrialization has been positive. The fact that most anybody reading this book can read this book, and probably works in something other than back-breaking agricultural labor, is due to the economic and technological growth described above. But none of it was easy, and none of it was without cost. The

---

[114] P.268 Webb, R.K. Modern England 2nd Edition

economic dislocation involved was extraordinary. Whole ways of life disappeared. It was rough in the center of the British World System, but it was far worse on the peripheries.

There's a lot of horror in the story of British Empire. The Indian subcontinent was probably the most abused of Britain's direct possessions. The forcible reorganization of India's economy towards British priorities led to a famine that killed as many as 5 million people in 1876-1878. That was only the largest Indian famine brought about by the British. The First War of Indian Independence was crushed with extraordinary British brutality in 1857, with men shot out of cannons, and tens of thousands of civilians massacred in multiple cities and across the countryside. Those were just the most infamous results of a multi-century system of racist oppression, and they are fairly well known. But to illustrate just how important industrialization and finance were, and to provide another little parable on the importance of informal rather than formal empire, I think it's worth adding a bit to the standard story of the horror of British India. Many historians now argue that one of the worst things Britain did to India was de-industrialize it.

European traders were first drawn to India in the 1500s and 1600s by the beauty and sophistication of its textiles. In 1750, twenty-five percent of the world's manufacturing took place on the Indian Subcontinent and thirty-three percent took place in China.[115] The history of the past two-hundred years has been all about the benefits that accrue to a country that can benefit from manufacturing. As important as it is in the twenty-first century to develop a high-tech service industry, the success of that industry still depends on a large manufacturing base. The differing levels of success of China and India today illustrate this. The modern Indian tech and business process outsourcing industries are far superior to China's. It doesn't really matter that much. China's development over the past forty years was

---

[115] P.6 Global Economic History: A Very Short Introduction

more focused on industry, and its GDP is now five times larger than India's rather than the fifty percent larger it was in 1970. The production manufacturing allows creates a greater level of production in all sectors, and a higher degree of specialization in the economy. Factory workers are probably better off than their parents who worked in agriculture, but whole new classes of owners, administrators, and urban dwellers also exist because of that manufacturing. Industrialization is the fuel that makes modern life and the very idea of widespread leisure possible. By 1913, the Chinese share of world manufacturing was down to four percent and the Indian share was down to one percent.[116] All of that potential was lost to these Asian powerhouses for over a century. And it wasn't just "lost". It was stolen. Mostly by the British.

It's common to look at the "Great Divergence" in economic performance between Europe and the traditional manufacturing powers of Asia as just a question of European inventors being cleverer at machine building. This is sort-of true. Europeans came up with more of the machines that facilitated industrialization. It was British inventors who drove the cost of textile spinning down far enough that India's export market was no longer viable. But it was also about coercion. It wasn't just that the Europeans were producing more, Asian countries were forced out of their traditional industries. There is probably no industry more important to the Industrial Revolution than cotton, and its use in the production of clothing and other textiles.[117] In the early modern era, India led this industry. Britain initially helped drive the growth of Indian textile production. "European cloth exports from India amounted to an estimated 30 million yards in 1727, but increased to some 80 million yards annually by the 1790s."[118] The British dominated this international industry, and used that power to steadily drive India into less and less valuable parts of that industry. In 1701 Parliament banned the import of printed textiles, so that the

---

[116] P.6 Global Economic History: A Very Short Introduction
[117] Sven Beckert's Empire of Cotton: A Global History forcefully makes this argument and I'm convinced.
[118] P. 46 Beckert, Sven, Empire of Cotton: A Global History

profitable finishing work could be done in Britain rather than India. In 1774, they went ahead and banned the import of all Indian manufactured cloth entirely.[119] Manufacturing was reserved for the British, while the Indians could only produce raw materials. Though Indian-produced textiles could still be exported to China and Africa for a time, the ships they were travelling in and the networks of wealth they were serving were British.[120] By the time Britain adopted the ideology of free trade, British manufacturers had reached productivity levels that Indian manufacturers could not compete with. Competition was a factor, but coercion came first. In the Indian province of Bihar, "The share of the work force in manufacturing dropped from twenty-two percent around 1810 to nine percent in 1901."[121] The British wanted raw materials for its own factories, so that's what India was forced to focus on, to the detriment of its own economic development. For centuries.

Informal empire meant that this wasn't just happening in places that flew the British flag. China's de-industrialization was a product of British men with guns as well. During the mid-nineteenth century Opium wars the British used their advanced gun boat technology to force open Chinese markets. Both of these vast countries, that had been used to doing things their own way, were now forced into the British system. This book attempts to cover the great horrors of British Imperial history. They are, quite rightly, the centerpiece of the national stories of countries all over the world. But the lost potential wrought by these commercial, industrial and financial changes is just as significant.

There's a flip side to all this. In committing all these horrors, the British and US World Systems also created vast new potential. China and India probably wouldn't have space programs at this point without the changes they had to make to respond to the British and US Empires.

---

[119] P. 48 Beckert, Sven, Empire of Cotton: A Global History
[120] P. 49 Beckert, Sven, Empire of Cotton: A Global History
[121] P.59 Global Economic History: A Very Short INtroduction

But we must always acknowledge the costs of these changes if we are to be honest about the achievement. Being honest about the horror makes it easier to sell the benefits. And the benefits were real, first for the British, but eventually for everybody else.

Reforming Thuggery

The wealth that was pouring into Britain, coupled with the unique stability bequeathed by geography, allowed British social and political systems to drift further away from their thuggish origins over the course of the 1800s, as they were imposing their thuggish world system on a progressively greater and greater sphere. Throughout the 1700s, ideas for reform and improvement had rocketed around Europe and over the Atlantic. These ideas are typically collected under the title of "the Enlightenment", but that implies a unity and agreement in these ideas that was not present. The fact that (small r) republican thinkers like Virginia's Thomas Jefferson, and "Enlightened Despots" like Catherine the Great of Russia were somehow both representatives of the same movement should give you a sense of the diversity of thought we're talking about here. Britain was uniquely well suited to put these reforming ideas into practice. The United States was still a sparsely populated place in the early 1800s, and after the French Revolutionary and Napoleonic Wars, Europe's aristocrats had had quite enough of new ideas. For the first half of the nineteenth century they fought a losing battle against any sort of reform while the British constantly experimented with it.

It's a fool's errand to attempt any systematic description of nineteenth century British thought in a paragraph. As one historian puts it: "The treacherous morass of early nineteenth century intellectual life offers one of the greatest challenges to historians of Britain today."[122] There were many conflicting strands, from the conservative emphasis on

---

[122] P. 184 Webb, R.K. Modern England 2nd Edition

incrementalism descending from Edmund Burke, to laissez-faire classical economics of folks like David Ricardo, and the more interventionist utilitarian ideas of Bentham and Mill. Utopian socialists like Robert Owen had an impact, and by the mid-century, Karl Marx was laboring away in the British library. It was all a glorious mess. Though the government was controlled by aristocrats well into the twentieth century, they had no monopoly on the development of ideas for reform, which bubbled up from new capitalist classes, and the first modern working classes. What made Britain different from everywhere else was the fact that wealth and stability meant that many of these ideas could be tried out, improved upon and developed further.

The Glorious Revolution had secured a place for Parliament in the governing of the country, but it was only during the nineteenth century that that institution began to evolve into something that we might recognize today. The tremendous dislocations brought about by wealth and industrialization inspired constant changes. The medieval British systems of law and society were never swept away, they were slowly changed. This meant that Britain, even today, retains many deeply anachronistic institutions, from royalty all the way down to the hilariously medieval government of the city of London.[123] But the British were also able to take steps that placed them decades ahead of any competitors. Small crises and electoral pressure led to a steadily evolution away from thuggery in the institutions governing law, trade, finance, and even labor. The predecessors of labor unions were already legalized, though quite constrained, by the 1820s.[124] To be sure, the plight of the British working person; child labor, the "satanic mills"

---

[123] The "City of London", the square mile at the heart of the mega-city, has an ancient government distinct from the "Greater London Area". There is a modern, popularly elected Mayor for Greater London. The "Lord Mayor of London" is a different office, with its own privileges and powers, some of which go back to the thirteenth century. The Lord Mayor is elected by businesses as well as people, in a convoluted system it's not worth any of our time to try to understand. This would all be very charming if the City of London didn't also have somewhat opaque and similarly confusing regulatory powers over the immensely powerful financial companies headquartered within it's borders.

[124] P. 182 Webb, R.K. Modern England 2nd Edition

and all that; was very, very dire. But the British system was already developing the outlets necessary to diffuse these pressures, and let them play themselves out in political concessions rather than bloodshed.

It's a standard argument that the reform movements of the 1800s allowed Britain to sit out the revolutionary cataclysm that rocked Europe in 1848. I'd go a bit further than that, and suggest that there were already forces at work in early-nineteenth-century Britain that helped inoculate the United Kingdom against twentieth century revolution as well.

The old aristocratic thugs were still present in Britain, and still controlled the government. Their openness to new ideas, and new men (after a generation or two), however, distinguished them from the desperately reactionary aristocracy on the continent. In 1832, the Parliament passed the Great Reform Act, restructuring parliamentary representation. It didn't massively expand the franchise, but it cleared out a lot of the dark ages debris that cluttered up the system, and in retrospect it is seen as another one of those great steps towards modern representative democracy and the eventual demise of the old British ruling class. Surprisingly, the government that brought about the Great Reform Act was the most aristocratic Britain had seen since the 1700s.[125]

In looking at England and Scotland in the 1800s you can begin to see the outlines of our modern world. A free press, public opinion, finance, labor, science, working life, the sandwich, everything we know today was popularized and improved upon in Britain in this period. It represented a decisive break from the thuggish system of government and society that had dominated human history since the agricultural revolution. Unfortunately, the wealth that underpinned this happy move forward came from a hyper-charged, industrialized thuggery

---

[125] P. 195 Webb, R.K. Modern England 2nd Edition

directed towards everybody else. This thuggery did come with a few silver linings for the rest of the world though.

Free Labor

Many claim that the British Empire's outlawing of slavery was a testament to the virtue of the British Empire… and they are absolutely right. There are a great many ways to explain away the inherent goodness of the move. I agree with all of them. The British were free to take feel-good measures against slavery earlier in the nineteenth century, while funding and profiting from its massive expansion in the United States. Chattel slavery was quickly replaced with slavery-like systems of indentured servitude exploiting Indians and Chinese as well as Africans. Britain's vile empire in Africa occasionally included forced labor into the twentieth century, even after the Second World War. But after the nineteenth century, thanks to the British, it was no longer legal for people to be property. This may seem like a low bar today, but it's a bar that no civilization in human history got over before the British.

From the later eighteenth century, the rising British mercantile classes became more and more disenchanted with the slavery that had generated so much of their wealth. The Slave Trade Act of 1807 banned the trade in slaves, over the opposition of the wealthy planters of the British Caribbean. By 1833, the wealth of those planters had been crowded out enough by newer industrial wealth to abolish slavery throughout the British Empire. There were numerous exceptions in the law itself. Slavery was preserved in territories (chiefly India) governed by the East India Company until the Indian Slavery Act of 1843. Slave owners received compensation, and the freed slaves were often forced into abusive apprenticeships and indentured servitude, a practice that would be used to replace slave labor across the empire. As we'll get into below, US independence allowed Britain to continue to benefit from slavery, and its abolition was enforced with differing degrees of rigor in different places. Regardless, hereditary chattel slavery was done away with by the British Empire and that's an accomplishment, even if an imperfect one.

Slavery had been an omnipresent institution. As its defenders loved to point out, it was endorsed by the Bible and endorsed by Aristotle. The horror of one human owning another was a key part of civilizations across the globe. Over the course of the nineteenth century, British influence helped to end it. But before the British worked against slavery, they perfected it. The revulsion that British reformers felt for slavery as an institution had a lot to do with the unique horror of European slavery as an institution. The plantations of the Americas are probably the first works of humanity that deserve the adjective "industrial". Long before textile work had moved out of homes and into factories, European-designed slave plantations in the Americas centralized production and the consumption of labor to an unprecedented degree. A few pre-industrial slave workplaces, like mines for example, may have offered similar levels of abuse and mortality, but it was the Europeans that introduced whole island, and finally continent-spanning economies based on little else. In their heydays in the seventeenth and eighteenth century sugar islands, and nineteenth century cotton states, these industries were the most lucrative and transformative businesses on the planet. The wealth that the vicious industrial thuggery of European and American slavery provided was a precondition to Britain's producing a society that could conceive of abolishing slavery. So the British World System's legacy with slavery was, in the end, positive, but more mixed than the British Empire's boosters will commonly let on.

Free Trade

The British Empire, formal and informal, had initially been put together with a Mercantilist mindset. Trade was something to kill for, and England fought three wars with the Dutch to win it. This began to change in the 1820s,[126] influenced by the ideas of founders of the discipline of economics like Adam Smith (1723-1790) and David Ricardo (1772-1823). In the 1840s, with the repeal of the Corn Laws in 1846, and other measures by Prime Minister Robert Peel[127], free trade became the dominant ideology of empire. The idea was that free trade would allow countries to focus on what they were best at. Of course, with its industrial and financial might, Britain naturally owned the higher value manufacturing and investing opportunities. The explicit intention of many British free trade advocates was that England become the "Workshop of the World". This relegated the rest of the world to raw material production. Those countries that managed to enrich themselves in a sustainable way under this system, like the US, Germany and Japan usually did so by breaking with free trade orthodoxy and implementing some degree of protection. The most important factor for industrial development was "a state's ability to isolate its domestic manufacturing efforts from competition, especially from Britain."[128]

The broader system and concept of free trade, and the interchange of goods and peoples that it brought about, however, did the world an immense amount of good in the long run. Though it's now clear that the full adoption of free trade in a nineteenth century context wasn't the best thing for the development of the global south, it was certainly an improvement over the earlier concepts of trade, which were little better than piracy. Scratch that, the dominant approach to trade prior to the British introduction of free trade concepts WAS piracy. It's clear that free trade did not instantly provide the benefits to the whole world that were promised. But the system of "War Capitalism"[129] that preceded it offered nothing but slavery and death. The ideas of comparative advantage and free competition have been tremendously

---

[126] P.224 Webb, R.K. Modern England 2nd Edition
[127] P.273 Webb, R.K. Modern England 2nd Edition
[128] P. 157 Beckert, Sven Empire Of Cotton: A Global History
[129] To use Sven Beckert's memorable phrase from the early chapters of Empire Of Cotton: A Global History

useful. Now that the rest of the world has gained the capacity to utilize the concepts and tools of the world system they were forced into, we're finally beginning to build that Utopia that was promised by British economists two centuries ago.

Freedom Through the Sword

The attempt to end slavery, and the beginnings of free trade go down in the win column for the British World System. They aren't unambiguous wins, but they are wins nonetheless. These concepts, however, were often utilized to justify coercive behavior. It was an earlier version of the weaponization of human rights that we see in the US World System. It was nowhere near as systematized or powerful as the US version, but anti-slavery, and pro-free trade enforcement was used as a tool of British foreign policy. The fact that Britain attempted to coerce the whole world into giving up the slave trade is hard to quibble with. The fact that it was done selectively is not. British allies got to keep trading slaves for decades longer than British enemies did.

Over the first half of the 1800s, the British slowly built up their West Africa Squadron, a naval group with the mission of capturing slave traders, and liberating slaves. The British felt their way forward carefully from 1807. They got the rest of Europe on board with the abolition of trade in slaves through negotiation. This was easier after the Napoleonic wars, when only the significantly weakened Spain still had a large slave empire. For the rest of the world, the British generally used coercion. But it was unevenly applied. The West Africa Squadron grew in force and effectiveness over the first half of the 1800s. But in East Africa the British didn't do much to stop slavery at all, and in fact may have aided it. Informal British Empire was exerted through a relationship with the slave-trading empire of the Sultans of Oman and Zanzibar.[130] These Sultans were promoted as a counterweight to the more threatening Ottomans and Iranians. Throughout the nineteenth

---

[130] P. 215 Darwin, John After Tamerlane: The Rise and Fall of Global Empires 1400-2000

century the British would repeatedly tell their allies to stop trading in slaves, despite being well aware that slave trading was their main business, and it was expanding rapidly. It was only in the 1870s, after the US abolition of slavery, that the British decided to finally enforce all the treaties on slavery it had made with the sultans.

In East and West Africa, and all over the world, with the adoption of these "globo-cop" responsibilities, the British claimed the right to interfere with shipping. The excuse for intervention may have been virtuous, but the power it gave Britain was immense. Anti-slavery enforcement added teeth to Britain's ownership of the seas. It also provided one of the "humanitarian" justifications for conquest when Britain decided to swallow up half of Africa in the latter nineteenth century. British anti-slavery is a positive legacy, but a more ambiguous one than we are customarily told.

British enforcement of their freshly minted free trade orthodoxy was considerably less ambiguous. We can all agree that slavery was something worth fighting against. Fighting to force the entire world to adopt new-fangled commercial ideas your Scottish philosophers just came up with is a lot harder to justify. Throughout the nineteenth century the British acted as if every civilization in the world was dealing with the same legal concepts they were. If a British merchant was abused somewhere, the British would hold the ruler of that territory responsible, whether or not that magistrate had any involvement with the interaction, or the power to deal with the situation one way or the other. If a territory had centuries-long traditions related to trade that conflicted with British ideas, then those ideas had to be changed by force. The Opium Wars against China, which we will deal with below, are the most famous example, but they are not the only ones.

Defenders of British Empire confuse the fact that positive elements of its system eventually spread all over the world with the idea that the

British Empire itself was somehow "good" or "virtuous". Some writers take nineteenth century British Imperialists at their word and pretend with them that they were acting out some sort of "civilizing mission". Many of them no doubt believed that they were doing good. But the true legacy of the British Empire was extraordinary destruction and dislocation in the name of profit. I believe that this did, eventually, produce a better world, but that doesn't mean the British Empire should be uncritically celebrated. The balance of this chapter and the next should make that pretty clear.

The Physical British World System ca. 1815-1860

Physical territory won during the Napoleonic Wars played an important part in British dominance, but it did so in a way that differed importantly from the massive swathes of land scooped up heedlessly in the later nineteenth century. Those later chunks of formal empire in Asia and Africa were economically useless to differing degrees. The Napoleonic War acquisitions in the early 1800s, on the other hand, were much more valuable, and served to improve and expand a massive, commercial, informal empire. Britain's naval and financial dominance, coupled with its desire to stake claims to strategic territory before the French could, changed the world entirely. "Where there had been twenty-three colonies in 1792, there were forty-three by 1816. The Empire had contained 12.5 million people in 1750: Seventy years later it was 200 million strong."[131] This growth occurred in part because of a less tolerant attitude towards local rivals. Everybody was a potential French ally, so other power centers could not be tolerated. The bulk of the growth of formal empire during the Napoleonic wars took place in India, where the last of the local rivals to British power were wiped out. It was India's wealth and complexity that made formal empire a viable commercial proposition there.

In defeating Napoleon, the British also picked up places like Malta, in the center of the Mediterranean, that allowed them to make that sea a British lake. Small, easily defensible ports on the island of Mauritius, and larger, strategically vital territories like the Cape of Good Hope at the southern tip of Africa, and the island of Ceylon (modern Sri Lanka)[132] allowed the British to dominate shipping lanes. Unlike later acquisitions, taking these places actually made strategic sense.

---

[131] Loc 815 Brendon, Piers The Decline and Fall of The British Empire
[132] P. 25 Evans, Richard J. The Pursuit of Power Europe 1815-1915

The control of the world's trade routes positioned Britain supremely well to take advantage of all the industrial, logistical, and technological expansion that flourished so extraordinarily in the mid-nineteenth century. Britain's position meant that everybody else's growth worked to their advantage as well. The development of the American and European interiors most often involved goods shipped on British ships, and produced raw materials for Britain's factories decades before industry really got going elsewhere. And British finance encircled the world.

Europe

The Napoleonic wars left Europe completely altered. The same five powers that had been emerging in the 1600s and 1700s were still present but they were all irrevocably changed. The Darwinian forces of twenty-three years of war had streamlined and altered them. The Holy Roman Empire that had nominally run much of Central Europe for almost 1,000 years, was abolished in 1806. Its **Austrian** rulers now formed a new empire, that was much less German, but had finally shed much of the Medieval politicking that had made its dominions so ungovernable. The German remnants of the Holy Roman Empire had been consolidated from well over 300 separate territorial entities to just 39. First among them was **Prussia**, which would eventually consolidate 38 of those 39 territories (not Austria!) into a united Germany in 1871. Venice, among many other independent Italian territories, had been swept away. Much of Italy was under direct or indirect Austrian control, though the Kingdom of Sardinia was more independent, and eventually became the main state mover in Italian unification, finally accomplished in 1871. **Russia** had gained new confidence as Napoleon's destroyer, and asserted a right to intervene against European Revolutionaries throughout the first half of the nineteenth century. **France**, under its briefly restored monarchy, was quickly welcomed back into the European state system.

Twenty-three years of war had left a Europe that badly wanted peace. Its traditional leaders were quite confident that they had had enough of revolution. Monarchs were restored everywhere in 1815, and even installed in places that hadn't had them for centuries, like the Dutch Republic (now the Kingdom of the Netherlands). Europe's great powers met at the Congress of Vienna in 1815 to organize a new order of peace and anti-revolutionary reaction. The United Kingdom was a key player at the Congress of Vienna. Lord Castlereagh, the British Foreign Secretary from 1812-1822 was tremendously unpopular by the end of his career. So unpopular that it may have contributed to his suicide. He was loathed by the British public for helping to set up a new system of aristocratic reactionaries on the continent. It wasn't seen as consistent with "English Liberties" but it served the British Empire very well.

The peace of Europe's nineteenth century is often over-sold. Neither German nor Italian unification came cheap. The Ottoman Empire's slow disintegration in Eastern Europe prompted brutal massacres and a series of ruinous wars of defense against Russia, the Austrians, and a range of newly independent peoples. In the long-term, restored absolute monarchy in Europe was a failure. A series of revolutionary movements, most famously those of 1848, forced a diverse array of constitutions and parliaments onto most of Europe's princes, with the exception of Russia. Austrian concessions to Hungary produced a new entity known as Austria-Hungary in 1867. France saw the fall of two more kings before mid-century. There were plenty of major and minor wars and revolutions. Hundreds of thousands died violently during Europe's "peaceful nineteenth century".

With the major exception of the Crimean War (1853-1856), however, all of these conflicts proceeded without lengthy intervention by British soldiers. The myth of Europe's peaceful nineteenth century is one of many artifacts of the fact that a lot of world history gets written in English. There was a ton of strife and suffering in Europe in the nineteenth century. It's just that the British didn't have much to do with it. So according to English-language world history, Europe had a peaceful century.

Britain's Informal Empire in Europe

Britain retained a leading role in Europe. London's position at the center of government debt markets meant that all governments in Europe sought British funding and British expertise. It's not common to see Europe in this period as part of the British "informal empire", but it probably should be. The general opacity and complexity of nineteenth century financial history makes this obscure, but it's likely that the role of British bankers across Europe was similar to the role played by Wall Street in today's US world-system. The sentiments of British markets limited and guided the kinds of projects, and types of governing systems that any country in the world could undertake. This was just as true in Europe as anywhere else.

Britain used force to exert its will in Europe, just as it more famously did in China and other regions. One largely forgotten historical episode illustrates the way that Britain's "informal empire" in Europe had a harder edge when it was judged necessary. Take the independent state of Belgium for example. It exists because Britain wanted it to. After the Napoleonic wars, what had most recently been the "Austrian Netherlands" was grafted onto the old Dutch Republic to create a larger Kingdom of the Netherlands. In one of Europe's many Revolutionary flare ups in 1830, the "Belgians" decided they wanted to be independent. The Dutch were prepared to fight to keep that from happening. None of Europe's other powers[133] wanted to give an inch to revolution, and they didn't like carving up kingdoms. But the British wanted to make sure "Belgium" didn't get attached to France, and liked the idea of a smaller, weaker state across the water. So they made it happen. The British recognized Belgium in 1831, got the other powers to agree that it would be a neutral state, and blockaded the Dutch in 1832 until they agreed to let the territory go.[134] This is exactly the sort of imperial skullduggery we all recognize in the US creation of Panama in 1903, or the British theft of Hong Kong from China in 1842. But we don't talk about it that way, because we're very invested in the idea that European countries were real competitors to Britain rather than just another part of Britain's informal empire.

The British government had a preferred side in all of Europe's revolutions and wars. They often used their Navy to make sure their side won. Britain's role as one of the five major European powers led them to be involved in everything to some degree, and British financial power meant that its preferences had to be considered, if not always followed to the letter. But the streamlined, reactionary Europe of the first half of the nineteenth century didn't cost the British government a great deal of soldiers or treasure. Europe only added to British wealth, through trade and government debt. For the first half of the nineteenth century, Europe was a well-balanced, well-managed profit center for the British.

The Mediterranean the Middle East

In earlier eras, Mediterranean trade was a great prize to be won. This was much less true in the first half of the 1800s, after the British had already largely won it. For millennia, prior to Portugal and Spain's

---

[133] The French were a bit more ambivalent, and more happy to play along with Britain on Belgium, perhaps because they'd just had a bit of revolution themselves.
[134] P. 303 Webb, R.K. Modern England 2nd Edition

development of maritime routes to Asia, the Mediterranean had been big business. All the Asian luxuries that Europe wanted came through the Mediterranean before the later 1400s. This was as true for the Caesars as it was for the early Habsburgs. The discovery of trade routes around Africa and across the Americas slowly but relentlessly chipped away at the Mediterranean's importance. The trade of the vast Ottoman Empire was still an important enough prize to the English in the 1600s to battle the Spanish and the Dutch over. From the 1600s through the Napoleonic wars, the Western Mediterranean had great significance for British conflicts against Spain and France.

The party was largely over by the early nineteenth century. The wealthy Italian cities of earlier centuries were no longer very powerful, and were most prized as tourist destinations for Britain's wealthy. In the 1810s and 1820s, the British partnered with France to finally crush the Muslim Pirate kingdoms of North Africa, not out of Christian crusading vigor, but out of a very modern crusade, the one against the slave trade. From the 1830s on, Britain was quite happy to let the French build a large but strategically insignificant West African empire starting from Algeria. There were occasional flare-ups over French actions in this arena, but they rarely lasted for long. France after 1815 had a relationship with Britain broadly similar to the proud but profoundly junior partnership Britain now has with the United States. The Ottoman Empire had transitioned from a threat to all Christendom up to the 1500s, to a valuable trading partner in the 1600s, to a fading power to be shored up by the later 1700s.

Britain had held the Western entrance to the Mediterranean at Gibraltar since 1713. In 1814, Malta became officially British as well. The Maltese islands sit in the middle of the Mediterranean, at its narrowest point between Sicily and modern Libya. These islands had been the subject of titanic struggles in the past, and would be again in the future.

Failing to take Malta in 1565 had been the high-water mark of Suleiman the Magnificent's Ottoman Empire. Failing to take Malta during the Second World War doomed Hitler's attempt to take North Africa as well. During the early 1800s though, holding Malta meant that the Mediterranean was essentially a British lake. The opening of the Suez canal in 1869 snapped Asian trade back through the Mediterranean, making the Middle East, and Egypt in particular much more important again. But that's a story for the next chapter.

Britain's main Mediterranean preoccupation before the 1860s was the Ottoman Empire in the East. And Britain's growing at the root of this preoccupation we find Russia. The Tsars were very interested in taking Istanbul and the entrance to the Black Sea. Russia had won an almost unbroken series of victories against the Ottoman Sultans from the late the 1700s and in to the 1800s. Britain wanted to keep the Russians bottled up in the Black Sea, so the government did what they could to shore up the Ottomans. This often conflicted with Britain's religious sympathies for the many different flavors of Christians the Ottomans ruled in Eastern Europe and the Levant. Government attempts to help the Ottomans were further complicated by broad sympathy for the "Greek home of Western Civilization" among learned Britons. "British sympathies were overwhelmingly on the side of the rebels; classically educated men who helped to make opinion, seeing (incorrectly) the resurgence of a great civilization, supported the revolt with their money, their military services, and their lives."[135] The events and progress of the Greek War of Independence (1821-1829) often had more to do with this clash within British politics than it did with the war itself.

One sympathizer with the Greeks in particular, Vice-Admiral Coddington, took it upon himself to disregard his orders, and destroy

---

[135] P. 171 Webb, R.K. Modern England 2nd Edition

the Ottoman-Egyptian Navy at the Battle of Navarino in 1827, in partnership with the French and the Russians. Prior to the battle of Navarino, the Ottomans had been largely successful in suppressing the Greek revolt. Navarino, combined with yet another Russian land war against the Ottomans, secured Greek independence. The European powers negotiated Greece's borders and installed a German king from Bavaria in 1832.

Britain's important strategic priority of Ottoman strength had been defeated by British public opinion and its effects on one belligerent Vice-Admiral. Greek independence encouraged the nationalist passions that ripped the Ottoman Empire to shreds over the next eighty years, culminating in the Apocalypse that ended the British World System, the First World War. This misstep is more glaring when we consider just how overwhelming British informal empire was in this region.

British sympathy for the Greeks was no bar to taking action when British commercial interests were disrespected. In 1850, the interests of some British merchants prompted the British to blockade the country, and quickly seize the Greek Navy.[136] British power was regularly exerted against the Greek's great enemy as well. Britain would not take a direct hand in the operation of Ottoman finances and government until later in the century, but the great Turkish need for help against the Russians meant that they were eager to keep the British happy. In 1845 a consul-general in Beirut felt that he was offended by the local Ottoman governor. A British warship was dispatched to make these feelings clear, but one historian claims that it wasn't really necessary to get the governor fired.[137] The Ottomans, even at this early date, were too reliant on the British to disregard their wishes.

---

[136] P. 176 James, Lawrence The Rise and Fall of the British Empire
[137] P. 176 James, Lawrence The Rise and Fall of the British Empire

In the first half of the 1800s, Britain's formal empire in the Mediterranean was just a few islands. But its informal empire made it the master of the region. Though this was a less important region than it had been for thousands of years, the British managed to knit the Mediterranean coasts together in a single network of trade and power for the first time since the Eastern Roman (Byzantine) project had failed at the hands of the Muslim caliphs all the way back in the 7th century. Growing French control of Northwest Africa was part of this system, not really a competitor to it. Britain's ability to quickly grab control of anything that mattered was demonstrated with the French construction of the Suez canal in 1869. The French quickly found themselves involuntary partners with the British, and in 1882, the British took all of Egypt, launching one of history's more shameful episodes, the Scramble for Africa, a topic for the next chapter.

The Settler Colonies

Britain's economic growth led to, and was in turn fed by, breakneck population growth. In 1800 the population of England, Wales, Scotland, and Ireland was around 16 million, and France's was 30 million. By 1900, those same British home territories had a population of almost 40 million, drawing more or less equal with metropolitan France. They had made up this gap despite spinning off large populations into places like Canada (5 million in 1900), Australia (3.7 million in 1900), New Zealand (800,000 in 1900). Not all of these people were from Britain of course, and Canada in particular had a significant population in 1800.[138] But the home territories had also spun off millions of people to the United States, and to many other territories throughout Britain's informal and formal empire.

---

[138] I think Canada had a European population of a little under a million in 1800, the figures are not super clear. https://en.wikipedia.org/wiki/Population_of_Canada

Make no mistake—Canada, Australia, and New Zealand were very much colored red on those British Empire maps. But the folks who set the policy for these territories had learned the lesson of the War of American Independence very well. There's a reason why we don't hear much about wars of independence for these colonies. There weren't any. There were controversies, and ideological struggles over sovereignty, but they were resolved peacefully for the most part. The policies for all of these colonies were set in this period of British dominance, and they were quite liberal. Canada was largely self-governing after 1848, and Australia was governed as five separate crown colonies from the 1850s. In 1901 the Australian colonies federated. These countries are independent today, but some of them still have the Queen of England on their currency and there is remarkably little bad blood between them and the "mother country". This is the result of an enlightened policy from the imperial center (towards white people). They were part of Britain's "formal empire" but they were intentionally allowed to fade into "informal empire".

This was quite an accomplishment, and unequaled among any of the European empires. Spain is successfully rebuilding bridges with its former colonies in the Americas today, but the separation was lengthy and unpleasant. The legacy of the largest French attempt at a settler colony in Algeria is remarkably vicious. For almost a century and a half, France attempted to turn Algeria into an integral part of their Kingdom (or Republic, Empire, or Commune) across the Mediterranean. Generations of French settlers worked to force French culture on a much more numerous Arab and Berber population that very much did not want them there. The Algerians won their independence in 1962 after a conflict that killed 300,000 people. As many as a million French colonists returned to France, some after generations in Africa. Canada and Australia are both among the top twenty largest economies in the world today, and New Zealand is becoming legendary as one of the nicest places to live on Earth. France retains many economic ties to Algeria, but despite its petroleum wealth, it's not a place people are usually very optimistic about.

The success of the British settler colonies was of course a legacy of viciousness to indigenous peoples as much as it was a legacy of Britain's mid-nineteenth century success. But even here we can see British imperial forces exhibiting some surprisingly good sense. In 1860s New Zealand, the conflict with the native Maori population escalated. At one point there were 18,000 imperial troops battling the vastly outnumbered and outgunned native population. Just 4,000 Maori fighters managed to tie down this force through innovative fighting and sheer determination. Eventually the British general involved had had enough, and decided that this was a terrible waste of time and resources, pulling out entirely by 1870.[139]

The repression of the Maori of course continued, but the sensible cost-benefit analysis of those running the empire kept it from being much worse. Despite the diminished but savage efforts of the white New Zealanders, the Maori are still 15 percent of the New Zealand population today. The Maori have real representation and power in New Zealand and world culture[140] that will endure. In later decades the British lost this ability to make good cost-benefit analyses, both with respect to indigenous populations, and the management of assertive white settlers. It was a key part of the success of the British World System in the 1800s, and its dissipation is a key part of the fall of that system.

The Largest Settler Colony—The Shortest History of The United States Ever

---

[139] I am grateful to Piers Brendon's Decline and Fall of the British Empire for making me aware of this extraordinary sequence of events.
[140] My favorite super hero movie of 2017, and quite possibly my favorite Marvel movie of all time was Thor: Ragnarok, a film helmed by Taika Waititi, a director of Maori descent.

The United States became formally independent with 1783's Treaty of Paris with Great Britain. But for the first century or so of our history it's hard to dispute that the United States was very much a part of Britain's informal empire. The volume of trade with Britain continued to grow exponentially after independence. British economic demands were a main driver of US expansion, if not THE driver. The American lack of squeamishness about slavery and the dispossession of natives accelerated growth. The British were deep in enlightened angst over both of those issues by the late 1700s. With US independence, British merchants and bankers could profit from the violent expropriation of land and labor without having to deal with the personal guilt of being slavers or brutalizers of noble natives.[141] The United States was chiefly a supplier of primary goods for British industry. This included wheat, tobacco, fish, and most importantly of course…cotton. All told, an independent United States was probably a better deal for the British than a dependent one was. London no longer had to worry about policing borders on the other side of the Atlantic Ocean, and North American goods streamed towards their markets in increasing volumes anyway. The British could also benefit from the trade produced by American expansion without feeling responsibility for the genocide that proceeded along with it.

Industrialization in Britain began with cotton textiles. It was the first industry to experience explosive growth, "…as early as 1795, 340,000 people worked in the spinning industry. By 1830, one in six workers in Britain labored in cottons."[142] Cotton was the industry that introduced the world to large scale factory work. The technological innovations that powered this development, including steam and rail, eventually branched off to create other industries. By the mid-1800s, early British industrialization was wholly reliant on the slavery that their empire had

---

[141] P. 112 Beckert, Sven Empire of Cotton: A Global History
[142] P. 73 Beckert, Sven Empire of Cotton: A Global History

supposedly banned. "In 1860, eighty percent of raw cotton for the [British] mills came from the American South..."[143] Remember that we're talking about the United Kingdom, a country that at this point had the entire cotton production of India, the industry's former home, under its control.

The British were deeply involved in every step of building the slave empire of the American South. The Louisiana Purchase of 1803, which doubled the size of the United States for just fifteen million dollars, was financed by a British banker. Thomas Baring provided the funds for this massive increase in US territory with the express permission of the British Prime Minister.[144] At the time of independence, many politicians in the United States were ambivalent about slavery. Thomas Jefferson, a slave owner, ended the (legal) importation of slaves into the United States in 1808. The industrial demands of Britain, however, coupled with the invention of the cotton gin in 1793, super-charged the institution. The western reaches of the already existing slave states filled up with cotton farmers, and new slave states like Mississippi were added to the union that were populated almost exclusively by slaves and their owners. Industrially super charged slave states created a dominant political force in the United States over the first half of the 1800s. These plantations were built in part with British capital. "The expansion of cotton agriculture depended on the advance of credit, sometimes secured by mortgages on slaves, most of which derived from the London money market..."[145] Between 1619 and 1808, roughly half a million Africans had been dragged into US slavery. A full third of them were brought over in just the final twenty-five years between 1783 and 1808,[146] largely to satisfy the needs of the British cotton industry.

---

143 P. 322 Webb, R.K. Modern England 2nd Edition
144 P. 106 Beckert, Sven Empire of Cotton: A Global History
145 P. 116 Beckert, Sven Empire of Cotton: A Global History
146 P. 109 Beckert, Sven Empire of Cotton: A Global History

By the middle of the 1800s, the days of southern politicians taking action against slavery were long over. Getting rid of slavery took a civil war, but the Northerners were no more innocent of profiting from African blood than the British were. Cotton was central to the entire US economy. "More than half of all American exports between 1815 and 1860 consisted of cotton"[147]. The defenders of British Empire all point to the banning of slavery as one of the main proofs of its virtue. Those defenders tend to leave out the central role Britain played in the horror of industrialized US slavery. The US was very much a part of Britain's informal empire, certainly up until the US Civil War, and most probably for many decades thereafter.

The War of 1812

The British could occasionally go too far in assuming that nothing had changed in their relationship with "the Colonies". It was chiefly the drafting of American sailors into the British Navy that started the war of 1812. Nobody really won that war, though the British did manage to burn down the White House, and the US Navy managed to beat smaller elements of the British Navy in a couple battles, so nobody really lost. If the British had not been so focused on the conflict with Napoleon, the results would likely have been quite different. Eighteen twelve was the year Napoleon invaded Russia, after all. All of Britain's large ships were tied up with the more important conflict around Europe. War with the United States limped on because the British didn't have the spare capacity necessary to crush the young country. What brought the war to a swift end in 1815 was the calamitous effect that it had on the US economy. The US simply needed British trade to function. The great US victory in the Battle of New Orleans, which launched the career of

---

[147] P. 119 Beckert, Sven Empire of Cotton: A Global History

eventual President Andrew Jackson, was fought after the peace treaty had already been signed.

After that blip the US-British relationship got back on track. In the US, we see ourselves as more powerful than we were, earlier than we were. The Monroe Doctrine, first laid out in 1823, asserted that European powers were no longer allowed to take territory in North or South America. This was a bit presumptuous, as we didn't yet have anywhere near the naval capability necessary to keep the Europeans out. Most Europeans were kept out of South America, but that was more about British power than it was about the US, as we'll document in the next section. The British felt free to carry out naval blockades against countries like Venezuela as late as 1903.

The US was certainly interested in asserting itself in the nineteenth century, it's just that all of our assertions served to broaden the reach of British investment rather than limit it. We had the Mississippi, Texas, California and everything in between to focus on developing. And with our growing need for railroads and industrial infrastructure, we were a better investment for the British than the Mexican and native peoples we displaced in the vast interior of today's United States.

The competition between North and South didn't help the US assert itself internationally either. It certainly doesn't fit the current British image of itself, but it was the slave-holding South that was more aligned with and eagerly subject to the British. The main concern south of the Mason-Dixon line was moving as much cotton as possible to British mills. The North was initially dependent on trade with Britain as well, but they were interested in building a manufacturing and trading empire of their own. This is what they set about doing through what became known as the "American System" of trade protection, internal improvements, and a central banking system. They were often opposed in this by the South, which preferred free trade for its cotton, and was perfectly happy with its reliance on slavery.

These conflicts came to a head in the US Civil War. The British seriously weighed coming in on the side of the South to protect their cotton supply, but ended up deciding not to, both on moral grounds, and perhaps because they were a little bit intimidated by the war machine that the North had built. After the Emancipation Proclamation, when it was no longer possible to pretend that the war wasn't about slavery, British sympathies turned against the South.[148] It took years and killed hundreds of thousands, but the US Civil War settled the question of the US path forward. Slavery and the hyper-production of raw materials were out, and industry and trade were in. It was now clear that the US was going to start playing a larger role in the world, but it wasn't yet clear what that role would be.

Latin American Empire

South and Central America were another arena for British informal empire. Their status in the nineteenth century also illustrates the degree to which the United States was not yet a power in its own right. The 1823 Monroe doctrine attempted to assert an exclusive American sphere of influence for the United States. Latin America would be the place where the United States took its first steps towards building its own empire and world system, but this didn't really get started until the early 1900s. In the 1800s Britain acted to keep the newly independent countries free of European influence, and in many cases the influence of the United States as well. The British wanted to keep these countries for themselves.

If you look at a map of the British Empire in Central and South America, only the slivers of Belize, Guyana and a bunch of islands in

---

[148] P. 318 Webb, R.K. Modern England 2nd Edition

the Caribbean will be shaded red. But that lack of coloration hides the commercial dominance that was a key part of both the British and the US World Systems. There is also the little-known detail that Latin American independence probably wouldn't have happened without British intervention.

Spain Loses Two Continents

After 1815, the British ruled the seas. The Spanish Empire, which had controlled most of North and South America for centuries, needed those seas to function. The reactionary European consensus after the close of the Napoleonic Wars was very much for the preservation of that Spanish Empire.[149] Spain had struggled for decades, and lost tens of thousands of soldiers attempting to crush the new Latin American republics. An extraordinary seventy-five percent of the more than 40,000 soldiers they sent were lost to disease and fighting. All of Continental Europe wanted Spain to hold onto the Americas. But it was Britain's world to shape.

In 1822, the French intervened in Spain to re-install a king after he had been overthrown by liberal revolutionaries. In response, George Canning, the British Foreign Secretary, recognized the independence of Argentina, Colombia and Mexico. British sailors and soldiers had played a part in these struggles prior to this point as well. The most famous participant was probably the temporarily disgraced Admiral Thomas Cochrane, known by Napoleon as "the Sea Wolf" who jumped from the British to the Chilean and Brazilian navies where he helped Chile and Peru win their independence. After British recognition of the independence of these countries the gig was up. No direct conflict between the British and Spanish militaries was necessary. British naval supremacy was such that the commercial and diplomatic support provided were enough to secure the continent's freedom. As the staggeringly self-important Canning put it, he had "…called the New

---

[149] P.171 Webb, R.K. <u>Modern England 2nd Edition</u>

World into existence to redress the balance of the Old".[150] This was pitched, of course, as a great feat of altruism. That's not what it was.

The growing consciousness of British economic superiority began turning the British into great advocates of free trade in the 1820s. The British tried to sell free trade to other countries long before they fully adopted it themselves with the abolition of the Corn Laws in 1846. By facilitating independence in Latin America, all forms of trade preference for Spanish goods were done away with. British traders could move in big. The independent countries of Latin America then quickly became part of the British trading and financial empire, as they became part of the US trading empire in the 1900s. It took very little time for a sad and familiar pattern to emerge. The business bonanza in mining and government debt unleashed by Canning's recognition of Latin American independence in 1822 quickly led to a boom, then mania, then bust.[151] The first of many Latin American debt crises was a large factor in London's Panic of 1825, which is seen as the one of the first dips in the modern world-wide business cycle. Britain was to maintain a dominant position in Latin American trade and investment for the rest of the 1800s.

After the United States ran off with California in the Mexican American War (1846-1848), US attempts to assert itself in the Caribbean became more serious. The quickest route between New York, the Mississippi River, and California cut across the thin isthmus between North and South America. Though Panama eventually became the focus, with and before the opening of its canal in 1914, in the mid-1800s the main transit point was Nicaragua.[152]

A series of provocations in 1856 made war between the United States and Great Britain over Nicaragua seem like a distinct possibility.

---

[150] Quoted on P.171 Webb, R.K. Modern England 2nd Edition
[151] P. 176 R.K. Modern England 2nd Edition
[152] The discussion of Nicaragua in this paragraph and the following paragraphs is drawn from Ben Wilson's Heyday: The 1850s and the Dawn of the Global Age

Despite the willingness of many in the British leadership to strike a blow for British prestige, the sense was that the British public wouldn't go for it. The two countries were just too economically inter-related. "As one Boston newspaper put it, if Britain burnt New York it might lay waste to $100 million worth of property, but it would be $100 million worth of its own property."[153] That is hyperbole of course, but the United States was a tremendous profit center for the nineteenth century British World System.

It's worth taking a minute to examine the lopsidedness of the tools used in the US-British fight over Nicaragua. The US tool was William Walker, a charismatic soldier of fortune who saw himself as a potential Central American Napoleon. He and his various gangs of ruffians were not officially working on the behalf of the US government. Walker invaded Nicaragua and set himself up as president in 1855. These actions were popular in the United States, especially in the South, but any US citizen who left to fight for him had to do so under false pretenses. Though US president Pierce did recognize Walker's presidency of Nicaragua, the decision was controversial within the United States, and came with no official support. US efforts to control Nicaragua were unofficial, and always completely reliant on the efforts of one charismatic warlord of dubious sanity.

The British just sent in its own warships. Walker's presidency was defeated in part by the British Navy's refusal to let his unofficial reinforcements from the United States land. Walker's supporters in the US could impotently rage against this, but they couldn't really do anything else. So much for the Monroe Doctrine. Despite its protestations to the contrary, in the nineteenth century the US lacked the ability to seriously challenge British interests in South America.

Trade Routes to Asia

---

153 P. 202 Wilson, Ben Heyday: The 1850s and the Dawn of the Global Age

For centuries, ever since Vasco Da Gama reached India in 1498, European powers had struggled to control the lucrative route around Africa to India and China. The struggle ended with the Napoleonic wars. The British controlled the route completely from 1815 until they were dispossessed by the Japanese in the 1940s. What follows is a brief tour of some of the highlights along the four continents between the British Isles and Australia. Any exhaustive story of every port and patch of land that was to some degree attached to even just the formal British Empire would take a much longer book.

In the wars up until 1815, all remaining French possessions were occupied, though there weren't all that many left after the Seven Years' War. One noteworthy acquisition from the French was Mauritius in 1810, a small but well populated island off the coast of Africa. The Dutch possessions that Britain absorbed during this period were much more significant. France swallowed up the Dutch Republic during the wars, so Britain took the Dutch colonies. The British first occupied the Dutch Cape Colony, (the coast of modern South Africa) in 1795, and finalized their takeover in 1806. In 1796 the British took the coasts of Ceylon (Modern Sri Lanka). The British fought two wars against the native Kandyan Kingdom, conquering the whole island in 1815. These three acquisitions alone provided highly strategic bases from which the whole route to China could be accessed. There were many more.

The British took the entirety of Dutch Indonesia in 1796. In a savvy bit of informal empire building, the British agreed to hand much of the territory back in the Anglo-Dutch treaty of 1814, in return for a number of Dutch territories in India. This meant the British didn't have to worry about running the territory, and that the Dutch had a much-needed source of revenue they could use to rebuild their country and their defenses. The new Kingdom of the Netherlands[154] soon found out,

---

[154] The Dutch come from the Kingdom of the Netherlands for some reason. It's also often called Holland. Irritating.

however, how little power they had if the British found a territory interesting. A second Anglo-Dutch treaty, in 1824, gave Britain the rest of the Dutch territory in India. Britain also got the right to develop Singapore and other colonies on the Malayan peninsula.

The 1824 treaty did guarantee that Britain wouldn't occupy any territory or set up any relationships with rulers south of Singapore, but that hardly mattered. Singapore, an island at the mouth of the strait of Malacca strait quickly became one of the most important places on the planet, economically and strategically. The British used it as a citadel and trading hub, jacking its population up from around 1,000 to around 80,000 in just forty years.

Throughout the nineteenth century, Britain's control of this network grew, first slowly then frantically. Treaties evolved into protectorates, and protectorates into directly held crown colonies. The entities that Britain put together, either directly or through the pressure of being a neighbor, still shape coastal Africa and Asia today. As just one example, a piratical group of emirates on the Arabian Peninsula were forced to sign a treaty with Britain in 1820 governing their foreign policy and shipping practices. They were forced to sign on to a more detailed treaty in 1853, and became an out and out protectorate in 1892. They remained as quasi-medieval emirates protected from all their neighbors until they emerged in 1971 to become the United Arab Emirates.

As much as I'd love to get into all this, at a certain point a history of the British World System becomes a history of the entire world. We don't have the space to get into all of it in granular detail. So let's move on to the big ones.

China—The British Narcos

By the mid-1800s China was very much a part of Britain's "Informal Empire". But it was a very recent development. Chinese goods had been popular in Europe for centuries. In the early 1600s, the English had joined with the Dutch to battle the Portuguese for access to Chinese trading posts. Chinese luxuries like silk, porcelain, and above all tea were high value products for the East India Company throughout the seventeenth and eighteenth centuries. But the British remained very peripheral in Chinese politics. One of the most famous episodes in European-Chinese diplomacy occurred in 1793. George Macartney, Britain's first envoy to China, visited the court of the Emperor. He hoped to secure trading privileges for British merchants. The embassy was a complete failure. Though he did succeed in meeting with the emperor briefly, it was very clear that the Qianlong emperor did not view the British as equals, and saw no need to acquiesce to any of their requests.

China had no need for anything from outside of China. Unlike the Mughals of India, the Chinese imperial system did not fall apart in the 1700s. There was no vulnerability for British traders and imperialists to exploit. The Chinese empire did not exhaust itself like the Mughals empire did. The British had to wait until they were powerful enough to destroy it themselves. In 1833, the East India Company lost her monopoly on trade with China, and a wide range of mostly British competitors crowded in to buy the luxuries the Western world craved. The traditional way of paying for Chinese goods was silver, an expensive good that the British did not control, and had many other uses for. To keep the volume up, they needed to find something else that the Chinese wanted. Their answer was opium. For British merchants, the trade was largely circular, drugs were produced in India, and shipped to China, with British middlemen reaping the majority of the profit. This proximity of supply and demand led to the British dominating this market, even in the era of free trade.

The Chinese despised this. Opium was nothing new, but the higher amounts that were showing up on the market at lower prices were creating an epidemic of addiction. Making things worse, they now had the problem British traders had had just a few decades prior. The silver that their currency was based on was rapidly flowing out of the country to pay for the narcotic. In 1839, the Chinese government acted to completely ban the opium trade (it was already illegal). Canton, the main trading port at that time, was closed, and tens of thousands of chests of opium were confiscated. After the destruction of the contraband, trading resumed. The British did not let it end there. They launched a war to defend their right to sell opium to the Chinese people, destroying a series of forts and armies. In 1842, the Chinese accepted defeat in the Treaty of Nanking, which gave the British Hong Kong and opened up five treaty ports for trade. It also set up the principle of "extraterritoriality", providing that the British would be tried by their own courts. The Chinese were not seen as fit to judge white men who committed crimes on Chinese territory. In the aftermath of the first opium war, other European and American countries achieved similar privileges for their merchants. The Chinese were desperate for anybody to counterbalance the British.

China had viewed itself as the center of the world for centuries. When they were conquered, as they had been by the Mongols in 1279 and the Manchus in 1636, the conquerors quickly assimilated themselves to Chinese culture. This was not the case with the new British invaders. Defeat in the first Opium War played an important part in the disintegration of Chinese Imperial power in the mid-1800s. The Taiping Rebellion (1850-1864), which is estimated to have killed *twenty to thirty million people,* is only the most famous of the insurgencies[155] sparked by the British crushing of the Manchu dynasty. European religion played a part in the Taiping Rebellion as well. It was

---

[155] P. 273 Darwin, John After Tamerlane: The Rise and Fall of Global Empires, 1400-2000

led by a charismatic student of Christian missionaries who claimed to be the brother of Jesus. China was never outright occupied by the British or any other foreign power (the Japanese came closest) but it was shaken to its core in the 1800s.

Gold rushes in California (1848) and Australia (1851) brought Europeans to the Pacific in even greater numbers, both drawing Chinese overseas and bringing foreigners to Chinese shores in unprecedented numbers. Tensions between China and the British led to the Second Opium War from 1856-1860. It didn't go any better for the Chinese, culminating in the burning of the Summer Palace outside of Beijing in 1860. That act of cultural desecration would be the rough equivalent of burning the Louvre and the Palace of Versailles combined, something that generations of German conquerors managed to avoid doing to the French. The ratification of the Treaty of Tianjin resulted in the complete opening of the country to European traders and missionaries.

As the nineteenth century wore on, other countries joined in the British crushing of China. The Second Opium War had included the French as a junior partner. By the crushing of the Boxer Rebellion in 1901, Britain was nominally an equal partner in a coalition including France, Russia, Germany, Japan and others. Over the course of the nineteenth century the Russians carved off sections of Chinese land in the North, around the Amur River and in Manchuria. The French took advantage of Chinese weakness to take land in Vietnam. Even the United States took over the Philippines in the Spanish-American War of 1898, far from China, but part of a play for the same markets. But it was Britain's informal empire, run from small outposts like Hong Kong and Singapore, that took the prize. As late as 1895, Britain still controlled two-thirds of China's foreign trade, and the opium trade remained a significant part of it.[156]

The operations of other empire builders in China was useful to Britain then, and it remains useful today for propaganda purposes. They all had their own little empires, but all these nations were fighting in the name of a free trade policy that the British set, and an opening of the Chinese economy that the British had created, and continued to benefit from more than anybody else. Informal empire was a powerfully useful thing. Britain's policy did much more to destroy Imperial China than Russia, France, or even Japan did.

India

It was in the later 1700s and early 1800s that India assumed the dominant position among British overseas possessions, and began to become a bit of an obsession for the British public and their leaders. The transition from informal to formal empire happened in India first, accelerating during the Napoleonic wars and reaching a new level of formality after the First War of Indian Independence in 1857. In the second half of the 1800s, the transition to formal empire accelerated everywhere, usually with the justification that it was necessary to protect India. India was important as the source of opium for the Chinese market and other raw materials. It was very important to Britain's budding industrialists as a market. But perhaps the most important thing it provided was soldiers.

The army of British India eviscerates one of the British Empire's greatest myths about itself. We still hear a lot about how the British were so much less militaristic than their French and German rivals. Even today, in certain sections of British media you can still find folks

---

[156] P. 240 James, Lawrence The Rise And Fall of The British Empire

rhapsodizing about how mere handfuls of plucky British soldiers held sway over millions of brown heathens.

> British India was 'the miracle of the world' according to the Marquess Curzon, who was appointed Viceroy in 1898. There was indeed something miraculous about the way in which less than a hundred thousand soldiers and administrators held in thrall two hundred and fifty million Indians.[157]

There was nothing miraculous about it. This ludicrous myth relies on a quite racist erasure of the hundreds of thousands, and occasionally millions of Indian soldiers and administrators that were essential to the running of British India and the larger British Empire. The British weren't less militaristic than the Germans or the French, they often had the largest armies on the planet. "Between 1789 and 1805 the Company's total strength increased from about 115,000 to 155,000, making it one of the largest European-style standing armies in the world."[158] At its height during the Second World War, British India enlisted around 2.5 million soldiers. These soldiers were first used to build empire in India itself in the 1700s, and then further afield, in Africa and Asia, and finally in Europe itself, in the trenches of the First World War and all over the globe in the Second. And it wasn't just soldiers. India's workers ended up everywhere. They often replaced slaves by working as indentured servants across Asia, Africa and the Americas. The conditions they worked in often weren't much of an improvement over those of the slaves they replaced. They could also rise to occupy more middle-class positions in colonies where the British were leery of giving power to the locals. This was the case across British Africa. The famous Indian freedom fighter Mohandas Ghandi (1869-1948) got his start in politics advocating for the rights of his people in South Africa.

---

[157] P. 217 James, Lawrence <u>The Rise And Fall of The British Empire</u>
[158] P. 85 Bayly C.A. <u>Indian Society and the Making Of The British Empire</u>

India was the engine of empire, and also its fuel. The people, markets and materials furnished by India's hundreds of millions allowed a small island in the North Atlantic to build a world system in the 1800s. Which is kind of surprising if you consider the views of most British in the 1770s and 1780s.

War Justifies Empire…

Before the French Revolution, many in London were looking for a way to step back from Indian governance. Wealthy "nabobs" like Robert Clive were resented, and there was some limited but real outrage at the way that Indian freedoms were being crushed in the name of profit. It would be nice to imagine that the ten million Indians who died in the Great Bengal Famine of 1770 were the main motivator of this anti-Indian Empire sprit, but it was probably more the fact that the East India Company required a massive £1.5 million bailout loan in 1773.[159] It's not that the British in India weren't making money, they were making obscene amounts of it, it's just that the folks working for the company took the money personally, not the company itself. The 1773 Regulating Act, and the India Act of 1784 sought to reduce corruption in India. They introduced the first governmental limits on the East India Company's administration. The India Act also "forbade any further territorial expansion".[160] British India was now to be limited, well run, and focused purely on making money.

War always gets in the way. The bar on territorial expansion lasted all of five years. Fear of a resurgence of French influence in the country prompted the British to go on an acquisition binge across Northern India. Richard Wellesley in particular, governor-general from 1798-

---

[159] P. 21 Read, Anthony & David Fisher <u>The Proudest Day: India's Long Road to Independence</u>
[160] P. 23 Read, Anthony & David Fisher <u>The Proudest Day: India's Long Road to Independence</u>

1805, made it his mission to destroy the two competing indigenous powers that were left in India, and ensure that France had no one to ally with. In 1799, Tipu Sultan, the last seriously independent Muslim ruler, was destroyed, and his territories were divided up between the East India Company and various puppet kings. The largely Hindu Maratha Confederacy as not fully subjugated until the third Anglo-Maratha war between 1816-1818, but the second Anglo-Maratha war between 1803-1805 was decisive enough to break them as a competing power. In pursuing these wars, the British took a broad swathe of territory across Northern India.

Though the British were building formal empire over more and more Indian territories, and did so with an increasingly racist system, there was a certain humility to this process that would be abandoned in the days of the "British Raj" in the second half of the 1800s. The imperial "glory" that would later be so jealously guarded by British monarchs was carefully preserved for the fading Mughal emperors in Delhi.

> Richard Wellesley, Governor-General 1798-1805, warned his aides to show respect to the Emperor 'as almost every class of people… continue to acknowledge his nominal authority' during the most expansive period of empire-building, and it is arguable that British success was facilitated by this scrupulous regard for Mughal authority.[161]

As India became more vital to the British Empire, and the European population of India grew, the administration became more explicitly racist. "The interest or even absorption in Indian life and culture, so evident in Englishmen in India in the eighteenth century, was giving way in the nineteenth to confident Victorian self-righteousness"[162]. British India's governing systems remained a collaboration between foreigner and native, but the Indians were pushed further and further

---

[161] P. 16 Bayly C.A. Indian Society and the Making Of The British Empire
[162] P.313 Webb, R.K. Modern England 2nd Edition

down the hierarchy. There is perhaps something about traveling along the spectrum towards formal empire that requires a racist ideology. Invading, holding, and shaping the territory of an alien culture has always required some assumption of superiority. Some of the most fervently anti-Muslim people I have ever met were US soldiers who were required to invade and oppress Muslim countries. To be fair, I have also met many US servicepeople who have great respect for the countries they occupied. There were plenty of nineteenth century Britons who deeply loved and respected India, as their countrymen shot Indians out of cannons. A racist ideology became more important in the nineteenth century, when the British imperial center had convinced itself that it was an admirer and defender of liberty. There had to be something wrong with Indians that meant they didn't deserve the same rights to freedom and self-government that the British did. A lot of energy went into crafting "scientifically racist" theories that were applied in India first, and in many other places later.

As India became more important, the British became more insecure about it. The thought that one lucrative territory might be vulnerable to the next territory over led to a never-ending succession of wars. Taking further territories led to longer borders, that took British territory closer to more threatening enemies, which led to yet more fighting. Burmese wars in 1823-1826 and 1852 took the borders of British India far to the east[163]. British India's responsibility for the sea lanes also took its control as far to the west as Aden, in modern Yemen, helping to create a distinct South Yemeni culture that continues to make that country's politics more interesting today. Neither of these expansions were as costly and damaging as the one to the northwest. The enduring British obsession with the illusory Russian threat to India… caused the British to move their borders relentlessly closer to the Russian threat. This led to bloody expeditions to Afghanistan in the 1840s and the 1870s. The

---

[163] P. 314 Webb, R.K. Modern England 2nd Edition

second expedition was to some degree successful, allowing the British to set up a protectorate. The first expedition was a catastrophe, involving the loss of an entire British army. This loss prompted the swallowing up of most of modern Pakistan in an attempt to save face. Sind and the Punjab were annexed to British India over the course of the 1840s.

This new turn towards formal empire produced one of the most savage incidents in the history of the British Empire in 1857. The British learned the lessons of the first war of Indian Independence in India, but they failed to apply them to the empire more generally. This conflict, often known as the Sepoy Mutiny, or just the Indian Mutiny, was caused in part by poor management of British India's own soldiers. The religious motivations behind this mutiny are well known. New rifle technology required that the soldiers use their teeth to tear open ammunition to prepare it for firing. Hindus were afraid that animal fat from cows was used in the preparation of the cartridges, and Muslims were afraid it was pig fat. This would be sacrilegious for each group. This may have been the spark, but the motivations for the uprising were more deeply seated. The growing racism of the administration was part of it, but the East India Company's continued land grabs were part of it as well.

The Company was still a money-making enterprise, but after the loss of their last monopoly in 1833, their business was government, not trade. More territories meant more tax revenue to be exploited. From 1848-1856 the viceroy Lord Dalhousie adopted a rapacious policy towards the swiss cheese of territories in India. He wanted to fill in the gaps with British control. The "Doctrine of Lapse" provided that if an Indian ruler died without an heir that satisfied the British legal conception of what an heir was, the territory would go to the British. This violated a lot of traditions of adoption and succession that had been observed in India for centuries. It also created a large pool of dispossessed rulers to rally around in opposition to the British.

The 1856 acquisition of Awadh (often spelled Oudh) was one of the many causes of the uprising. India remained, and remains today a very diverse place. Some were benefitting from British rule, and many were more concerned with their traditional enemies than they were with fighting the British. The insurgents rallied around the old Mughal king, and took his old capital of Delhi. The uprising was largely centered on the north of the country and did not spread to the south or to the newly acquired territories in Sind and the Punjab. Had the uprising been more general or unified, it would probably have been successful. Even as it was it took months for the British to crush it. That crushing involved indiscriminate violence and reprisal that would have made a Roman blush. The last Mughal emperor was exiled, and his sons were murdered in cold blood, along with every soldier captured in the re-taking of Delhi.[164] Whole villages were wiped out, and some rebels were dismembered by being shot out of cannons. British claims to a higher degree of civilization rightly took a hit from this harsh repression. Disregard for the life and property of the governed was not unique to the unrest of 1857. "…the systematic burning of villages, crops and granaries, and the slaughter of livestock … marked every frontier operation."[165]

The British learned a few lessons from the mutiny. The old fashioned, profit focused governance of India was done away with. The East India Company was abolished with the Government of India act in 1858. Respect for the religions of the locals was more rigorously observed. And the "Doctrine of Lapse" was ended. India's petty rulers were now recognized as a useful tool. Many dynasties lasted all the way down to independence in 1947. Unfortunately, this lesson was not applied to the

---

[164] P. 54 Read, Anthony & David Fisher The Proudest Day: India's Long Road to Independence
[165] P. 234 James, Lawrence The Rise And Fall of The British Empire

world more generally. The policy of sucking up new territory that had led to cataclysm in India was soon applied more broadly.

The subjugation of India provided the armies necessary to build a larger formal empire, and the existence of that tool made such an extension more likely. But it's unlikely that this provided much real economic benefit to the UK itself. The whole rickety apparatus largely paid for itself, because India subjects could be forced to pay for it, but was there really much of a point to it?

> There was no reason to believe that British Manufactures, textiles and machinery needed formal empire to penetrate Indian markets. After all they had commanded markets throughout Asia, Europe and Latin America without benefit of collectors and judges. In fact, modern economic historians speculate that without easy colonial markets British industries might have modernized more rapidly in the later nineteenth century to face growing European and American competition. India would have sold raw materials on the world market regardless of her formal colonial status[166]

In 1876, Queen Victoria was declared Empress of India. All that pomp and pretension was a great source of pride to the British people, but this love of formal empire may be another result of the historical hangover I keep taking about. British wealth and power had much more to do with newer means of production than the old school thuggery of land and titles. But the British people wanted the old school thuggery to convince themselves that their power was real.

The Myth of European Empire

This short, desperately incomplete, survey should give a sense of just how dominant the British World System was in the nineteenth century. The period between 1856-1860, recounted directly above, is especially striking. India and China, two ancient and powerful civilizations, countries of hundreds of millions even back then, were crushed by

---

[166] P. 201 Bayly, C. A. Indian Society and the Making of British Empire

Britain at **the same time**. The Second Opium War in China, and the crushing of the first War of Indian Independence involved the sacking of multiple cities across vast continents, and the coordination of hundreds of thousands of British and Indian troops, subjugating hundreds of millions. The destructive power, and the arrogance necessary to wield it are absolutely staggering. Britannia ruled the waves, but it also ruled most of the coasts that those waves touched, directly or indirectly. The industrial, financial and technological resources that Britain brought to bear desperately outclassed all rivals throughout the nineteenth century. Everybody else was playing catch up. But this is not how we remember it.

The nineteenth century is still largely seen as an era of "European Empire" rather than British Empire. We hear a lot about it from both sides of the political spectrum. Left leaning folks like to talk about the vile white oppressors who raped and murdered their way across the world. Resurgent white nationalists across Europe and the United States agree with this, though they tell the story differently. They, either explicitly or in thinly veiled terms, like to talk about the genius of Western Civilization, and the natural superiority of white folks. They are both getting the story wrong. What they are talking about isn't European Empire, it's the British Empire.

We should not attempt to exonerate other European Imperialists, or claim that they didn't do horrible things. They absolutely did. The Belgian Congo, with the European massacre for profit of as many as ten million Congolese is the go-to example for a reason. But almost all of these crimes came in the context of the British World System that ran the world throughout the nineteenth century. As we covered above, the independent country of Belgium itself was set up by Britain in 1830, mostly to keep a potential launching pad for British invasions out of the hands of other European powers. The British set the tone.

The earlier Spanish and Portuguese empires had an impact in the Western Hemisphere, but it was only in the nineteenth century that Europe housed a system powerful enough to seriously exploit the interiors of the American continents. And where was all that cotton produced in the Southern United States, and all that sugar produced in Brazil going? Into the markets that the British World System created.

Nobody is blameless here. Almost all European countries have some some dark and brutal nineteenth century history of exploitation to live down. But in the most intense period of European Imperialism, the non-British Europeans were followers, not competitors. The British hold a much larger share of responsibility for what went on in the nineteenth and twentieth centuries than we are currently told. The imperialist abuse of China and India's millions, and the Scramble for Africa, that saw a continent savagely carved up in a decade or two, are all very British stories, that were primarily driven by the dominant British World System. Many European countries got a slice of Africa to brutalize, but it was only the British bits that were really useful.

Nineteenth century British Imperial ideology has survived to shape our ideas of history today. The British justified their expanding informal and formal empires as necessary acts of self-defense against grasping, expanding competitors. British participation in the First World War was and is also justified as a necessary act of self-defense. They consistently sold their competition as being much more impressive than it was. Because the British write the history in the world's dominant language, we still hear a lot about Britain's imperial rivals.

The French had large, largely economically worthless tracts of land just across the Mediterranean in West Africa. They also had a few possessions in Asia. The British controlled all of the lucrative trade routes and most of the coastal land between French Algeria and French Vietnam. The Russians took over much of central Asia in the nineteenth century but there just wasn't much going on there in terms of trade or even people. The British had significant chunks of the trade in Russian Asia, and used Russian expansion as an excuse to swallow up much of modern Pakistan. Germany was a much more serious threat than either France or Russia, but as we'll cover in more detail in the next chapter, British mishaps had a lot to do with Germany's creation, and their threat to the British World System was also greatly exaggerated. All of these enemies were to some extent manufactured. Both in the sense that British actions made them more powerful, and that they were never as powerful as they were portrayed to be then, and are portrayed now in the historical record.

All historians fall into this trap. One of this book's most useful sources has been Sven Beckert's Empire of Cotton. It's an extraordinary book that does a brilliant job of knitting together the history of the nineteenth century with the thread of its most important industry. But its introduction can still feature sentences like this:

> The cumulative result of this highly aggressive, outwardly oriented capitalism was that **Europeans** came to dominate the centuries-old worlds of cotton, merge them into a single empire centered in **Manchester**, and invent the global economy we take for granted today.[167] [**emphasis mine**]

Historians everywhere know that something special and important was happening in Britain in the nineteenth century, but they are quick to ascribe this to a broader "Europeanness", even when they are describing phenomena centered on British cities. The new economic, social and political models pushed out from London were adapted at different rates everywhere, both between and within countries. Winners and losers were also distributed in complex patterns. A well situated Indian Merchant or Banker might feel significantly better about the British World System than a very European child laborer in Belgium to take one extreme example. A convincing argument can be

---

[167] P. xvi Beckert, Sven Empire of Cotton: A Global History

made that some North West European countries did a better job of succeeding in the British World System than others, industrializing quickly and prospering under the new dispensation better than most of the rest of the world. That doesn't mean they were leading the charge. Europe was not the surging home of Imperial rivals to Britain that we are typically sold. It was one very important section of the British informal empire that the British mismanaged apocalyptically. After Napoleon, Europe saw a range of copycat empires that never really succeeded in freeing themselves from British and later US domination.

It's tremendously important to get this story right. The British created the first unified world system, and the United States has crafted the second from its wreckage. If we allow these self-serving British ideas of what happened to go unchallenged, we miss one of the most important lessons of the fall of the British Empire. As the US system ages and decays, its masters are getting obsessed with the same sorts manufactured enemies that the British did. Some of them are more credible threats than others, but none of them are really that important yet. Washington DC tells itself that it needs to be more worried about rivals like Iran or China than the ever-accelerating mistakes that Washington DC itself keeps making. I think dismantling the myth of European Empire is an important part of correcting these mistakes. We should stop blaming others for the mistakes of the folks who really run the world. Today those rulers are found in the United States. In the nineteenth century they were found in Britain.

Bye-Bye, July

By the latter half of the nineteenth century the world was beginning to change. Britain was still very much on top, but many of Continental Europe's revolutionaries no longer saw the English system as the goal, as they had as late as France's July revolution of 1830. In 1848, much of Europe burst into revolution simultaneously, from France to Hungary, Prussia to Sicily, and many places in between. Thanks to new transport and communication technologies, revolution could spread quickly, and the disparate movements began to resemble each other in at least one important respect. Similar ideas of Nationalism underpinned all of the uprisings, though the details varied widely. The 1848 revolutions saw plenty of "liberal" pro-British demonstrations, but it also witnessed the birth of newer, less British-friendly forces. Karl Marx's Communist Manifesto was published in 1848, a bit before its time. The easy alliance between liberal reform and nationalist thought was still strong in 1848, but with hindsight we can see the tensions beginning to form. In 1871, the birth of the German Empire saw nationalist dreams satisfied by Bismarck's blood and iron rather than Germany's many liberal parliaments. That Empire was declared, not in Germany, but in France, after the crushing defeat of Napoleon III at the battle of Sedan. The revolutionaries that took over Paris in the aftermath of France's defeat were more inspired by Marx and other Communist thinkers than they were by John Locke and David Hume. Their claims to be working on the behalf of "The People" were quite socialist, but there was a lot of nationalism in that soup as well. The extraordinarily bloody crushing of the Paris Commune hinted at a darker future for Europe's ideological wars. The British didn't own the future anymore.

But perhaps we're getting ahead of ourselves. The next chapter will deal with the fall of the British World System. The rise of nationalism, in one guise or another, was the external force that prompted Britain's disastrous turn to formal empire. This shift was first evident in Britain's nearest informal empire in Europe, but nationalism became more and more important throughout the world as the nineteenth century wore on. The British "…never really grasped nationalism. Perhaps their own nationalism had been around so long that they could not recognize its analogues elsewhere"[168] Britain reacted to everybody else's growing

---

[168] P. 318 Webb, R.K. Modern England 2nd Edition

wish for self-determination with a worldwide attempt to stiffen its control. It's none too surprising that that went poorly.

"They allow themselves to be ruined and altogether undone by their own instruments, governments of their own making, and a press of which they are the proprietors"

John Maynard Keynes[169]

Chapter 6
Losing the British World System

So When Did the British Empire End?

Dating the end of the British World System is a difficult task. There are a number of different dates that all have great arguments in their favor. Was it 1914? 1945? 1956? 1968? 1997? 2016? The 1956 Suez Crisis, with its abject humiliation of Britain's leaders, has always appealed to me, but researching this book has persuaded me that 1914, the beginning of the First World War, is probably the right year to go with. This chapter will tell the story of how the British got to 1914. Before we get into it though, a brief look at the other contending dates for the end of empire will be useful. The British World System fell apart piece by piece, and is still falling apart more than a century after WWI, but it's 1914 that was important. The Great War cost the British their position on top, and every humiliation since has just been a result of that initial loss.

It's difficult to pinpoint the end of any empire. Scholars of Rome have contending dates for the Empire's end that range over 1,500 years, to

---

[169] P. 140 Keynes, John Maynard <u>The Economic Consequences of the Peace</u>

cite what is probably the most extreme example. Politicians actively work to obscure the facts. Successors, from Charlemagne to Nigel Farage, try to wrap themselves in the glory of empires that have faded. This question gets even harder when we're talking about empires that are true world systems. When the United States took over world governance from Britain, it was happy to preserve many elements of the existing system, and even preserve some British privileges. The United Kingdom still has a seat on the United Nations Security Council, for example. Though the transition from US Empire to whatever comes next is likely to be less friendly, it's possible that much of what we've created will be preserved as well. The extent to which Britain has benefitted from being replaced by a friendly hegemon prompts another question however:

Did the British Empire End?

This book has tried hard to emphasize the importance of informal empire rather than formal empire. It's the economics, the financial relationships and business ownerships that matter far more than borders, numbers of aircraft carriers or military bases. If you look at it this way, it's just possible to claim that the British Empire never really ended. From the oil monarchies of the Persian Gulf, to the enforced market-friendliness of South America, there are consistencies between the British and US World Systems everywhere you look. This has led to some fun conspiracy theories. The following of Lyndon Larouche, a perennial no-hope US presidential candidate[170], asserts that the British Empire is still alive and well today, and that its machinations are responsible for everything from the war in Iraq to the Trump-Russia investigation.[171] They contend that the dastardly financiers of the City of London have corrupted US elites in an effort to undermine the heroic

---

[170] No longer! Lyndon Larouche died at the age of 96 in February of 2019.
[171] "Britain Empire Still No. 1 Enemy Of The Civilized World" https://youtu.be/5Zl2FBvZm9o

legacy of Alexander Hamilton, Abraham Lincoln and FDR! It's a fun theory to think about, but quite nuts.

Some form of this story is important to the British. Today's leadership of the UK claims that a "special relationship" exists between Britain and the US, and politicians like Tony Blair have gone to great lengths to preserve it. Some in London like to imagine that their relationship with the US Empire is more of a partnership than a feudal one. Harold Macmillan, UK Prime Minister from 1957-1963, liked to imagine Britain as the wise Greek predecessor, guiding the Roman-ish American Empire that had replaced it.[172] These imaginings range from the sad to the farcical, but there are definite through lines between the two world systems that give the idea of continued British power and influence some credibility. But it's easy to refute.

Who decides what happens? The UK Prime Minister or the US President? Donald Trump's 2018 abandonment of the Iran Nuclear Deal answers this question quite firmly. Despite the opposition of British PM Theresa May, as well as the leaders of France and Germany, Trump has been successful in unilaterally reinstating sanctions on Iran, and dragging everybody else along with him. European leaders have made a big show of creating alternatives like INSTEX to preserve the trading relationship with Iran. This declaration of independence from the US banking system certainly has great future potential, but it is unlikely to work in the short term (and despite desperate Iranian entreaties, it hasn't been working so far). British and other European companies can't follow the lead of their countries' leaders because they are too afraid of the US government regulators who control world financial flows. This is only the latest in a century long line of US humiliations of British Prime ministers, from WWI down to today. Elements of the British World System and British privilege survive under US control, but the British Empire itself is dead.

---

[172] Loc 9968 Brendon, Piers The Decline and Fall of the British Empire 1781-1997

Nonetheless, British financial power is very real. Or at least it was.

2016—Brexit

In the years to come, Lyndon Larouche and Company are probably going to have to find a new bogeyman. On June 23rd 2016, I found myself at dinner with a bunch of British folks in Istanbul, Turkey. At the end of the evening everybody breathed a sigh of relief. The exit polls indicated that the United Kingdom had voted to stay in the European Union in that day's "Brexit" referendum. The next morning we woke up to find out that it wasn't true. This extraordinarily stupid choice by the British people represents the final death of British informal empire in Europe.

For decades, as the remnants of Britain's formal and informal empire evaporated almost everywhere else, British financial leadership had become more entrenched in Europe. After British entrance into the EU's predecessor, the European Economic Community (EEC) in 1973, and especially after Margaret Thatcher's opening up of UK financial regulation in 1986, the UK became the indisputable financial capital of Europe. Britain's informal empire in Europe survived and flourished. London managed to hang on as a financial center, one that sometimes even challenged New York in size and power. Brexit is currently in the process of ending the City's dominance.

Many confidently assert that London will hold on to its financial leadership. It won't. The prime position of places like New York and London isn't about special skills, or better service. It's essentially regulatory. New York has all of the United States, still the world's largest single market, to use as a "home-hinterland" for financial business due to the access that a unified set of laws and regulations provides. London had a similar "home-hinterland" in all of Europe in the later twentieth and early twenty-first centuries. In some years, by some measures, counted all together, the EU was a larger market than the United States. Brexit, in whatever form, will eviscerate London's access to the EU market. Finance as a business is entirely reliant on the regulations that govern it. Brexit will terminate the UK's ability to influence those regulations in Europe.

"But English is the international language of business!", some cry. That's absolutely true. It has been for decades now, and thanks to US wealth it's unlikely to change quickly. But English has been too successful to preserve London's dominance. Somewhere between fifty-to-sixty percent of Germans self-report the ability to speak English.[173] Those numbers are likely inflated, and the some of the self-reporting probably refers to half-remembered school days phrases, but as you move up the socioeconomic distribution, and into the relevant fields of finance and law, that figure represents more complete fluency. In my legal work in Istanbul I interacted with hundreds of Turkish professionals who were significantly better at legal English than I was. Germany, a wealthier country, with a much better education system, is significantly better equipped with English speakers than Turkey is. Modern digitized finance requires fewer and fewer actual humans to operate anyway. In October 2017, Goldman Sachs CEO Lloyd Blankfein famously tweeted about "spending a lot more time in Frankfurt"[174] and he's not going to be the only one.

London's fall as a financial center won't come in months or even years, but it won't take decades. It's the slow drip of financial companies to places like Frankfurt and Paris that will make the difference. As crises and the natural churn of fortune leads to businesses closing in London, their successors will open on the Continent. As WhateverBank shutters a trading floor to open up some new shop for crypto-wankery, the few jobs that are left will quietly drift south and east over the English Channel. If the negotiations around Brexit are mishandled, which

---

[173] Reports vary. This is a fun article on the topic, google should be able to translate it for you. "Germans Speak Bad English" https://www.zeit.de/karriere/beruf/2013-06/studie-englisch-kenntnisse-berufstaetige

[174] Finch, Gavin "Lloyd Blankfein Tweets About Spending 'A Lot More Time' in Frankfurt" October 19, 2017 https://www.bloomberg.com/news/articles/2017-10-19/goldman-ceo-tweets-about-spending-a-lot-more-time-in-frankfurt

seems likely, the process may be quicker. Regardless, the 2016 Brexit vote was an extraordinary renunciation of informal empire and the most recent candidate for the death of the British Empire.

1997—Hong Kong

In 1997, the British let go of its last slice of formal empire in Asia. That vast network of trading entrepots from Sierra Leone along the coasts of Africa and Asia all the way to Shanghai, had boiled down to a dwindling handful of assets, with Hong Kong being the most important. The most significant legacies of this system were bases like Diego Garcia, in the Indian Ocean, that had been turned over to the United States. Britain had officially acquired Hong Kong after the first Opium War back in 1843. For a century and a half, Hong Kong prospered as the British doorway to China. In 1898, the British signed a ninety-nine-year lease for much of Hong Kong's territory with a desperately weak Chinese government. A century can make a real difference.

The Empire still had a hold on the emotions of the British public, as was demonstrated by Margaret Thatcher's popular 1982 war against Argentina over the Falkland Islands in the South Atlantic. Imperial nostalgia allowed British politicians to score points at the expense of minor geopolitical actors like Argentina, but there was no possibility of challenging a country with the weight of China, even the China of 1997. Margaret Thatcher tried hard in the 1980s, in fact, to get a better deal out of the Chinese. She failed. The British didn't have anything to offer the Chinese other than arrogance and terrible history. It was a return to 1793, when the Chinese emperor turned away the Macartney mission because the idea of treating it as an equal was ludicrous. The British handover of Hong Kong to the Chinese Communist government was orderly, but prompted a great deal of hand-wringing. It shouldn't have—it was just the final step in processes that had started long ago.

1968—The End of East of Suez

By the later 1960s, much of the old formal British Empire was independent or about to be. The 1950s and 1960s had witnessed some of the most squalid and vile episodes in British imperial history, as they employed the techniques of the Nazis they had defeated to try to hold on to territories like Kenya and Rhodesia (Zimbabwe). Thankfully the British couldn't afford these tactics, fiscally or politically, and eventually let the bulk of its remaining colonies go in a rush. "…between 1961 and 1966, independence was granted to Sierra Leone, Tanzania, Western Samoa, Jamaica, Trinidad and Tobago, Uganda, Zanzibar, Kenya, Malawi, Zambia, Malta, Singapore, Gambia, the Maldives, Guyana, Botswana, Lesotho and Barbados."[175] Together, those new nations represented most of the territory that was left of Britain's formal empire. But the British still had pretensions of being a world power. They were out of the vast tracts of land business, but they hoped to hold on to their world-wide system of military bases.

The years leading up to 1968 had seen a series of financial reverses for the UK, the most important probably being the first Arab oil embargo after the Six Day War with Israel. The grim financial picture resulted in a decision to devalue the pound in the name of maintaining international competitiveness. In the new post-imperial world of trade flows and latter twentieth century consumption, the network of Asian bases was just too much to maintain. The Brits decided to abandon all the bases beyond the Suez Canal, in places like Singapore, Malaysia, the Persian Gulf and the Maldives. They simply couldn't afford it anymore. This was a delayed reaction to the fact that they had already had their fall from great power status powerfully illustrated ten years prior.

1956—The Suez Crisis

In the 1950s, the British were still quite convinced that they had an empire. India had been lost in 1947, but the sun didn't yet set on British

---

[175] Loc. 6450 Darwin, John Unfinished Empire: The Global Expansion of Britain

territory. Winston Churchill, the hero of WWII, and a grand old imperialist, had found his way back into the Prime Minister's office between 1951 and 1955. His successor Anthony Eden managed to dispel these imperial illusions quickly and forcefully. After the demise of British India, the Suez Canal had lost its old strategic significance. But that didn't keep Eden from wanting to fight to preserve British power over it. Oil flows had given it a new importance. British influence over Egypt had steadily diminished since the rise of Egyptian nationalist and Pan-Arab icon Gamal Abdel Nasser in 1952. But the British government, along with the French government and individual shareholders still owned the canal.[176] Nasser nationalized the canal in July of 1956. Eden hatched a plot with the Israelis to create an incident that the British and French could respond to by invading to "restore order". It worked. At first.

Dwight Eisenhower, the US president at the time, did not approve, and he told the British to go home or lose the financial support of the USA. The British had no choice but to obey. This humiliation made it very clear that Britain's time as an independent actor on the world stage was finished. The blow was somewhat sweetened by the fact that they could claim a "special relationship" with the new boss.

It was a tremendously significant moment in the demise of the British World System. The US's decades of dithering over whether or not to assert world-wide hegemony were over. Actions that hurt US propaganda efforts against the Soviets were no longer acceptable. Smacking down Eden, who lost his job over the Suez Crisis, made the power relations that had already emerged painfully clear. Few missed the significance of Britain's humiliation. But it merely publicized a dynamic that had begun to form long ago.

1945

---

[176] P. 593 Webb, R.K. Modern England 2nd Edition

In 1945 Winston Churchill got tossed out. The great old British Prime Minister had achieved victory over Hitler in World War Two, a threat that he was among the first to truly recognize, but the people of his country had had enough of him. Churchill epitomized an old school vision of Britain and its empire. He still saw the British Empire as the world spanning titan of his youth, and he believed in fighting to maintain that power. His vision did not match post-war reality or the aspirations of the British people in 1945. They elected Clement Atlee, a man who promised a number of social programs, chief among them a National Health Service, to compensate the British people for all of the suffering they had done for Empire. Atlee also took the first steps towards decolonization, pushing forward the simultaneously long overdue and undercooked independence of India and Pakistan in 1947.

Losing the Raj was Churchill's nightmare. During the war, "Churchill was increasingly desperate to hang on to India because Britain was slipping from its position as a great power as the United States and the Soviet Union came do dominate the wartime alliance."[177] Britain had been barely hanging on as the world power for quite some time, but it was WWII that made the collapse clear for all to see. The First World War had turned the British into a debtor nation, but the carcass of the British World System was still powerful enough that they could playact at primacy in between the wars. They couldn't handle a Second World War level effort.

In WWI, the British had independently played a central role for three years before needing US help. In WWII, the British strategy from the beginning was to desperately hold on until the US could be convinced to save them. We tend focus on the heroism of the Battle of Britain, but looked at honestly the Second World War was a tale of non-stop British humiliation prior to US entry, from Dunkirk to Norway to North Africa to Singapore, Hong Kong and Burma. The fall of Britain's

---

[177] Loc. 8162 Brendon, Piers The Decline and Fall of the British Empire 1781-1997

"impregnable fortress" in Singapore in February 1942 was an important moment. Defeat at the hands of Japan was a blow to the prestige of Britain, and European colonizers more generally. The Japanese pushed the British out of the Pacific in 1942. When the Japanese were defeated in turn, it was the Americans who profited, not Britain. By 1945, fiscally, morally, and, as Churchill's fall illustrated, politically, the gig was up. Wars are really bad for the country on top.

Some like to see the end of the British Empire as quite civilized. It was not. The decline and fall of the British Empire, and this first wave of deleveraging in particular, was a world-wide disaster. The British Raj—extending from modern Afghanistan to modern Thailand—ended in 1947 with the creation of a Muslim Pakistan and a Hindu India. The problem was that at the time, the two religious populations were mixed across the entire territory, and to effect their division, they had to be *moved*. Partition cost over a million lives in brutal intercommunal fighting. In 1971, "East Pakistan" became Bangladesh with another savage war that is estimated to have killed between 300,000 and 3 million civilians. The most likely candidates for the first mutual exchange of nuclear weapons remain India and Pakistan.

The immediate post-war era also gave us the never-ending crisis in Israel and Palestine. The British withdrawal from Palestine in 1948 led to the first of many ruinous and bloody wars between Israelis and Arabs, and a problem that is with us still. These are the most high-profile problems, but almost every country in the world is still dealing with the legacy of the British Empire's fall to some degree.

The US's approach to this legacy was and is the most important. In the first years after WWII, the US government adhered to its traditional hostility to empire (when the US wasn't doing it). The US's quick post-war withdrawal of support certainly had something to do with Britain's precipitous withdrawal from India. "…when the war was over and American lend-lease – of so much help during the war despite its somewhat capricious administration – was abruptly terminated, Britain could not survive on her own resources."[178] The US anti-imperial vigor faded as the Cold War began in earnest. The tattered British and French empires came to be seen as useful bulwarks against Communism. The US supported those empires with its treasure, and eventually, in Vietnam, with its troops. By 1948, with the Marshall Plan, the US was doing what it could to prop up what was left of Western Europe, including the British and their empire. Many of the formal elements of the British World System would limp on for another twenty years, though without its Indian center, the empire had no future. The outcome of the Second World War may have made British decline and American accession more obvious, but it was the century's first great conflict that truly stuck the killing blow.

1914—1918

We have a winner. "The First World War and its outcome destroyed the legitimacy of international order, the political framework on which globalization depended."[179] That globalization was for British benefit first and foremost, and the international order that was ended was the British World System. It wasn't immediately obvious, but 1914 was the year that killed the British Empire.

A world system dies in many ways, but at root it's about the money. Historians talk at length about the fatigue of the British people, changing international views of what was acceptable in international relations, "imperial overreach" or a failure of will on the part of British leadership, among many other explanations. All those factors were present, but at root, it was all about the money. Financially speaking, the war turned Britain into a debtor nation. This switch in Britain's status cut to the root of both their formal and informal empires. Though

---

[178] P. 580 Webb, R.K. <u>Modern England 2nd Edition</u>
[179] P. 422 Darwin, John <u>After Tamerlane: The Rise and Fall of Global Empires, 1400-2000</u>

they celebrated their "victory" in the First World War by sucking up some new territory in Iraq and Palestine, the British quickly learned they couldn't afford to play the game the way they used to. Everything was more expensive. Everything was more difficult. If it weren't for the expense of the world wars, perhaps there would still be a British Empire today. The British World System ended because it won two wars against Germany.

The whole period between 1914 and 1945 also provides another answer the "did the British Empire ever end?" question. The apocalypse of the two world wars certainly provided an ending. Britain's dominance, and even its power to act independently on the world stage definitively ended. It's the sort of thing this book is designed to help the United States avoid. And the tale that ends in 1914 provides many, many examples to avoid. The world wars were a result of Britain's catastrophic failure in world system management.

It's just possible to imagine the British piecing it all back together if the Second World War hadn't happened. But I find it unlikely. What made the post-Great War empire so expensive was the same force that had led to that war: nationalism, and a fundamental British misunderstanding of what it was, and the extent of the threat it posed to outside oppressors. The roots of this failure go far back into the nineteenth century. It's common to limit discussion of the causes of the First World War to the few months and years before it happened. That narrow focus makes it easier to pretend it was Germany's fault, or everybody's fault. A wider view reveals a different story. Britain's WWI wounds were self-inflicted.

1853–1914—Driving the World Off A Cliff

In the nineteenth century, the British leadership and public were focused on inordinately complex and expensive machinations against imperial rivals that didn't really exist. The Russian, French and even German empires outside of Europe were just as dependent on the British World System for their prosperity as any non-European polity was. The British were so focused on these **manufactured enemies** that they missed the real "great game" of the nineteenth century, the spread and weaponization of nationalism to every people and region in the world. The brutality and cost of the fight against imperial "rivals" ended up powering the drive towards national self-determination everywhere.

From the perspective of British interests, this was the "Historical Hangover" at its worst. The nationalist inclinations of the British Public interacted with the war-focused pretensions of the still aristocratic British leadership in an extraordinarily detrimental fashion. The British mistook the glorious military details of their victory over Napoleon for the true economic, financial and legal nuts and bolts of their imperial power. If the British Empire was forged by war and military competition, then surely war and military competition was the way to preserve it?

Not So Much.

In an earlier version of this book, published as a brief essay back in 2012, I claimed that the British Empire was led astray by a nasty aristocratic elite, mired in a thuggish medieval obsession with conquest. My more libertarian politics at the time led me to imagine that the more virtuous bourgeois leanings of the British middle and lower classes could have righted the ship, if they had only had the necessary power. Having now spent a couple years looking at this, I have to conclude that that's simply not the case. It is very true that sometimes desperately ignorant aristocrats had too much power in politics and the military, all the way through the end of The Second World War. It's also true that the British franchise only grew slowly, with universal manhood suffrage only attained in the early twentieth century. But public opinion was much more important than I thought it was, and public opinion was often more viciously imperialist than the bloodthirsty aristocrats who ran the government.

Empire was popular. Over the course of the nineteenth century, news from the Empire became big business. Regulatory and technological changes led to more widely available and cheaper newspapers. Thanks to the expanding network of telegraph lines in the mid-nineteenth century, the news could come quicker, and with less mediation by polite opinion.

> The newspaper revolution of the [18]50s significantly altered Britain's relationship with the wider world... The deeds of heroic men on Britain's colonial frontiers and accounts of "small wars" in faraway places offered lower-, middle-, and working-class readers a banquet of patriotic adventure stories set in exotic locations. Millions of people in Britain who had never picked up a newspaper before became deeply involved in the unfolding drama of empire. The "new journalism" helped foster a new imperialism— and an imperial ethos that would reshape Britishness.[180]

The mid-century master of this sort of politics was Henry John Temple, better known as the Viscount Palmerston. He had a staggeringly long career in politics, entering Parliament in 1806, and dying as Prime Minister in 1865. It would be silly to pin Britain's turn towards hyper-aggression and failure on one man, but he certainly managed to play a

---

[180] P.302 Wilson, Ben Heyday: The 1850s and the Dawn of the Global Age

large role in a lot of it. He was Foreign Secretary when the British forced Greek independence, and essentially invented Belgium in the 1830s. He was also Prime minster during the empire's extraordinary peak in the latter 1850s, managing to oversee the destruction of Chinese power in the Second Opium War (1856-1860), and the vicious subjugation of India after the first War of Indian Independence (1857-1858).

Thanks to a press that shamelessly harped on the deaths of English colonists, real and imagined, no one was opposed to the harrowing of India. Many in government were embarrassed by the China policy, however. Even in the nineteenth century, destroying one of the world's great civilizations to sell some drugs struck many as being a bit out of line. Palmerston's China policy was subject to a vote of censure in the Parliament, which led to an election in the spring of 1857. The aristocrats who ran the country thought Palmerston's policy was too aggressive. The voting public at the time, limited as it was, did not. Palmerston was confirmed in power, and Britain forced China into a humiliating capitulation that is rightly resented to this day.

In the century leading up to 1914, the British Empire faced a series of choices much like the ones we face today in the United States. Its people had revolutionized the way the world lived. They were instrumental in building unheard of prosperity. If they had stuck to the principles that built that prosperity, informal empire, free trade and a strong navy, British dominance could have slowly faded, giving way to a richer, freer world. Who knows, it is unlikely, but perhaps they could have remained the world's greatest power into the 21st century. That's not what happened.

It's the Nationalism, Stupid

Over the course of the nineteenth and early twentieth centuries, the British squandered the true wellsprings of their power in pursuit of ancient ideas of grandeur and formal imperial expansion. What they failed to recognize was the power of nationalism, in their supposed rivals, and in the many disparate peoples that made up their empire. The British strategists, caught up in their historical hangover, took a series of actions to preserve their power that in retrospect almost seem calculated to inflame the nationalist passions of the rest of the world's peoples. The British World System was built with an emphasis on a loose, deniable informal empire that was obscenely profitable. In the Crimean War starting in 1853, and for the six decades thereafter, the British consistently acted to make their Empire more formal, more obvious, and more offensive to everybody they were exerting their power over. It was offensive to everyone from the Germans to the Chinese to the Zulu. The US World System figured out how to make the world's nationalist passions work in its favor after 1945. The British Empire's complete failure to manage these passions led to its fall.

A merely chronological recounting of this period won't get at the full scope of the slow-moving disaster. In this chapter, the narratives of individual countries take center stage. By taking a look at the decay of the British World System from the perspective of just a few of the peoples affected, we'll get a better sense of how relentlessly mismanaged the whole thing was. By spending some time on the main "rivals", we'll demolish the idea that Britain's failures were justified by competition. As we go through each story, keep in mind that similar processes were taking place in many places that we don't have the time to cover. The British World System was so all-encompassing that to comprehensively cover every element of its fall would make this chapter longer than the entire rest of the book.

Ireland: The First Colony, the First to Go

The Irish were Britain's first colonized people, both in the modern era, and long before. The Welsh became part of England's political system so far back in time, that as an outsider I find it hard to see their experience as very different from the Northumbrians or Mercians. Every good Welsh patriot bridles at that suggestion, ready with a thousand reasons why their ancient kingdoms should be seen as different and separate from the seven early English kingdoms, from their descent from the Romano-British to a still-surviving language. All that is true-ish, but in a book that focuses on modern political development, and sees everything, everywhere before the 1640s or so as an unbroken string of vile thuggery, separate Welsh identity and political agitation just doesn't figure much. As much as I'd like to get into the details of fascinating controversies like the battle to disestablish the English church in Wales, this book is meant to be a brief survey not a comprehensive one.

The Scottish were involuntarily absorbed into British identity as well, and much more recently than the Welsh. But the Scots were bullied into Union with England on much more equitable and profitable terms than the Irish. The first British kings were Scottish kings first after all, and the fact that the Scots voted to stay in the United Kingdom as recently as 2014 indicates that they have had an experience, since the 1707 Act of Union anyway, that was for richer rather than for poorer.

The Irish were just a little too distant, a little too numerous, a little too poor, and a lot too Catholic to ever be absorbed on the same generally positive terms as the Scots or the Welsh. It has been a centuries long tale of oppression, one that every English ruling group, from the Normans in the 1100s, to Cromwell's New Model Army in the 1650s, to twentieth century UK prime ministers has added to. It's easy to characterize the experience after the Reformation as one of the

Protestant English repressing the Irish Catholics, and there is some truth to that, but it's nowhere near that simple.

Ireland's brutalization was made worse by the fact that England's control of Ireland throughout the medieval period was so tenuous. A weak king would lose control, and a strong king would come back a decade or decades later and start the process of conquest all over again. "Each of the reconquests of Ireland had involved some confiscation of land held by the Catholic Irish and its transfer to successive waves of English landlords, speculators or farmers..."[181] Each wave of conquerors, and the populations used for settlement were different. Around 1610 James I sent over the Scottish Presbyterians that formed the nucleus of the Northern Ireland that remains with the United Kingdom today. It's somehow fitting that the king who first united Scotland and England did the most to shatter Ireland, but there were many waves of colonization before and after James's "Plantation of Ulster". Each new wave of English conquest oppressed the Catholics, but also left earlier waves of English and Scottish colonizers dissatisfied to differing degrees.

Over the course of the 1600s, the start-stop history of English conquest ended. The growing "Empire of Wealth" described in Chapter four gave England the resources it needed to complete its control and deepen the oppression over the course of the century, culminating in the 1690s. William III's crushing of Ireland, as part of the post-Glorious Revolution consolidation of English power over the "British Isles", left Ireland particularly brutalized. The country's subjugation was so comprehensive that London politicians didn't really need to worry about Irish questions until the later 1770s when the British troops based in Ireland were diverted to fight against American Independence. Ireland was the first victim of the broader thuggery of British

---

[181] P.67 Webb, R.K. Modern England 2nd Edition

Nationalism. It was also the first country to free itself by turning the tool of nationalism against the British oppressors.

Modern Irish nationalism took a while to develop. In the earlier stages, and to a steadily diminishing extent across the 1800s, the Catholic and Protestant Irish could make common cause against the English on certain questions. This seems strange from the modern perspective, where conflicts in Northern Ireland are usually between the Catholic and Presbyterian Irish. One of the many tools of oppression was the Irish obligation to pay for the established English Church. This fueled both Catholic and Presbyterian resentment. Unlike in the North American colonies, the Navigation Acts were strictly applied to Ireland throughout the 1700s. These laws imposed onerous tariffs and requirements on trade for the benefit of England and Scotland. This irritated everybody who had an interest in Irish land, whether they were absentee English nobility, resident landowners, or peasants.

The early political fights against British oppression, like the fight against the Navigation Acts, won in 1779, and for Catholic Emancipation (basic political rights), won in 1828, were fought for by a more united Irish political class. Its success was due in part to the fact that there initially weren't many Catholics in this political class. Poverty and oppression had kept Catholics from even the most basic participation in the government of their own country. Successive waves of conquest added diversity to ownership interests, but mostly just brought misery for the Catholic peasantry.

The ceaseless misery of the Catholic majority began to break down in the 1700s. In the context of relative peace after the brutal 1690s, not even the Protestant Ascendancy could keep all wealth from trickling down to some Catholics. By the early 1800s, Irish Catholics began to develop a more independent voice, through groups like the Catholic

Board (est.1811), the Catholic Association (est. 1823), and powerful Catholic politicians like the Dublin lawyer Daniel O'Connell (1775-1847).[182] As differing power centers grew up in Ireland, London continued to play them off of each other. In return for Catholic Emancipation in 1829, the property requirement for voting was jacked up considerably, disenfranchising many of the Catholic voters that had made Emancipation possible. Three years later, with the First Reform Act in 1832, a broader slice of the English and Scottish population got the right to vote. The Irish franchise was reformed as well. But the property restrictions were not eased in any meaningful way, essentially giving the nothing to the broader Irish Catholic public.

Despite this, at the dawn of the 1840s it was easy to imagine that Ireland's issues had been managed to a degree. Parliament now had both Protestant and (limited) Catholic Irish representation, and the generalized bourgeois drive against corruption and aristocratic abuses couldn't be kept entirely out of Ireland. The Irish Catholics were beginning to carve out a meager but growing slice of the British Empire's prosperity through organization to keep landowners more honest, and through more profitable roles in the military and in England's rapidly expanding industrial cities.

Then the "Irish problem" turned horrific.

The Great Famine

Nothing fuels nationalism like an atrocity, and the Irish Famine was one of the worst the nineteenth century had to offer. The potato crop failed in 1845 and 1846 due to a virus known as potato blight. The destruction of the crop was so widespread that what little was left had to be eaten, leaving nothing left over to plant in 1847. The Irish census

---

[182]p. 190-191 Webb, R.K. Modern England 2nd Edition

in 1841 recorded 8,175,124 people. In 1851 it was 6,552,385. Somewhere between half a million and a million people died from outright starvation or related diseases. The rest left the country. The famine supercharged the already extensive practice of Irish emigration. The combined population of Ireland and Northern Ireland in 2017 still has not reached the numbers attained in 1841. The population of the Irish diasporas in the United States, Canada, and Australia are larger than the independent Irish population today. This too is a legacy of the famine.

The British at the time saw this as an unfortunate, primarily biological event. Outrageously, in some British circles and history texts, this is still the way the Great Famine is viewed today. The country that had violently taken and repressed Ireland for centuries, the country whose aristocracy owned and managed much of the land of Ireland, and the country who set and ran the terms of trade and the economy in Ireland, essentially took the attitude of "Gee whiz, that's too bad!". The government made a few desperately inadequate attempts to stem the horror, but private charity did far more. It wasn't nearly enough. During the famine, the English continued to import food from Ireland as the Irish starved. Anger over the Great Famine is still a large part of Irish identity today, in Ireland and in its vastly more populous diaspora. And it should be. Other than the Great Bengal Famine of 1770[183], there is no clearer illustration of the contempt that the British had for their subject peoples.

The political damage done was not immediately apparent. The Irish were focused on survival. There was a brief uprising in 1848, inspired both by the famine and the Europe-wide upheaval of that year, but it was quickly crushed. "Indeed, for more than fifteen years, many Englishmen thought that the Irish problem had been solved, however

---

[183] Discussed in Chapter four

dreadful the remedies that Providence had chosen to apply."[184] Those Englishmen couldn't be more wrong. The famine became one of the founding grievances of modern Irish nationalism. It was important to the politicians and people of Ireland, but it was perhaps even more important to the large Irish diaspora that built up across the British Empire and in the United States.

Crucially, embittered Irish migrants in the United States were free to organize against British control of Ireland, and organize they did. Those who stayed in Ireland could occasionally be placated by progress in political representation and the all-important issue of land reform. The hierarchy of the Catholic Church in Ireland also tended to disapprove of more radical solutions to Ireland's problems. The Irish in the US diaspora were not similarly constrained. They were more focused on British crimes than incremental solutions, and more likely to advocate for independence. They provided organization, funding, and occasionally arms for more radical groups and politicians. This dynamic was present from the Famine through to the foundation of the Irish Free State in 1922, and remains a factor in the troubles in Northern Ireland down to today. The Irish diaspora was one of many factors that kept British and Irish politicians from finding any true solution to the "Irish Problem" across the 1800s.

Too Close, Too Far, Irish Power in British Politics

The United Kingdom of Great Britain and Ireland came into existence in 1801. It was established by two Acts of Union in 1800, one in the British Parliament, and one in the Parliament of Ireland. With the passage of this act, the ancient Irish parliament dissolved itself. This parliament had represented the interests of the Protestant landowners, not the vast majority of the Irish people. Nonetheless, the "repeal" of

---

[184] P. 281 Webb, R.K. Modern England 2nd Edition

Union was a rallying cry for Irish Nationalists throughout the nineteenth century. The landowners who lost their voice in the Irish parliament were not cut out entirely. They were given representation in the UK parliament that sits in London. Until the establishment of the Irish Free State in 1921, this Irish representation remained contentious, and it remains contentious today. At the time of this writing, the Northern Irish Democratic Union Party (DUP) holds the power in the UK's shaky governing coalition, making the Brexit process more difficult for everybody.

At the outset, in 1801, the Irish members of Parliament reliably represented the interests of Irish landowners. They were just another fairly predictable interest group to be managed in British politics. Individual nationalist politicians, like Daniel O'Connel (Member of Parliament (MP) from 1828 to 1847) had a real impact, but most Irish MP's were manageable. Over the course of the nineteenth century, the UK slice of the British public that could vote for parliament slowly grew. The First and Second Reform Acts in 1832 and 1867, pointedly excluded any expansion of the Irish franchise. With the Third Reform Act in 1884, however, the number of men in Ireland who could vote tripled, and the floodgates of Irish nationalism truly opened.

The Irish MPs became a powerful political bloc that kept Irish land issues and advocacy for "Home Rule" at the forefront of British Politics for four decades. To oversimplify dramatically, the British Liberal party tended to want to satisfy these demands, while the Conservative party tended to side more with the landowners and later the Protestants of Northern Ireland. The Liberals could also act oppressively, of course, and Conservatives occasionally put forward legislation that satisfied Irish Nationalist demands. It all depended on the give and take of the politics of the day.

Long before 1884, however, the effects of the Great Famine were disordering both Irish and British politics. The Irish Republican Brotherhood, or Fenians, a forerunner of later pro-independence groups, was founded in the United States in 1858.[185] By the mid-1860s, they were having an impact in Ireland and the UK, both in organization, and with some active freedom-fighting/terrorism. They didn't have much mass appeal in Ireland, but their actions served to put British politicians on notice that all was not well in Ireland. William Gladstone in particular became convinced that something had to be done, and he made Irish issues a centerpiece of his legendary political career. Between 1868 and 1894, the Liberal Gladstone served as Prime Minister an unprecedented and never since matched four separate times.

Even before the advent of the Irish bloc in Parliament, in the later 1860s, Gladstone attempted to make Ireland happier, with the disestablishment of the English Church in Ireland, and some attempts at land reform. In later governments he put forward multiple attempts at Irish "Home Rule" legislation. As you can probably guess, judging from the fact that a UK prime minister supported it, "Home Rule" did not mean independence. The proposals varied over decades of discussion, but the idea was often to treat Ireland similarly to the overseas dominions like Canada and Australia. Throughout the 1880s, Gladstone and other British politicians worked with, and had to deal with one of the universally recognized titans of Irish and British politics, Charles Stewart Parnell.

Parnell

Parnell's formation and leadership of the Irish Parliamentary Party (1875-1890) may be one of history's great missed opportunities.

---

[185] P. 342 Webb, R.K. Modern England 2nd Edition

Parnell was a scion of the old Protestant landowner class, but he transcended his roots to become a formative figure in Irish nationalism through savvy political maneuvering, a deft touch for public opinion in Ireland, and great personal charisma. He managed to portray himself as a firebrand for the Irish nation, thanks to an arrest by the British authorities, while also working through the system to attain the possible. Many imagine that if Parnell had lasted longer, a unified Ireland would have attained something like Canada status, and eventually emerged unified and independent, without all the bloodshed. I tend to think this oversells the great, lost leader, and undersells the extraordinary obstacles erected by the legacy of British oppression and the Famine.

Parnell and Gladstone's efforts faced repeated obstruction from the British House of Lords, Ireland's radical diaspora community, and the pro-United Kingdom Protestants of Northern Ireland. When Parnell fell from power in 1890, over his adulterous relationship with Kitty O'Shea, naming Irish bars across the world, the great moment had passed. The Irish Parliamentary Party survived under different leadership, and UK politicians continued their process of incremental reform, but it was never enough. The British always thought that a few more hand-outs would solve the problem. They never understood that the Irish might have the same aspirations for independence and dignity that they did. As will become a theme throughout this chapter, the British just didn't understand nationalism, in Ireland or anywhere else.

Land reform efforts did help. Between Parnell and the First World War, the power of landowners was dramatically curbed, and the general rise in world prosperity couldn't be kept completely out of Ireland. The fall in misery only added to Irish demands for dignity and independence. These urges were channeled primarily into the Home Rule movement, but the passion for full independence grew inexorably in Ireland and in the Irish diaspora. Finally, after the quelling of the House of Lords' veto in 1911, the Government of Ireland Act was passed in 1914, devolving significant powers to Ireland, while keeping it in the British Empire...

... And then it was postponed.

The First End of The British Empire

The First World War was expected to be a brief engagement, and it seemed only natural to politicians in London that the tricky implementation of Home Rule should be delayed. Many Irish politicians acquiesced initially, and tens of thousands of Irish soldiers fought and died for the British Empire in Continental trenches. But then the war dragged on. We will see this again and again. The demands of Britain's ruinous competition with illusory rivals repeatedly killed the chances for a happier ending to an imperial relationship. The World Wars had similar effects across the Empire.

In 1916, a group of Irish Nationalists took it upon themselves to declare independence. The Easter Rising of the Irish Republican Brotherhood only lasted six days, but it ended the old incremental era of Irish politics. Initially, the Irish public blamed the nationalists as much as the British for the destruction of Dublin that their crushing had required. That changed with Britain's brutal reaction. They executed most of the Rising's leaders, as well as other figures who had not participated directly. In the December 1918 British election, the old Irish Parliamentary party was wiped out by Sinn Féin, a party supporting Irish independence.

On January 21, 1919, the Sinn Féin members who had won the election formed an independent Irish parliament, and the War of Irish

Independence began. This bloody conflict involved fighting between the Irish Republican Army on one side, and the British Government and Protestant militias on the other. The British put together their own poorly-governed auxiliary forces, including the infamous "Black and Tans" to attempt to reassert control. Hundreds were killed, cities burned, and the sectarian animosities that have made the history of Northern Ireland so fraught were fully forged. This period gave us the division between the modern country of Ireland, and the Northern Irish territory that remains with the United Kingdom to this day.

The Anglo-Irish treaty of 1921 established the Irish Free State, and formalized Ireland's division. This prompted a brief but bloody civil war between opponents and supporters of the treaty within the Irish Free State, killing noted Irish patriots like Michael Collins. The Irish Free State was still technically a dominion within the British Commonwealth, with nominal loyalty to the British king. These minor imperial trappings were chipped away over the course of decades, but for practical purposes the Irish attained their independence in 1921. The Irish, Britain's first colonized people, became the first people to make themselves free.[186]

The Irish Inspire

Aspects of the Irish experience were unique. Their proximity to the seat of the British Empire made their period of suffering longer, but it also provided some advantages. Significant portions of the British military were Irish, as were significant portions of the working class of England and Scotland's industrial cities. The large Irish populations of the United States and the British settler colonies meant that coercion of Ireland could cause strains with vital allies. This imposed limits on the

---

[186] As opposed to the Thirteen Colonies, which were made up of *colonizers* rather than being a colonized *people*.

repression that the British could impose on the Irish people. British treatment of more distant peoples, like those in Africa and Asia, was significantly more monstrous. The Irish were spared concentration camps. While British propaganda deplored the behavior of the German "Huns" in Belgium, they could only go so far in repressing the countrymen of soldiers that were dying to fight the Germans. Familiarity forced the British to treat the Irish like fellow human beings, though not equal ones.

Nonetheless, the Irish struggle became an inspiration to subject peoples throughout the world. From India, to Africa, to non-British struggles in Algeria and Vietnam, the Irish victory over their imperial oppressors shone like a beacon. The lessons of the Irish struggle were applied in independence struggles everywhere. If only the British had learned these lessons better, they might have avoided not only the domestic economic catastrophe of decolonization, but the external violence that attended it, *and* improved the post-imperial lots of its former colonies in the bargain. British incomprehension of nationalist urges, followed by repression, followed by failure was a pattern that recurred over and over in the first half of the twentieth century.

Europe—Informal Empire Mismanaged

Europe in the mid-nineteenth century was getting richer, but that was no bar to continued British dominance if that dominance could be managed well. All of Europe was ensnared in a financial web that brought great profits back to London. Even after its industrial dominance began to slip in the later decades of the 1800s, no European power could hope to rival Britain's position at the center of world banking and finance. The profits of Britain's head start at industrialization were continually re-invested all over the world, and in European empires as well. A lot of the continental European capital and infrastructure destroyed in the First World War had been paying dividends straight to London. There's an inertia to financial relations. Without some form of disruption, profitable systems will remain in place. The Great Wars that Britain allowed to happen disrupted the financial relations that made their world system possible.

The United States was a vastly greater threat to the British World System than anything the French, Russians or Germans could put together. This is obvious in retrospect—we're living in the US World System after all—but perceptive thinkers at the time could see the threat as well. Large chunks of the extraordinary wealth developed in this continent-wide country flowed back to London as well, but the United States didn't have any natural checks on its power. Canada and Mexico didn't provide any meaningful military competition, allowing the US to focus on economic development. The size of the US economy surpassed the size of the UK economy at some point in the last decade of the nineteenth century, and then continued to zoom ahead. The US colossus only awaited a disruption of the old system to take the leading role. The British mismanagement of Europe provided that disruption.

Britain's newly enriched informal empire in Europe was caught up in its own historical hangover in the second half of the nineteenth century. They were inspired by Britain's brutal empire more than the freedoms that built it. This meant that every European country had to deal with the ambitions of every country it shared a border with. The French had to deal with the Germans and the Italians. The Germans had to deal with the French and the Russians. The Russians had to deal with the Japanese and the Germans. The Austrians had to deal with a bewildering array of competitors, large and small. The British didn't really have to deal with any of it. To be sure, the European natives could put up a bigger fight than the Maori or the Zulu, but that's an argument for staying out of European wars, not getting into them. If the British had done a better job of managing their European informal empire, Germany would never have unified. Even after that failure, there was no reason to get involved in Germany's attempts to control Europe other than reasons the British had created for themselves.

One of the central ironies of the run-up to the two World Wars, is that the British weren't all that focused on the Germans they ruined themselves fighting. Up until the decade and a half prior to 1914, and even within that crucial decade, the British were far more focused on two other obsessions: Their hilariously diminished French rival, and the farcical idea that Russia posed a threat to British India.

The Hilarious French

For a millennia prior to their Revolution in 1789, the French had led Europe. In the days of the old school thuggish equation, when (land + peasants) times organization equaled power, France's vast size, population and agricultural resources were unequalled in Europe. France was rarely unified, but even when it wasn't, French armies wrought havoc across the Continent and into North Africa and the Middle East. French-ish Norman armies took England in 1066, Jerusalem in 1099, Constantinople in 1204, and large tracts of Italy and Germany at various times. When Henry IV (r.1589-1610) and his successors finally unified France, it bestrode the continent like a colossus.[187] After 1789, under the Revolutionary governments and Napoleon, the French had taken the weaponization of nationalism to new heights. Napoleon briefly surpassed the accomplishments of any French king or Norman Duke, only running out of steam at Moscow.

After all that, the French nineteenth century experience just looks kind of comical. British propaganda from the 1800s up to today has

---

[187] Name that Shakespeare reference...

portrayed the nineteenth century French Empire as a meaningful rival. Closer inspection reveals that to be ridiculous. They were desperately outclassed by their "rivals" across the English Channel. The result of the Napoleonic wars makes this clear. France, with a world-historically great general, weaponized nationalism, and the human resources and wealth of France, Italy, Germany, and much of Eastern Europe to draw upon…lost to a nation of shop-keepers and sailors.

France's nineteenth century reputation and power was a legacy of better days. Paris still led Europe culturally, as it had for centuries. France still controlled a large territory, and like Britain, it could rely on a more unified national identity than most. Unlike the Germans, the Austrians and the Russians, their battles for national unity and against minorities had already been won. It still controlled a land army that was larger and arguably better run than the British one. France's large unified market and proximity to the British economic dynamo also positioned it well to benefit from industrialization and grow wealthy and prosperous.

Politically France was a basket case. The country had a grand history that was impossible to live up to. British political history is one of occasionally jerky but constant evolution from 1689 until today. The French had at least seven separate forms of government in the nineteenth century alone. They went from Republic to Empire (1804), to two separate new Monarchical systems (1814 and 1830), to another brief republic (1848) to another Empire (1851) to another Republic (1870). Throughout this development, they desperately tried to reassert their dominance in Europe, doing such a terrible job that they managed to bring about the Unification of Germany, a country that beat France in the Franco-Prussian war before it was even officially born. The German empire was declared in the French palace of Versailles in January 1871. The French didn't invite them there. The Republic set up in the aftermath of loss to Germany in 1870, France's third, managed to last all the way up until the Second World War, and another conquest by Germany.

The French imagined that Britain's large land empire was a factor in *its* extraordinary power, so they decided to build one too! They expended an extraordinary amount of blood and treasure to build a large and largely economically useless land empire in Western Africa and in a handful of other places. The glorious French Empire had outposts in Algeria, Madagascar, and Vietnam. The British controlled, directly or indirectly, almost everything else on the lucrative sea routes between Algeria and Vietnam.

The French were very, very proud. The British were occasionally wise in their indulgence of French nationalist sympathies. Letting the French build an empire in North West Africa, made it easier for the British to control Egypt, the most useful bit of North Africa. But the British shouldn't have allowed this indulgence to convince them that French power was real. Part of this was history. You can't struggle against a country for a century, and beat them utterly, without suspecting that they're perpetually about to make a resurgence. The US's current obsession with a fading Russia is a good example of this. Nineteenth century history is filled with famous "incidents" where prickly French honor butted up against overwhelming British power. War supposedly threatened on multiple occasions. But upon examination, none of these incidents are particularly credible. The British worked to soothe French feelings, and prop them up, because French pretensions were such a useful tool. They allied with the British in the Crimean War, in the carving up of China, and involuntarily in the cultivation and suppression of Egypt. The relationship between the British Empire and France in the 1800s is strikingly similar to the relationship between the United States and the United Kingdom today. France could only exert itself outside Europe in junior partnership with their much more powerful ally.

The Fashoda Incident

To put this hilarious idea of French power to bed once and for all, it's worth looking at one of these famous diplomatic incidents in detail. We'll cover the obscenity that was the "Scramble for Africa" below, but let's dive in on one of the crowning episodes here, the "Fashoda Incident". Fashoda, today known as Kodok, is a small town situated on the White Nile river in what is currently South Sudan. On September 18, 1898, French and British colonizing forces met here. Major Jean-Baptiste Marchand, and Lord Kitchener met civilly, both politely insisting on their country's right to Fashoda. They parted peacefully, but this confrontation ignited a diplomatic firestorm. War loomed, supposedly. France ended up backing down for a number of reasons, from British naval superiority to Russia's notification that their alliance with the French did not extend to war with the British Empire over minor African towns. The way that this story is typically told leaves out some pretty important details.

The British came down the Nile from their Egyptian protectorate, through Sudanese territory that they had just conquered. The French came by land. Earlier in 1898, Lord Kitchener had led a force of 7,500 British and 12,500 Egyptian soldiers into the heart of Sudan, battling all the way, with a flotilla of gun boats, aided on some legs by a single-track railway constructed for the purpose. It was a logistical feat that would still be impressive in 2019. On September 2nd 1898, at the Battle of Omdurman, Kitchener destroyed the 50,000 strong army of the Mahdi, a Sudanese religious figure who had embarrassed the British Empire fourteen years previously. On September 3rd Kitchener's army raised the Egyptian and British flags over Khartoum, the Mahdi's capital. British forces remained there until 1956. The British forces that raced to confront Marchand in Fashoda two weeks later were smaller, a mere 1,500 British, Egyptian and Sudanese soldiers in five gunboats.

The French major showed up on a wide wheeled bicycle. With 12 French troops and 120 Senegalese infantrymen. [188]

Some rivalry.

Russia—Useful and Abused

The Russian rivalry was a bit more credible, but it too was oversold. This had disastrous results for European history, and for colonized peoples all over the world. The British leadership and public were **obsessed** with Russia. The obsession persists today, and it has spread across the Atlantic to the United States. The typical nineteenth century Briton saw herself as forward thinking and freedom loving. She saw Russia as a backward home of oriental despotism, with hordes of soldiers ready to be deployed according to the Tsar's absolutist will. The Russians were the great bogeyman of Britain's century on top. This is odd, because they were a tremendously useful tool for the British. They kept Britain's informal empire in Europe in line for the first half of the nineteenth century. This ended when the British destroyed Russia's European power for a few crucial decades after the Crimean War.

The Crimean War was the great exception to Britain's "peaceful" nineteenth century in Europe. The war, fought between 1853 and 1856, was the only British fight against a European great power between 1815 and 1914. The conflict in Crimea was particularly disastrous, but

---

[188] This story is drawn directly from James, Lawrence The Rise and Fall Of the British Empire pps. 281-284. Mr. James doesn't find this whole interaction as hilarious as I do.

the Russian obsession dominated Britain's nineteenth century. Fear of the threat that Russia supposedly posed to Britain's formal empire in India, and informal empire in Ottoman lands, is at the root of most of the worst policy decisions the British made in the 1800s. These range from the disastrous invasions of Afghanistan in the 1840s and the 1870s, to the occupation of Egypt in 1882 that launched Europe's "Scramble for Africa". Over and over again, fear of Russia provided the justification for the expansion and militarization of British Empire. It was the propaganda gift that kept on giving to British Imperialists. The Russia obsession was probably the main driver behind the British Empire's catastrophic shift in focus from informal to formal empire.

It is one of history's greatest ironies that in the two twentieth century wars that destroyed the British World System, Russia was allied with the UK against Germany. You would think that this would have prompted some reevaluation of the nineteenth century. It hasn't.

> The threat that Russia posed to Britain grew like a cancer in the century before the assassination of Franz Ferdinand [in 1914], as Russia transformed itself from a ramshackle, archaic kingdom with an agrarian economy into a reformed and ambitious Empire. This set alarm bells ringing in London with increasing regularity and at increasing volume as it became clear that Russian growth and expansion had not just brought its interests into competition with those of Britain but threatened to overwhelm them. [189]

That account isn't taken from some two-hundred-years-past imperial fantasist, or some Cold War historian projecting twentieth century facts back on to the 1800s. It's taken from a book published in 2015. The Silk Roads: A New History of the World is one of the more successful pop history books of the decade. If you're in the English-speaking world, it is probably prominently displayed on the bookshelf at your

---

[189] P. 280-281 Frankopan, Peter The Silk Roads: A New History of the World

local airport's newsstand. The book is a fun survey, but its treatment of Britain's rivalry with Russia is basically just regurgitated British imperial propaganda. Let's dismantle it, shall we?

Russia's Vast, Empty Empire

It's undeniable that Russia's size and scale are impressive. In 1900, the Russian empire was estimated to have ruled over 136 million people, compared to the mere 40 million found in the United Kingdom at the time. Throughout the nineteenth century, the Russian empire's borders did get much closer to British India, and Britain's informal empires in China and Ottoman Turkey. In the 1700s and 1800s, they steadily encroached on the Ottoman and Iranian empires, a growth which British strategists imagined might eventually threaten the sea routes to India. In the latter nineteenth century they scooped up a series of khanates on the territories of modern Kazakhstan, Uzbekistan, Tajikistan and Turkmenistan.

You may have already noticed the amount of special pleading that went into the case for Russian power in the last paragraph. Russia ruled over three times as many people as Britain… if you don't count the British Empire. In 1900 it's estimated that 384 million people lived under the British flag. Mind you, that's just the formal subjects of the British Empire. That figure does not include the hundreds of millions of people outside formal control that labored to make Britain's informal empire more wealthy and powerful.

Up until 1945, the British Empire was always around three times more populous than the Russian one, and its peoples were in much more useful places. Even today, a quick glance at the population density map will tell you that most of Russia's population and economic activity is concentrated far to the west, up against and interacting with Europe. This was even more true in the nineteenth century, when Russia's borders included modern Finland and the Baltic countries, most of modern Belarus and Ukraine, and significant chunks of Poland. This was very uncomfortable for the peoples of Central and Eastern Europe, but the Russians never seriously threatened British interests.

"The March to India"

Those endless Asian territories Russia took in the nineteenth century look super impressive, but there weren't all that many people there, and there wasn't much economic activity either. In the glory days of the Silk Road, before the Portuguese and Spanish developed the oceanic trade routes between Asia and Europe, cities like Tashkent and Samarkand were a big deal. By the time Russia captured central Asia in the mid-nineteenth century, those glory days were long, long gone. Those once-magnificent cities were dusty ghost towns loomed over by the architectural glories of Tamerlane and other centuries-dead world-beaters.

There aren't many glorious tales of Russia's conquest of the center of the world island, because there wasn't much to it. The largest Russian army involved in the central Asian conquest was 13,000 men in 1873, used for the conquest of Khiva, a desert oasis Russia had failed to take multiple times. Most central Asian conquests typically involved smaller detachments of two to five thousand men. Those are not nineteenth century great power war numbers. The main challenge in this conquest was not the people the Russian forces met, but the logistical challenges of getting there. The time-honored war-making methods of the steppes did not present much of a challenge to Russia's nineteenth century armies, if they could get there.

In the unlikely event that the nineteenth century Russians could get a sizeable army to the borders of British India, it would have faced one of the larger and better equipped fighting forces on the planet at the time. I'm no military expert, but my understanding is that supply lines are important. The Russians were unable to capture Khiva, relatively close to the Russian controlled Caspian Sea, before 1873. The idea that they would be able to move a land army at least ten times as large, many times as far, across Afghanistan, and maintain a serious campaign against the extensive and quickly ocean-supplied forces of British India, is beyond farcical. Prior to the advent of the railways, nobody in official circles took this seriously. "The British government knew that such an expedition was not feasible. One British intelligence officer thought that any Russian invasion of India 'would amount to little more than the sending of a caravan'".[190]

Even though the government knew they were groundless, fears of Russia were a dominating factor in foreign policy discussions throughout the nineteenth century. One of the most absurd results of this was the history of the western border of British India. All of modern Pakistan was taken by the British due to fear of Russia. They feared Russian encroachment, so they moved the supposedly vulnerable border closer to Russia. The British attempted to move into Afghanistan between 1839 and 1842. It was a desperate failure, involving the loss of Britain's entire expeditionary force. Supply lines were important to the British too. To make themselves feel better, the British snapped up Sindh in 1843 and the Punjab in 1849. Modern Balochistan was added to British administration through negotiation with local princes in the 1870s. Britain conquered most of the territory of modern Pakistan to confront a Russian threat that was not real.

The picture changed somewhat with the advent of the railways, but not considerably. Russia lagged far behind Britain in rail construction. It only surpassed the British Isles in mileage in the 1880s, and it may have taken until the 1890s for the entire Russian empire to have more rail than British India alone. As with its population and priorities, the Russian empire's rail network was concentrated in the west, forming a dense network of connections among Russia's European subjects, with a few lonely lines shooting off into the east. The great Trans-Siberian railway, from Moscow to Vladivostok on the Pacific, was not

---

[190] P. 48 Figes, Orlando The Crimean War: A History

completed until 1916. The Trans-Caspian network, connecting Russia's mid-century central Asian conquests was completed in 1898, but it didn't even connect to the rest of the Russian rail system until 1906. The completion of this Orenburg Tashkent link did finally make the movement of large bodies of Russian troops to the borders of British India seem somewhat plausible.

But what would the Russians do if they got there? Leaving aside the challenge of getting masses of Russian soldiers across Afghanistan, they would then face a British India that had been massively hardened by a comprehensive railway infrastructure of its own.[191] In the decades after the first War of Indian Independence in 1857, 40,000 miles of rail infrastructure had been built in India. It was designed both to keep the Indians down, and keep any competitors out.[192] The sheer density of the network is worth a google. Many stations were fortified, and it was well integrated with British India's impressive navy and armies. The British could bring the force of a subcontinent, and a world system to any point that needed to be reinforced. British India was always secure from Russia. A serious invasion of British India from Russia was about as likely as an invasion from the Moon.

"To Constantinople!"

The Russian threat to the Ottoman Empire, however, was not a joke. The Russian Empire's population and power was concentrated in the west, and that's also where the Ottoman Empire's European lands were. The Russian quest for a warm water port came to fruition in the 1770s and the 1790s, with Catherine the Great's conquests of traditionally Muslim lands to the north of the Black Sea. The dispossessed Crimean Khanate was not directly controlled by the Ottomans, but it was a tributary state, and the Ottomans keenly felt the

---

[191] Bogart, Dan and Latika Chaudhary "Railways in Colonial India: An Economic Achievement?" http://www.socsci.uci.edu/~dbogart/railwaysahievjune2012.pdf
[192] Loc. 3102 Brendon, Piers The Decline and Fall of The British Empire

loss. Throughout the nineteenth century, the Russians consolidated power around the Black Sea, sending streams of ethnically cleansed Muslim refugees into the Ottoman Empire, and making other traditional powers in Southeastern Europe very nervous.

The Russians shared a religion with the many Eastern Orthodox Christians who lived under Ottoman rule. This helped create the Russian autocracy's fantasies of taking Istanbul back for Christianity and resurrecting the Eastern Roman Empire. Ottoman armies were only occasionally a match for Russian ones, and once the Black Sea ports began to be developed in the later 1700s, there was little physical bar to the realization of the dream.

The Russians made it to the outskirts of Istanbul twice in the nineteenth century, taking Adrianople (Edirne) in 1829, less than 150 miles from Istanbul, and making it to San Stefano (Yeşilkoy) in 1878. Yeşilkoy is close enough to be on the Istanbul subway system today. On each occasion Russia was forced to give up its gains. The threat of the British Navy, and the European armies they could subsidize, was enough to keep the Ottomans propped up. Russia's physical ability to conquer the Ottoman Empire simply didn't matter.

Proximity didn't help the Russians dominate the Ottomans economically either. The Russians could briefly conquer Ottoman territory. The British conquered the Ottoman economy. In 1838, through a combination of bribes and threats, they imposed free trade on the Ottomans. This weakened the central government by reducing its customs revenue, but led to a surge in economic activity, dominated by the British. British exports to the Ottoman Empire went up by a factor of eleven in the 1840s.[193] The Russians watched helplessly as the British economically colonized a region that they had thought was a part of their sphere of influence. These tensions led to war.

---

[193] P.47 Figes, Orlando The Crimean War: A History

The Crimean War

The Crimean War (1853-1856) was the great exception to Britain's "peaceful" nineteenth century in Europe, and it was fought against Russia in partnership with the French and the Ottomans. Its consequences were profound, but it has been pushed out of the historical consciousness by Europe's two great twentieth century wars. Its legacy for most can be boiled down to Florence Nightingale's founding of modern nursing, the Cardigan sweater, and the disastrous but poetic-to-some Charge of the Light Brigade. Among the historically-minded, the Crimean War is remembered as a bit of a scandal. The Light Brigade's suicidal horseback charge into Russian artillery was just the most famous screw-up. The British military showed itself to be unprepared, poorly-led and ill-equipped. The British-French-Ottoman invasion of Russia ended up as a long siege rather than a quick victory. Despite the even more staggering lack of preparedness of the Russians, hundreds of thousands of British and allied soldiers died accomplishing not much at all. Historians now see it as having been a wake-up call for Britain, and an important step towards the modernization of warfare generally, and the British army in particular.

The scandal is considerably bigger than that, though. It upset the balance of informal empire that had kept Britain relatively safe from European problems since 1815. The war didn't cover anyone with glory but it did satisfy one of Britain's main aims. It set Russia back decades and destroyed its influence in central Europe.[194] After the defeat of Napoleon in 1815, the Tsars had taken a leadership role on the Continent. Their armies enforced the balance of power, and acted against national and liberal revolutionaries across the length and breadth of Europe. As recently as 1848-1849, Russian armies had

---

[194] P.237 Evans, Richard J. The Pursuit of Power

supported the Habsburg Monarchy against rebellious Hungarians, and helped to defend it against the Prussian monarchy that eventually ended up unifying Germany.[195] The Crimean War ended that ability, handing Russia a large defeat, and reducing its ability to even access Europe militarily through the Black Sea. "Russia did not recover the dominant position it had held in Europe until after 1945."[196]

Though the Austrian Habsburgs did not actively fight against Russia in the Crimean War, they didn't support Russia either, which the Russians saw as a betrayal. The cozy understanding between Austria and Russia, that had kept revolutionary nationalism contained for half a century, ended. It's possible that Germany's unification in 1871 and subsequent rise to power would have happened anyway, but this strikes me as unlikely. At the least, Russian power could have maintained a better balance in Europe, one that wouldn't have required such costly British interventions in the two world wars. But the British destroyed that power, and through that destruction they created the German threat that would eventually bankrupt the British World System. All to defend against an illusory Russian threat to India.

Russia's Vast, Useless Armies

Russia has a formidable military reputation. If you look at it seriously though, it's hard to see what this reputation is based on. As any armchair historian can tell you, invading Russia is a suicidal mistake. Across the centuries, Russia's vast empty tracts of land, harsh winters, and willingness to be extraordinarily cruel to its own people has made it essentially unconquerable. Invaders from Napoleon, to Hitler, to Woodrow Wilson have found this to be the case. Russia on defense is

---

[195] P.233 Evans, Richard J. The Pursuit of Power
[196] P.442 Figes, Orlando The Crimean War: A History

unbeatable. Russia on offence is essentially useless. Russia's record beyond her borders is not mixed. It's nigh-universally disastrous.

The great exceptions, of course, would be 1813 and 1945. In both those years, victorious Russian armies swept across Europe to crush the invaders who had been foolish enough to march on Moscow. But the Russian winter did a lot of the softening-up. Napoleon had lost over half a million men to his campaign in Russia. Hitler had lost millions. The victorious Russian armies were not acting alone in either year. In 1813 they were part of the Sixth Coalition, allied with almost every non-French people in Europe. Napoleon had to deal with allied armies marching up from Spain as well as from Russia. After Napoleon had fled Russia, it was the Prussians who took the lead in the great European battles that finished him off.[197] In 1945, Hitler had to deal with two other allied fronts, coming up from Italy and down from Normandy. The victorious Russian armies of both eras were heavily subsidized and supplied by better organized British or US allies.

Outside of those years, it's hard to find examples of Russian success against any army that wasn't vastly outnumbered, like the Swedish or the Finnish, or desperately behind the times, like the Ottomans, or both, like the Austrians. Sometimes the Russians couldn't even beat these supposedly outclassed opponents. The British and French campaigns in the Crimean War were deeply absurd. The war had been launched to defend the Ottomans from a Russian invasion across the Danube in 1853. The problem was that the Ottoman armies under Omer Pasha defeated the Russians before the British and the French even got there, kicking the Russians out of Ottoman Europe. Everybody just sort of ignored the fact that the "Sick Man of Europe" had handily defeated the "Terrifying Russian Colossus" and the French and the British

---

[197] P. 365-372 Clark, Christopher Iron Kingdom: The Rise and Downfall of Prussia 1600-1947

wasted the next three years providing another great illustration of why you should never invade Russia.

Again and again across the nineteenth century, the British were told that this, this was the time to take Russia seriously! They had recovered and reformed from their last humiliating defeat. They had finally figured out how to leverage their vast population, and create a truly threatening military machine! It was never true, no matter how badly British and German militarists wanted it to be. After being desperately embarrassed in the Crimean War, the Russians spent half a century reforming their society, economy and military. Their great push for Asian empire came in China, not India. It all looked very impressive, but the Russian armies and navies in Asia were completely destroyed in the Russo-Japanese war (1904-1905). The Japanese accomplishment here shouldn't be sold short, but once again, Britain's great bogeyman had been slaughtered by what was seen at the time as a "second-rate" power.

After that humiliation, European strategists assured themselves, Russia was finally to be taken seriously. The supposedly steadily growing power of Russia was one of the main reasons that the Germans participated in the First World War. The Russians had to be defeated before they got too powerful! The Germans shouldn't have been worried. In the first contact between German and Russian forces at the Battle of Tannenberg in August 1914, the Germans destroyed two Russian armies in four days. The Russians had enough people and allied support to keep limping on for another three years or so, but their defeat in WWI was so humiliating that they needed to try a whole new system of government.

Even under the Soviets, Russian power was exaggerated. Their attempt to control Afghanistan in the 1980s lasted half as long as the current

US effort, and cost them more than five times as many casualties (which is not to say that the US attempt has been much more successful). At the time, the USSR shared a border with Afghanistan, and while US civility is exaggerated, the Soviets were much freer to brutalize the Afghans. Russia's invasion of Georgia in 2008 was also an embarrassment. Russia's war aims were accomplished, but the antiquated nature of Russian doctrine, and the inoperability of many Russian systems were on full display. Things have supposedly improved lately. But five years after the start of hostilities, the vaunted "asymmetric" powers of Russian intelligence have failed to take much of Ukraine, a country that's half Russian. After investing a decade of "peak oil" earnings in their military, and with nobody shooting at them, Russian air force operations in Syria aren't completely embarrassing, but those victories are coming in the context of a strong alliance with the long-established government of Syria, and significant support from Lebanese and Iranian ground forces. Oh, also Syrian rebels they are bombing don't have an air force or any serious anti-aircraft capabilities.

For centuries now, the "threat" from Russia has been consistently exaggerated to justify violent actions by the British and US World Systems. This remains the case in 2019. A declining power, with a falling population, and a GDP per capita that's about to be surpassed by China, is key to the strategy and budget demands of the US military. The farcical idea that Russia is a serious rival in "Great Power Competition" is costing the US taxpayer hundreds of billions of dollars. Our continued indulgence of nineteenth century British myths of the "Great Game" with Russia is a big part of this.

The threat from Germany was not a myth. The necessity of confronting it is a myth we believe in to this day.

Germany—The European Natives Discover Nationalism

The most important thing about Germany is not Adolf Hitler. Hitler, Germany's mad dictator from 1933 to 1945, is one of history's most compelling figures. He murdered tens of millions. He captured the hearts and minds of a country that many saw as the world's most civilized, and directed that country towards savage barbarism. He's a big deal. But he wasn't inevitable, and there's a lot more to German history than Hitler.

2017 saw the release of Wonder Woman, a film beloved by millions. I hated it. For most of my life I've been hungry for pop culture treatments of the First World War. It's a tremendously important part of world history, and it's almost never depicted on screen. Not even Steven Spielberg could do it successfully. Remember 2011's War Horse? Very few do. I was very excited to see what Wonder Woman made of the Great War. It was infuriating. The filmmakers seemed to have done enough Wikipedia-ing to pick up a name or two, and some of the trench warfare stuff was amusing, but beyond that they just made a WWII flick. The bad guys were Nazis in First World War uniforms. They were portrayed as the same bunch of screeching exterminatory lunatics we see in the multiple depictions of the battle against the Nazis we get every year. Wonder Woman's filmmakers owe the German people an apology.

The ignorance of the Wonder Woman filmmakers is only different in degree from many historical treatments of the rise of Germany. The very real evil of Germany in the 1930s and 1940s is cast back to taint everything about German history. This is most egregious in the way that it colors descriptions of the run up to the First World War. The Germans are depicted as Nazis, and Kaiser Wilhelm II steps into the role of Hitler. It's absurd to conflate an incompetent quasi-constitutional monarch with the demonic force that was Hitler and the

Nazis, but it helps to justify first the British choice to involve itself in the Great War in 1914, and second the US choice to jump in in 1918. The fact that that US decision to jump in and pick a winner probably did more than anything else to create Hitler is conveniently left out of discussions. Discussions we don't have, because the First WWIs a blind spot in popular culture. Which is how you get treatments of the topic as bad as Wonder Woman's.

There's a reason why British and US historiography is obsessed with Hitler. It serves to distract us from noticing something important. The most important thing about Germany is not Adolf Hitler. The most important thing about Germany is that it did not exist at the beginning of the British World System. It was a series of British choices and British mistakes that created a unified Germany. And once the Teutonic titan was created, confronting it was not necessary. Hitler had to be confronted, of course, but the circumstances that created him were as British and American as they were German, if not more so. Without the war that the British allowed to start in 1914, and the ending of the war the Americans imposed in 1918, there would never have been a Hitler.

Also, without Britain's two "victorious" wars against Germany, the British World System might have survived.

German Nationalism

Peoples that could plausibly be called Germans have occupied the center of Europe for well over a thousand years. From medieval times, German colonists weaponized Christianity to crusade against pagan peoples further east. The Holy Roman Empire, an entity that claimed the Europe-wide legacy of Rome, most often spoke with a powerful German voice. But the tools that had served Germany so well for centuries failed miserably after the Reformation got going in the 1500s. Power built on war-happy aristocratic classes and a universal church fragmented with horrifying results. The long-lived Holy Roman Empire (800 or 964 -1806) had accreted a degree of power over a staggeringly diverse assemblage of administrative units. Land could be controlled by free cities, bishoprics, religious orders, and a full range of aristocratic landholders, with a bewildering range of titles. Each sub-division had its own privileges and legal peculiarities. This was barely manageable with a unified church. When Christianity fractured into Catholic, Lutheran, Calivinist, and other denominations, the empire descended into centuries of crisis.

States like Bavaria, Saxony, and most importantly Prussia rose up to challenge the Austrian Holy Roman Emperors. In the best argument for great man history I can think of, Prussia won out, thanks to what very serious historians describe as "…a freakish run of abnormally gifted Hohenzollern leaders"[198] from the Great Elector Frederick William (r.1640-1688) to King Frederick II "the Great" (r.1740-1786). The Hohenzollern dynasty's run of quality ended with Frederick II, but Prussia had already been set on a winning trajectory. By the time Kaiser Wilhelm II, the last of the Hohenzollerns, ran Prussia in to the ground in 1918, he was also running a united Germany. Prussia's lead had a lot to do with the serial disasters it was subjected to. The formative one for what was then known as Brandenburg-Prussia was the Thirty Years' War (1618-1648). The handful of disconnected Northern European territories under the Hohenzollerns were some of the most abused territories, at the mercy of invading armies from multiple powers. This prompted Prussia to develop one of the most skilled and largest armies in Europe, proportional to its size. This great founding embarrassment prompted Prussia's, and later Germany's,

---

[198] P.246 Clark, Christopher Iron Kingdom : The Rise and Downfall of Prussia 1600-1947

extraordinary zeal in pursuit of martial, technological, and societal accomplishments.

New Prussia versus Old Austria

To oversimplify massively, from the early 1700s to German Unification in 1871, German and central European politics were about the tensions between Prussia, and the Austrian leaders of the larger bodies of the Holy Roman Empire, and later the German Confederation, that Prussia was still technically subject to for this period.

> The struggle between Prussia and Austria represented in this sense a conflict between the 'state principle', based on the primacy of the state over all domestic and supra-territorial authorities, and the 'imperial principle' of diffused authority and mixed sovereignty that had been a defining feature of the Holy Roman Empire since the Middle Ages.

Austria and Prussia were sometimes aligned, and sometimes not. But Austria was always playing catch-up. The novelty of Prussia as a state left it freer to innovate. It also had powerful outside patrons when it counted. During the Seven Years' War (1756-1763), Austria, France, and Russia all teamed up to destroy what was still a second-rate power. Luck, and Frederick II's military prowess kept Prussia going, but so did British subsidies. Over the course of the 1700s, Prussia moved up the rankings, joining in with Russia and Austria in carving up Poland in the 1770s and the 1790s. No matter how talented Prussian kings were, or how skilled their armies were, a larger "Germany" wasn't yet on the cards. It took a new disaster to make that possible.

Napoleon destroyed the Holy Roman Empire first physically, through a series of conquests, and then institutionally. He also powerfully demonstrated the value of nationalism, fielding armies that were both much larger and much more motivated than his competitors. This ignited a passion for German unity. The whole revolutionary and Napoleonic period, from 1794 to 1815 was not just a war, it was a generation-long upheaval for central Europe. The old German politics of dynastic intrigue and civilized battle buckled under the constant pressure. Many smaller states were swept away, and the necessity to modernize everything, from education to military administration, was repeatedly reinforced by humiliation. After losing the battles of Jena and Auerstedt in 1806, Prussia lost two-thirds of its territory, and was forced into an alliance with France that lasted until 1813. The grinding catastrophe of these two decades forced innovation in Prussia and across the German states. Other polities, like Baden, Wurttemberg and Bavaria went further towards constitutional reform than Prussia, but Prussia led the way in economic reforms.[199]

German nationalism was a key facet of Prussia's ability to reassert itself. In 1813, as the alliance with France disintegrated, the Prussian king called up all the able-bodied men in his kingdom to join militias to defend the homeland. Though the king would loathe the comparison, this was similar to the 1793 *levée en masse*, when France's Revolutionary government conscripted the entire public. 1806 had been an embarrassment that left many wondering whether Prussia would survive as a great power, or even an independent one. The Prussian citizen militias, combined with a restructured regular army, reestablished Prussia's great power status after 1813. Prussian armies took the lead and a disproportionate amount of the losses in many of the great battles that ended Napoleon's power.

German nationalism was a powerful force in the reconstruction and restoration of Prussia and the other states. The victories from 1813 to

[199] P. 340 Clark, Christopher Iron Kingdom : The Rise and Downfall of Prussia 1600-1947

1815 made its value clear. But this was inconvenient for the two largest states. Prussia controlled large Polish populations, and depending on the period, there were usually more Slavs than Germans in Austria's empire. Nationalism was also deeply tied to revolution, and no hereditary monarch was going to be a fan of that. Prussia would eventually make its peace with these ideas, but that lay decades in the future. The reforming zeal that Prussian and other German leaders had used to survive and triumph during the Napoleonic wars quickly dissipated after they had been won.

A successor of sorts to the Holy Roman Empire, the German Confederation, was put together. The number of German states had been cut down from hundreds to just thirty-nine. This confederation was used primarily as a tool for repression of all revolutionary ideas, including liberalism and nationalism. The Carlsbad Decrees of 1819 instituted federation-wide censorship, and banned many nationalist groups. Following the Congress of Vienna in 1815, the Austrian and Prussian aristocracies joined together with the ruling classes across the continent to attempt to reconstruct the pre-Revolutionary world. The center of this reactionary dispensation, and its muscle, was the relationship between Austria and Russia. The Austrians had done well out of the war, picking up Italian territory they had craved for centuries, and shedding a lot of painful complexity in Germany with the demise of the Holy Roman Empire. Austrian territorial reach and Russian numbers provided a forceful counterweight to a series of revolutions in the first half of the 1800s.

At the Congress of Vienna, Britain once again stepped in to help Prussia, who they saw as a helpful counterweight against France. They made sure that Prussian borders included territories further west. These territories, especially the Rhineland, eventually became the industrial heart of Germany. "The creation of a large western wedge of Prussian territory along the river Rhine was a British not a Prussian, idea."[200] This ensured that Franco-Prussian rivalry became an important dynamic throughout the nineteenth and twentieth centuries. This early promotion of Prussia makes more sense than British choices later in the century. Directly after a century-long struggle with France, it made sense to set up a natural competitor to it.

In the first half of the 1800s, Prussia most often supported Austrian and Russian crushing of revolutionary and nationalist uprisings. The fact that these uprisings kept happening, though, was an indication that the days of the thugs on top were numbered. The monarchs managed to preserve their position until the First World War, but the demolition of traditional privileges and structures continued. The traditional peasant duty to work on aristocratic farms was done away with. In 1834 a German Confederation-wide customs union was established. And the national ideas that had been so important to the fight against Napoleon continued to percolate, capturing the minds of many, including Frederick William IV (r.1840-1861), the King of Prussia himself.

Thanks to modern communication technologies, the upheaval of 1848 proved much harder to stamp out. Revolution spread everywhere in Continental Europe, and nationalism was a larger factor than before, in every country. The government of Metternich, the architect of Europe's reactionary system, fell in Austria. France lost another king. Multiple Italian and German countries got constitutions and overthrew monarchs. The list goes on and on. The Prussian monarchy is probably the only aristocratic interest that was helped by these events. The Prussian King's view of nationalism was necessarily idiosyncratic, but he saw the attraction of the idea. During 1848, he went further towards endorsing German nationalism than any other European monarch, using it to defuse the Berlin mob, and at least initially participating in

---

[200] P.388 Clark, Christopher Iron Kingdom : The Rise and Downfall of Prussia 1600-1947

the attempt to set up an all-German legislative body in Frankfurt. He played his cards rather well, choosing the right times to be carried along by events and the right times to be repressive. In doing so, he helped to link Prussia to the idea of unification in German minds.

On the surface at least, the reactionaries managed to win in 1848 as well. It was a close-run thing, but it was Russia that made the difference. The Russians shored up the Austrian empire by taking a direct hand in crushing Vienna's rebelling Hungarian subjects. It also served to deter the Prussians from making any more attempts to use nationalism to further assert itself against Austria. Once again, Russia had proved vital in keeping Germany from centralizing. Russia helped keep Britain's informal empire in Europe manageable.

German Unification

Throughout the contest for primacy in the German lands, the Prussians held more cards than the Austrians. They were free of the burden of medieval rigamarole, usually had a better organized and more modern military, and long before 1848 they took a lead in exploiting German nationalism. The only thing Austria had was Russia, the reactionary titan to the east. With the Crimean War (1853-1856), the British destroyed this relationship. ""…the Austrians had made the fateful decision to join the anti-Russia coalition, a move that was seen in St. Petersburg as rank treachery. Vienna thereby irretrievably forfeited the Russian support that had once been the cornerstone of its foreign policy."[201] By drawing Austria into the Crimean War, even though the Austrians didn't do any fighting, the British had opened the door to German unification and the apocalyptic wars of the twentieth century.

---

[201] P. 512 Iron Kingdom : The Rise and Downfall of Prussia 1600-1947

Britain's Russia obsession broke Europe's old order for good. The loss of Russia's support led to a decade of humiliation for Austria. Their territories in Italy went first. Just three years after the end of the Crimean War, the Second War of Italian independence broke out. Piedmont-Sardinia, an entity that is to modern Italy roughly what Prussia is to modern Germany, allied with the French and took most of Austrian Italy in 1859. In 1864, in the Second Schleswig War, Prussia's legendary chancellor Otto Von Bismarck manipulated Austria into helping his country war against Denmark. The Schleswig-Holstein question is reputed to be one of the most complicated in European history. An old-fashioned dynastic succession dispute was supercharged by the clash between German and Danish nationalism. The Germans won, but this left Austria and Prussia to tussle over what to do with that Northern European chunk of land, far from Austria's borders.

Two years later this led to what Bismarck had wanted all along, the Austro-Prussian war of 1866. It ended in a decisive Prussian victory. Austria's borders were not changed, but Prussia annexed long desired territory elsewhere in Germany. The German Confederation was replaced by a North German Confederation under Prussian control. This new mega-state in the center of Europe was alarming to the French, the Austrians (obviously) and the South German states like Bavaria that still retained a tenuous independence. If the British were focused on the right things, they would have been worried too.

The British were focused on Belgium. They were still obsessed with the French[202] and the possibility that they might threaten the Belgian state that Britain had forcibly torn from the Netherlands in 1830. So the British let the balance of European power that had served it so well float away. In 1870 Bismarck successfully goaded the French into

---

[202] P.318 Webb, R.K. Modern England 2nd Edition

attacking Prussia, knowing that it would help him rope in the Southern German states who remained independent. In 1871, the establishment of the German Empire was proclaimed in the Versailles Hall of Mirrors, after the Prussian armies trounced the French. Prussia had used German nationalism to become Germany. This created a state in the middle of Europe that was a genuine European great power. Not a power on the scale of Britain, of course, but one that could cause tremendous trouble if Britain was silly enough to get militarily involved in nearby territory. A force, in other words, like the Maori had been in New Zealand. Germany made things tremendously more complicated.

Manufactured Enemies

All of the rivals that Britain faced in the run up to the First World War were manufactured by Britain itself. The threat that they posed to the British Empire did not grow up organically. In the case of France and Russia, countries that existed long before the nineteenth century, it was the threat they posed to Britain that was manufactured. It was an illusion that helped British political and commercial interests meet their goals. The illusion helped press barons sell papers. It helped justify the enrichment of expansionary imperial functionaries and businessmen on the ground around the world. The fear of French and Russian hordes helped politicians of all stripes whip up passions for a range of causes.

The illusion of competition also helped the British World System justify itself. Subjugating the entire world to a single system was hard to justify for the exclusive benefit of one country. Beyond competition, the idea of the supremacy of a broader "white" civilization provided powerful justification for the shift that was occurring. The idea of the triumph of a broader civilization, passed from Romans and Greeks down through the Renaissance, was more attractive than the idea of grubby British merchants bending the world to their will. "Christian Civilization" was another useful mental framework for these purposes. So other European empires, as petty as they were by comparison, provided valuable ideological cover for the British World System.

The German boulder that eventually derailed the British World System was manufactured in a different sense. Germany came into being during the period of British dominance. There were multiple opportunities for Britain to avert the creation of this country, and many more opportunities to avoid conflict with it once it had been created. The British chose not to take up any of those opportunities. Germany's hyper-nationalist birth meant it harbored the same exaggerated sense of its power and rights that France had. In some ways, the German national idea was even more prickly, because it was more recently constructed, and its fragility inspired more fervent responses. This made the relationship between Germany and France volatile, but it also added to the list of countries who would get snippy when Britain added more territory to its empire. It's important to remember that Germany, France, Russia and even Austria believed in the illusion that they were Britain's rivals just as fervently as the British public did. Britain's repeated illustration of its overwhelming superiority in the last decades of the nineteenth century was infuriating to all other powers.

Britain's facilitation of German independence was deeply unwise, but not unsalvageable. If the British had done a better job of managing the feelings and expectations of Continental Europe's four main powers, there was no reason an apocalyptic war was necessary. Up until the mid-nineteenth century, Britain had excelled at becoming wealthy off of informal empire, the sort of thing that wasn't going to throw German or French nationalists into a tizzy. Unfortunately, the British seem to have lost that skill after mid-century, opting again and again for exactly the sort of expansions of formal empire that seemed almost calculated to inflame national passions, and make Europe less manageable.

The Scramble for Africa

In the latter years of the nineteenth century, Europe's great powers engaged in what is known as the "Scramble for Africa". Much of Europe's colonization of the world followed some sort of logic. The conquest of the Americas was about gold and silver, and later on about sugar and tobacco. Eventually those continents became large markets unto themselves. Imperialism in Asia was about capturing the trade and luxuries that had fired European imaginations since ancient times. Textiles, tea, and spices came from Asia. The ancient civilizations had grand palaces to plunder, and complex economies that could be bent to serve outside forces.

For most of the period of colonization, Europeans only saw Africa as a source of labor. People were purchased at coastal entrepots, and Europe's footprint outside of the continent's extreme north and south remained small. Africa's great civilizations were hard to access, and malaria and other illnesses made it difficult for Europeans to survive, let alone prosper. The British, of course, took the lead in what little European colonization of Africa there was. British territory in South Africa, formally taken from the Dutch in 1814, steadily grew over the course of the century. In West Africa, the fight against the slave trade generated a small protectorate or two. There were British explorers, missionaries, and the occasional massive punitive expedition, like the one against the Ethiopian Empire in 1868. These brutal stabs at the African continent added to European knowledge, and very occasionally added to wealth, but they did not yield much formal territory. Other European powers had smaller holdings as well. Very few of these amounted to much more than a handful of coastal forts.

The French project in Algeria, after 1830, was probably the most impressive non-British piece of territory-grabbing. Until the final decades of the nineteenth century, the European foothold in Africa was quite small.

In 1870, less than 10 percent of Africa was under European control. By 1914, Wikipedia puts the figure at around 90 percent.[203] Back before the 2008 economic crisis, there was a vogue for insisting that everything was about economic rationality and the efficiency of the market. Some Marxist thinkers maintain that everything outside of the economy is just "superstructure" guided and predicted by the power structures of dollars and cents. The "Scramble for Africa" may be history's best counterexample against both of those theories. There was next to no economic rationale for Europe's economic empires in Africa. It was purely about prestige. The great plans for development and markets are only coming to fruition now, over a century later. Much of the earlier British Empire was run by great trading companies that lasted centuries. The Royal African Company, centered on the slave trade, lasted in some form from 1660 to 1821. The East India Company lasted, in many different forms, from 1600 to 1857. The companies of the scramble era rarely lasted a decade. The German East Africa Company sold out to the German government after just six years (1885-1891). The Imperial British East Africa Company only lasted from 1888 to 1896. There was no viable rationale to exploiting most of Africa in this era. But most of Africa's 11,730,000 square miles of territory were swallowed up anyway, in just a few short decades. Each European Empire desperately wanted to ensure that they wouldn't miss out on a scrap of land that could plausibly be useful to some other empire, somehow, someday. So the whole continent got swallowed up at incalculable cost to the folks who actually lived there.

---

[203] https://en.wikipedia.org/wiki/Scramble_for_Africa

This scramble was undignified, unproductive, and immediately disastrous. It was the British who launched the whole nightmare in the first place. As the world's leading empire, the British set the tone, making it clear that African empire was something you needed in order to be taken seriously. In launching and winning the Scramble for Africa, the British set tensions between European powers very high and kept them there.

Egypt—Making Dominance Obvious

Egypt is one of the world's great "what if?" stories. Decades before Japan ended its isolation, it looked like this African country might be able to beat the Europeans at their own imperial game. The French invasion of Egypt and the Middle East, lasting from 1798-1801, provided an early illustration of the impossibility of threatening British India in a world of British naval supremacy. It was a costly side show in the early years of Napoleon's trajectory. But for the region's Muslims, it was world-shaking. The French armies were eventually starved out by British blockade, but for a few years they ranged all over the holy land. This was deeply humiliating to peoples who saw themselves as naturally superior to the infidel. Steps had to be taken.

Egypt was nominally under the control of the Ottoman Empire, but it was a light and pre-modern sort of control. After the British and French left in 1803, an Albanian soldier of fortune named Muhammad Ali managed to set up his own dynasty in 1805, with grudging Ottoman recognition. Muhammad Ali, who reigned from 1805 to 1848, and his son Ibrahim Pasha, created a North African super state. They had great material to work with. Egypt had been the agricultural powerhouse of the ancient world, and the Ottoman Empire as well. The Muhammad Ali Dynasty took a fierce approach to modernization, using often repressive means[204] to build an impressive military force, and push economic development. In the process, they threatened the Ottoman Sultans and the budding imperialists of Europe. At its greatest extent, nineteenth-century Egypt controlled modern Syria, Crete, Sudan, the holy cities of Mecca and Medina and parts of Greece as well. The Europeans were used to dealing with the Ottoman "sick man" of Europe. They were not happy to be dealing with a healthy new Islamic empire in the Middle East.

In the initial decades of the Muhammad Ali dynasty, modernization was very much a top down process. But as Egypt accumulated more of the furniture of modernity, especially a westernized army, the same sorts of nationalist phenomena emerged there that had cropped up elsewhere. Egypt being a largely Muslim country, religion was of course wrapped up with nationalist ideas in ways that were distinct from Europe, but not as distinct as we tend to think. The German Empire's Chancellor Otto Von Bismarck celebrated unification by launching a fifteen-year struggle against what he saw as the scourge of Catholicism.

Britain used the same carrot and stick approach to the Egyptian empire that it used with everybody else in its informal empire. The British actively fought the Egyptians on a few occasions, most notably sinking much of the Egyptian fleet at the Battle of Navarino in 1827. The Egyptians had quite successfully crushed the uprising in Greece for the Ottoman Sultan, before a diverse group of Europeans intervened to establish Greek Independence. These sorts of setbacks were frustrating, but it was European finance, combined with a war on the other side of the world, that truly sank Egypt. One of the greatest successes of the Muhammad Ali dynasty was the establishment of a flourishing cotton industry. When the US Civil War broke out, the supply of cotton from

---

[204] P. 132 Beckert, Sven

the Southern US was severely impacted, sending prices into the stratosphere. For a few short years, Egypt experienced an extraordinary boom. The successors to Muhammad Ali and Ibrahim Pasha were not as wise. They used the boom to take on high levels of debt that were desperately unsustainable once the US Civil War ended. The British owned significant portions of this debt, but the French owned more.[205]

More French Failure

The French saw North Africa as their sphere of influence. They were especially keen to exert their will in Egypt. In the first half of the nineteenth century, when the Eastern Mediterranean was a bit of a backwater in geopolitical terms, the British let the French have a freer hand. The British intervened when the French got a bit too ambitious. Between 1854 and 1869 a French company labored to construct the Suez Canal. They did so over the opposition of the British, and a range of other physical and diplomatic obstacles. Tens of thousands of Egyptians were forced to work on the project, and thousands died in the process. But finally, in 1869, the French had built their canal, sealing their control of North Africa, and giving the great British Empire a black eye!

The period of French control of the canal lasted about a third as long as the period of time that it took to build it. Ismail, the grandson of Muhammad Ali, who had attained the title of Khedive from the Ottoman Sultan, was allotted a number of shares under the agreements that governed the canal. Thanks to Egypt's steadily disintegrating financial picture, in 1875 Ismail sold his nearly controlling portion of the shares in the canal to the British government. With each step in the Egyptian government's fall into servitude, the French found themselves pushed further out. The British steadily took control of

---

[205] P.303 Webb, R.K. Modern England 2nd Edition

Egypt's finances and politics, with France as a junior partner. In 1879 the two European countries deposed Khedive Ismail, in favor of his son Tewfik, prompting a reaction they did not expect.

The Egyptian people rose in what is described as "…one of the first truly nationalist uprisings…"[206] against European Imperialists. The movement was a product of increasing literacy, and the growing wealth and national consciousness of the Egyptian peoples over the course of the nineteenth century, but especially in the 1860s and 1870s. Their leader was Colonel Urabi, a man who had risen from a peasant background because of his successful career in the modernized military. Urabi and his followers were not only protesting against the privileges of European empires, but also against the Muhammad Ali dynasty, which originated in Albania. It was the sort of process we have seen end happily throughout the twentieth century. A dictator of some sort enriches a country to enrich himself, but produces a more empowered populace in the process. This populace then demands more rights, and a larger say in the running of the country. Urabi set up a chamber of deputies to provide more representation for the people.

Unfortunately, it was the nineteenth century, rather than the second half of the twentieth. Urabi's nationalist movement prompted a savage response from the Europeans. His new, democratic government was a threat to the absolutism of the Khedive, but it was also a threat to the interests of French and British business interests. In January 1882, the French and British governments weighed in on the struggle between Urabi and the Khedive, sending a Joint Note to the Egyptian government in Khedive Tewfik's favor. By the spring, they had a fleet off of the Egyptian coast. In July, rioting in Alexandria prompted the British bombardment of that ancient city, and the invasion of Egypt. By September, Urabi's forces had been defeated and he went into exile.

---

[206] P.364 Webb, R.K. Modern England 2nd Edition

The French were nominally participants in this crushing of Egypt's national aspirations, but it was the British Navy and the British Army doing the fighting, and it was Britain that ended up occupying Egypt.

The occupation was meant to be a temporary measure to shore up the Khedive, but the British ended up staying for the next seventy-four years. The shifting politics of that long period required different names and approaches to British occupation, but it kept continuing, despite multiple promises that it was ending shortly. "According to one estimate, Britain made sixty-six official declarations of intent to quit Egypt in the four decades after 1882."[207] As with the Irish, it was the constraints of Britain's foolish competition with European "rivals" that prompted the next stage of conflict with Egyptian nationalism.

Up until WWI, Britain's "veiled protectorate" in Egypt was still officially subject to the Ottoman Empire. The Ottomans joined the Germans and the Austrians against the British, so this was no longer viable. In 1914 the British declared a more official protectorate over Egypt, once again failing to reckon with the power of superficial changes to disrupt if they offended Egypt's nationalist sensibilities. WWI itself prompted great hardship and forced labor for Egyptian laborers on Britain's behalf.[208] When the United States entered the war, Woodrow Wilson brought a lot of high-minded language about the freedom of peoples. In practice, Wilson was mostly talking about European peoples, but the Egyptians thought they deserved their own say. Saad Zaghloul, an Egyptian politician, petitioned the British government to be allowed to attend the peace conference in Paris. The British arrested him and exiled him to Malta. His exile prompted the Egyptian revolution of 1918. Impoverished by the war, the British

[207] Loc. 3706 Brendon, Piers The Decline and Fall of The British Empire
[208] Loc. 6618 Brendon, Piers The Decline and Fall of The British Empire

government belatedly realized the power of symbols, and declared Egypt independent.

Over the next four decades, Egypt had its own independent government, but its freedom of action was nominal. Britain retained control of Egypt's foreign policy and the Suez Canal. It took another world war, and the advent of a new world hegemon, the United States, to finally get the British out of Egypt. In the aftermath of the Second World War, another conflict that imposed great hardship on the Egyptian people, President Gamal Abdel Nasser rose to power in 1952. He deposed the last Khedive, and instituted a range of nationalist and socialist policies that chopped away at British power. As we discussed above, when Nasser nationalized the Suez Canal in 1956, British Prime Minister Anthony Eden came up with an elaborate scheme to take it back. By using British debt to the US as a weapon, President Eisenhower made it clear that this kind of British behavior was no longer acceptable. The world wars that Britain had allowed to happen finally swept away this element of the British World System as well.

But, long, long before that, the British occupation of Egypt in 1882 set events in motion that would lead to those world wars. When Britain took Egypt, it took an empire. Muhammad Ali had invaded Sudan in 1821. When they occupied Egypt in 1882, British politicians wisely decided that they were willing to let Sudan go. Sudanese Muslim fanatics—the Mahdi army—were successfully rebelling against the Egyptian army, and Prime Minister William Gladstone didn't see the point of fighting to keep this large swathe of African territory. He was frustrated in this sensible decision to cut the Sudan loose by the half-mad British General Charles Gordon. Gordon was a religious fanatic as well, and he was thrilled by the idea of confronting Muslim hordes. Ordered to evacuate the Sudan, he instead chose to hole up in Khartoum, leading to a dramatic multi-month siege. Gordon and everybody who followed him were slaughtered in January of 1885. Gordon had proved how costly, pointless and stupid the occupation of Sudan was, but the British public loved him for it, and demanded that he be avenged. Ten years later, Lord Kitchener set out for Sudan, destroying the Mahdi army at the Battle of Omdurman in 1898, bumping into a French bicyclist at Fashoda, and establishing British control of Sudan that lasted until 1956.

The Scramble

The British occupation of Egypt in 1882 fired the starting gun for a two-decade orgy of violence and conquest. Between November 1884 and February 1885, representatives from the United States and thirteen European powers met in Berlin to set down some "civilized" rules for European theft of African land. The Berlin Conference imposed a sort of rule of "occupiers keepers" holding that European countries couldn't just make wild claims, they had to be able to demonstrate "effective occupation". This was, of course, much worse for the people who had been living on African territory. To make their claims, European countries now had to waste tremendous amounts of manpower and money, creating great discomfort for the occupiers, and living hells for the Africans. The European public loved it. The British came out on top of this struggle as well.

According to sheer land mass, France can be seen as "winning" the Scramble for Africa, but most of the territory it "won" was in the sandy wastes of the Sahara. In terms of population and wealth, Britain was far and away the most successful colonizer, putting together an unbroken line of protectorates and territories from Egypt down to South Africa. A "Cape to Cairo Railway" across this vast territory was discussed and built in part.[209] Egypt had one of the most developed

---

[209] https://en.wikipedia.org/wiki/Cape_to_Cairo_Railway

economies in Africa, and the Suez canal provided real strategic value. The growing colonies in Southern Africa were similarly strategic, and eventually provided serious economic value through diamond and gold mining. But Britain had many territories of negligible value as well, swallowing up plenty of territory thousands of miles inland from the coasts. The Sudan was only the most prominent example of this needless complexity.

The most well-known horror stories from the Scramble for Africa era are not British. King Leopold of Belgium, heir to a monarchy the British set up, is now recognized as the most savage of the imperialists. His use of the Congo as his private property between 1885 and 1908 is estimated to have killed as many as ten million people. Even Europeans of the time recognized the outrageousness of this behavior, and the Belgian state took the Congo from the King in 1908. On a smaller scale, the Herero genocide in German East Africa from 1904–1908 is also shocking. It's estimated to have killed 30,000–100,000 people. The numbers aren't as horrifying, but the clarity of the policy was. The German military engaged in a quite straightforward program of genocide. In public proclamations and official communiques, Lieutenant General Lothar Von Trotha calmly explained that his policy was one of annihilation.[210] The British always did a better job of couching their policies in humanitarian language. It's not clear, however, that the effects of their policies were all that different from those of the Germans. What is clear is that the British were present in vastly more places than the Germans and Belgians were, with a wide range of experience, from the mildly repressive to the genocidal.

Kenya

---

[210] P.605 Clark, Christopher Iron Kingdom: The Rise and Downfall of Prussia 1600-1947

There are fifty-four countries in Africa today, and that barely scrapes the surface of the ethnic, religious and cultural complexity of the world's second largest continent. Every city, state and people on the continent was affected by Britain's launching of the Scramble for Africa, whether their oppressors flew British flags or not. We simply don't have the space necessary to cover those experiences in detail. To stand in for everybody else, we'll pick just one story to tell.

European influence had a great impact on the country that would become Kenya long before the British. The Swahili culture that had grown up around trade across the Indian Ocean was severely disrupted by Portuguese raids after 1498. As we covered in Chapter Two, the Portuguese and Spanish empires had negligible impact in the interior of any continent, but they created a trading empire up and down the coasts of Africa and Asia. The Portuguese fought to maintain trading centers on modern Kenyan territory in the ancient cities of Mombasa and Malindi. They were finally booted out by Omani Arabs in 1698.

The Zanzibar sultanate that split off from Oman in 1856 controlled the Zanzibar islands and parts of the coastline of modern Kenya and Tanzania. The sultanate had more direct control of the islands and coasts but its trading links spread as far inland as modern Burundi, Rwanda and Uganda. The Zanzibar sultanate benefitted from the links that were being forged between world markets in the 1700s and 1800s, creating a more robust trading network than had previously existed in the region. Unfortunately, that robust trading network was based primarily on the trade in slaves. In the "British" nineteenth century, the Zanzibar and Omani Sultanates preserved their power against other Europeans by moving closer and closer to London's orbit. The continued importance of slavery was an embarrassment to the British that was finally resolved in 1873 with a quick siege and capitulation from the Sultan.

The Sultan of Zanzibar's rule had survived for decades acting in complete contravention of the principle of anti-slavery, something that was nominally very important to the British. The Sultan's rule barely lasted a decade in the new hyper-nationalistic scramble era. Prompted by German interest in the continental African tribes of the Sultanate, Britain moved to take more direct control of Kenya. They first did so in the classic colonial form, setting up the East Africa Company in 1888 to meet the requirement of "effective occupation". The company quickly proved to not be economically viable, so the British government set up the East Africa Protectorate in 1895.

As was the case elsewhere in Africa, European control began with an appalling loss of life. In the 1890s, a third of Kenya's population is estimated to have died due to a combination of famine and disease.[211] In this earlier period the numbers of settlers were small, and government policy was inconsistent. The British were never impolite enough for an explicit policy of genocide, and the government in London often claimed that they kept the interests of the native foremost in their minds. They managed to kill a third of the population anyway. British colonists and officials in Africa, not London platitudes, drove the facts on the ground. There were plenty of small-scale massacres, but it was the expropriation of the best land and the unsettling of accustomed ways of life that led to famine and the diseases that stem from malnourishment.

Kenya become the site of one of the most fantastic strategic boondoggles of the British Empire, the Uganda railway. It stretched from Mombasa on the coast, across Kenya, to Africa's great lakes region. Because of Russia and France's illusory threat to India, the British had gotten involved in Egypt. To safeguard their unnecessary

---

[211] Loc. 7191 Brendon, Piers The Decline and Fall of The British Empire

position in that country, the British had also taken the almost entirely useless territory of Sudan, at great cost. The Nile ran through both Sudan and Egypt, so somebody decided it was deeply important that Britain control the source of the Nile as well. This led to the construction of the Uganda railway, finally completed in 1901, functioning mostly to heighten tensions with the Germans who had taken adjacent territory, and to facilitate the murder and expropriation of the local inhabitants. As is often the case with Chinese development of Africa a century later, the locals didn't even get the benefit of jobs in construction. Britain imported most of the labor force from its Indian territory. The Indians ended up far outnumbering the white settlers in Kenya. They also ended up occupying many of the "middle-class" positions in Kenyan society. This too helped to keep the native population down.

The railway made it easier for white settlers to come inland in greater and greater numbers. Kenya's highlands were seen as an attractive place for these vicious entrepreneurs. According to one British diplomat, the settlers subjected the locals to the same sorts of atrocities that were taking place in the Belgian Congo.[212] They just weren't on the same scale, so they did not attract as much notice. "The new settlers were forever threatening to take more land by force, while demanding government protection against the native uprising they expected to provoke."[213] The settlers reserved the best land for themselves, with no respect given to ancestral privileges or the most basic ideas of justice. The British self-conception as liberators made enslavement of the locals an impossibility, but the conditions inflicted on workers were often little better than slave-like. Physical and sexual abuse and forced labor were all common.[214]

---

[212] Loc. 7246 Brendon, Piers The Decline and Fall of The British Empire
[213] Loc. 7246 Brendon, Piers The Decline and Fall of The British Empire
[214] Loc. 7293 Brendon, Piers The Decline and Fall of The British Empire

Repression in Kenya got significantly worse during and after the First World War. East Africa saw significant fighting, with German forces carrying out a stubborn guerilla fight throughout the war. The British established a Carrier Corps of Africans to deal with the logistical hurdles of the fighting. The eventual 400,000 men who made up this force did not join voluntarily. As many as a fifth of them died.[215] After the war, the British government decided to take a firmer hand in Kenya, "promoting" it from a protectorate to a colony in 1920. Apartheid type measures to enforce white supremacy and wring more value from the subject population were a big part of this "promotion".[216] The population of white settlers quickly accelerated after the war, thanks to a program settling WWI veterans on Kenyan farms. The population of 5,500 whites in 1914 almost quadrupled to 21,000 settlers in 1939.[217]

As the British Empire shook and then fell elsewhere, the British started focusing more on their African domains. They wanted to replicate earlier successes elsewhere on African territory. They hoped to create new settler colonial societies like the ones in Canada and Australia. After Indian independence in 1947, they hoped to replace their vast Indian armies with African soldiers. These efforts failed or were never attempted due to lack of resources. Through racism and repression, the British managed to set up some of the most brutally unequal societies in human history. White settlers lived with all the modern conveniences, and lorded it over a subject population that was treated little better than slaves. That atrocious setup at last managed to turn a profit. Zimbabwe is a country that had an even more lengthy ordeal freeing itself from British colonialism than Kenya did. Every article you read about Zimbabwe will snidely point out that it was the "bread basket" of Africa under white rule, and can now hardly feed itself. That characterization leaves out the extremes of repression and humiliation

---

[215] Loc. 7307 Brendon, Piers The Decline and Fall of The British Empire
[216] Loc 7315 Brendon, Piers The Decline and Fall of The British Empire
[217] Loc. 7300 and 7375 Brendon, Piers The Decline and Fall of The British Empire

that made that earlier "success" possible. Africans were not allowed to choose where they lived. They were not allowed to choose their work. They were often beaten as a tool of work discipline. If they chose not to participate, they starved. If they objected, they were murdered.

Kenya was luckier than Zimbabwe or South Africa. There simply weren't enough white settlers to make apartheid viable without the support of the larger British Empire. South Africa didn't truly attain its freedom until the 1990s, while Kenya was able to win it in the 1960s. But not before one of the most disgusting episodes in the history of the British Empire, the repression of the Mau Mau Uprising (1952-1960). The Mau Mau remains controversial today. The question of whether it was a Kenyan national movement, rather than a movement of a particular tribe or collection of tribes is too complicated for me to dive into. What is not controversial is that the British reaction to the Mau Mau was a spur to Kenyan nationalism and Kenyan independence. The British response involved mass arrests, collective punishment, and a massacre here and there. In 1954, the British put the entire population of Nairobi, Kenya's capital, under martial law in Operation Anvil. They detained over a quarter of the city's population as Mau Mau sympathizers were sought out. Those who were deemed to be affiliated with the Mau Mau were shunted into a sophisticated totalitarian system of detainment camps. Other populations throughout the country were forced into similar camps. The British inflicted torture, judicial and extrajudicial murder, aerial bombing, and the full range of authoritarian techniques on the Kenyan population. It was often noted at the time that the British were using the techniques of the Nazis they had just defeated against another subject population. This is hyperbole, but not as extreme a version as we might hope. The repression of the Mau Mau is estimated to have killed 20,000 Africans directly. Estimates of the deaths caused by relocation and deprivation related to British repression in the 1950s go as high as 300,000. The fight against the

Mau Mau was eventually successful, but it also helped kill the legitimacy of the British Empire in British eyes. It never had any legitimacy in Kenyan eyes.

Kenyan nationalism had many less-violent manifestations than the Mau Mau. The Kenyan African Union dated back to 1944. Its leader from 1947, Jomo Kenyatta, would eventually become the first President of Kenya in 1964. The Kenya Colony's Legislative Council only accepted its first black African member in 1944, under the pressures of the Second World War. But change came much more quickly thereafter. The British attempt to crush the Mau Mau also included some carrots to go along with the sticks. The legal privileges of white settlers began to diminish, as native Kenyans attained more basic economic rights. In the latter 1950s and early 1960s, more and more desperate attempts were made to set up a "free" Kenya under white domination, similar to the situations in South Africa and Zimbabwe. There just weren't enough white people in Kenya to get away with it. It wasn't worth risking the cost or the degradation of another Mau Mau level uprising. The Kenyans won their freedom.

Versions of this much-abridged story took place all over Africa and Asia. Defined more broadly, the story of every people in the world in the first half of the twentieth century was one of surviving the failure of the British World System. Unfortunately, because of the concerns of the time, a few more paragraphs on one group in particular are necessary to describe the history of the Scramble for Africa.

The Boers—White Lives Matter

The British are most pilloried not for what they did to indigenous black Africans, but what they did to the Boers, white settlers descended from the Dutch. The emphasis on the plight of the Boers was important historically, but also, shockingly, remains important today. Most sophomore history majors can tell you that the first concentration camps were British, set up to contain Boer families during the Second Boer War (1899-1902). The British are rightly condemned for this policy, and the horrible conditions within those camps. But British policy towards white Africans was never consciously exterminatory. A great deal of the extraordinary expense of the Boer wars came from British recognition that the white Boers had rights and couldn't merely be treated as animals.

That wasn't the case for Britain's non-white subjects in Africa. Black Africans who resisted Britain rarely made it as far as concentration camps. After the crushing of Boer resistance in 1902, these viciously racist colonizers became trusted partners in the administration of British South Africa. In 1910, they were granted dominion status on similar terms to Australia and Canada, and were given a progressively freer and freer hand in the abuse of black Africans, until the full institution of "independent" apartheid government in 1948. Black South Africans would not receive the benefits of independence until the demise of apartheid in the 1990s. The Second Boer War was a tremendously significant event for the British World System. Both for its absurd expense and the way that it antagonized Britain's European "rivals". But it's important to remember that this concern with the Boers, over any other repressed people in Africa, was quite racist, at the time and today. Regardless, the Second Boer War requires a couple paragraphs, because of its impact on the attitudes of the other European powers.

The Boers were the portion of the Dutch colonists that refused to reconcile themselves to British rule. Significantly, their celebrated trek out into the wilderness did not come when British control was formally established in 1815. The Boers instead left for the bush in 1835, in response to the British abolition of slavery. These courageous defenders of their right to crush the rights of others formed a series of independent republics. After losing the First Boer War (1880-1881), the British had decided that subjugating these republics wasn't worth the effort. The idea of a white led independent republic in Africa didn't bother them that much. It's instructive to compare this to the seething resentment that came with the Sudanese Mahdi army's defeat of a British army in 1885. That defeat was seen as requiring revenge. After that revenge was carried out in 1898, Sudan was pointlessly subjugated for the next sixty years. The British were content to let the white South African republics go. What changed this was not renewed anger at the Boers, but gold.

Gold cropped up in Transvaal, one of the Boer republics. The discovery quickly transformed Transvaal from a poor and dusty home of bigots (even by nineteenth century standards), to the richest country in Africa. A rapacious constellation of British politicians decided that Britain needed to take these republics and started plotting accordingly. The most powerful among them was Joseph Chamberlain, the Secretary of State for the Colonies, who I compared to Trump at the outset of this book. Imperial entrepreneurs like Cecil Rhodes had been a factor in aggressive moves like this for centuries. Sometimes their schemes were resisted in London, sometimes they were encouraged. Chamberlain went further than most in letting the empire builders run, and war broke out in 1899.

The Second Boer War initially did not go well for the British, so they drowned the territory in British troops. Another comparison with that bicycle borne French Expeditionary force we talked about above might be helpful. In Fashoda a year earlier, France had declared her rights in Africa with a force in the low hundreds. The force that Britain sent to crush the Boers eventually numbered around 500,000.[218] The British crushed the official Boer military, occupying Johannesburg and

---

[218] https://www.britannica.com/event/South-African-War

Pretoria by mid-1900. The war dragged on for another two savage years, however, after the Boers opted to continue fighting as guerrillas. The British invented the use of concentration camps for counterinsurgency in this conflict. A fifth of the Boer women and children in these camps are reckoned to have died from disease and malnutrition.[219] This atrocity against white Africans outraged Europeans in a way that atrocities against black Africans could not. Perhaps because most European powers were in the process of committing similar atrocities against black Africans at the time.

The Boer War gave the Europeans a chilling illustration of British power. The complete disregard for the principles of liberty that Britain claimed to hold dear also made an impression. This was not a war to save black Africans from Boer repression—the British had already made it clear they were fine with that. This was a war for gold. In the words of one historian, the rest of the world saw that "...the greatest imperial power in the world was willing to stoop to any villainy to extend her grasp over small, defenseless nations".[220] The ability to move half a million soldiers across the world to crush a single insurgency demonstrated the vast extent of British power. The European powers, Germany in particular, were made keenly aware of how far behind the British they were. The old British caution of taking on too much had dissipated. From North to South, the British led the Scramble of Africa, and used it to make the power of their empire obvious and obnoxious to the fragile nationalisms of the European continent. British greed had used the African continent to push the European continent towards an apocalyptic war.

Who Really Started the First World War

---

[219] P.448 Webb, R.K. Modern England 2nd Edition
[220] P.446 Webb, R.K. Modern England 2nd Edition

As the twentieth century dawned, the British found themselves diplomatically isolated. Their victory in the Scramble for Africa, and their crushing of the Boers in particular, left them without an ally in Europe's power struggles. In retrospect this was a great place for Britain to be. The Boer War had illustrated how much trouble the British could get into by fighting even the smallest and weakest of enemies on their own turf. The half million troops it had taken to beat the Boers were not cheap. Naval superiority and vast financial resources made less of a difference if all your opponent needed to do was walk to the battlefield with a rifle. This made an incredibly good argument against getting involved in any sort of European conflict. Britain's vast world-wide power lost much of its efficacy if it was bogged down fighting locals for a South African plain or a Belgian forest. The Boer War should have made the British much less eager to make commitments that might result in European war, not more.

Unfortunately, the British of the time were incapable of learning this lesson. They had convinced themselves that the French, British and Germans really were rivals for world-wide power. They felt left out in the cold, and took steps to end their isolation. In so doing, they created the encircled and terrified Germany that put the Continent on the path to war. The British took the wise step to get closer to Japan and the United States. These powers had growing interests and capabilities in territories that were crucial to British wealth and power like China and Latin America. The British choice to cozy up to France and Russia didn't bring any of these benefits.

The French were already a junior partner in British foreign policy. They had loud disputes with the British, but the threats of war were mostly public relations exercises. The French could probably have taken Belgium against British wishes, but they would have done so at the cost of their navy, Vietnam, Algeria, and the rest of their hard-won and not very impressive world empire. The Russians had just been booted out of China after their humiliating defeat in the Russo-Japanese war (1904-1905). Neither of these allies were worth a commitment to shedding British blood on the continent, but Britain began to develop a defensive axis with them anyway. The British leaders and public had spent a century telling themselves that these countries were threats, so they saw alignment with them as an accomplishment.

In 1904, the British signed a series of agreements with France known as the Entente Cordiale. The agreements settled territorial disputes in North Africa and elsewhere. In 1907, the British entered the Anglo-Russian convention which settled disputes between the two countries in Afghanistan, Tibet, and Persia. These agreements were not an explicit defensive alliance, but they did away with most of the historic obstacles to relations between the three countries. The French and the Russians had set up an alliance for mutual defense in 1894 that was clearly aimed at Germany. At the time, Germany shared long borders with both countries. The fact that Britain had resolved all its conflicts with the surrounding powers was quite threatening to Germany. British behavior over the next decade only made it more threatening. Though there was no formal alliance Britain kept aligning with France and Russia, on dispute after dispute.

Scramble Everywhere

The Scramble for Africa was the most atrocious manifestation of what became known as the "New Imperialism," but the tensions it created played out everywhere, and on every front, geographical, commercial and even cultural. Geographic areas of competition included Africa, Southeast Asia, and the Chinese ports, Eastern Europe, the Pacific Islands and the Middle East, among many others. The decade leading up to 1914 played host to a series of escalating crises, usually related to one fault line or another. Morocco was lucky enough to be the location of two separate incidents (1905-1906 and 1911). Britain usually took the side of their new French and Russian friends against Germany.

The crises came in the context of a booming world economy. Between the Panic of 1873 and the mid-1890s, the world had experienced a long depression. But growth accelerated for the decade or so leading up to the First World War. As ever, the British scooped up the lion's share of the wealth that was generated, but the fact that more was spilling over to everybody else made the British very nervous. This manifested itself in two ways that were particularly nerve-wracking: a naval arms-race with Germany and accelerating industrial production in Continental Europe and the United States. As with much in the standard story of the lead-up to the First World War, historians tend to give both of these phenomena a more prominent place than they deserve.

The great naval race with Germany was atrociously expensive. The competition to build armored battleships, the aircraft carriers of the day, required an obscene amount of money. To make matters worse, the rate of technological advancement was accelerating, and ships were obsolete almost as soon as they were built. Between 1898 and 1908, the Germans attempted to build a fleet that could compare with Britain's, and the British spent vast sums to stay ahead of them. Britain relied on naval superiority, and they perceived a German naval buildup as a serious threat. What most retellings of this story leave out is how comprehensively Germany lost this first great modern arms race. By 1908, the expense was getting so outrageous that the civilians in Germany's government called a halt to it. During the eventual war, these great battleships were judged to be too expensive and too important for morale purposes to risk in actual battle. The 1916 Battle of Jutland's results were either inconclusive, or favored towards the Germans, depending on the account you read. Regardless, the British had vastly more ships, and the German over-sea navy sat out the rest of the war. Britain's naval blockade of Germany was attacked by submarines, but the British battleships ended up being almost as useless as the German ones. The naval race with Germany cost a lot of money, and made the British very nervous, but it ended up signifying very little.

The threat the British should have been worried about, of course, was the United States. Its anti-militarist tradition kept it from posing a real challenge to British power outside of the Americas before 1917. Figures like Teddy Roosevelt (President 1901-1909) did their best to get the US to compete in European power struggles, but the US public wasn't interested. They were largely content to be a profitable and growing part of the British World System. When that equilibrium was unsettled by the British failure to avert world war, things changed immediately. In 1916, President Woodrow Wilson decided the US should have a navy. Within just five years, that newly founded force was considered to be the equal of the British,[221] ending more than a century of naval supremacy.

Another key part of the standard story of British decline is the idea that US and German industrial production was beginning to catch up. In certain sectors, like chemicals, this was the case. British thinkers of the time, and since, were convinced that they were falling behind. The stereotype was that the dusty, old school British capitalism of sole proprietors was not equipped to keep up with the fully corporatized predators of German and American business. Historians have been

---

[221] Loc. 884 Tooze, Adam <u>The Deluge: The Great War, America and the Remaking of The Global Order 1916-1931</u>

questioning this conclusion for some time. Even in industry, it's likely that in the aggregate, outside of a few cherry-picked sectors, Britain remained far ahead of the competition.[222] And in the rest of the economy, Britain remained extraordinarily dominant. The ballooning world economy made the British richest of all.

> As more and more regions were drawn into the commercial economy, specializing in the export of staples (in which their market advantage was greatest) and buying more imports, their need for exchange banks, insurance companies, shippers and shipbrokers, as well as the hardware of railways, harbours, ships and cables rose astronomically. These were all services in which the British enjoyed a long lead, and through which they could levy a large rent on the new streams of trade. [223]

When this ballooning world economy needed to finance something, London was the source. In the decade and a half leading up to the war, British overseas investment doubled from 2 to 4 billion pounds.[224] Governments, corporations, individuals, whoever... British finance was there to help them do what they wanted, and British financiers were there to profit. The extent of this extraordinary privilege is hard to quantify. It's not as straightforward as pointing to the raw numbers of US or German steel production. We also don't hear about it much because it doesn't serve the narrative of British weakness that is a key part of the justification for the Empire's participation in two world wars. In fact, it was the wars themselves that brought about British decline, not the extremely profitable run-up to those wars. Wars are never good for the country on top.

The First World War—The Revolt of the European Natives

---

[222] P.384 Webb, R.K. Modern England 2nd Edition
[223] Loc. 3110 Darwin, John Unfinished Empire: The Global Expansion of Britain
[224] Loc. 3171 Darwin, John Unfinished Empire: The Global Expansion of Britain

The "Everywhere Scramble" finally ended in the Balkans, the territories in South Eastern Europe that were throwing off the Ottoman yoke. The flashpoint was between Germany's now quite junior partner Austria, and the Slavic Serbs, who could rely on the support of Russia. If we ignore the century of British power before 1914, and just focus on the months that lead up to the war, it's easier to see the Germans as the bad guys. A case can be made that the Germans, encircled by what looked to be a solidifying alliance between Britain, France and Russia, wanted war sooner rather than later, and that WWI is therefore Germany's responsibility. That case has been made repeatedly. But even that case is beginning to fall apart. Christopher Clark's The Sleepwalkers, published in 2012, is probably the most well-known recent reevaluation. In the book Clark exhaustively (and exhaustingly) details the way that the European governments fell into WWI almost inadvertently fell into the First World War. Nobody quite realized what they were getting into, and nobody was innocent. This reevaluation is welcome. The last of the First World War veterans has died, we should be able to talk about these things more honestly now. We should go considerably further than Clark.

The issue of Belgium is one fruitful topic for reevaluation. Despite the solidifying "Triple Entente" between Britain, France and Russia, British leaders were always careful to point out that they had made no commitment to defend their partners. When it was clear that war was breaking out, many tried to keep Britain out of it. What made the difference was German violation of Belgian neutrality in the summer of 1914. Britain did have clear treaty commitments to Belgium, and used the German invasion of France through Belgium as their justification for war. But why did Britain have those commitments to Belgium? Why was Belgian neutrality British business? Why did an independent Belgium exist? As we covered earlier, independent Belgium was created by British naval power in the 1830s. Britain had set a trap for itself, and created an obligation that eventually killed their world system.

Britain's experience over the nineteenth and early twentieth centuries had made it very clear what their power could and could not do. Through financial, commercial and naval power they could organize the entire world for their benefit. They could use that organization to destabilize older power centers, and they made spectacular inroads into older empires like Manchu China and Mughal India. Things got more complicated if they faced the committed *military* opposition of a cohesive group tied to particular territory. Because they were so far out ahead economically, the British could focus overwhelming power on any people that challenged them. But it was ruinously expensive. Peoples as diverse as the Maori, the Sudanese, and the South African Boers had managed to give the grand British Empire a black eye, most often losing eventually, but sometimes even winning. Looking at this history, the British choice to get into it with the European natives in 1914 just looks insane.

The First World War Kills the British World System

Most assumed that the First World War would be brief. The last major clash on the continent, the Franco-Prussian war, had taken less than six months (July 1870-January 1871), and the major battles had been concluded within three months. No one had fully understood what the mechanization of war since then meant. The war began in August of 1914. By the end of the year, the Western Front between Germany and France had stabilized into a murderous system of trenches. Britain's Empire did relatively well, losing just under 1,000,000 soldiers to this horror show. The French, from a much smaller base of population, lost about 1,200,000. The Germans lost an estimated 2,000,000, and the Russians an even ghastlier 2,200,000. The numbers of dead are hard to fathom. No one was prepared for the cost in life, but more importantly for British power, nobody was prepared for the cost in money.

At the outset of the First World War, US president Woodrow Wilson was eager to keep the US out of the conflict. The decision was largely taken out of his hands by US bankers. There was too much money to be made by supplying Britain and her allies. This eventually ended up committing the United States to supporting their war aims. "By the end of 1916, the American investors had wagered two billion dollars on an Entente victory."[225] Back then, a billion dollars was real money. If the US wanted to keep their banking system stable, they would have to get into the war.

Britain, France, and Russia probably looked like a good bet at the beginning. Britain ran the world, after all, and seemed to own half of it. But as the war went on, piece by piece Britain began to liquidate its investments abroad. Private holders of foreign securities were forced to exchange them for British government debt.[226] Large swathes of the US economy were converted to supplying war materials for the Entente powers. The British and French governments paid for this with dollar-denominated debt to the US. The United States didn't just get a tremendous amount of war materials business out of WWI, it got ownership of the debt that funded that business too. By August of 1916, under the pressure of the cost of the Battle of Verdun, France's credit sunk to the degree that Britain had to take over the whole funding operation.[227] By the summer of 1917, the British were in danger of default themselves.[228] They had reached their limit. The extraordinary

---

[225] Loc. 925 Tooze, Adam <u>The Deluge: The Great War, America and the Remaking of The Global Order 1916-1931</u>

[226] Loc. 908 Tooze, Adam <u>The Deluge: The Great War, America and the Remaking of The Global Order 1916-1931</u>

[227] Loc. 908 Tooze, Adam <u>The Deluge: The Great War, America and the Remaking of The Global Order 1916-1931</u>

[228] Loc. 1716 Tooze, Adam <u>The Deluge: The Great War, America and the Remaking of The Global Order 1916-1931</u>

cost and destruction of funding the war brought them to the brink of insolvency. The fruits of a century of dominance had been pissed away in just four years of great power war. The British world system was over.

The Americans saved the British from a richly deserved loss in the First World War. Germany had outlasted all of the world's imperial powers, in a deeply impressive multi-front performance. It's hard to argue against the idea that Germany's destiny was to lead Europe, as it finally does today. But the British owed the US too much money to be allowed to lose. The United States's entrance into the war in April 1917 came with an additional loan to the Entente of 3 billion dollars.[229] American money, and eventually soldiers, kept Britain and France in the war for long enough to exhaust Germany in November of 1918. The United States, through war loans and war debt, had replaced Britain as the world's banker.

Woodrow Wilson got over his earlier reticence, and warmed to his role as arbiter of the world. The US Senate had not. After stepping in to impose the wrong winner, the US decided to step back. This allowed the British, and to a lesser degree the French, to act the part of victors. They carved up the Middle East, and continued to make imperial glory a part of their propaganda. But it was hollow. The US held the purse strings. London still held great financial importance, but it was subservient to New York. Many of those great rivers of capital still flowed through London, but they now all ultimately terminated in New York. "In the 1920s loans continued to flow from the City of London to the world, but this increased Britain's dependence on funds from America."[230] Hollow imperial pretense, mixed with the US lack of

---

[229] Loc. 1716 Tooze, Adam The Deluge: The Great War, America and the Remaking of The Global Order 1916-1931
[230] Loc. 7677 Tooze, Adam The Deluge: The Great War, America and the Remaking of The Global Order 1916-1931

interest in international power led to a couple extraordinarily unstable decades, the 1920s and 1930s.

The inter-war period, the Great Depression, and WWII are all fascinating topics, but they are outside of the scope of this chapter. The British Empire limped on, but the British World System was dead. They had allowed cheap, profitable informal empire to become ruinously expensive formal empire. Obsession with illusory enemies had gotten Britain bogged down in costly imperial adventure after costly imperial adventure, until the last one in Europe turned them into a debtor country. What followed from here was a sad story, but it's not a British one. It's an American one, covered briefly in the next chapter, but it won't be covered in detail in this book. To close out the story of the British World System, Let's take one final look at the most important part of Britain's empire.

India Wins Its Independence

British planners weren't right about the threat to India, but they were right about India's importance. The comprehensiveness of the British World System would have been impossible without the resources of manpower and wealth that India provided. The US World System is lucky enough to have great population, resources and wealth in one country at its core. The British World System found its weight in India. The soldiers of British India were instrumental in building British Empire. Indian laborers and Indian merchants functioned as non-uniformed emissaries of Empire as well. Much of Britain's Asian Empire, from Yemen to China, was administrated from India. By the later twentieth century the financial benefits of the scale of India became more and more important. The large European and Indian military was paid for by Indian taxpayers, not British ones. India was not a drain on imperial coffers. In fact, it owed large involuntary debts to London bankers and the British government. All those Indian railways were paid for by loans from Britain.[231] The remnants of the British World System simply couldn't function without India, which is why they disintegrated so quickly in the decades after Indian Independence in 1947.

That independence is another in a long line of ironies in the history of the death of the British World System. The eventual success of Indian and Pakistani nationalism[232] was a direct result of the stresses of the two world wars. These wars were undertaken, at some remove, in the name of protecting British India. But those glorious fights against manufactured enemies ended up destroying British control in India. In the aftermath of the Indian Rebellion in 1857, the British had successfully created a system of control that, with the right mixes of carrots and sticks, could plausibly have ruled India for decades longer. But the world wars imposed too many costs on Indians, and on the systems that the British had set up to govern them.

Hindu vs. Muslim

After 1857, the British abandoned its old habit of expropriating local notables, instead choosing to incorporate them in the governance of the subcontinent, and encouraging the participation of Indian princes in imperial pageantry and governance. A key pillar of this method of control, and all others, was the tension between Muslim and Hindu. Some claim that the British invented the animosity between Muslims and Hindus in India. That's ludicrous. It's a rivalry that goes back about as long as Islam. Early Arab expeditions made it into parts of modern Pakistan by the 700s, and made serious inroads in modern Indian

---

[231] Loc. 3216 Darwin, John Unfinished Empire: The Global Expansion of Britain

[232] And Burmese nationalism too! Myanmar is one of the many topics this book has neglected. The perils of writing about a system that encompassed the world.

territory after the 1100s. But there is no denying that the British made the situation worse.

Religious differences always exist, but their importance and danger from decade to decade is dependent on politics. The Muslim Mughal Empire (1526-1857) pushed farther into India than any of its predecessors. Some emperors were renowned for their tolerance and eagerness to work with people across faiths, some were infamous for their bigotry. These waves of tolerance and intolerance were always subject to the political concerns of the time. In the aftermath of the 1857 rising, the British consciously made use of these tensions in a policy of "divide and rule". The British justified their rule in India by claiming that they were preparing the Indians for self-government, so they invested resources in education and preserving, translating and publishing the laws and literature of India's great traditions. In doing so, they were careful to maintain and foster the separateness of these traditions. Depending on the decade, they would move back and forth between favoring Muslim and Hindu, usually centered on opposing whichever community seemed most threatening at the time.

In part because of this successful program of division, most early Indian nationalists focused on inclusion in governance rather than independence. Some always wanted the British out immediately, but they were in the minority before 1914. Indian nationalists wanted a larger say in their government, along the lines of what Canada or Australia had. "Home Rule" became a rallying cry in India just as it was in Ireland. To some extent, the British believed their own mythology on self-rule. They took a series of actions designed to placate this desire. Unfortunately, the British World System would never be viable under Indian Home Rule. If India was free to make its own domestic choices, then it would choose to stop sacrificing its own well-being to subsidize British imperial efforts around the world.[233]

---

[233] Loc. 6670 Darwin, John Unfinished Empire: The Global Expansion of Britain

So, Britain engaged in a largely successful campaign of half measures, slowly conceding enough power to keep Indians happy and more suspicious of religious rivals than their overlords. In 1861, the Indian Councils Act had set up provincial and national legislative councils across British India. The role of these councils, though, was only advisory. In 1909 the British expanded the electorate and increased Indian participation in these legislative councils was increased. At the same time, the principle of separate electorates was established, guaranteeing seats to Muslims. This too fostered divisions the British could use. All real power was retained by the British Viceroy and the ninety-five-percent-white Indian Civil Service.

The First World War

This easy trajectory of glacially slow devolution of power, eased by the promotion of sectarian strife, was derailed by WWI. As that conflict dragged on, the British demanded more and more from India. As war production spun up, the Indians began to produce more goods for the imperial war machine. This should have resulted in profits for Indian businesses, but most of those profits were forcibly maintained in British banks and cycled into British government debt. The return for heightened Indian labor was more scarcity. Over a million Indian soldiers served abroad. Despite the alliance with France and Russia, and the quick end of the German presence in Asia, British paranoia about Indian dissent increased. India had rallied to the support of Britain, and its reward was the insult of the Defence of India Act of 1915, which suspended a number of basic rights for the duration of the war. This and other outrages led to the Lucknow Pact, a brief unity between Hindu and Muslim political elements. In response to Lucknow, and growing unrest, the British took a "carrot and stick" approach. The Government of India Act of 1919 enlarged the participation of Indians in provincial government, and established a partially elected national government. The system established in 1919 was known as "Dyarchy", dividing up government functions between the British overlords and elected Indians at the national and local levels. Unfortunately, the end of the war did not end British paranoia, and coercive efforts continued. The much loathed Defence of India Act was reaffirmed by 1919's Rowlatt Act, despite the end of the war. This led to a massacre that turned the previously incrementalist Indian nationalists into fierce advocates for independence.

On April 13th, 1919, Brigader General Reginald Dyer ordered his troops to fire on an unarmed, non-violent crowd in Jallianwalla Bagh, in Amritsar. Estimates of the number massacred range from the British government figure of 379, to as high as 1,600. Regardless of the number this was outrageous. Dyer neither apologized, nor thought he had done anything wrong. He saw it as an appropriate measure to keep the Indians in line, and many British agreed. In the end, Dyer did lose his position in India, and was forced to retire, but the damage was done. He faced no real consequences for the willful murder of hundreds of Indian citizens. Despite all of India's loyal service in the war, and all the lip service paid towards freedom and self-government, British contempt for Indian life was made crystal clear.

Gandhi and the Indian Independence Movement

There were many great Indian advocates of self-determination before Mohandas Gandhi (1892-1948). Some followed Bal Gangadhar Tilak (1856-1920), an early and fierce advocate of complete independence from Britain. More were aligned with figures like Dadabhai Naoroji (1825-1917), who took his quest for Indian dignity and participation in government all the way to London, as the first Member of Parliament of wholly Indian descent.[234] It was Gandhi, however, who turned

---

[234] If you stretch the definition, the Anglo-Indian David Ochterlony Dyce Sombre, may deserve the title of first Indian in parliament. His brief tenure in Parliament in 1841 was more traditionally British however. He was

Indian Nationalism into a mass movement. His political journey, and his ultimate successes were inseparable from Britain's disastrous exploitation and disrespect of Indians during WWI.

Gandhi first entered politics through the study of British law. In South Africa, he advocated for and won rights for Asian minorities. Most English language accounts of the Indian independence movement emphasize the degree to which the important figures were influenced and shaped by British culture and ideas of liberty. This is true, but it is overdone, and is used to sell an unhelpful narrative. For example, if you read a three-sentence summary of the life of Muhammad Ali Jinnah (1876-1948), Pakistan's founder, typically at least one of them will refer to his fondness for British suits, and his theatrical adoption of the mannerisms of an English lord. If the account is a paragraph long, it will probably somewhat snidely mention that this first leader of a Muslim country sometimes enjoyed a civilized drink or two. Jawaharlal Nehru (1889-1964), the first prime minister of India, and a prominent member of a political dynasty that remains very important today, was educated at Cambridge in England, and is famously rumored to have enjoyed the company of the wife of a certain British official.

These biographical details, coupled with the fact that British individuals sometimes occupied prominent positions in the early days of the Indian National Congress (est. 1885), have been used to put forward the idea that the British Empire was a good thing for India. The British supposedly did the Indians a service by bringing them the concepts and culture of representative government. This is a lot like saying that Slavery and Jim Crow in the United States were OK, because some white people helped to found the NAACP, and Protestant

---

there to advocate for his own considerable land and business interests. Naoroji was an actual advocate for Indian interests.

Christianity helped form the world views of Civil Rights leaders like Martin Luther King Jr.

The Indians who eventually kicked the British out were influenced by British forms of law and government because they had to be. There was no alternative. Jinnah and the Nehru family rose to wealth and prominence as attorneys, because there was no other avenue to reach success for Indians who were not already hereditary royalty. They mastered the tools of the oppressor because they had to. Jinnah in particular was such a skilled advocate that during a period in the political wilderness he moved to London and quickly founded a fabulously lucrative law practice.[235] These people did what they had to do to speak up for their country. They used British ideas of liberty and nationalism because they knew that those ideas would speak most powerfully *to their British oppressors*. The British should not be applauded for providing the tools to solve a problem the British created.

The emphasis on the supposed Anglophilia of the Indian and Pakistani founders also underestimates the degree to which these British ideas were adopted throughout the world. India was a special case in every sense, but most of Europe and the world found itself establishing forms of government that mirrored British parliamentary practice over the course of the nineteenth and twentieth centuries. Nobody makes a big deal of how closely the French and German forms of government of today mirror British models. But we *do* always point out how 'British' the Indian movement for self-government was. It's an irritating historiographical tick that smacks of white supremacy.

Emphasizing the British-seeming elements of Indian independence also gets sillier the more you study the actual events. The career and philosophy of Gandhi was so very much its own idiosyncratic thing that I'm hesitant to even try to describe it from my Western perspective.

---

[235] P. 242-243 Read, Anthony & David Fisher <u>The Proudest Day: India's Long Road to Independence</u>

But one obvious element of Gandhi's appeal to the masses that eventually gathered around him was that he *distanced* himself from British forms and ideas. Many of the early Indian nationalist talking shops may have had British overtones. That contributed to the ease with which the imperialists ignored and co-opted their concerns. Few early nationalists had much connection to the masses of Indian people. Gandhi had that. Gandhi moved millions with the force of his personality and his ideas. His principles of self-reliance, non-violence and self-rule were drawn from many sources, Western and not. There's a surprising amount of Tolstoy in there. But at root they were very, very Indian. From his adoption of traditional dress and industry, to his mix of political and spiritual authority, to his (heroic but failed) rejection of the attempt to divide Muslim and Hindu, Gandhi was far, far removed from the image of a British politician. And it was that distance that made his movement successful.

Across the 1920s and 1930s, that "low dishonest decade"[236], as the British Empire and the Western world in general fell into disarray, the Indian people rose. Through a series of inspired movements, Indians slowly chipped away at the crumbling edifice of European rule. This story, from the Khalifat movement, to the Salt March, to the quit India movement, to the triumph and tragedy of victory and partition makes for extraordinary reading.

With the 1935 Government of India Act, the British Parliament granted most of the traditional wishes for self-rule. The Viceroy and other elements of British rule were pushed into more of a traditional executive function, devolving many more powers to elected Indian legislatures. That level of devolution probably would have been quite satisfying to an Indian nationalist of 1910. But events, and the British abuse of India during WWI, had proceeded too far for a little loosening of the reins to satisfy anyone. Regardless of the sincerity of the

---

[236] Auden, W.H. "September 1, 1939"

Empire's wish to step back, its declining financial position required too much of India for the offered "freedoms" to be legitimate. Before the reforms could be fully implemented, the demands of WWII intervened. A far less willing British India was again called upon to make extraordinary sacrifices. Millions of Indians served abroad, and the British once again sacrificed the Indian economy to war production. British weakness was brutally exposed in the fall of Singapore, and the Japanese march through Burma, up to the borders of India. The old mythology of White Supremacy was impossible to preserve in the face of these reverses. These great humiliations led to great British promises for the future, but India had heard that before. What they got in the short term was starvation. British rule had begun with a great famine in Bengal in the 1760s. After 180 years of "enlightened" British rule, 1943 saw another Bengal famine, costing upwards of three million lives. Another million lives were lost in broke Britain's hasty scuttle out in 1947. The division of India between Hindu and Muslim that the British had done so much to foster resulted in lasting enmity between independent India and Pakistan.

Famine: The Gift of The British

The 1943 Bengal Famine, and its direct connection to the British war effort, was particularly disgusting, but it was nothing new. Mass starvation stalked almost every decade of British rule in India. Indians died in British-created famines in far greater numbers than the Irish. Five million people died in the Great Famine of 1876–1878 alone. The recent reappraisal[237] of Churchill and his role in the Bengal famine is welcome. Churchill, like most British imperialists, thought that famine was just something that "happened" in India. Yet the independent Indian state, as famously mismanaged as it is, has somehow managed to go seventy years now without mass starvation. Even in India's early

---

[237] Safi, Michael "Churchill's policies contributed to 1943 Bengal famine – study" The Guardian March 29, 2019

decades of extreme poverty, mass starvation was not a thing. This is something that should be thrown in the face of the smug commentators, from Prager University to Harvard University, who want to lecture you about how awesome the British Empire was. British leaders like Queen Victoria and propagandists like Rudyard Kipling, liked to depict themselves as benevolently looking after their Indian "children". Yet the richest, biggest and most powerful entity in human history to that point couldn't get it together enough to feed its own people. The basic, affordable measures that could have been taken to avert the deaths of millions were simply never taken. I'm sure those far off English freedoms were terribly comforting to all those Indian mothers who watched their children starve to death to help the British balance of payments.

On British Responsibility

The story I have laid out above is different from the standard approach to "European Imperialism" we are taught in our universities and popular culture across the world. There is quite rightly a lot of emphasis on the evils of the era, and the guilt that the white man should bear going forward. I don't want to diminish by one iota the guilt of actors in countries from Belgium, to France, Spain, the Netherlands, Germany, the United States, Japan and Russia, among others. In fact, I'd like to add to it a bit. The standard story is that all this bloody swallowing up of other people's land was justified by a competition between empires of existential importance. The imperialist countries needed to act in these barbaric ways to protect themselves from each other.

In truth, as I hope this chapter has shown, there was no such competition. There was a tone, set by the British system that ran the world between 1815 and 1914. The British were not the peace-loving business people, bullied by nasty militarist Germans and Russians, that they portrayed themselves as at the time, and continue to portray themselves as today. The British set the terms of the imperialism game, led the charge towards the exploitation of every continent, and handily won the imperialism game as well. It wasn't even close. The US, the Japanese and the European players, with all their savagery, were just playing catch up, and failing to catch up.

It's important to emphasize that all of this horror, all of this exploitation and insanity took place in the context of a system that the British built. The expansion of all of the "competing" empires worked in Britain's favor as well, helping to force the world into an economic system where Britain reaped the majority of the benefits. The story of the evils of this system and its eventual, apocalyptic end has plenty of guilt to go around, but the lion's share belongs to the British and their failure to manage the world they had taken. Let me be very clear...

The British ran the world between 1815 and 1914, so the primary blame for the World Wars at that system's end belongs to the British.

WWII is one of history's most well-trodden topics. If you find the right group of people (usually older, whiter and male-r), you can spend hours picking apart the minutiae of campaigns and heroic personalities from Churchill and Eisenhower to Rommel and Patton. In my youth, the History Channel in the United States was affectionately known as the "Hitler Channel" for the amount of time it spent telling and retelling the story of the rise and fall of the Third Reich. The second World War is a great story about good and evil. The few who bother to think about why this satisfying story came about acknowledge that it had a lot to do with the first World War, and see that conflict as a great tragedy. The even smaller group of people who wonder why the first war came about fall for a glorious or sordid story of imperial competition. They accept century-old British imperial propaganda as the real story.

I don't doubt that the people of the time, and today, believe(d) these stories. But by letting these stories become our history of the past two centuries, we fail to understand what really happened. We ignore the vast power that the British piddled away on the "Great Games" they were playing with Russia, France, and finally Germany. We ignore how avoidable the world wars were, and how much responsibility Britain deserves for letting them happen. Whether we focus on the "nobility" or the melancholy futility of these conflicts, we are very much missing the point.

Would More Brutality Have Done the Job?

What if the British had been more brutal? What if they had arrested Charles Stewart Parnell, Mahatma Gandhi, Jomo Kenyatta, and the nationalists of every country, paraded them through London and had them decapitated in front of Buckingham Palace? What if they had treated the Irish and Indians as brutally as they had treated the Kenyans? This question obsesses many neo-Imperialists in the United States today. What if we had **really** tried to win the war in Vietnam? What if we had had the iron will to disregard the niceties of the Geneva Conventions even further than we did, and **really** fought to win in Afghanistan and Iraq? Wouldn't that have worked?

Nope.

It didn't work out too well for the British in Kenya. The US's scorched earth approach to nationalists in the Philippines (1899-1902) killed hundreds of thousands, and US Empire didn't take there. The British attempted a more brutal policy towards Ireland between 1919 and 1921, and it only provided fodder for the Irish Nationalist cause. We've got models for vigorous, ends justify the means empires in the twentieth century. We rightly see the Nazis and the Communists of the Soviet Union as great villains, but they didn't see themselves that way. They thought they were making the world a better place too. It's possible that a more Nazi-like British or US Empire, with the much greater resources at the command of their world systems, could have succeeded. But at what cost?

Despite all the horror I've recorded here, I do think that there's something worthwhile in the British and US Empires. What makes them worthwhile is exactly the transition away from more thuggish methods of control that a more brutal policy would erase. The transition from formal to progressively lighter methods of informal imperial control was a good step. Now we have the potential to move to a prosperous world-wide informal "imperial" system run by no one. That potential would not exist if the British had managed to construct a modern Orwellian system in India, or if the United States had genocided its way across Vietnam and Iraq as successfully as it did the American West.

I have zero interest in rehabilitating the war-mad imperialists and interventionists who often ran the British and US systems. But I do think that the world has been left in a better place than it was in all the centuries before the world systems. I think all this suffering, political struggle and discussion has in some sense been worth it, or it could be if we don't screw up what we've currently got going. Stalin and Hitler were monsters, and a world created by them would have been a horror show. A world created by British Hitlers and Stalins would have been similarly worthless. We could still get a world created by American monsters. Let's try to avoid that.

On the Responsibility of the United States

I want to re-evaluate the history of the British Empire, not because I hate the British, but because I want to learn from their mistakes. We are now living in the second world system. My country, the United States, sits at its center and calls the shots. We are vastly more powerful than the British were. The British were defeated by their misunderstanding of nationalism, and the way that their turn to formal empire offended national sensibilities everywhere, leading to an apocalyptic war they could not afford. Thanks to savvy propaganda, and a more successful attempt to convince the world that it respects self-determination, the United States has figured out how to work the world's nationalist instincts into the functioning of our world system. But now we're losing the plot. Rather than focus on being a better steward of the world we run, we are focused on an even more surreal cast of manufactured enemies than the British were. We are making exactly the same sorts of mistakes the British did, and are even building what's beginning to look like formal empire in places like the Middle East and Afghanistan.

The United States runs a global trade and financial system that more thoroughly penetrates every nation on the planet than the British system ever did. But by making the same mistakes that the British did, I fear that we may be driving towards an apocalypse that will make Britain's world wars look like a tea party. But we don't have to, if we apply the lessons of Britain's failure to the US World System we all live in today.

"The dirty little secret of empire is that for all the rhetoric of 'burden', it is often psychologically fulfilling for those who run it and provides a good living for those who justify it."
Charles S. Maier[238]

Chapter 7
The Disturbingly Similar US World System

This book has shown that the British Empire was a lot more powerful than is typically appreciated. It has also emphasized that that power was much more about the system of informal control that the British had forced the rest of the world into than it was about formal imperial territory. I hope it has become clear, too, that the British and US Empires are more alike than is popularly believed. This chapter will briefly outline the rise of the US World System, show that in most respects it is a super-charged version of the British system at its height, and document the painfully obvious warning signs of a British-style decline.

The British as the Dutch

The US politicians and businessmen of a century ago were more interested in carving off economic benefits than taking on any of the responsibilities of world government. For most of the nineteenth century, the conquest of the North American continent was enough to keep the United States occupied, launching one of the greatest economic expansions the world had seen to that time, doubling per capita income while more than tripling the US population between 1850 and 1900. With the financial panic of 1893 and the ensuing

---

[238] p.77 Maier, Charles S. Among Empires: American Ascendancy and Its Predecessors

depression, it was clear that the country's economic focus had to shift. The frontier was closed. The low hanging fruit in continental expansion had been plucked. It was time to look outward.[239]

Like the initial architects of the British Empire, the US leaders of the 1890s and early 1900s were chiefly preoccupied with commercial concerns. The first English imperialists had built an empire of wealth by violently dispossessing the Dutch. The US merchant princes were now turning their sights on the seas and markets controlled by the British. But their path was considerably easier. The nineteenth century was very different from the seventeenth. The British Empire in the nineteenth century was slowly killing itself through a senseless shift from informal to formal empire. All the US had to do was sit back and eat its lunch.

The US started close to home. As far back as 1823's Monroe Doctrine, the US had declared its opposition to European interference in the Americas. It was only in the latter nineteenth century that we had the power to enforce it. The Spanish-American War (1898) saw the US embark on more straightforwardly European-style imperialism, with our new acquisitions in the Philippines, Puerto Rico and Guam. But the United States was always lukewarm on formal empire. The concept of "American Empire" always inspired vocal disgust as well as pride. Informal commercial empire was always more the goal than acquiring territory. Teddy Roosevelt's carving Panama out of Colombia to construct the canal in 1903 was to become more typical. It was always preferable to meet goals without too much military expenditure or the need for extensive formal control. Even though Panama's independence was very much in service to US interests, the imperial implications were deniable, at home and abroad.

---

[239] This point in particular is a concern of William Appleman Williams's great The Tragedy of American Diplomacy, which inspired much of the discussion in this section

Wealth Does Not Equal Power

There was nothing inevitable about the US rise to power. By the first decade of the twentieth century, the US was the world's largest economy. Its potential was immense. If raw economic power was all that mattered, the "American Century" would have been declared in the 1890s rather than 1941.[240] But the US had the same problem that China should have in the mid-twenty-first century. There was already a big guy in town. Though many in the US, most famously Teddy Roosevelt, were eager to compete directly with the British, most were content to profit from the system in place.

The Open Door policy, laid out in two notes from US Secretary of State John Hay in 1899 and 1900, was a statement of intent of sorts. The notes were a response to the scramble for China that the British had inspired through their two Opium Wars and other machinations. Hay wrote that China was not to be divided up, and all countries were to have equal access to the treaty ports that fallen country had been forced to open. The US government was nowhere near done with protectionism in its own country, but it was beginning to aspire to open access to all of the world's markets. Not at all surprisingly, the hegemon to come was getting more interested in free trade just as the old British hegemon was losing interest, devising systems of "imperial preference" pushed by politicians like Joseph Chamberlain. At the time of its formulation, the Open Door policy was more aspirational than anything else. Japan and the European powers kept on carving up China anyway. But it's easy to see this emphasis on free trade and markets in our government's rhetoric all the way up to January 2017, and the election of our very own Chamberlain, Donald Trump.

---

[240] That intriguing term was popularized by Henry Luce the publisher of Time Magazine in an editorial in 1941.

If the British had been more savvy about the way they ran their world system, it would have lasted a lot longer. The First World War cleared the path for the United States. The British Empire exhausted itself in a pointless battle on the European continent, with a German enemy it had done more than most to create. The fact that Britain was on the winning side was immaterial. The war flipped the British government's finances, leaving it owing more money to the periphery than the periphery owed to it. At wars end in 1918, Britain was in better shape than all its historical "rivals", but it was now financially subservient to a newer one, the United States. Britain's physical empire had grown, but it no longer had the resources necessary to exert itself over the peoples and territories it controlled. From Ireland to India and everywhere in between, the compromises with nationalist forces were adding up. This process was happening more quickly in some places (Ireland), and more slowly in others (India), but the trajectory was clear. The British hope was to draw the United States further into world governance. They needed the Americans to take on roles that they could no longer afford.

Woodrow Fricking Wilson

President Woodrow Wilson (from 1913-1921) swept in at the end of WWI to choose a winner and dictate terms to Europe's beaten down belligerents. He may be the most disastrous president we have ever had. Woodrow Wilson's messiah complex had some momentous effects. If you set up a line of dominos and kick one over, all the rest of them fall down. The history of the twentieth century was largely the result of dominos that Wilson set up and kicked over. He decided to use our wealth and power to settle WWI in the Allies' favor. He also invaded the Soviet Union in an attempt to help the losing side of its civil war. Any fair account would date the Cold War between the US and the Soviet Union from that intervention rather than the late 1940s. In my old age I've gotten a bit more charitable, but I think you can still make a pretty compelling case that Wilson was the historical figure most responsible for both Hitler and Stalin.

When Wilson arrived in Paris in 1919 to participate in the peace talks at Versailles, he was a worldwide celebrity. His Fourteen Points and his (more perceived than actual) support for the self-determination of all peoples made him the idol of millions. He intended to impose a "Peace without Victory" on his allies and set up a new world order under the auspices of the League of Nations. He was far, far out of his depth. There are plenty of theories about what happened at the Paris Peace Conference. John Maynard Keynes portrayed him as a provincial Presbyterian fanatic.[241] One theory claims that his previously impressive vision failed him because he was a victim of the Spanish flu.[242] Whatever the reason, he got snowed by Britain and France and failed to keep them from imposing the punitive Treaty of Versailles on Germany. Despite the very debatable question of war guilt, the Germans were required to pay massive reparations in territory, industrial goods and gold. The various payment plans agreed to over the next decade forecast payment structures lasting into the 1980s.[243]

When Wilson returned to the United States he failed to get the Treaty and the League of Nations past his own Congress.[244] The Senatorial refusal to get involved with the League wasn't isolationism. It was a reluctance to be constrained in foreign policy. Wilson disagreed with the Congress on the shape of US dominance, not the idea that it should exist. Many accounts tend to collapse the 1920s and 1930s, and portray the rejection of the League as a US withdrawal from the world. That came later. In fact, even after Wilson left for his very brief retirement, the United States was already acting as a hegemon, just on its own terms. In 1918, the British and the French hoped that the US would

---

[241] Keynes, John Maynard Economic Consequences of the Peace
[242] Barry, John M.
[243] P. 76 P. 74 Adler, Selig The Uncertain Giant: 1921-1941 American Foreign Policy Between the Wars
[244] https://www.senate.gov/artandhistory/history/common/generic/Feature_Homepage_TreatyVersailles.htm

take on Britain's traditional role as a forgiving paymaster. In the Napoleonic wars, the British had outright subsidized its allies for decades. The Europeans hoped that now that a new US-led order was in the offing, the US would forgive the billions of dollars of debt that the allies had taken on to fight the First World War. They were very, very disappointed.

Meet the New Boss… If She's Interested

In fact, paying off US debt was the dominant factor in European politics in the 1920s. The punitive German reparations requirements were directly tied to US requirements. The British at least were eager to forgo German indemnity payments, if the US would forgive British war debt. It never happened. The US imposed bilateral debt settlements and payment plans on all parties. A series of crises in the early 1920s, including German hyperinflation, and the French reoccupation of German industrial areas, convinced the US to take a more active hand. The US wasn't going to get paid at all if the continent dissolved into chaos. The 1924 Dawes Plan and the 1929 Young Plan both attempted to deal with the issue. Significantly, both plans were named after US citizens. Both plans consisted of large US loans to Germany. These loans were then paid more or less directly to the Allies as reparations, through an agency with US oversight, and then the money was used to pay allied war debt… to US banks. The debt kept racheting up, with a focus on continued interest payments but limited thought given to the possibility of eventual payment of the principal. This absurd situation was brought to an end by the Great Depression and the rise of Hitler, who repudiated the reparations payments. The Allied powers then promptly defaulted on their war debt to the United States. "When this banking merry go-round stopped, foreign debtors owed the United States and its citizens about twenty one billion dollars."[245] The United

---

[245] P. 74 Adler, Selig The Uncertain Giant: 1921-1941 American Foreign Policy Between the Wars

States was already acting as a hegemon in the 1920s. It just wasn't doing a very good job.

The Washington Naval Conference of 1921 and 1922 is also worth mentioning. For over a century, Britain had based its world system on its naval dominance. When representatives of the other powers arrived in Washington, DC in the fall of 1921, the US representatives already had sweeping program of naval disarmament put together. The proposal was that the US and British fleets be agreed to be the same size, and other naval powers, chiefly Japan, be given a lower limit on numbers of ships. What was the reaction of Britannia, the proud ruler of the waves? Gratitude. They could no longer afford naval dominance and were delighted to share responsibility with the United States. Japan's acceptance of these limits settled the balance of power in Asia for at least a decade. The United States had come a long way from its mostly ignored Open Door Policy. [246]

The US was no longer interested in sharing power in the Western Hemisphere. During and after WWI, the US eagerly jumped into Britain's old role of Latin America's enforcer. The first three decades of the twentieth century remain the high point of the US's physical interventions in Latin America. US troops were frequently sent to enforce US commercial interests and to, in Wilson's shockingly arrogant phrase, teach Latin Americans "how to elect good men". The United States invaded and occupied multiple countries south of the border and in the Caribbean, some, such as Panama and Honduras, as many as four or five separate times. [247]

This was a period of experimentation for the United States, and its leaders quickly realized that an aggressive policy, much like its

---

[246] The analysis of Allied War Debt and the Washington Naval Conference is taken directly from Tooze, Adam The Deluge: The Great War, America and the Remaking of The Global Order 1916-1931
[247] http://www.zompist.com/latam.html

experiment in direct imperial rule in the Philippines, wasn't yielding much. Soldiers on the ground bred resentment and destruction, not profit. The builders of the US Empire wanted markets, not subjects. Roosevelt adopted a Good Neighbor policy that took a more hands-off approach to Latin America. At least on paper. The Cold War would see almost every country south of the border subjected to a damaging tool-box of coups and subversion. Regardless, like the British before them, US policy makers discovered that informal empire was much more profitable than formal empire.

Latin America was the proving ground for the techniques and approaches that would make up the broader US World System. But the Depression consensus in the US saw no value in expanding their system to the much more complicated Old World. They had been burned by their decade of experimenting with financial hegemony in Europe. In the 1930s, the United States turned inward. The results were disastrous.

Powers from Fascist Italy, to Nazi Germany, the USSR and Japan saw an opportunity. They saw Britain as the falling hegemon it was, and the US as the rising hegemon it didn't want to be. They tried to use this time of flux to seize the initiative. The nascent US order that opposed them wasn't interested in sacrificing anything to oppose these powers and the British simply couldn't afford global dominance anymore. American inattention to what would have been British responsibilities—Japanese expansion into the Pacific and Manchuria, German expansion into Austria, attempted Italian expansion into Ethiopia—allowed the development of the situation that led to war. Much like the first world war, the second was the product of decades of power dynamics. WWI was brought about by British mismanagement of their world system. WWII happened because there was no world system. Instead of grappling with those failures, the US foreign policy community of today believes a fairy tale.

Learning the Wrong Lesson

The only piece of nineteenth or twentieth century history that those in US government seem to remember is Munich. In 1938, British Prime Minister Neville Chamberlain travelled to that German city to meet with Hitler, and try to stave off another war. He chose the path of appeasement, and gave Hitler what he wanted in Czechoslovakia in the rightly loathed Munich agreement. In the constrained window of the politics of the late 1930s, the lessons typically drawn from this historical anecdote are correct.

There are revisionist interpretations, suggesting that Chamberlain gave Britain time to finish preparing for the war. But the Czechoslovakians were prepared to fight Hitler in 1938, and they had fortified and mountainous territory with which to fight him. Unlike the Polish the next year, they had the industrial base and military they needed to be a real partner in stopping Hitler. It was Munich, in part, that convinced the Soviets to join Hitler in 1939's Molotov-Ribbentrop Non-Aggression Pact, giving Germany the free hand it needed to conquer Poland and France. The world would have been a much better place, and WWII would have been much shorter if it had started in 1938 rather than a year later. So yes, looking at the late 1930s alone, Chamberlain's policy of appeasement is rightly reviled.

But we shouldn't just look at this from the perspective of the 1930s. Unfortunately that's exactly what US policy makers, politicians, and even supposedly serious scholars do. The rallying cries of "Appeasement!" and "Munich!" have been used in every single US conflict since 1945 from Vietnam to Iraq. It's a key part of the way that the Iranian and Syrian regimes are viewed in the US today. If we get into an apocalyptic war with China a few decades from now, the morons that lead us into it will be shouting "Munich!" at the top of their lungs as they do it.

World War II was not a conflict that existed on its own. It was instead the clear and natural result of failures by the British Empire that went back a century. And these were failures of aggression, not timidity. It was the British Empire that chose to move imperial competition from the realm of trade and finance it dominated to one of dumb military power and formal empire. The choice to opt for this competition left British power at the mercy of any regional power that could get it together to master some of the tools of industrial war. And in the final analysis that's all Germany ever really was—a more technically advanced version of regional powers the British had already faced, like Tipu Sultan or the Maori—serious regional threats and powerful peoples in their own right, but *not* competitors for global hegemony.

It was the British Empire that chose to neuter Russia in the Crimean War in the 1850s, clearing a path for German unification in 1870, and German dominance in Eastern Europe. It was Britain that launched the Scramble for Africa and brought imperial competition to a fever pitch. It was the British Empire that chose to exacerbate this situation in the 1910s by creating an alliance system antagonistic to a German regime that was mildly more distasteful than the French but had endless potential for peaceful development. And finally, it was the British Empire that chose to involve itself in the First World War on the European continent, in the end replacing a distasteful German regime with a truly evil one.

After that point, it makes sense to talk about Munich as a failure. But the true failure was one of a hundred years of British leadership. That's the narrative thread that US policy makers ought to be following. By the time the 1930s rolled around, Britain had already given up its leadership. The leaderless world of the 1920s and 1930s took us back to that pre-1815 world where aggression was necessary. That is not the world we live in today, no matter how diligently US policy makers seem to be working to create it. The narrative of appeasement has been used for every US foreign crisis since the 1940s, and every tin pot regime that has ever mildly embarrassed us has been compared to Hitler. In the process, the appeasement narrative has justified exactly the sort of dumb aggression and militarism that really killed the British World System and led to Munich. Neville Chamberlain and Winston Churchill are not the British Prime Ministers US policy makers should focus on. Both of those guys were fighting battles that Britain had already lost.

The Second World War

In WWII there was no question of the British being able to fight independently. Their war strategy from the beginning was to just hang on long enough for the US to join up. Prior to 1941, and for the year or so before the US "Arsenal of Democracy" really got going, the story of the Second World War was the rapid rolling up of British Empire by Germany and Japan, from North Africa to the gates of India. When the US did eventually join up, they took the British-style "Napoleonic War" approach that they had refused to take in the aftermath of the First World War. "Lend-Lease" was a gussied-up way of subsidizing the war efforts of Britain, the Soviet Union and others. The British did end up even further in debt to the United States after WWII, but without the outright gift of weapons and material through Lend-Lease the British would never have been able to fight Hitler at all.

The Soviet Union ended up providing the cannon fodder necessary to defeat Nazism, and ended up a lot more important to the new world order than it would have been if the war had never happened. It was the fear of the Communist enemy that finally persuaded the United States to set up the world system we all live in today.

When Does the US World System Begin?

The British Empire provides a much easier dividing line between rise and victory. There is great clarity about when the British world-wide system got started. France provided a challenge for over a century, and a much more intense challenge from the French Revolution in 1789 on. And then with the end of Napoleon's power at Waterloo in 1815 that challenge ends, and British world dominance begins.

There is no hard and fast dividing line with US dominance. How do you treat the Cold War? It's traditional to measure the start of US hegemony from the fall of the Berlin wall in 1989, or the collapse of the Soviet Union in 1991. I think that puts the date way too late. The Soviet Union had been limping along since the 1970s at the latest, propped up by its growing status as a petrostate. Another approach is to date the start of the US World System from 1945. Historians correctly point to the fact that the United States was the only country in the world that still had advanced industrial capacity. The industries of most countries had been bombed to dust. Japan and Germany, once and future industrial titans, had experienced the complete destruction of multiple cities under Allied bombers. The war had wiped out as much as seventy percent of Europe's industrial capacity.[248] It was the United States alone that was unscathed. In 1945 the United States is commonly thought to have represented a full fifty percent of world GDP, a peak that has never since been matched, and hopefully never

---

[248] https://en.wikipedia.org/wiki/Aftermath_of_World_War_II#Economic_aftermath

will be again. A lot of the elements of the US World System were also put in place in 1945, from the United Nations to the World Bank and the IMF and the rest of the Bretton Woods system.

But I don't think it makes sense to talk about US hegemony beginning in 1945. The Cold War was a real struggle in the early decades. US dominance was no longer an open question by 1989, or even 1979, or possibly as far back as 1956. But there's no single date you can point to. The emergence of US domination was a continuum rather than a discrete moment. As with a lot of this book, I think it's a question of informal empire rather than formal empire. The main belligerents in the Cold War got in the most trouble when they let their militaries get involved in actual fights for territory, in places like Vietnam and Afghanistan. The battle for informal empire is the one that the US won unequivocally, and it's the battle that mattered.

The Communists

For younger readers, US culture's ongoing obsession with communists might look kind of silly. It must seem mystifying that geriatric-centered news sources like Fox News constantly inveigh against Communism with little explanation of what it is or why it is bad. The largest "Communist" country still existing today is China, a country whose support for capitalism and globalization often seems more convincing than that of the current US president. Smaller countries like Vietnam and Cuba seem to be on or aspiring to the same path. Of course, there is still the gangster state North Korea, hanging out there, scaring everybody. But it's hard to see Communism as a global threat in 2017. It's a struggle that most people see as over. I certainly see it that way. But it was a very real struggle.

If you look for the history of the "Cold War" in pop culture, you'd be forgiven for thinking the most important thing about it was the over-reaction to Communism in the United States. Most people have heard of Joe McCarthy and the Hollywood blacklists, because that's the aspect of the Cold War that gets the most attention. *Bridge of Spies*, from 2015, is emblematic of this trend. I loved the film, but I'm afraid that it minimizes the Cold War. Some scenes towards the end do an excellent job of conveying the horror of Communism, but most of the film just doesn't. Everybody's favorite character is the Communist spy, the scariest character actors are reserved for the CIA, and much of the first half of the film is dedicated to the anti-communist excesses of the American legal system. It is a great film. If it were one of five or six big movies that dealt with the Cold War this decade, I would have no complaints. Unfortunately, it's the only recent major film I can think of that has covered the subject at all seriously.

What made Communism so dangerous, and allowed it to be so successful between the 1920s and the 1960s, was a time of great flux in geopolitics. It was the two world wars of the early twentieth century that allowed international Socialism to transition from a bugaboo for Babbitts to a legitimate world power. Revolutionary left ideas had percolated throughout the British World System of the nineteenth century. London's imperial masters probably wouldn't have minded too much that Karl Marx was scribbling away in the British Museum, if they were even aware of it. Revolutionaries were more of a threat to the shakier monarchies on the continent than they were to Britain at the peak of its powers.

Ironically, it may have been the rise of the United States itself that made Communism's rise more likely. It was clear by 1900 that the world's equilibrium was getting shakier. The nineteenth century system, with Britain ruling the seas, and a fairly well-balanced Europe full of mini-empires, free to conquer and despoil in all directions, was threatened by the rise of the United States. Russia's rise was important as well, but its backwardness kept it from posing anywhere near the threat that the United States did. To paraphrase Napoleon's famous quip about Britain, the United States wasn't a "nation of shopkeepers", it was a continent of shopkeepers. By 1900, the United States already had the world's largest economy. It wasn't organized for world domination yet, but it clearly had the potential. As early as 1878, William Gladstone, the legendary British prime minister, stated that America would "probably become what we are now, the head servant in the great household of the World, the employer of all employed."[249] Everybody saw it coming, but nobody really knew what to do about it. This impending shake-up gave international affairs a new frenzy, made chaos more likely, and gave revolutionaries more opportunities.

The struggle against Communism came in two phases, somewhat like the Spanish and French eras of the British struggle against Catholicism. The first phase of competition in each case probably involved a lot more over-reaction than was warranted. The second did not.

Phase One: Red Scare

What is conventionally known as the first "Red Scare" isn't seen as beginning before the end of WWI, but you can see its elements everywhere in the beginning of the twentieth century, and before. The Progressive movement of reform in the early 1900's was sometimes explicitly, but always implicitly about heading off the possibility of radical unrest. US elites often crushed labor movements with great violence in the late nineteenth century and early twentieth century. As with the British, the ideological fear became wrapped up with nationalist fear. The socialists that were coming for your goods were often portrayed as Jewish or southern European or Slavic in some way

---

[249] P.406 Jenkins, Roy Gladstone: A Biography

that was un-American. The most famous example of this would probably be Sacco and Vanzetti, two anarchists who were executed for murder in Massachusetts in 1927. Their guilt was not well established, and they became a bit of an international cause celebre. That didn't keep the good people of Massachusetts from killing them. The US obsession with Communism was and is strikingly similar to the bone deep fear of Catholicism that was so important to the rise of the British World System in earlier centuries.

Phase Two: Red Scarier

Imagine if after decades of worrying about it, Islamic fundamentalist terrorism suddenly crystallized into a state. Now imagine if this Islamic State, instead of being made up of a solid media strategy and a few easily bombed losers,[250] took over multiple continents. That's what the US was dealing with in the middle of the twentieth century. Unlike the largely US intelligence-community-created flash in the pan that is "Radical Islamic Terrorism" today, Communism after the Second World War was a real mass movement, with serious adherents, territories, armies, navies and nuclear weapons.

In 1945, the Soviet Union (150-200 million people depending on the source you trust) was larger than the United States (140 million). It also had an anti-imperial ideology that understandably appealed to most of the developing world, and direct access to the Eurasian world island where much of the conflict would be carried out. The US's allies in Britain, Germany, Japan and Western Europe were all in ruins. The

---

[250] Just as an aside, we got an object lesson in how intimidating the Islamic State was not in the early months of 2018. Our "fearsome allies", the various Kurdish militias of northern Syria made fairly quick work of ISIS when our offensives got going. When Turkey decided to invade that Kurdish region in January 2018, I was expecting a prolonged quagmire type situation. Turkey, however, quickly met its objectives. This is despite the fact that the Turkish military has just been through successive waves of purges. By a transitive property you can probably conclude that neither ISIS nor the Kurds presented much of a threat to a real military. Yes, the Kurds did have the US air force to use against ISIS, which it did not have against Turkey, but I think the lesson still applies.

conflict started out quite poorly for the United States, with the USSR taking over all of Eastern Europe, and Communist ideology triumphing in China between 1945 and 1950. The Chinese communists ended up as a great enemy of the USSR, but that wasn't clear until the 1970's. While Joe McCarthy was leading his witch hunts, the United States was engaged in a savage war with Communist legions on the Korean peninsula. As ludicrous as it may sound today, it wasn't illogical to see the US as an underdog at the beginning of the Cold War, and it was certainly the way that the United States saw itself at that time.

In the first flush of victory in 1945, many imagined that the US could demobilize and again turn away from the world. The swift end of lend-lease put Britain in a difficult position. The United States did not want to be seen to be propping up the old British and French empires. There was even some residual affection for "Uncle Joe" Stalin. This dissipated quickly. It became clear that the US was not going to have the world of open, capitalist markets it wanted without a fight. By 1947, the British, in the process of their calamitous exit from India, informed the United States that they could no longer afford to suppress Communist influence in Greece or Turkey. Despite a lack of support from Stalin, it was looking like Communist partisans would win the Greek civil war, giving the Soviets an outlet on the Mediterranean, and further encircling the Turkish strait between the Black Sea and the Mediterranean that Stalin coveted.

In a speech to Congress in March 1947, Harry Truman put forth what became known as the Truman Doctrine. In the words of one historian, "In two years, the US government had gone from ambivalence toward a Soviet sphere of influence limited to central and eastern Europe to an apparently open-ended obligation to defeat left-wing insurgencies in every part of the world."[251] In 1949 the Soviet Union developed an

---

[251] P. 148 Bulmer-Thomas, Victor Empire in Retreat: The Past, Present, and Future of the United States

atomic bomb, and from then until the early 1990s human civilization really was just a few bad decisions away from ending on any given day.

The highlights of the Cold War are familiar to those who lived through it and to most students of US history. The Berlin Airlift, the Marshall Plan and the Formation of the North Atlantic Treaty Organization in the 1940s. The 1950s brought the Korean War, trouble in the Suez, the Soviet Invasion of Hungary, the launch of the Soviet satellite Sputnik and the Space Race. The 1960s brought the Cuban Missile crisis, the Vietnam war, and great social unrest across the world. The 1970s brought Détente, Nixon in China with Zhou En Lai, and humiliations for the US from the oil crisis to the end of US presence in Vietnam. The 1980s brought the Soviet invasion of Afghanistan and the miraculous fall of the Berlin wall, as well as Rock and Roller Cola Wars. Yes, this is the Billy Joel version.[252]

It's a dramatic but comfortingly heroic epic. It vastly undersells the scope of the conflict. The Cold War was a time of horrors. Many were perpetrated by the United States. The Soviet Union was certainly the main villain in Eastern Europe, China and Central Asia, but it was a much more even fight of brutes in South East Asia, and the US almost certainly took the lead in horror in Latin America and Africa. The Truman Doctrine implied involvement all over the world. The United States was everywhere in a sense that the British were never capable of. From coups to proxy wars to massacres to more benign electoral manipulation and commercial subjugation there is not a country on this planet that does not bear the scars of the Cold War. All the conflicts of the second half of the twentieth century, from all the endless civil wars of the Global South, to India and Pakistan's brutalization of each other and Bangladesh, to the endless suffering in the Middle East, were accelerated if not created by the Cold War as well. I'd love to dive in, but doing it justice would take another couple years of writing, and this book is supposed to be about the lessons we can learn from the British

---

[252]Apologies if you're not familiar with Billy Joel's "We Didn't Start the Fire". It's a great song.

Empire, not the American one. It's enough for now to say that the origin stories of the two empires are quite similar. The British built the first world system out of fear of the Catholics. The United States built the second, immensely more powerful one out of fear of the Communists.

With 20/20 hindsight I think you can place the Soviet Waterloo somewhere in the early 1960s. The formal empire of the Soviets fell with the Berlin wall in 1989, but its informal empire was defeated long before that. The US-funded Marshall Plan that rebuilt Western Europe in the late 1940s was incredibly costly. The thirteen billion dollars spent at the time is equivalent to around 110 billion in 2016 dollars. But the investment paid. The resurgence of Europe and Japan provided great opportunities for US business, and built a planet that made a world-wide Communist victory, which had seemed so close in the late 1940s (at least to American foreign policy elites), essentially impossible. At some point we'll never be able to locate exactly, a Japanese, or Californian, or German teenager reached for a Coke, and Marx and Lenin's hopes went up in smoke. The economic emergence of Japan, Germany and the rest of our European allies in the decades after WWII was unmatched in the Communist world. The USSR had done a fairly good job in the 1950s. The Soviets had experienced a roaring recovery from WWII, and continued their pre-war success in brutally marching the agrarian empire of the Tsars into an industrial future. The Soviets also racked up some impressive technological achievements. In 1957 the Soviets launched the first satellite, Sputnik, terrifying 1950s America. But the Soviet system couldn't compare with Western consumer culture. Krushchev could scream about producing more steel all he wanted, but Communism had no idea what to do with all that steel. Advertising beat central planning.

The US World System, Super-Charged Informal Empire

On every metric, the US World System is vastly more powerful than the British one that came before it. In the chapters above I took pains to emphasize that British informal empire was more important than its formal empire. The obvious parts of the map that were shaded "English Red" were quietly held together by the financial, legal and commercial dominance that the British had attained. The United States doesn't have much of a formal empire because it doesn't need one. The financial and human resources Britain stole from India and used to fuel its empire can all be found in our continent-sized country. Our unprecedented dominance in military force is impressive, if not particularly useful, but the power of the US World System is so much more than that. We've also wrapped the whole world into systems of institutional, financial, legal and banking control that would stun nineteenth century London bankers with their scope and power. To start this section off, it's worth summarizing some of these elements.

Ideological

The US World System has succeeded in the arena that defeated the British Empire. We've managed nationalism much more effectively. This is based on the US's perceived commitment to the ideals of national self-determination. The extraordinarily powerful US informal empire is based, to a larger degree that we acknowledge, on the fact that the US has been able to portray itself as uninterested in formal empire. The idea that the US world empire is committed to the freedom of all peoples has its detractors, especially now, but it's always had real power as well, and it was a real improvement on the image that the British conveyed to the world.

What the United States did is apply that initially-English idea of self-government to a much vaster canvas. In the process, we helped to make liberty an ideal for the whole world rather than just a North

Atlantic island. At first this liberty was just the ability to belong to a weirder sect of Christianity and do back-breaking agricultural labor on land that was more truly your own. And Freedom was something that only belonged to a limited class of propertied white men. It has grown from there. At our best we have been dedicated to the idea that you can figure out what is best for yourself, and go for it. A massive tide of immigrants has been attracted to this promise. Those who stayed home were inspired by America as well. From the French Revolution down to the Arab Spring, people world-wide have been inspired by elements of our experience. Liberty has changed. Over the course of the nineteenth and twentieth century the US became an urban and suburban society, where self-sufficiency was lost, but the potential of every individual was expanded. The energy unleashed by all these different pursuits of happiness changed, and continues to change the world. More than anything, else, what the United States has done right is be big, rich, and happier than most over 200 years. This may seem simple, but it was hard won.

At every stage of the US's jerky rise to power, respect for national self-determination was always a selling point, even if it was often disrespected by Washington, DC. Wilson's Fourteen Points were the justification for participation in WWI. FDR's WWII-era Atlantic Charter was based on self-determination as well, adding moral opprobrium to the insolvency that forced Britain to give up India. Early Cold war presidents like Eisenhower provided real support for independence minded nationalists in the developing world, supporting Egypt's Nasser during the Suez struggle against Britain and France (as long as, as in Nasser's case, the interests of those nationalists aligned with the interests of the White House).

This perceived support for self-determination allowed the US to build a profitable world system on the ashes of the British one with the consent of most of the planet. From Greece, Guatemala and Iran at the outset of the Cold War, to Vietnam and dozens of other countries in the decades since, the US has repeatedly violated these principles of self-determination. US actions have included the full imperial range of covert subversion, financial manipulation, and if all else fails, blockade, sanctions and war. But the US almost always prefers to use the carrot rather than the stick. There is almost always more money to be made than spent when the military isn't involved.

It's not just about profit though. The core belief in liberty and self-determination is real, and it continues to be one of the main pillars of the US World System's legitimacy. Even the Trump administration, whose blind support of Saudi aggression in Yemen has reached new depths of hypocrisy and horror, still occasionally acts in service to these ideals. In Sudan, throughout the first half of 2019, a peaceful protest movement has been battling against a military dictatorship. The same Saudi-UAE coalition that has been brutalizing Yemen has weighed in on the side of the Sudanese dictatorship with billions of dollars. But in Sudan they don't have the bogeyman of Iran to point to, so they do not have US support. The US State Department, even under Trump consigliere Mike Pompeo, has refused to back the Saudi play, and as of this writing the Sudanese generals have been forced to negotiate with the protesters. The US commitment to liberty and self-determination has always been conditional, but it has led to a degree of world-wide buy-in that the British never had. The British had to violently impose their financial, legal and commercial system on the world. The US World System has been adopted much more voluntarily. Violence has only occasionally been a factor.

Ideological Victory

Since 1989, the United States has enjoyed the same sort of cultural dominance that the British had in the first half of the 1800s. Like the British before them, the US had won a colossal struggle, but much more so than the British victory over Napoleon, the longer battle against the Soviets implied an ideological victory. Long after the totalitarian Soviet model had begun to fail internally, Communist ideals of equality, anti-imperialism and anti-capitalism still held great appeal. Russia's abandonment of Communism discredited it almost entirely. It was clear to many that the US model was better at providing wealth throughout the twentieth century, but after 1989, it became undeniable. From the 1990s, the "Washington Consensus" has been what reforming countries aim for. There are disputes as to what exactly the term means, but most agree that it includes a basket of "neo-liberal" reforms, including trade liberalization, macroeconomic stabilization, and, depending on the time and place, sometimes austerity and privatization.

Since the 2008 financial crisis this model has supposedly fallen out of favor. But it is still enshrined in US founded and controlled institutions like the World Bank, the International Monetary Fund (IMF) and the World Trade Organization (WTO). There have always been elements of coercion in this of course. The US-dominated IMF and the World Bank famously impose these reforms before bailing out or lending money to troubled countries, which bothers many. But this approach has been useful to many countries, on every continent, and it continues to be so. It's also, even at its most coercive, a big improvement on British gun boats.

The death of the "Washington Consensus" has been much exaggerated. Across Africa we have seen countries like Tunisia and Sudan establish, or attempt to establish representative democracies. Ethiopia's rock star Prime Minister Abiy Ahmed, in power since 2018, has promised to transform China's favorite protégé with a program of free elections and privatization. Countries have benefitted in the longer term as well. The focus on maintaining large financial reserves in the developing world, in the aftermath of 1997's Asian Financial Crisis, can be seen as following from some interpretations of the "Washington Consensus". That focus saved numerous emerging economies during the 2008 crisis. In fact, Washington Consensus reforms allowed some, like Turkey for example, to grow explosively in the easy money years after 2008, as Europe and the US suffered. These pro-market approaches worked very well for some countries, and not so well for others. But it always worked out well for the United States, making nations on every continent more receptive to US business and capital. The British would be extraordinarily jealous of the system we have going.

Re-Formatting the British World System

The US World System takes its legitimacy from the US's perceived (and much-propagandized) support of everybody's self-determination. This crucial reformatting of hegemony allowed the US to pick up the broken pieces of the British system and reshape them into something new and more powerful. Four decades of Cold War competition between the United States and the Soviet Union gave an extra incentive to the extension of the vast informal commercial empire Britain had bequeathed to the US. Countries needed to be convinced of the benefits of a Capitalist approach rather than a Communist one.

In the nineteenth century, the British, through the holding of strategic territory and the cultivation of local elites, controlled the world's trade routes. In the decades following WWII, that control fell apart due to the expense which Britain's diminished resources could no longer bear. The large territories of the formal British Empire, in places like India and Africa, often suffered violent transitions to independence. But the control of the world's trade routes shifted directly to the United States. US informal empire was usually on such a larger scale that the old British bases were no longer necessary. What was the point of physically holding Malta or Cyprus to control the Mediterranean if

Italy, Greece, and Turkey were "eager"[253] to sign up for the US-run NATO architecture and bases? Why bother with Singapore, the British Navy's Asian citadel, if Japan and Taiwan were "happy" to host a string of bases? Relationships were important here as well. The relationships Britain had with Saudi Arabia and the "Trucial Sheikhs" of what became the UAE were just transferred to the US wholesale. This straightforward control of the world's trade routes makes a good case that the date for US defeat of the Soviet Union should be seen as earlier than even the 1960s date I proposed above.

The British legacy was much more than physical. The British spread English everywhere. The United States speaks that language too. The British uses its almost unique Common Law system to govern commercial relations. The US uses that system too. The nationalist minded elites all over the world that chafed under the British World System have been happier under a US one that pretends to respect self-determination, and tends to pay them much better than the British one did. In my work as a corporate attorney abroad, I was surprised to find that the most valuable skill in worldwide business remains the English language. The British violently battered down barriers to force the world to accept their commercial and legal ideas. The richer, more literate world of today sends millions of students to the United States to absorb those ideas voluntarily.

Modern Industry and Technology

As I emphasized in Chapter Two, an understanding of the vastly greater scale of the US World System is inseparable from an understanding of just how far we've come over the past two centuries. When British dominance began in 1815, most of the world's people were still engaged in rural agriculture. By the twentieth century, modern life was

---

[253] As one irate reader of this text points out "Greece was made pro-NATO and pro-Western by an anti-communist, pro-monarchist coup orchestrated by the British with the help of Greek Nazi collaborators against the incredibly heroic communists who'd fought the Germans every day of the war."

dependent on an extraordinary range of manufactured products. Countries across all continents had created complex industries and supply chains to service these needs. The exponential leap from wood or coal fired steam engines to internal combustion engines is just one example of the extraordinary progress in complexity and power we're talking about here. I've spent long hours trying to wrap my head around the principles of what is known as the "first industrial revolution" in the decades around 1815. This includes concepts like steam condensation and textile spinning. I lack an engineering mind, so my studies have been largely fruitless, but I've got a limited grasp of some of it, which has been helpful. When it comes to the "second industrial revolution" of the latter nineteenth century or thereabouts, I don't even bother. Chemical industries in dyes, and proto-pharmaceuticals, flight and machine tools are beyond me, and they always will be. Suffice it to say, the progress was mind-blowing, and by the mid-twentieth century, opportunities, both for progress and horror, were extraordinary.

Nineteenth century British industrialists profited mightily from industries that used centralized machine production to produce consumer goods. Twentieth and twenty-first century US industrialists profited from industries that put incredibly complex machines in the driveways and pockets of consumers worldwide, from Model T Fords to iPhones. Each smart phone includes technologies, and is backed by supply chains, that would mystify the most powerful nineteenth century engineer-industrialists. US politicians love the refrain that "we don't make anything anymore!" and maintain that other countries are stealing our know how and industrial dominance. This is true, but only in a very limited sense. Some of the production happens elsewhere, but these vast supply chains, and most of the ideas that drive it are still directed by US business and capital.

Finance and Acronyms

As with the British Empire before it, the profits of a century of industrial and trade dominance have been deposited into what is possibly the most important underpinning of the US World System, the country's tremendous pool of capital. New York leads the financial world, with the same dominance London once had. There's no higher sign of success for a company, even those from an emerging rival like China, than a listing on the New York Stock Exchange. This privilege has led to another sorely under-appreciated aspect of the US World System: in the financial world, we control everything. The tremendously complex and (let's be honest) rather boring intersection of international finance and imperial laws laid down by Congress and regulatory agencies is where the US World System's power really lies.

When Trump unilaterally took the United States out of the Joint Comprehensive Plan of Action (the Iran Nuclear Deal) in May of 2018, reactions from our European allies were immediate and defiant. They angrily proclaimed that the Iran Nuclear Deal was a multi-lateral agreement, they were independent actors, and their companies would continue to do business with Iran in the face of US sanctions. Then German Chancellor Angela Merkel heard from Siemens, the German industrial giant, and French President Emmanuel Macron heard from Total, its biggest oil company. The sad fact was that these companies, economic champions of their respective countries, were completely incapable of operating without US approval. Total S.A. is one of the seven biggest oil companies in the world, and it's one of France's largest and most powerful businesses. Unfortunately for Macron, it also relies on US banks for 90 percent of its financing, and 30 percent of its shareholders are American.[254] Despite the wishes of the French government, France's largest oil company was incapable of acting in the face of US disapproval.

---

[254] Rosenberg, Elizabeth and Edoardo Saravalle "China and the EU Are Getting Sick of US Financial Power" Foreign Policy November 16, 2018 https://foreignpolicy.com/2018/11/16/us-eu-china-trump-sanctions/

Not every foreign company is as exposed to US investors as Total is. But any company that hopes to operate internationally has exposure to the US dollar, and US banks, if only to process transactions. Institutions like the IMF, the WTO and the UN are important venues for the exercise of US power, but it's another set of lesser known acronyms that truly strikes fear into corporate lawyers and businesspeople worldwide. Since 9/11, the United States has been pushing more and more of world management into its own court system. Under the guise of fighting terrorism, the US government has been quietly expanding its jurisdiction over almost anything it wants to.

OFAC, the Office of Foreign Assets Control, has run the US sanctions program since the 1950s, but since 9/11 it has been expanding a system of "secondary sanctions" against a growing list of "malefactors." A secondary sanction is one that is not just enforced against any US national that attempts to do business with a targeted country or individual, but anyone in the world who attempts to do business with a target. When wielded carefully by a suave diplomat like Obama, this very imperial assumption of power can avoid ruffling feathers. Under Trump, European leaders are waking up to just how much sovereignty they have lost to the US over the past couple decades.

FATCA, the Foreign Account Tax Compliance Act, passed in 2010 and implemented in 2014, is even more sweeping. In order to catch US tax cheats, FATCA forces every bank in the world to formulate a reporting relationship with the US Internal Revenue Service (IRS). This law created outrage among those who could understand it, but the consequences were so draconian, and the details were so mind-numbingly complicated, that the world just knuckled under and complied. As with many of these issues, complexity leads to consent. You basically need a law degree to understand what's happening, but if you spend a month or two looking at the issues generated by one of these acronyms, or others, the effect is stunning. The US World System is vastly more powerful than the British one.

The US Department of Justice (DOJ) has been going further and further afield in recent decades. The two acronyms discussed are only two of many. There are many more agencies and legal doctrines that are capable of entrapping businesses and countries that have very little to do with the United States. The United States's jurisdiction has been steadily expanding, case by case. For his part, Donald Trump has been using trade and legal policy in ways that violate supposedly long-cherished norms. The December 2018 arrest of Chinese tech executive Meng Wanzhou in Canada over Iran sanctions, and the multiple attempts to use trade policy to bully Mexico over immigration come to mind. Trump is making these efforts look more clownishly sinister, but US Presidents have been developing the tool box he is using at least since the close of the Second World War.

Hollywood

The power of US culture goes far beyond the ideals that motivate our governing system. Cinema and television produced in the United States has a wide reach, but "Hollywood" is only a shorthand. To an extent that British propagandists could only dream of, the United States influences the dreams and aspirations of every individual in the world with an internet connection or access to a television. The British successfully co-opted rich elites who could afford the educations necessary to learn European languages. US culture, by contrast, is everywhere. "Hollywood" isn't just a place, or a particular industry. It's an entire way of viewing of the world, and mode of cultural production that has infiltrated everywhere. The US World System profits from this, either directly, or through world-wide adoption of lifestyles and ideological approaches that serve it.

Turkish television has a famously wide reach.[255] Across the Middle East, North Africa and Eastern Europe, Turkish soap operas are phenomenally popular. They do better than US programming because they are more modest, and more respectful of traditional societies and family structures. But they are still selling formats, ideas and aspirations initially cooked up in the United States. They aren't salacious enough to get banned, but they are certainly more salacious than anything that was previously on offer in Arab lands. Among much else, the Turkish soaps have prompted some popular reevaluation of the role of women everywhere they have been viewed. They advertise a glamorous Turkish lifestyle that sells the same range of consumer products US prestige TV does.

Thanks largely to the internet titan Reliance Jio, over the past couple of years, low-cost internet has brought over 300 million Indians into the digital age.[256] The world's largest YouTube channel is now Indian. Channels across the subcontinent are provided in a bewildering array of languages, and they deal with a wide range of local concerns, economic, educational, social, and religious. But the formats these concerns are being presented in were cooked up in Silicon Valley. Every entrepreneur with a YouTube channel is using similar tricks, and similar tools, and is packaging local culture into more US-style snippets. It's a global exercise in cultural self-colonization. And the profits are streaming back to Google.

This internet-enabled aspect of US cultural dominance is only in its early days. China has managed to set up its own internet, with rigorous government control. But Chinese companies are selling the same visions of wealth and self-actualization that American firms do. China's internet giants sell their shares in New York, and China's

[255] Gurmen, Esra "How Turkish Soap Operas Took Over the World" Fader March 1, 2016
http://www.thefader.com/2016/03/01/turkish-soap-operas
[256] Hawkes, Rebecca "India's Internet Subscriber Base Rises to 636.7MN" Rapid TV News July 11, 2019
https://www.rapidtvnews.com/2019071156647/india-s-internet-subscriber-base-rises-to-636-7mn.html#axzz5tUOEWL8A

wealthy are more interested in buying into the American dream than the Chinese one. It's entirely possible that this aspect of US dominance will fade away as countries become more savvy, and the market for internet media gets larger. But it's just as likely that the profits and the influence will continue to stream back to the first mover, the United States, for decades to come.

Institutions and International Law

The British Empire enforced its ideas of international law—for example, imposing its versions of free trade and the abolition of slavery—on an often-unwilling world. The United States has at least a dozen multi-lateral institutions that enforce our conceptions of international law, on a vastly wider scale, and on a wider variety of topics. The British attempt to ban slavery was a legitimately great thing. But it also provided many of their first footholds in Africa, and it was not applied to useful allies like the Sultans of Zanzibar. The growing attempts to enforce international concepts of human rights after the middle of the twentieth century has absolutely been a good thing as well. But these concepts also functioned as a bludgeon to use against US enemies like the Soviet Union, while the US blocked human rights enforcement and investigation of its allies. This unequal enforcement of human rights persists today. The US State Department trumpets human rights violations by Iran, while attempting to cover up much worse abuses by Saudi Arabia. The use of these concepts by the United Nations and other institutions is a good thing, but the United States also uses those institutions to advance its own ends, moral and immoral, with great effect.

As more countries have built up the capacity to utilize institutions like the UN and the WTO to make international law work for them, a backlash against those institutions has grown up in the United States. It's important to remember however, that these institutions have charters that were all written by the United States. If other countries, large and small, have learned how to occasionally use these institutions to give the US a minor black eye, that actually serves the US system as well. It's a sign of the adoption a general system that the United States benefits from immensely.

The Pax Americana, Nukes or Nationalism?

One of the greatest virtues of the US World System has been the extraordinary seventy four years of great-power peace that we have experienced since the end of WWII. The Cold War saw great horrors perpetrated by both sides, but nothing on the *scale* of the world wars in the first half of the twentieth century. And since the Cold War, the world has gotten even more peaceful. The conflicts in Syria and Yemen are horrific, but any decade of the Cold War featured a dozen Syria-level conflicts. The fact that none of the top twenty economic powers in the world have engaged in a shooting war with each other in three quarters of a century is a gift. And unlike the Pax Britannica of the nineteenth century, the great powers of this era have been competing for markets more than imperial territory. How this came about is a very important question.

The standard answer is "Nuclear Weapons". The US and the USSR never started a shooting war, ostensibly out of fear that it would inevitably escalate to a mutual nuclear exchange and the effective end of the world. Those fears were real, but they do not explain why the Cold War, and the period of US hegemony since, has seen such a fall in violence worldwide. The Pax Britannica saw a long period of rarely-interrupted peace between great powers as well, but it also included savage wars of destruction against indigenous peoples and empires on every continent other than Europe. Both the US and the USSR were terribly embarrassed when they attempted to establish more formal power over countries like Vietnam, Afghanistan and Iraq. Overwhelming military force is not what it used to be. The answer here is nationalism. More wealthy and educated twentieth and twenty-first century populations were enraged by any attempt to occupy their territory, and used all the tools at their disposal to thwart it. The almost universally-adopted weapons system of nationalism has been just as important to the past seventy-four years of peace as nuclear weapons.

The soft-power elements of the United States's informal empire were and are much more important than the harder power aspects in maintaining the US World System and world peace. The United States's actual or perceived commitment to the self-determination of peoples has been just as important to preserving our hegemony as nukes have been. Healthy respect for nationalism and sovereignty, combined with the broader US tools of financial, commercial, legal and cultural management, and other elements of "soft power" are much, much more important to continued US power than the formal "hard power" of US military dominance.

Culture and politics in the United States tend to obscure this simple point. We are caught up in our own version of the "historical hangover". We associate US power with our defense establishment, and look to great military victories, above all WWII, as the true source of our power. This is a terrible mistake. I am not some pacifist who thinks that the US World System would be possible without military dominance. We could get by with spending half as much on our military, but I recognize that it remains necessary for now. The problem is that the United States has spent the past three decades making the exact same mistakes as the British Empire did. We believe our power comes from military force, so we look for more reasons to use it. By doing so we have been steadily chipping away at the true sources of our ideological, institutional and commercial power. It's a terrible contradiction. The United States still needs our military industrial complex. But it is trying to kill us.

Formal Empire

There are many more physical manifestations of US Empire than we acknowledge, from Puerto Rico and other territories in the Caribbean, to a chain of Pacific islands stretching halfway to China. But unlike British India, none of that formal empire is an important part of our self-image. US formal empire is seen as an inconvenience or an embarrassment, if it is seen at all. We don't let it get in the way of our self-image as liberators. But we do have a quietly growing web of formal empire that is little mentioned but straightforwardly imperial.

The United States has hundreds of military bases abroad. Any attempt to come up with a concrete number will fail, due to the lack of agreement on what constitutes a base, US government secrecy about some bases, and the political vagaries of each individual relationship with the host country. As just one example, Honduras has had a US base defined as "temporary" since 1982, to circumvent the Honduran constitution's prohibition of foreign military installations.[257] In 2018, the Pentagon admitted to 514 overseas installations[258], but the same report includes restrictive definitions of what constitutes a base.[259] While it purported to list non-base installations under the "other" category as well, it's clear that there is a lot of wiggle room here. Reading the report, one gets the sense that the Pentagon accountants were struggling to figure out what was going on as well. And nobody disputes that there are plenty of installations that are kept secret. The US special forces are thought to maintain plenty of facilities in foreign

---

[257] Vine, David "Where in the World Is the US Military?" Politico July/August 2015
https://www.politico.com/magazine/story/2015/06/us-military-bases-around-the-world-119321
[258] P.8 2018 Department of Defense Base Structure Report
https://www.acq.osd.mil/eie/Downloads/BSI/Base%20Structure%20Report%20FY18.pdf
[259] P. 4 2018 Department of Defense Base Structure Report

countries that meet any popular definition of "bases," if not the Pentagon's definition. For years now, the round number of 800 or so foreign bases has been the figure critics gravitate towards. This has remained alarmingly constant in the face of multiple troop draw-downs and expansions in places like Iraq and Afghanistan. Any number provided is an estimate.

These bases are examples of formal empire. Recall that most of the British Empire's break-neck expansion in the run-up to the First World War was about denying other powers influence in a given area. That's what these bases are designed to do as well. Though some of them, like those in Western Europe, primarily act as staging areas for other conflicts, many also take a more direct hand in the politics of their host countries. Across Africa, bases act as training grounds for local militaries, propping up whatever faction we have deemed to be useful to our interests. It's ruinously expensive. It also prompts other powers to get in on the game. Ridiculously, the tiny African nation of Djibouti hosts US and Chinese bases on either side of a coastal city. Each of these hundreds of bases is an opportunity for international incidents, and quite possibly new wars. The US involvement in Vietnam started out as a training and advisory mission. The British had to win two wars with Germany to bankrupt itself. On the current trajectory, we risk doing it with bases alone, long before WWIII gets a chance to start.

The Useless but Essential US Military Industrial Complex

The bases, however, are just one manifestation of what I like to call the metastasized military industrial complex. WWII and the Cold War gave the United States the most dominant and terrifying military force in history. A crucial, ignored lesson of the Cold War and the decades since is just how useless this military tool is. A massive infrastructure of death is necessary to maintain credibility and effectively participate in the dick-waving contest that is international politics. We could probably do with a military half the size, and we absolutely need a military industrial complex that produces cheaper, more useful tools than the current one.

We view our nuclear forces as a deterrent, their use unimaginable, maintained to keep anybody else from imagining using their own. This is the way we should view our conventional military forces as well. They can be effective deterrents, but useless in action. Seriously, since WWII, or debatably Korea, where have they done any lasting good? Vietnam in the 1960s and 1970s? Grenada in the 1980s? Somalia in the 1990s? Iraq after 2003? Afghanistan in the 2000s, 2010s, and probably the 2020s? To be sure, the Pentagon occasionally does great work in disaster recovery, and smacking down pirates, but those are not the purposes for which it was built. Our war machine is pretty shit at war, and the irrational compulsion to keep using this big, shiny, lethal tool is what will probably end the US Empire.

The Metastasized Military Industrial Complex

The problem of the military industrial complex is one that has long been recognized. US President Dwight D. Eisenhower, a military man, left office with a very explicit warning against it in 1961:

> This conjunction of an immense military establishment and a large arms industry is new in the American experience. The total influence-economic, political, even spiritual-is felt in every city, every state house, every office of the Federal government. We recognize the imperative need for this development. Yet we must not fail to comprehend its grave implications. Our toil, resources and livelihood are all involved; so is the very structure of our society.
>
> In the councils of government, we must guard against the acquisition of unwarranted influence, whether sought or unsought, by the military-industrial complex. The potential for the disastrous rise of misplaced power exists and will persist.[260]

---

[260] Eisenhower's farewell address, televised 1961. You can find a copy here.
https://www.ourdocuments.gov/doc.php?flash=false&doc=90&page=transcript

Everyone from campus leftists to the late war-mongering Republican senator John McCain acknowledges the pernicious triangular relationship between the Pentagon, the US Congress and weapons manufacturers. Congressmen want jobs for their constituents; high-ranking Pentagon officials, military and civilian, want good jobs after government; and the defense industry is happy to provide both. This leads to an endless cycle of ballooning costs, expensive weapons of dubious merit, and a political class that worships the military and likes to use it. I'd like to introduce two factors that are less appreciated. These two factors, protection and time, have made the problem of the military industrial complex infinitely worse than it was in Eisenhower's day.

The first is the special, protected status of the Defense industry. Prior to the 1980s, political classes in the United States and across the world had a great deal more discretion in the economic arena. Presidents of a half century past thought nothing of price controls, strategic nationalizations, and other interventions in the economy that we currently associate with failing dictatorships. Since the Reagan Revolution, and the accumulation of rules around economic globalization in institutions like the WTO, economic discretion has fallen mightily. Politicians who seek to protect a given industry now have to face both international regulation, and the condemnation of a chattering class that prefers to let markets work. The defense industry is completely free of that. The purposes of "National Security" quite rightly shield weapons companies from the scrutiny of the WTO and Wall Street free marketeers. A given congresswoman is happy to have a widget factory in her district, but if China makes a cheaper widget there is very little she can do to preserve that factory. If a bomb factory opens in her district, however, she has complete freedom to use her powers to make that factory eternal. This special status of defense companies makes sense, but it also gives the weapons industry power over our congresspeople that is massively disproportionate to its already large role in our economy.

The second factor is time. In 1961, Eisenhower and many others in positions of power could remember a time when the United States did without an "immense military establishment". Before the Second World War the United States had never maintained more than a handful of men under arms between wars. Everyone who grew up under that version of the United States is dead now. This is what I mean by metastasis. Over four decades of Cold War and the three decades since, the cancer of military money has steadily spread throughout our governing system and society. The military industrial complex doesn't just include the Pentagon, defense contractors and Congress anymore. It includes most of our established media, which hates Donald Trump and everything he stands for…unless he's bombing something. It includes our universities, almost all of which take large grants from the Pentagon and other branches of the government, creating an intellectual climate that unthinkingly assumes that the US military must be everywhere forever. A staggering array of companies you would never think of, from McDonald's to Amazon, benefit from large military contracts as well, adding their weight to the perpetual war machine. In some sense we're all a part of the problem. Inertia has set in. Even after the past two decades of disaster, "Hey, maybe we shouldn't start another trillion-dollar war in the Middle East?" is only now, during the 2020 Democratic Presidential primary, ceasing to be a marginal, radical opinion. This metastasized military industrial complex prompted us to miss one of history's greatest opportunities.

A Missed Victory

The years between 1989 and 1992, which saw the mostly-peaceful collapse of the Eastern Bloc, were miraculous. Far-sighted statesmen in the United States rightly refused to declare victory. The fact that the Cold War remained cold was a victory for all humanity, and as good a case for divine intervention as you can find in the twentieth century. All of the dominoes that Woodrow Wilson had kicked over in 1917 by picking a winner in WWI had fallen. Hitler had been defeated, and now the Soviet Union had voluntarily dissolved itself as well. The world was ready for a new era of peace, or at least "not our problem". It was not to be.

Rather than wind down, the military industrial complex we built for the Cold War dedicated itself to finding a purpose. The US military, government and media have spent the past thirty years manufacturing fear with which to justify the existence, growth, and (mis)use of American military power. This didn't happen because people are evil. It happened because people want to keep their jobs. George H.W. Bush, who had done a great job overseeing the end of the Cold War, was still a military industrial complex man at heart. In Iraq, he took what could have been a negotiation, or a quick police action, and turned it into an air-force-sustaining permanent occupation by no-fly-zone, that his son turned into an across the board military spending bonanza a decade later. There was a limited peace dividend in the 1990s. Some bases closed, and some programs ended. But most of the Cold War establishment remained, and they continued the desperate search for something to do. They invented something to do after September 11, 2001, that had very little to do with the attacks that day.

The War on Terror Was Another Scramble for Africa

It's in the US security establishment's actions since 9/11 that we see the clearest parallels to the screw-ups that ended the British World System. In a superficially understandable response to the attacks of September 11th, the Bush administration launched a sweeping program, supposedly designed to go after Jihadi terrorists wherever they could be found. That's not what the Bush or Obama administrations actually did.

Global "Radical Islamic Terrorism" was a tool created by the US and two fundamentalist Sunni Muslim countries to kick the Soviets out of Afghanistan in the 1980s. Over the course of the decade, the US intelligence community worked closely with Saudi Arabia and

Pakistan to form networks of militias to combat the Soviets. In so doing, they collected and funded Sunni extremists, and helped them build international networks. One of these US-sponsored networks grew into Al Queda, the organization that attacked the United States on 9/11.

Ensuring that 9/11 could never happen again required a few simple steps. First and foremost, ending the sponsorship of Saudi Arabia and the terrorists they created in collaboration with the CIA. An Afghanistan invasion was inevitable, less because of the intransigence of the Taliban than because of the anger of the US people. Maybe ten percent of the extraordinary expenditure and sacrifice of rights brought about under the Department of Homeland Security and the Patriot Act has been useful. Maybe ten percent of our vast network of Special Forces trainers and assassins does useful work. Very little of this, after the quick defeat of the Taliban, offered much in the way of profit for defense contractors. So we destroyed Iraq and Libya, providing an excellent showcase for our bombs, planes and missiles. We turned what should have been a straightforward punitive expedition to Afghanistan into two decades of what is almost certainly human history's largest and most pointless waste of wealth and military material.[261] The continued idiocy of the CIA and Saudi Arabia created ISIS, a threat in Syria that was so malign we could justify destroying multiple cities from the air over the course of years.

The War on Terror was a half-hearted attempt to attack only the most obvious elements of Jihadi terror. But it had great and understandable support from a public mired in fear and anger. To my eternal shame, I was a big supporter for the first five years or so of this effort as well. The War on Terror led to record defense expenditure, and the US public's acceptance of constant war and intervention. The global War

---

[261] It's obviously been a catastrophic waste of innocent human life, as well, but this is at least one category in which past monsters have outdone the ones running our wars right now.

on Terror didn't just involve the more public destruction of Iraq, Syria, Somalia, Libya, Yemen and Afghanistan. It also involved the spreading out of US military contractors and personnel to dozens of countries in Africa and Asia. This US-sponsored intensification of military spending and capabilities provoked panic and overreaction in the US government's official targets: China, Russia and Iran. The toppling of Iraq and Libya, and the massive effort to topple Syria, countries that had little to nothing to do with 9/11, also added to this panic. Though Russia, Iran, and the China of 2019 are much smaller players in the US World System than the official adversaries of the British World System were, their reactions are very similar to the reactions of Germany, France, and Russia to Britain's Imperialism. US militarism over the past two decades has inspired a massive rise in Chinese, Russian and Iranian militarism in self defense.

Much like the British Scramble for Africa, the US War on Terror has failed in all of its stated goals. The scramble was supposed to make Britain safer, more secure, and more prestigious. Instead it added to the expense, complication, and world-wide resentment of the British Empire. The US War on Terror has led to the creation of more Middle Eastern instability and Jihadism rather than less. Inconveniently for the Pentagon, however, radical Islamic terrorism is now fading away. This is a result of falling oil prices, not military success. American allies in Gulf countries like Saudi Arabia and the UAE can no longer afford to bankroll the Jihadists they have supported over the past three decades. While declaring a victory they do not deserve, the US national security state is currently pulling a fast one on us. The War on Terror is over. We are now moving on to a new justification for our hyper-militarization, one that is even more reminiscent of the foreign policy that ended the British World System.

Great Power Competition

The Trump administration has ended the War on Terror. They're not even hiding this massive shift in focus. They don't have to. The supposedly opposing sides in the eternal dumpster fire of the Trump presidency, Trump and the national security state, are completely unified in their sweeping expansion of US strategy, goals and potential targets. News organizations focus on the outrageousness of a single figure, while Trump works closely with all his supposed enemies in government to force a more truly imperial program on the US public. This isn't a conspiracy theory. It's laid out in public information that we don't have the mental bandwidth to pay attention to anymore.

Trump's first Secretary of Defense was James "Mad Dog" Mattis. Known as the "warrior monk", this Marine general distinguished himself with his knowledge of history and strategy, and as a brutally efficient war fighter in the early days of the Iraq war. The complete failure of all of the wars and policies he served didn't detract from his reputation, it added to it. Mattis is a rare and valuable commodity. He's an admirable figure that the US foreign policy establishment and its enablers in mass media can point to. He's something "good" that came out of two decades of disastrous, aggressive failure. Trump and the national security state used Mattis's prestige and his position as the "adult in the room" to push a sweeping and ignored switch in national strategy.

The victory over the territorial Islamic State, an entity that would not have existed without the multibillion-dollar CIA/Saudi effort to destabilize Syria after 2011, has been adopted as a turning point. It's a recognizable victory over "terror" that the military industrial complex can use to justify moving to a new strategy. They don't want to give up a single penny that the US public gave them to fight terrorists–in fact they want hundreds of billions of dollars more. On January 19, 2018 Defense Secretary Jim Mattis announced the new strategy:

> The U.S. military has put countering China and Russia at the center of a new national defense strategy unveiled on Friday, the latest sign of shifting priorities after more than a decade and a half of focusing on the fight against Islamist militants.[262]

If you get your news from Fox News or the New York Times, this can seem completely rational. All US and British media has been filled with stories of Russian and Chinese perfidy for years now. Over the past two years, it has intensified. All this reporting over-emphasizes the power and threat that these countries pose today, but they do have real aggressive acts by China and Russia to point to. What's almost always left out is how the War on Terror, just like the Scramble for Africa launched by Britain's invasion of Egypt, was seen in the rest of the world. It was a constant aggressive act, that had very little to do with terrorism, and it antagonized everybody. This has helped the foreign policy establishment in its mission to justify current and expanded expenditure on weapons. Mattis's switch in policy was the fruition of three decades of pumping up a group of failed, or largely cooperative states into something that could plausibly pose a threat. Chinese, Russian and Iranian military expenditure and adventuring has increased over the past two decades. But this foreign expenditure and adventuring increased as rational response to the insane aggression of the US War on Terror.

Manufactured Threats

---

[262] Ali, Idrees, "U.S. military puts 'great power competition' at heart of strategy: Mattis" Reuters January 19, 2018 https://www.reuters.com/article/us-usa-military-china-russia/u-s-military-puts-great-power-competition-at-heart-of-strategy-mattis-idUSKBN1F81TR

The long list of threats that the US government presents to us are all really just Cold War hangovers. None of them really amount to much, but US government over-reactions to threats now function to make the world much more dangerous. The wars in Iraq, Syria, Libya and Ukraine have all come about because the US government has scared us into letting it do stupid things. Our worldwide network of military bases functions mostly to present future options for idiocy. The threat that Russia and Iran pose to the US today is even more illusory than the threat that France and Russia posed to the British Empire. The slightly more rational threat posed by China only becomes real when the contemplated battlefield is close to their turf, as was the case with the German threat to Britain in the early twentieth century. The massively greater scope, power and wealth of the US World System makes the "threats" it focuses on even more ridiculous than those the British obsessed over.

Let's take a look at some of these "threats":

China: This is a country with naval pretensions that spent fifteen years rebuilding someone else's aircraft carrier.[263] A first homegrown carrier was launched in 2017, but it's not clear whether it will be fit for service or just a training vehicle. China's fragile social peace is largely dependent on our taste for consumer electronics. Their territory is ringed by a group of more technologically and economically advanced countries that are firmly united in opposing its rise when a US president isn't trying to slap tariffs on them. China couldn't be further from our problem. Twenty or thirty years from now, if absolutely everything continues to go right for China (it won't), the country might pose a threat to the United States, and even then, only if *we* continue to antagonize *them*. If we do everything wrong, and China is a real threat to us twenty years from now, all the weapons and materiel we are currently stockpiling will be outdated and useless. Massive armies

---

[263] "China's First Aircraft Carrier Enters Service" BBC September 25, 2012 https://www.bbc.com/news/world-asia-china-19710040

built up to fight wars do not win them, they lose them (See Germany, Japan ca. WWII).

In 2015, China's construction of artificial islands in the disputed Spratly Islands in the South China Sea became an international controversy.[264] These islands are name-checked in any article listing China's aggressive activity. What is rarely mentioned, however, is the wide range of actions that the United States was taking against China in the same period. After 2012, the Obama administration pursued its "Pivot to Asia", a re-focusing of diplomatic and military resources towards China. It was largely ignored in all the noise over the Syria debacle, but it was far more significant than another sordid spin on the Middle East death-go-round.

Diplomatically speaking, the US managed to carve off the only two countries bordering China that could plausibly be seen as China friendly. Communist Vietnam was more closely tied into the US trading and security system and the sale of US weapons was approved. Myanmar, previously run by a military junta close to China, held elections in 2015 that brought the previously-incarcerated Aung San Suu Kyi to power. Myanmar's transition is ongoing, and the military remains powerful, but the elections led to an economic opening up that is very threatening to the Chinese. The Obama administration also negotiated the Trans-Pacific Partnership (TPP) a trade deal excluding China that was aimed directly at its economic life's blood.

Looked at in this context, China's dredging up a few islands looks more like a desperate attempt to hold on to influence and self-respect rather than the action of a rogue state. It's likely that the story of the twenty-first century will be one of competition between China and the United States. But it's the US that is very much in the driver's seat. We get to

---

[264] Watkins, Derek "What China Has Been Constructing in the South China Sea" New York Times, October 27, 2015 https://www.nytimes.com/interactive/2015/07/30/world/asia/what-china-has-been-building-in-the-south-china-sea.html

decide whether it is one that is carried out in an economic or diplomatic realm or a military one. It would be vastly better for the world, the United States, and China if the US government opts for diplomatic and economic competition rather than warfare. Unfortunately, there is little in current rhetoric or recent history that makes it seem likely that US policy-makers will choose wisely.

Russia: The threat of Russia is slightly more plausible, but only because our bi-partisan foreign policy has done its best to make it so. Our treatment of this country is the best example of the foreign policy establishment's lack of ideas. The USSR chose to end itself in 1989, but we have continued to wage the Cold War against a largely peaceful, enthusiastically capitalist country. We now have military personnel all over the territory of what used to be the USSR. Despite our promise to Gorbachev not to extend NATO (an institution that largely exists to consume the products of the US defense industry), we have expanded the organization up to Russia's borders. The fact that they occasionally thwart our EU and NATO based charm offensives is a pretty weak response.

The truth is that Russia is nowhere near our class as a military power. In 2008, Taiwan-like enclaves Russia has maintained in Georgia since the Cold War were attacked by that tiny country on Russia's border. The Georgian President who ordered that attack, Mikheil Saakashvili, is not only still alive, but continued to run Georgia for a few more years, and is still running all over Eastern Europe annoying Russia. This would be the equivalent of a Cuban government surviving after attacking the US base at Guantanamo. The idea that Russia can threaten the United States, or even Europe anymore, is nostalgia, nothing more. Six years of "asymmetric" adventuring in Ukraine, prompted by a US-supported coup, has failed to take back more than a sliver of that former Tsarist and Soviet territory, even though the population is half Russian. Russia's "triumph" in Syria did the people of the United States a great service, helping to avert the full-on Iraq-style intervention that the US foreign policy community so desperately wanted. Russia's minor commitment of troops and planes to Syria was backed up by the long-established government of the country as well as massive support from Iranian and Lebanese militias.

A quickly hushed-up news story from February 2018 neatly illustrates Russian impotence. Fevered YouTubers and cable news commentators love the idea that WWIII is perpetually on the cusp of breaking out in Syria. It's an idea that both governments like. The United States loves to pump up the potential Russian threat, and the Russians are deeply flattered by the idea. It's a fantasy. Did you know that the US has already killed somewhere between dozens and hundreds of Russian soldiers in Syria? US and Russian forces clashed outside of Deir-ez-Zour in Eastern Syria on February 7th and 8th 2018. The Russians were obliterated.[265] This was it, an escalation to WWIII was certain! Except it wasn't. The Russians quickly disavowed their nationals, depicting them as unaffiliated mercenaries. When the United States lost some military contractors in Fallujah, Iraq in 2004, we razed a city. The Russians did their best to cover it up. To this day, it's not entirely clear what happened, because it didn't serve the narrative of either country to talk about it. Russian power and "triumph" in Syria is an *illusion* that helps inflate US defense budgets. Neither Putin nor Mattis wanted to threaten that illusion.

Also, if we lived in that magical candy land where conventional hostilities broke out with China or Russia, whichever of the two countries it wasn't would automatically invade the other on our behalf. Despite our best efforts, they feel more threatened by each other than they are by us.

---

[265] Nechepurenko, Ivan, Neil MacFarquhar and Thomas Gibbons-Neff "Dozens of Russians are believed killed in US-backed Syria attack" New York Times February 13, 2018

Iran: Good lord. The only reason they still have a religious government is because George Bush decided to put the Iranian theocracy in his 2002 Axis of Evil speech. The US foreign policy establishment was working fairly closely with the Mad Mullahs to jack up arms sales during the Iran/Contra affair back in the 1980s, and I occasionally wonder if they have ever stopped. The idea that Iran would reclaim Islamic holy land held by Israel by nuking it and irradiating hundreds of millions of their fellow Muslims is a Foggy Bottom fever dream.

Obama's foreign policy was largely a continuation of Bush's with one shining exception. The more I study it, the more I am impressed with his attempt to solve the Iran problem with the Joint Comprehensive Plan of Action. If Obama's Iran Nuclear Deal had been followed up on, we would now finally be witnessing a Middle East transitioning towards peace. Instead we got Trump's withdrawal from the deal, supported by most of the Washington, DC establishment that claims to hate Trump. Many claim that this extraordinarily bone-headed move was prompted by nefarious Israeli interests. They are missing the truly sinister fact that the US defense establishment desperately needs Iran as an enemy. Israeli Prime Minister Benjamin Netanyahu works for that establishment, not the other way around.

North Korea: Please. The country is basically a Pentagon/State Department jobs program. South Korea could conquer this place in a week. Not our problem.

Much of 2017 was spent in another one of our periodic world-wide panic attacks on the topic of North Korea. This was rooted in our inability to acknowledge that the North Korean regime is actually quite rational. They know that their monarchical system of gangster rule isn't particularly viable in the twenty-first century. The famines prove that. And they also know, thanks to US actions in Libya and Iraq, that giving up a nuclear deterrent is a mistake. Gaddafi and Hussein gave up their

WMDs and let inspectors in. They were each crushed within a decade of making that decision. My great fear is that Trump's interaction with Iran has been another object lesson in the perils of engaging with the United States on the topic of Nuclear Disarmament.

But the crucial fact remains this: If the North Korean regime ever uses a nuclear weapon it is the end of the North Korean regime. So they won't do it. They have successfully driven the costs of regime change too high for any actor to contemplate undertaking it. It's been quite a successful policy. North Korea will continue on this path until they fall apart. As with any dictator, belligerence on the part of the United States will only serve to entrench the regime.

Radical Islam: Thanks to lower oil prices, this threat is now fading away. It's sad that we are now opting for Great Power Competition, but it's nice that we will be spared the ridiculousness of watching US politicians continue to pretend to take this threat seriously. An enemy that needs to hi-jack your hardware with box-cutters to make an impact is clearly not operating in the same league. Some small percentage of the law enforcement efforts after 9/11 have been useful. The only useful thing our armed forces could do against this threat, depose the Taliban in Afghanistan, was accomplished within six months of the attacks. But, because we can only think militarily, we spent two decades pursuing this undefinable and ever-expanding enemy by bombing allies like Pakistan and Yemen, and stepping up military involvement across Asia Africa. And, after twenty years of that, we're now in talks with Taliban in Afghanistan.

The most frustrating thing about this "threat" is that it was entirely created by the United States. Saudi Arabia, the ideological home of every twenty-first century terrorist, from 9/11 to ISIS, has been protected and maintained by the United States for well over half a century. The radical ideology that has come back to bite us in the 2000s and 2010s was a tool of US policy against the Soviet Union in the 1970s and 1980s. To our shame, we've continued to use the tool of Sunni radicalism against Iran, in places like Syria and Iraq. We've continued to do this despite the way this weapon has blown back on the United States over and over.

There is a real problem here. That problem is Saudi Arabia. As soon as we stop backing that country, this particular flavor of terrorism will evaporate, and the Middle East will be allowed to recover from the Cold War the same way the rest of the World has.

Remember the State Department?

The most frustrating thing about this pitiful rogues gallery is the fact that we know how to solve all these problems. We're just not interested in doing it. The answer is the extraordinary diplomatic and commercial resources of the US World System. When I was born in 1979, much of the world was run by dictators that make the Assad family look about as threatening as a Chicago mayor. Half of Europe was controlled by brutal Communist oligarchies and dictators. Latin America was mostly run by people who considered dropping people out of helicopters to be a sound governing strategy. Our great democratic Asian Tiger friends in South Korea, Taiwan, the Phillipines, Indonesia and more were all run by petty despots. Our Indonesian guys alone slaughtered upwards of a million of their own people in 1965 and 1966. The Soviets' guys in Cambodia, the Khmer Rouge, murdered 1-3 million people from 1975-1979. We hear a lot more about the Khmer Rouge in the US for some reason. Africa didn't have many bright spots either. Even Japan and Mexico were one-party states until the 1990s.

In the four decades since, the world has improved immeasurably. Outside of the Middle East, a region where the Cold War never ended, democracy has broken out everywhere. Results have been uneven of course, some dictatorships persist, and many of these democracies have serious problems. The US has serious problems too. None of the vanished dictatorships of my youth, Soviet-aligned or US-aligned, fell because of massive military interventions. They were largely bribed and cajoled out of it. The carrot and stick of trade treaties and human rights scrutiny was what it took. One of the greatest tragedies of the Syrian conflict is that in 2010 it looked like Assad was very open to this kind of transition. These transitions did not just happen naturally. The US used to have a massive diplomatic apparatus that coordinated all of this. The State Department was a useful tool back during the Cold War when things were serious. It was neglected and aggressively de-funded long before the Trump administration's more public attempts to destroy it. Foreign policy has been a tool of the defense contractors for decades now. A properly funded and supported State Department would risk ending these dictatorships and rogue states. But the US government doesn't want to end them. It wants to profit from "fighting" them.

Government by Boeing

Undersecretary of Defense Patrick M. Shanahan took a leading role in the implementation of the new "Great Power Competition" defense strategy that Mattis announced in January of 2018.[266] He never served in the military. He never served in the government prior to 2017, in fact. His entire career, starting in 1986, had been spent at Boeing, one of the country's largest defense contractors. Boeing makes civilian planes as well, and it seems like Shanahan spent some time in those divisions as well. But his most relevant qualification for the Defense Department was his leadership position at Boeing Missile Defense systems from 2004. In December 2019, Jim Mattis resigned in a huff over one of Trump's sanest policies, the proposed withdrawal of US troops from Syria. Patrick M. Shanahan was the acting Secretary of Defense for the first six months of 2019. Mike Pompeo, the current

---

[266] Anonymous "Bringing out the Big Guns" The Economist March 2nd, 2018 That's the title in the print edition, online the title is Pentagon changes its focus to Russia and China
https://www.economist.com/united-states/2019/02/28/the-pentagon-changes-its-focus-to-russia-and-china

Secretary of State, was also a defense contractor in civilian life. The foxes are now guarding the henhouse.

The Trump administration has the virtue of making things more explicit. All the sordid, greedy underpinnings of the US World System are shorn of their more polite façade, in the Defense Department more than anywhere else. Shanahan spent six months gleefully rampaging through the Pentagon, "reinventing the way we fight war"[267], and putting in orders for expensive new weapons systems for WWIII. When Shanahan lost his job due to one of the saddest domestic violence stories I have ever read, he was replaced by Secretary of the Army Mike Esper. Esper's most relevant experience was as a Vice President of Government Affairs (lobbying) for Raytheon, another important weapons company. Defense contractor ownership of US foreign policy is more explicit now, but it has been the case since 1989, and certainly since 2001. It's a cancer that has been advancing over decades, not a Trumpian novelty.

The military industrial complex does help the US economy. The go-go economy of the pre-crisis Bush years was supported by the housing boom, but the destruction of Iraq and Afghanistan pumped a lot of money into the economy as well. The vaunted "Trump Economy" is very straightforwardly Keynesian. The Republicans let Trump do the sort of "pump-priming" they kept Obama from doing. The past three years have seen at least half a trillion dollars of stimulus in the form of military spending. The past two decades of unnecessary war fighting have been an extraordinary bonanza for the US economy, but for US military contractors most of all.

The Cost

[267] Anonymous "Bringing out the Big Guns" The Economist March 2nd, 2018
https://www.economist.com/united-states/2019/02/28/the-pentagon-changes-its-focus-to-russia-and-china

Post-9/11 wars have cost well over a million lives. But since the intense Iraq War years in the middle of the last decade, very few of the lives lost have been American. Through drones, long-range missiles, and light footprint special forces, the human cost to the United States has been minimized. It's now easy for the US voter to put the forever wars out of her mind. We continue to fall into massively lethal adventures like the ones in Yemen and Venezuela[268], mostly because very few people in the United States are aware that they are even happening. Most Americans who become aware of these US government actions oppose them. But the majority assumes the experts are handling things, as the war machine profitably rumbles on. This is a terrible mistake.

US soldiers may not be dying in large numbers yet, but the foundations of the US World System is being steadily chipped way by our permanent wars. That ideological commitment to self-determination that made the US World System succeed where Britain failed is getting harder to see. We've been in Iraq since the early 1990s. We're rounding three decades. The British Empire's tenure in Iraq only lasted around a decade. US soldiers have been in Afghanistan for almost two decades now. The Soviets were only there for a decade. The British had semi-formal control over Afghanistan for a number of decades, but they never managed to occupy it for more than a year or two.

Our formal empire is growing, while our informal empire makes more and more demands of the rest of the world's nominally independent countries. The growing power of acronyms like FATCA, OFAC and many others is slowly making our empire more explicit. Most US presidents aren't as in your face about it as Donald Trump, but we've been letting the precious fiction of international equality slip away for decades now.

---

[268] Sanctions kill too.

What's happening today is very similar to Britain's complete mishandling of nationalism in the decades leading up to the First World War. Alternatives are emerging. The "Washington Consensus" still has power, but other models are being taken more seriously. European leaders like Viktor Orban can proclaim themselves opponents of "Liberal Democracy" and survive in power. Proponents of everything from the "Chinese Model" to crypto-currency anarchism are beginning to chip away at the margins. It's not that any of these arguments are persuasive or mass phenomena yet. But Marxism and pan-German nationalism were failed ideas in 1848. By 1871 they were changing the world. The financial crisis of 2008, and the world's souring on the vision of "Anglo-Saxon" capitalism, fair or not, may be the modern equivalent of 1848. The ideological foundations of the US World System are cracking.

The financial foundations are cracking as well. The US financial lead is now eroding, for the same reasons that the British lead did—pointless, ruinous war. The expense and complexity of the wars that the US fights is much greater than those the British fought. The costs of the past fifteen years of fighting vastly weaker states like Afghanistan and Iran is measured in trillions of dollars. These investments haven't paid, and the loans we took out to make them haven't been paid off. The Washington Post recently reported that the costs of servicing the US national debt will rival the US Defense Budget by early 2022.[269]

To be sure, unlike Britain, the majority of US national debt is still held in the US and by client countries like Japan. It's now become

---

[269]Paletta, Damian, and Erica Werner Washington Post April 16, 2018 How Congress's and Trump's Latest Deficit Binge Paved the Way for The Next One https://www.washingtonpost.com/business/economy/how-congress-and-trumps-latest-deficit-binge-paved-the-way-for-the-next-one/2018/04/15/2d198608-3f2f-11e8-8d53-eba0ed2371cc_story.html

fashionable in the US to maintain that "deficits don't matter", in the immortal words of Republican Vice President Dick Cheney. The federal government's shortfalls have been going up since the Clinton presidency, and have gone into overdrive under Trump. The forecast inflation has failed to show up, and the appetite for US debt has not diminished. But this may have more to do with the similarly parlous status of any potential rival. The European and Chinese economies of 2019 are even sketchier looking than the US economy. We can probably rely on that being the case through the first half of the 2020s. But what about after that? Europe or China could finally get their acts together, and the US government might wake up one day to find that nobody is interested in funding the war machine anymore. We may not even need a world war to find ourselves in the Suez type circumstances that showed everyone how hollow British power had become.

One of the most fundamental lessons of the fall of the British Empire is the fact that war is the enemy of the country on top. Primacy, or hegemony or whatever you want to call it, presents a lot of advantages. The privileges of being on top accumulate and there is a sense of inertia. The relationships and infrastructure that make up world hegemony don't necessarily have to go anywhere. It takes a war to destroy them. It's therefore in the interest of the country on top to keep things as peaceful as possible. If it wants to preserve its primacy that is. Win or lose, the expenditure and complication of warfare drains the financial wellspring of modern hegemony. No matter how dominant the military power on top is, the locals will always care more about the place you are fighting for than you will. Eventually, the US's multiple wars will catch up with it. If they haven't already. Every new war could be the one that blows up to be our next trillion-dollar debacle. Every war has the possibility of turning the rest of the world against us. This makes Washington DC's eternal quest for the next conflict absolutely insane.

As much as I'd like to blame the sinister wiles of the military industrial complex, the sad truth is that to some extent we're now doing this to ourselves.

Everybody's Turning Militarist

> For a long time, America enjoyed a geographical advantage in the world with oceans on both sides to protect it, Now, social media has created cyber-bridges over which those who do not have our best interest in mind can cross and we are allowing it. No wall is going to protect us from that.[270]

So, who do you think that is? Some Trump-addled Breitbart columnist? Or perhaps just an overly paranoid member of the Military Industrial Complex, occupying a spot in a think tank or defense department agency somewhere? Nope. That's Jim Fricking Carry, a famous US comedian and film star from the 1990s.

One of the most striking signs of the British Empire's decline was the way that public support of empire and aggression grew. The elements of society that were not happy with Empire were silenced or simply ignored. Politicians who once took principled anti-Empire stances like Gladstone found themselves overseeing imperial expansion.

We can see that same turning happening right now. For decades conservatives have treated Hollywood as a "Fifth Column". It's a generalization, but I think it's fair to say that the attitudes of our celebrities were generally more internationalist and left-leaning than that of the country as a whole. When it comes to issues of foreign policy post-2016, though, that's changed. It's usually particular events that change these attitudes. Individual massacres of Bulgarian and

---

[270] https://www.cnbc.com/2018/02/06/comedian-jim-carrey-delete-your-facebook-account-and-dump-the-stock.html

Armenian Christians in the Ottoman Empire built support for British intervention, for example. In the US, it's the election of Donald Trump that has done the job. Unwilling to accept that Hillary Clinton was not a very good candidate, we have crafted a very elaborate story of Russian skullduggery. There are elements of truth to this, but some hacking that any teenager could carry out, coupled with the purchase of a couple hundred thousand dollars' worth of Facebook ads is not the Republic ending threat that Jim Carrey's account makes it sound like.

This is not just about Russia. It's about a generalized feeling of discontent. Our military doesn't win wars anymore. Our government is manifestly incompetent. Ironically, this creates an urge to grab hold of and celebrate the institutions that have caused these issues. The fact that Intelligence Community brutes like James Comey have become Progressive darlings is mystifying, but it actually makes a lot of sense in a story of Imperial decline. As the great twentieth century historian William Appleman Williams pointed out long ago, we desperately want to externalize our threats. We can't believe that we've been doing things like Trump to ourselves. Somebody else must be to blame.

And we're losing the ability to see things in any sort of proportion. On Friday, February 16th, 2018, the Mueller investigation released the indictment of 32 Russians in his years long Russia investigation. It made some damning claims about Russia's involvement in the 2016 election. An organization with ties to the Russian government had set up some anonymous groups and identities on social media to promote Donald Trump and general division in the United States. This provided a storm surge to the already high-running river of outrage flowing through the national discourse. This proved it! We were at war!

That same week details had emerged about an actual war being fought in Syria. It had been reported earlier that the US government had killed a number of Syrian army soldiers attempting to take control of Syrian oil fields. Around the 14th of February it became known that the US had actually killed a few dozen, or perhaps as many as hundreds, of Russian military contractors. The two events were never connected. The frantic declarations that war had been declared on us through fake Facebook groups never acknowledged the fact that the US military had been waging actual, physical war on Russia and her allies for years. As other powers begin to catch up to the US economically, we get more and more threatened. We are so used to being able to effortlessly dictate to the entire world, in our language, that we become deranged at the most minor reverses. This stems from the one arena where the US system is unquestionably weaker than the British one.

American Empire Is Dumber than British Empire

It pains me to admit this, but US Empire is just dumber than British Empire. This is a function of two things: A: American Empire is more powerful than the British Empire ever was. B: The world is better equipped to satisfy a hegemon's demands than it was during the British era.

The United States got to start its period of dominance as an 800-pound gorilla. The British Empire had to figure out how to bend initially larger markets like China and India to its will. This required deep local knowledge, feats of entrepreneurial brilliance, and Machiavellian manipulation. The British foot-soldiers of Empire, uniformed and not, spent decades learning about the territories they controlled. It should go without saying that this included deep knowledge of local languages. British scholars wrote the first dictionaries for many of the languages of their empire.

For the past century or so the United States has had the largest market in the world. Our imperial subjects came to us. Our wealth and power has enabled a shocking level of ignorance. Our foreign service officers visit countries in two to four-year stints. These stints are usually preceded by a few months taking language crash courses. Some foreign service officers get a working knowledge of the local language. Most do not. It doesn't really matter. Everybody speaks English now. Each country has its own literate elites, that make the work of the US World System much easier for Washington, DC. This also makes Washington, DC much dumber than London ever was, however, leading to the horror show that is the modern Middle East.

British India vs. American Saudi Arabia

The deep ignorance of the masters of the US World System can best be illustrated by looking at each empire's deepest engagement with foreign religions. For centuries, British thinkers and administrators wrestled with the many conflicting religious streams they found in their vast Indian territories. This influence is deeply disturbing to modern eyes. It involved cultural appropriation and a conscious warping of the belief systems and cultural priorities the British imperialists found in India. But I think it's possible to look at the experience as on the whole positive, especially because it ended up giving power to the forces that eventually kicked the British out of India. The US's unthinking promotion of the most brutal and intolerant ideological stream in Islam, Saudi Arabian Wahabism, resulted in the tremendous own goal of 9/11 and what I think can be fairly characterized as a world-wide form of cultural genocide against the many diverse forms of Islam that existed seventy years ago. There's no upside to that story.

British Scholars

As the East India Company began to build British India in the mid-1700s, they knew they had to reckon with the many diverse forms of religion that were present. They had to deal with the Muslim, Hindu and Sikh Princes and warriors, bankers and landlords, that were present in differing mixes in every city and tract of land they attempted to control. The efficacy of these systems of control, and the level of profit that could be extracted, depended on how successfully the British could engage with all these cultural strands. They didn't just engage, they attempted to shape these strands into something that looked more familiar to them, and that fit more readily into their systems of revenue extraction.

The "Hindu", "Muslim", "Sikh", "Christian", and many other smaller religious strands in India, looked nothing like the way these strands are defined today. The British attempt to force all this diversity into a few smaller, more easily manageable strands was all about control. This effort was ultimately unsuccessful, but it worked for a very long time. The British founded multiple educational institutions to collect information about India's many religious traditions, and attempt to jam them into more "rational" and consistent schools of thought.

> [First de-facto Governor-General of British India] Warren Hastings's desire to master India through an understanding of her languages and scriptures was accompanied by the publication of Halhed's Grammar of the Bengalee Language in 1778. In 1781 the Calcutta Madrassa was founded. [Another Governor-General of British India] Wellesley's Fort William College, designed for the education of civil servants, published Hindu works of mythology and scripture as did the Hindu Sanskrit College (founded 1821).[271]

This effort was unquestionably an assault, but it prompted a flourishing of Indian intellectual life. The students of these schools contributed to the ideological response that eventually liberated India. These institutions were created for the purpose of control, but they involved real intellectual curiosity and sometimes awe-inspiring dedication on the part of British scholars. I like to think that the kernels of goodness in some of these efforts helped to sow the seeds of the liberation that India eventually experienced. But perhaps that's my Eurocentrism talking. The motivations behind these broader intellectual projects were malign, and they certainly made for savvier imperialists. The

---

[271] P. 162 Bayly, C. A. Indian Society and the Making of British Empire

early British at least knew that Wahhabi Islam was something to be avoided at all costs.[272]

American Morons

Alas, the same cannot be same for the later British, and the US imperialists that followed them. In their last gasp attempt to swallow up a chunk of the Middle East after the First World War, the British created Saudi Arabia. The Saudi state had had a number of ups and downs. By the later nineteenth century the Saudi royal family and the extremist Wahhabi clerics they were allied with were living in exile in Kuwait. The British knew that their ideology was malign, but they also saw their fanaticism as useful. It was divisive by nature. By sponsoring it, the British could spoil any attempts to create a unified Arab state. The British paid annual subsidies to the Saudis and gifted them large amounts of surplus armaments post-WWI. The Saudis swept across Arabia, taking Mecca and Medina in the 1920s. In the defense of the British, they didn't know quite how large a gift they were giving to the Saudis.

The US World System builders don't have that excuse. From 1938, American engineers worked to make this backwards Wahhabi state one of the richest countries in the world. Saudi Arabia's hyper-rich theocracy was just as useful a spoiler for the Americans as it was for the British. It was used to crush the Pan-Arabist movement under Egypt's Gamel Abdel Nasser in the 1950s and 1960s. This may have been defensible from a certain realpolitik perspective. What the Saudis were encouraged to do to worldwide Islam was not.

In the latter decades of the twentieth century, the US government encouraged Saudi Arabia to export its ideology. Washington, DC was gleeful to find that its Saudi clients shared their loathing of Communist atheism. Wahhabi cultural imperialism was encouraged world-wide,

---

[272] P.167 Bayly, C. A. Indian Society and the Making of British Empire

and outright facilitated and armed in the Afghanistan conflict in the 1980s. Communism was a threat everywhere, so spreading extremist Islam everywhere was thought to be useful. As we all well know, this was a calamitous failure to read the fine print. Even now, as the extent of Wahhabi distaste for all western thought and civilization has become more well known, and the US government has supposedly spent the past eighteen years fighting that ideology's various permutations, the US government has very few Arabic speakers to call on. The US government just doesn't do its homework.

The most obvious result of this ignorance was the attacks on the United States on September 11th. The majority of the hijackers were from Saudi Arabia, and the Al Qaeda network that supported them had been built by US and Saudi intelligence. It's very likely that the attack itself was directly supported by elements within the Saudi government and royal family. But that's not the worst of it.

What's worse is the effect that Saudi Arabia has had on broader Islamic thought and culture over the past seventy years. Saudi Arabia the country contributed to the defeat of the Pan-Arabism and Arab nationalism ideology. And Saudi Arabia the cultural superpower provided the ideological contagion of Wahhabi Islam that claimed it could succeed where earlier ideologies had failed. The situation is thankfully changing now, but throughout the second half of the twentieth century, Saudi Arabia was one of very few Muslim countries with great wealth and influence. Much of the Muslim world was mired in post-colonial poverty. Saudi Arabia was happy to build mosques and provide other charitable institutions in all of these countries, as long as they got to choose the preachers. This has led to the world-wide phenomenon of "Islamic" fundamentalist terror, but it has also crushed a lot of the diversity that was still present in Islam just seventy years ago. I think it's fair to characterize this as a form of cultural genocide.

British scholars built a sophisticated system of control, that eventually yielded positive results in flourishing religious diversity and national liberation. American idiocy built a wasteland, in lower Manhattan and across the Middle East.

It's Not Getting Better

The Islamic world is now finally emerging from the US encouraged era of Saudi theological ascendance. The oil price is falling, and other Sunni Muslim powers are emerging, putting their weight behind other, healthier interpretations of Islam. But the United States hasn't learned anything. The US government, and not just the President, seems to be at war with expertise.

The case of Robin Raphel is justly famous, recounted in the Wall Street Journal[273], and a recent book by Ronan Farrow.[274] A career foreign service officer, Raphel developed decades worth of contacts in Pakistan. Her expertise and influence within Pakistan were so great that she was called out of retirement in 2009 to help sort out the US's disastrous and eternal engagement in Afghanistan and Pakistan. She struggled for five years to accomplish that Sisyphean task. Her struggle ended in October 2014 with an espionage investigation by the FBI.

Raphel lost her security clearances and lost her job. The investigation upended her career, and ruined her ability to work with the US government, an institution she had served for her entire adult life. The problem was that she knew too many Pakistanis. As a diplomat. The FBI found it strange that a US diplomat focused on Pakistan and Afghanistan had conversations with figures in Pakistan. The investigation closed in 2016 with no charges filed. But it ended a great career, and sent a clear message to any diplomat working for the US government: Don't get to know the countries you work in too well.

---

[273] Entous, Adam and Devlin Barrett, "The Last Diplomat", The Wall Street Journal December 2, 2016
[274] Farrow, Ronan War on Peace: The End of Diplomacy and the Decline of American Influence

This is insane.

A Personal Anecdote

I lived in Turkey from 2011-2016, and I can testify to how strange Robin Raphel was. There were many US foreign service officers on the outskirts of my social circles. The problem was that they didn't leave their compounds much. They were all very nice, upstanding, reasonably clever folks. They didn't know Turkey very well.

There were plenty of Americans floating around who did know Turkey. English teachers, business people, and a variety of other professionals and layabouts who knew Turkey, and a range of other countries and languages quite well. People like that, and people like me, are generally not welcome in US government. Applying for a security clearance requires an exhaustive list of the places you lived, and a range of easily contacted references. The longer you've been outside of the US the harder this list is to put together. I'm quite boring by the standards of the people I met in Turkey, and there is no way I'd be able to put together a list like that. The US government isn't interested in hiring people who actually know things about the outside world.

The institutional gatekeepers of our prestigious academic institutions aren't much better. I know a gal from California who learned fluent Turkish, and managed to travel Iran for three months on an artist's visa. She learned Persian. That is an incredibly rare thing for a US citizen to pull off. She certainly knows more about Iran, supposedly one of our greatest foreign policy challenges, than ninety-nine percent of the people working on those countries in Washington, DC. She applied to get a grad degree at Harvard so she might be able to work in policy circles. She didn't get in. Of course she didn't. The masters of the US World System don't know the world, and they don't want to. This, among many other things, needs to change. We won't be able to effortlessly dominate the world for much longer.

The US World System is in slow decline. We're still powerful enough that the world is unlikely to fall into another apocalyptic war for a couple decades. But WWIII should be a real possibility by the late 2030s. If we keep on the current, "British but dumber" trajectory, WWIII is what we will get. But we don't have to.

"Things Could be walked away from and made anew. No one would ever have to fight"

-Cory Doctorow

Chapter 8
Transcendence

It's easy to make fun of people who see a better world.

Almost every book on the run-up to the First World War takes a paragraph or page or two to mock Norman Angell. In 1909 this British Labour Party politician published a book that became an international sensation under the title <u>The Great Illusion</u>. His argument was that war was now impossible. The Great Powers of Europe were just too interconnected economically. The men running Europe would be insane to take such a suicidal course. Any "great power" war would result in disaster for all of the countries involved, and a tremendous loss of power, wealth and prestige. The war proved his point quite ably. Angell was only incorrect in assuming that the European leaders wouldn't be dumb enough to go ahead and fight a suicidal war anyway.

Angell's incomplete prophecy was also name checked in much of the risible deluge of "2014 could be 1914!!!" articles that came out on the 100th anniversary of the launch of WWI.[275] Neither 2014, nor 2019 has

---

[275] Here's one from the Globe and Mail that name checks Angell. There were literally dozens of these articles. Just google 2014 and 1914. https://www.theglobeandmail.com/opinion/read-and-vote-is-2014-like-1914-a-prelude-to-world-war/article19325504/

much to do with 1914, for reasons I will get into shortly. But these articles were right to point out that our globalized, interconnected world is no guarantee against the return of war. They mocked Angell's misplaced confidence in the impossibility of war, rather than lauding his proven and still very relevant points about the pointlessness of war. Irritatingly, most of these articles took the exact opposite lesson from Angell that they should have. The articles tended to advocate for more militarized preparation for war, and an accelerated hyper-vigiliance. These are exactly the sorts of policies that brought about the apocalypse Angell didn't think was possible.

The Free Trade evangelists of the early British and US World Systems get made fun of a lot too. Early on in British Empire historian John Darwin's <u>After Tamerlane</u>, a key source for this book, he sets up their view to be taken down.

> Among the first to imagine a globalized world were the British free traders of the 1830's and '40s, who drew their inspiration from Adam Smith. Worldwide free trade, so they reasoned, would make war unthinkable. If every country depended upon foreign suppliers and customers, the web of mutual dependence would be too strong to break. Warrior aristocracies that thrived in a climate of conflict would become obsolete. The bourgeois ideal of representative government, spread by traders and trade, would become universal.[276]

In early 2018, we saw another raft of takedowns of a different generation of "naïve free traders". The Clinton administration's choice to incorporate China into the World Trade Organization was supposedly going to inaugurate a new era of peace and prosperity for all. Trade would liberate China. In March of 2018, the Economist magazine declared this policy to be a failure.[277] China fooled us. It has failed to morph into a bigger version of Switzerland. The Communist

---

[276] P. 8 Darwin, John <u>After Tamerlane: The Rise and Fall of Global Empires, 1400-2000</u>
[277] The Economist "How the West Got China Wrong" March 1st, 2018

party is still firmly in power, and this civilization-state of over a billion people has failed to submit to international trade norms with the meekness of Belgium. The Trump administration weighed in on this topic as well, with an extensive report from the US Trade Representative that used many similar arguments.[278]

As may already be clear, I don't buy these arguments. The fact is that the "bourgeoise ideal of representative government" has become almost universal, as those century-and-a-half-dead propagandists suggested. Everybody's got a parliament. The countries that are lagging in this arena, and there are many, feel the need to at least pretend that they function in this way. Even North Korea claims to be acting in the interests of its people rather than the old school clique of thugs that actually run the place. The visions of the reformers of the 1840s have succeeded beyond their wildest dreams.

China's accession to the WTO has also been a miracle for the world. China remains a deeply unfree and authoritarian place, but it could have been so, so much worse. Think North Korea is bad? What would the world be like if it had a North Korea like state of 1.4 billion people rather than just 25 million? A large capitalism-oriented country that fails to honor free trade dogma to the letter, a characteristic it shares with every developed country, is vastly better than the alternative. This isn't some pie-in-the-sky counter-factual I'm selling here. I'm talking about China as it existed between 1949 and 1979. China's evolution was never going to be as straightforward and simple as the politicians who sold WTO accession claimed. But the world is much richer, and much safer because of that WTO accession. China's newly inaugurated "president for life" Xi Jinping is terrified of his people. He's no Chairman Mao. The sort of Chinese leadership that could blithely launch tragedies like the "Great Leap Forward" that starved 15 to 30

---

[278] United States Trade Representative, <u>2017 Report to Congress On China's WTO Compliance</u> published January 2018

million people is long gone. Xi Jinping can't launch a middle-class destroying "Cultural Revolution" either. Honestly, I'd be surprised if he could pull off a Tiananmen Square Massacre. The Uighurs of Xinjiang province are trapped in an Orwellian nightmare of reeducation camps and cultural replacement. But they aren't being executed wholesale. The China of 2018 is not the China of 1959 ("Great Leap Forward"), 1966 ("Cultural Revolution) or even 1989 (Tiananmen Square). It's exactly the forces that our mocked utopians championed that transformed China.

Angell and the Free Trade evangelists are not clowns to be laughed at, they are prophets of a dream deferred. The path to their utopias has been a lot longer, and a lot more tragic than they thought, but much of what they dreamed of has come to pass. This is what I'm talking about when I talk about "Transcendence".

Transcendence

The history laid out above is pretty grim. Not just the story of the US and British World Systems, but everything before those systems as well. Chapter Two explained how most of history has been a story of various collections of thugs on top, battling it out for land and power at the expense of pretty much everybody else. There were brief moments of light, here and there, but on balance it was rough stuff. Chapter Three documented the tricks of geography that gave Britain and the United States the potential to build systems of thuggery that incorporated the entire world. Chapter Four, on the beginnings of the British World System, started to document the ways that these world systems provided the opportunity for new and different forms of thuggery, that had their own disastrous effects, but also broke the old equation of Land+ People to exploit = Power. Chapter Five documented how new technologies super charged the British World System, bringing new oppression to the entire world, but also new vistas and opportunities as well. Chapter Six documented how the

"Historical Hangover" of old ways of thinking and running empires destroyed the British World System. Chapter Seven documented the way that the United States has, because it serves our own interests, built a world system that at least claims to respect the self-determination of all peoples. The US has constructed a world system that would look Utopian to those 1830's British economists, but US policy makers are now falling into their own version of the "historical hangover". The forever war and the metastasized military industrial complex is chipping away at the foundations of the US World System, risking another apocalypse.

The chief mistake of utopians past was in arguing that the futures they saw were inevitable, or that they could be arrived at without cost. They emphatically were not and could not. Another world war is possible. Probably not this decade or the next, but it remains a possibility if the world, and the United States in particular, doesn't get its act together. But by the same token, we are not irrevocably doomed to war. There are all manner of theorists who argue that there is something fundamental about capitalism, or the nation-state system that leads to war. I haven't seen much evidence for that. War is the product of stupid decisions. The history of the British and US World Systems makes it pretty clear that it's the hegemon's penchant for smaller wars that leads to bigger wars. There's nothing inevitable about it. We can make better decisions and keep war from happening. Not forever. Nothing is forever. But for centuries. We can transcend the violent, petty history described in this book. Nobody else needs to die. Seriously.

US foreign policy is now dedicated to preserving an impossible degree of power, trying to keep any other country from becoming a global or even regional power. This is a recipe for collapse, and an ugly collapse. But if we shift the focus of our foreign policy to resolving the few flash points that remain, and spreading prosperity, the potential is extraordinary. The United States has always reaped the lions' share of the rewards under the US World System, but peoples across the world have been able to grow and prosper as well. What needs to happen now, if we are to avoid another apocalypse, is that the US World System needs to evolve into something the whole world can truly benefit from. Two-hundred years of enlightenment and economic development have given us all the tools we need. We have the opportunity to transcend military competition entirely. The United States can use its remaining power to build not a utopia, but a new, larger stage for human endeavor. People are better than the question of how best to throw rocks at each other. There is, at this historical moment, the opportunity to start working on grander challenges, with more meaningful victories. We can take this opportunity, or we can squander it. This vision may seem impossibly optimistic, but there are many reasons to believe it is already happening.

Reasons for Hope

2019 is not 1914, or even 1900. 1914 saw the British World System dissolve into world war. There are many reasons to fear that the US World System could go the same way, but there are many, many more to believe that it could go in a different direction. The most important of these is the US's still very real invulnerability.

Modern technology, from cyber-war to cheap missiles, has made the Atlantic and Pacific Oceans seem a little smaller than they used to be, but that's only because we continue to insist on making all the world's problems our own. If we actually prioritized nuclear non-proliferation over silly geopolitical grudges, we would be even safer. Contrary to the dreams of fevered nativists like Jeff Sessions and Steve Bannon, Latin America now reproduces at a similar rate to the rest of North America. There are no barbarian hordes to come. The US is well-situated to thrive in a post-US-hegemonic world. Our involvement with the world outside our continent has always been a choice.

The invulnerability the United States has historically enjoyed allows for some deeply silly thinking about war. American friends I usually think of as serious people occasionally muse about how what the US needs is "another war to unify us again". Can you imagine a Russian, a German, a Chinese person or an Israeli arguing that the twentieth century's wars were a good thing? It's a lot easier to fantasize about war when you're almost certain it won't be fought on your territory. It's troubling that US geography has produced hegemons with this attitude towards conflict, but isolation has been great for government in the United States. If we can spend more time focusing on the benefits of peace and distance, and less on historical hangover glorification of war-making, we will lessen the risk of catastrophic mistakes. Thankfully, the world has also changed since 1914, in ways that make this shift in focus more logical.

The Death of the Aristocrat

People love the idea that things haven't changed. Aren't we in exactly the same position? Academics who should know better, like Graham Allison of Harvard, push the idea that the World Wars could be explained by the simple dynamic of the rising power and the declining power. In this view, WWI broke out primarily because the established British Empire was being challenged by the rising power Germany. Doesn't today's dynamic, with the established United States and the emerging China mean we're headed for another war?

In one sense, this book is dedicated to the idea that there is in fact a dynamic to be worried about. We want to avoid a crash similar to the one that the British Empire created. But in another sense, these analogies, and certainly the fevered insistence that a new war is imminent, is poppycock. The world of 2019 has about as much in common with the world of 1914 as it does with the HBO TV series

Game of Thrones. In Chapter Two, I claimed that much of world history can be boiled down to a tale of thugs on top abusing each other, and everybody else, forever. This dynamic was breaking down by 1914, but the thugs were very much still setting the tone. Parliaments were making progress in most countries, but the interests of old noble families were key in the move to war, across Europe and even in Britain.

Landed aristocracy in Europe did fairly well out of the first stages of industrialization, as late as the first half of the 1800s. The growing demand for mines and factories could be very good for the folks who owned large swathes of mineral rich land, and had the capital necessary to build factories. It was rarely nobles who came up with these projects, but if they weren't too dense, they could figure out how to profit from them, too. The growth of cities and demand for agricultural products was also great for landed aristocrats. This ended in the mid-nineteenth century. Railroads gave European metropolises easier access to bread baskets in Ukraine and the American Mid-West. Demand for food continued to rise, but supply went into the stratosphere. In Britain, the price of wheat fell by half between 1871 and 1901.[279] The landed aristocracy started disintegrating. Great manors were sold off, and the practice of marrying those with hereditary titles off to wealthy commoners, which already existed, went into overdrive.

But those manors and those noble marriage partners were in high demand. Europe's aristocracy may have been falling apart, but the new elites were very interested in keeping up those traditions. Even though the hereditary thugs were fading out, the wealthy newcomers were eager to adopt their thuggish ways. "Honor", idiotically defined, remained the order of the day. Dueling survived into the twentieth century, even though the elites doing it were less and less

---

[279] P.282 Evans Richard J. Pursuit of Power: Europe 1815-1914

aristocratic.[280] The nobles still set the tone. This was the mindset that brought us the First World War. In 1914, the folks running European countries still largely saw the control of land as the highest value. If you got rich, you bought an estate. Your country's ability to control land was what mattered, even if it made no economic sense at all. The Scramble for Africa was a prime example. War was glorious, and it was the only way for the men running Europe to truly prove themselves and the worth of their societies.

The World Wars were horrible things. As I've delved into the histories of these empires, one "what-if?" question has bugged me more than anything else. What if they never happened? What if this or that interaction had gone differently? Think of all the lives that could have been saved. But there is one irreducible value that the world wars gave us. They allowed us to see that the mindset in the foregoing paragraph is insane. Throughout the twentieth century, and into this one, people who argue for the glory of war are generally laughed out of the room. Any war must be justified in terms of aggression by the other party. The United States doesn't even have a War Department anymore. It's the Department of Defense now.

We still have elites today. And those elites certainly profit from our modern wars. But it's not like Chuck Schumer is going to call out Tucker Carlson for pistols at dawn. All manner of horrible things still happen, but the old-fashioned aristocratic lust for land and glory truly is dead. I'd argue that that transition has not gone far enough, but the progress we've made over the past century may already have saved us from WWIII. We should all be grateful for the death of the classic idea of aristocracy.

---

[280] P.290 Evans Richard J. Pursuit of Power: Europe 1815-1914

Vanishing Flash Points

The falling away of aristocratic ideals makes the world a much safer place. The few flash points that are left are quickly fading away. There are a couple of resource and national disputes that you can shoehorn into the old frameworks of national interaction, but they are not what justify our extraordinary defense budgets. It is mostly just an old way of seeing things.

In fact, it may be our defense budgets that bolster these conflicts and issues, rather than the other way around. There are a lot of academics and government bureaucrats that rely on arms industry money, and have a vested interest in keeping it flowing. The world has a number of "frozen conflicts". The demilitarized zone between North and South Korea, and the Armenian-Azerbaijani dispute over Nagorno-Karabakh, are just two of many that come to mind. Unsettled territorial issues can lead to decades of angry stasis, with heavily-armed militaries facing each other across disputed borders. Quickly resolving any and all flashpoints that can lead to war would be the goal of any sane foreign policy. But defense contractors everywhere, Russian and American in the two examples above, benefit from the continuation of these conflicts. So they stubbornly continue. The persistence of these "frozen conflicts" is completely unnecessary and frustrating, but it's also a sign of how far we have come. The fact that there are just a few of these to focus on, in a very wide world, is great progress. In prior centuries every border was a bone of contention.

The new focus is resource constraints. We are solemnly told that war over oil, or water or food is a likely occurrence in the future. In 1994, Robert D. Kaplan, a celebrated journalist, and well-paid consultant for defense interests, wrote an article entitled "The Coming Anarchy",[281]

---

[281] Kaplan, Robert D. "The Coming Anarchy" <u>The Atlantic</u> February 1994

arguing that despite the end of the Cold War, things were about to become much more dangerous. He warned that "Disease, overpopulation, unprovoked crime, scarcity of resources, refugee migrations, the increasing erosion of nation-states and international borders, and the empowerment of private armies, security firms, and international drug cartels"[282] were going to make the world a much more dangerous place. It was an incredibly influential article. These claims should be familiar to you. You can find them everywhere.

Today they lean a little more heavily towards climate change than 1990's obsessions with crime and drug dealers, but the goal of these think pieces remains the same. The point is to say: "The world is going to become more dangerous! We still need our military spending and more of it too!". Environmentalists love to point out that the US military sees climate change as a great threat, and the Pentagon tends to list it in their various defense strategies and threat analyses. It's not because the generals are "woke." It's because they're desperately looking for any sort of threat to justify their budgets.

Kaplan remains respected, and the impact of his article is well known enough that its twenty-five-year anniversary prompted some reappraisals. Kaplan portrayed himself as vindicated,[283] but even military industrial complex house journal the Washington Post had to concede that he had been almost completely wrong.[284] The developing world was in dramatically better shape than he had portrayed. Africa has spent the past quarter century getting richer and stabilizing. Mexican immigration to the United States is essentially over. In fact, the only anarchy that was produced over the past twenty five years was turned out by the US military industrial complex itself, with its

---

[282] Kaplan, Robert D. "The Coming Anarchy" The Atlantic February 1994

[283] Kaplan, Robert D. "The Anarchy That Came" The National Interest October 21, 2018

[284] Drezner, Daniel W. "Reckoning With the Coming Anarchy" The Washington Post November 1, 2018

destruction of Iraq, Libya and Syria. The United States military didn't protect us from instability and refugee flows, it created it.

The justifications for conflict keep fading away. The search for oil remains a flashpoint, but only barely. New sources and technologies, most famously in US shale patches, but from everywhere in the world, have banished "peak oil" fears for at least a decade to come. It's entirely possible that climate change will lead to water or food crises, but it's hard to see how military force would be helpful in resolving these crises. If we're going to fall into another world war, we need there to be something to fight over, and those potential flashpoints are all quickly fading away.

The World Has Bought in Already...

Under the British World System, most of the world was subjugated. Imperialists subjected whole continents, and the majority of humanity to violent racial hierarchies. War between great powers was rare, but exterminatory campaigns against indigenous populations were common. None of that is true of the US World System. Sure, you can argue that there are neo-colonial aspects of the current system. We should always be striving to be better. But the idea that surfing YouTube is somehow as bad as starving to death or getting blown out of a cannon by an angry British soldier is ridiculous.

The US World System has been clever about offering a narrative and real opportunities for prosperity to the entire world. Every country on the planet has elites, if not general publics, that are eager to interact with the economic and social systems that the United States has fostered. English speaking lawyers and businesspeople are eager to figure out how they can help themselves by helping the US World System. In much of the world, we've already reached that transcendent utopia I'm talking about. The US government is the only thing that seems likely to stop it. Our insistence on flooding the world with weapons and brutalizing a series of Middle Eastern countries is the main thing placing the US World System in jeopardy. The rest of the world has already bought in to the US system.

This is even true of China. I'm writing this in an absurdly expensive apartment in a very undesirable part of New York City. There are a lot of factors making real estate expensive in the United States, but at the high end it's the Chinese. It's not just the city. Jack Ma, the founder of Chinese tech titan Ali Baba, purchased twenty-three million dollars' worth of upstate New York in 2015.[285] Even the future competitors of the United States have bought in to the US World System. So, in the final analysis, "Avoiding the British Empire" could be quite easy to do.

Conclusion

The world was once one of peasants and thugs. Most of us had to look to the thugs to protect us from other thugs, and the strength of our thugs depended on the amount of land they had, and their proficiency at war. This equation has been broken for a long, long time now. But we all still operate as if it's the case. We use our miraculous rise in productive and technological power to build spectacular weapons for pointless fights.

Politicians who take an aggressive stance towards the world and its conflicts are seen as tough-minded sorts who see the world as it really is. This couldn't be further from the truth. It's getting more and more difficult to sustain the illusion that our current level of military expenditure is necessary and good. But politicians still work hard to do so. Actions taken for short term political and economic goals are portrayed as essential, eternal conflicts.

In 2015, I watched the President of Turkey re-start an ethnic civil war to win an election. Prior to 2013, Erdogan had been a great force for

---

[285] http://www.businessinsider.com/jack-ma-buys-adirondacks-property-for-23-million-2015-6

peace between the Turkish government and the large Kurdish minority. In June of 2015, however, his party lost its parliamentary majority in part because of the defection of some Kurds. So he used a terrorist attack to re-start the Turkish government's war against the Kurds, knowing that fear would win him a new election, as it did in November 2015.

Erdogan's actions were only possible because of the nightmarish war in Syria. It too is depicted as being about high-minded, eternal questions of religion and democracy, when it's really about some very short-term and grubby priorities on the part of NATO countries. Across all of Eastern Europe, Latin America and Asia, the past few decades have thrown up a tremendously useful tool of regime change: Let economic development bribe authoritarians out of existence. Nobody dies, nobody kills, everybody gets richer. This process was accelerating in Syria in 2010. But the intelligence communities and military industrial complexes of the West decided they had a better solution. Yielding half a million deaths and the possible end of the European Union.

It's stunning how many of the world's problems can be traced back to dumb choices out of Washington, DC. The US World System as a whole has been great for the world, but a few politicians caught up in a military obsessed "historical hangover" are endangering US power and privilege, and the continued peace of the world. Almost every crisis the US has focused on since the end of the Cold War has been a complete waste of time. George H.W. Bush's misunderstanding with the US client Saddam Hussein could have been resolved in a million better ways. Instead it was resolved in the way most likely to maintain the jobs of the hundreds of thousands of recently irrelevant Cold Warriors in Washington, DC. This choice, more than any other, gave us 9/11, ISIS, and the destruction of millions of lives in the Middle

East. Even worse, it put Russia and China on notice that the end of the Cold War was not in fact the end of history, and they needed to build up arsenals of pointless, self-destructive military toys to compete with the US. It's all very pointless.

The US World System is unique. But the lessons of the fall of the British Empire can be instructive. At the beginning of the twentieth century, the British could have sat back and marveled at the world they built. Instead they chose to viciously hang on to the pointless trappings of empire and killed their world system. We in the US World System have the same choice today.

The rules of the game are still ours to write. By changing our approach, and truly acting for the benefit of the world in general, we can take advantage of an extraordinary opportunity. We can help to transcend the violence and pettiness that has marked the conduct of international affairs to date. This is the lesson that the history of the British Empire is trying to desperately to teach us.

For more analysis and videos on this topic and many others, please join us at...

www.MoreFreedomFoundation.com

Acknowledgements: This project took a lot longer than expected. When I started this book in the summer of 2017 I expected to have it done by the end of the year. Two and a half years, two countries and at least four apartments later, this book is finally in your hands. I'm eternally grateful for the patience of family, friends, patrons and fans, who only engaged in a little light eye-rolling as I blew through deadline after deadline.

One factor in the length of the writing process was the pressure of maintaining a weekly schedule of YouTube uploads. But the book would not have been possible without the emotional, intellectual, and monetary support I get from all my digital friends on various platforms. The supporters on my Patreon crowd-funding page have been particularly helpful in keeping body and soul together.

I'm grateful to Gillian Morris, Nathan Ruffing, and especially Jon Coumes for reading part or all of multiple versions of this text. It's an immeasurably better book than it would have been without their input. The fact that these reviewers strongly disagreed with me (and continue to disagree) on certain points and perspectives also made for a stronger book. The responsibility for any errors in the text is of course all mine.

Last and foremost, I have to thank Susan Taylor Morris, and Robert Earl Morris, Jr. My parents have been an unstinting source of encouragement through my past half decade of odd choices. The life of an itinerant political and historical critic is probably not exactly what they envisioned for their over-educated, middle-aged son, but nary a discouraging word has been uttered. Their choice to raise their children with books rather than televisions is at the root of my ability to attempt anything like this. I owe it all to them.

Printed in Great Britain
by Amazon

16546161R00235